Communication and Cyberspace

Social Interaction in an Electronic Environment

The Hampton Press Communication Series
Communication and Public Space
Gary Gumpert, supervisory editor

Communication and Cyberspace: Social Interaction in an Electronic Environment
Lance Strate, Ronald Jacobson, and Stephanie B. Gibson (eds.)

Modernity, Space, and Power:
The American City in Discourse and Practice
Katharine Kia Tehranian

forthcoming

Voices in the Street: Exploration in Gender, Media, and Public Space
Susan J. Drucker and Gary Gumpert (eds.)

Communication and Cyberspace

Social Interaction in an Electronic Environment

Edited by
Lance Strate
Ronald Jacobson
Fordham University
Stephanie B. Gibson
University of Baltimore

Second printing 1997

Printed in the United States of America

Library of Congress Cataloging-in-Publication Data

Communication and cyberspace : social interaction in an electronic environment / edited by Lance Strate, Ronald Jacobson, Stephanie B. Gibson.
p. cm. -- (The Hampton Press communication series). Communication and public space)
Includes bibliographical references and index.
ISBN 1-57273-50-1. -- ISBN 1-57273-51-X (pbk.)
1. Communication--Data processing. 2. Communication and technology. 3. Computer networks. 4. Cybernetics. 5. Social interaction. 6. Virtual reality. I. Strate, Lance. II. Jacobson, Ronald L., 1956- . III. Gibson, Stephanie B. IV. Series.
P96.D36C66 1996
302.2'0285--dc20 96-12044
CIP

Hampton Press, Inc.
23 Broadway
Cresskill, NJ 07626

Contents

Acknowledgments

The editors of this book would like to extend their deep and sincere appreciation to Gary Gumpert and Barbara Bernstein for making this project possible, for their confidence in us, and for their support of our efforts.

We would also like to thank the following individuals for their help: Sue Barnes, James Capo, Richard Cutler, Raymond Gozzi, Jr., Nancy Kaplan, Neil Kleinman, Judith Yaross Lee, Roger Musgrave, Christine Nystrom, Everett C. Parker, John M. Phelan, Janet Sternberg, and Edward Wachtel.

Acknowledgments are due to Fordham University's Office of Research for two supporting grants, and to the McGannon Communication Research Center, Fordham University's Department of Communication and Media Studies, and the University of Baltimore's School of English and Communication for more indirect forms of assistance. Special thanks go to the *TINAC* Collective, and to *Girls Just Wanna Have Drums*.

We would like to thank the following individuals for deepening our understanding of communication and cyberspace: Tony L. Arduini, Jr., Eva Berger, Kay Fielden, Michael E. Holmes, John McDaid, Joshua Meyrowitz, Pat O'Hara, Henry Perkinson, Rita Rahoi, Susan Mallon Ross, Amy Sauertieg, Charles J. Stivale, and David Thompson.

Finally, a special thank you to Barbara, Betty, Benjamin, and Sarah Strate, to Akiko, Brando, and Suki Jacobson, and to Orton, Bear, Cleo, and Percy Gibson for their love and support, and understanding and patience.

About the Authors

Sue Barnes is an Assistant Professor at Marymount Manhattan College in the Communication Arts Department. For the past six years, she has been developing computer-oriented curricula and computer-aided instructional materials. In 1993 she received a SUNY Faculty Grant for the Improvement of Undergraduate Education to improve hypertext literacy skills. Dr Barnes has written about and researched interpersonal computing, computer-mediated communications, virtual communities, and internet relationships, and her work has appeared in *Communication Education, New Dimensions in Communications, the CIT94 SUNY FACT Conference Proceedings*, and *Interpersonal Computing and Technology: An Electronic Journal for the 21st Century (IPCT-J).* Currently, she is the Editor of *IPCT-J,* a scholarly, peer-reviewed journal, focusing on computer-mediated communication, and the pedagogical issues surrounding the use of computers.

Joseph Barrett is a copy editor for *The Wall Street Journal.*

Michael P. Beaubien is a New York-based writer interested in technology and culture. He is currently managing editor of the *Encyclopedia of Molecular Biology and Biomedicine.*

James R. Beniger is an Associate Professor at the University of Southern California's Annenberg School of Communication. He is the author of *The Control Revolution: Technological and Economic Origins of the Information Society.*

Jay David Bolter is a Professor in the School of Literature, Communication and Culture at the Georgia Institute of Technology. He is the author of *Turing's Man: Western Culture in the Computer Age* and of *Writing Space: The Computer, Hypertext and the History of Writing.* He is also the co-author of the hypertext authoring software program *Storyspace.*

Margaret Cassidy teaches at New York University and is currently conducting research in media education.

Richard Cutler is an instructor in Interactive Media in the Department of Communication and Media Studies at Fordham University, currently researching the formation of identity, norms of behavior, and social position in voluntary, interactive electronic message groups.

Susan J. Drucker is an attorney and Associate Professor of Speech Communication at Hofstra University. She is the co-editor with Robert Cathcart of *American Heroes in a Media Age* and with Gary Gumpert of *Voices in the Street: Gender, Media, and Public Space*. Her primary areas of interest include media law and the impact of laws on social interaction and public space. Her work has appeared in *The New York State Bar Journal*, *Communication Quarterly*, *Communication Theory*, and *Critical Studies in Mass Communication*.

Stephanie B. Gibson, one of the co-editors of this anthology, is on the faculty in the School of Communication at the University of Baltimore where she teaches communication theory and hypermedia design. Her major research areas are the relationship between culture and technology, hypermedia and pedagogy, and feminist studies, and she has directed several conferences about interactive media. In collaboration with Stuart Moulthrop and Nancy Kaplan, she is working on a critical study of the World-Wide Web. She belongs to a women's drumming circle in Baltimore known as *Girls Just Wanna Have Drums*.

Mark Giese teaches broadcasting and cable courses at The Pennsylvania State University at Hazelton. His research interests include virtual communities and social uses of new electronic communication technologies.

Gary Gumpert is Professor Emeritus of Communication Arts and Sciences at Queens College, City University of New York. He is the author of *Talking Tombstones and Other Tales of the Media Age* and has co-edited with Robert Cathcart three editions of *Inter/Media: Interpersonal Communication in the Media World*. He has also co-edited with Sandra Fish *Talking to Strangers: Mediated Therapeutic Communication*, and with Susan Drucker *Voices in the Street: Gender, Media, and Public Space*. His articles have appeared in journals such as *The Quarterly Journal of Speech*, *Critical Studies in Mass Communication*, and *Communication Theory*.

Ronald Jacobson, one of the co-editors of this anthology, is an Associate Professor in the Department of Communication and Media Studies at Fordham University and the author of *Television-Related Cartoons* in *The*

New Yorker Magazine, and *Television Research: A Directory of Conceptual Categories, Topic Suggestions and Selected Sources.*

Neil Kleinman has written about propaganda, intellectual property, international law, Renaissance literature, design and architecture, and the influence of technologies on society. On the faculty of the University of Baltimore, where he teaches in a program he helped create that links writing, design, and the new digital technology, he is director of the Institute for Language, Technology, and Publications Design and is co-director of the University's School for Communications Design, which is a part of the Yale Gordon College of Liberal Arts.

Charles Larson is a Professor in the Department of Communication Studies at Northern Illinois University, and the author of *Persuasion: Reception and Responsibility*, now in its seventh edition. He has published numerous articles and monographs concerning political communication, advertising, dramatism, and the need for community.

Judith Yaross Lee is an Associate Professor in the School of Interpersonal Communication at Ohio University, where she teaches communication theory and historiography. She is the author of *Garrison Keillor: A Voice of America*, co-editor (with Joseph W. Slade) of *Beyond the Two Cultures: Essays On Science, Technology, and Literature*, and Is a founder of the Society for Literature and Science, serving as Executive Director from 1987-93.

Paul J. Lippert is an Associate Professor of Speech Communication at East Stroudsburg University. His research interests include cinema studies, orality-literacy theory, and media epistemology, and he is currently working on a book on the media theory of Walter Ong.

Mark Lipton teaches at New York University and Fordham University, and is currently conducting research on visual literacy.

Stuart Moulthrop is an Associate Professor in the School of Communications Design at the University of Baltimore. He is the author of *Victory Garden*, a critically acclaimed electronic fiction, as well as numerous essays on hypertext and new media, and the co-editor of the journal *Postmodern Culture*. In collaboration with Stephanie B. Gibson and Nancy Kaplan, he is working on a critical study of the World-Wide Web.

Terri Toles Patkin is an Associate Professor in the Department of Communication at Eastern Connecticut State University. Her research interests include organizational communication and telecommunications policy.

John M. Phelan is a Professor in the Department of Communication and Media Studies at Fordham University, and Director of the McGannon Communication Research Center. He is the author of *Apartheid Media: Disinformation and Dissent in South Africa, Disenchantment: Media and Morality in the Media,* and *Mediaworld: Programming the Public.* Recently, he was appointed to the United Nations NGO Committee on Disarmament by the Union of Concerned Scientists.

Neil Postman is University Professor and Chair of the Department of Culture and Communication at New York University. He is the author of over twenty books, including *The End of Education, Technopoly, Amusing Ourselves to Death, The Disappearance of Childhood, Teaching as a Conserving Activity, Crazy Talk, Stupid Talk,* and *Teaching as a Subversive Activity* with Charles Weingartner.

Lance Strate, one of the co-editors of this anthology, is an Associate Professor in the Department of Communication and Media Studies at Fordham University. He is co-author, with Neil Postman, Christine Nystrom, and Charles Weingartner, of *Myths, Men, and Beer*, and is currently working on a book on media theory entitled *Understanding Media Ecology*. He is also the supervisory editor of Hampton Press's Media Ecology Content Area Series.

Philip A. Thompsen is an Assistant Professor of Communication at William Jewell College, Liberty, Missouri, and General Manager, KWJC radio. His research interests include computer-mediated communication, human-computer interaction, and new communication technologies. Prior to his career in academia, he was a professional radio announcer for nine years.

Elizabeth Weiss is a Los Angeles-based screenwriter and teacher.

Herbert Zettl is Professor of Broadcast and Electronic Communication Arts at San Francisco State University. His major research areas are media aesthetics and video production. He has published extensively in both fields. His CD-ROM "Video Producer: A Video Production Lab," developed with the Cooperative Media Group for Wadsworth Publishing Company, has won the Macromedia People's Choice Award for Best Educational Product 1994, the New Media CD-ROM 1995 Gold Medal in the Higher Education category, and Silver Medals in the Continuing Education and Best Use of Video categories.

Surveying the Electronic Landscape: An Introduction to Communication and Cyberspace

Lance Strate
Ronald Jacobson
Stephanie B. Gibson

The title of this book begins with the word *communication* because our primary concern is with the processes by which human beings create messages, transfer information, and make meanings; the ways in which individuals form relationships and create communities; and our capacity to construct identities and realities through discourse. Social interaction never takes place in a vacuum, however, and this anthology is devoted to the new communication contexts made possible by computer technologies. Again, our emphasis is on communication as it is mediated by computers, not on computer technology itself. And we take the position that computer media—in fact, all media—are best understood not just as means or agencies *through* which communication takes place, but as environments or scenes in which communication occurs. Thus, in this volume we are specifically concerned with communication in the electronic environment known as *cyberspace.*

WHAT IS CYBERSPACE?

We realize that the meanings of *cyberspace* have evolved and multiplied as it has grown in popularity and diffused through different sectors of society. Although we are especially concerned with cyberspace as a contemporary phenomenon, it is important to acknowledge that the word was coined by author William Gibson (1984), who used it as part of a science fiction scenario in which individuals could directly connect their nervous systems to a global computer network referred to as *the matrix* and experience a form of *virtual reality*:

> "The matrix has its roots in primitive arcade games," said the voice-over, "in early graphics programs and military experimentation with cranial jacks." On the Sony, a two-dimensional space war faded behind a forest of mathematically generated ferns, demonstrating the possibilities of logarithmic spirals; cold blue military footage burned through, lab animals wired into test systems, helmets feeding into fire control circuits of tanks and war planes. "Cyberspace. A consensual hallucination experienced daily by billions of legitimate operators, in every nation, by children being taught mathematical concepts. . . . A graphic representation of data abstracted from the banks of every computer in the human system. Unthinkable complexity. Lines of light ranged in the nonspace of the mind, clusters and constellations of data. Like city lights, receding. . . . (p. 51)

Gibson's neologism and his vision of the future originate in popular culture, a fact that has prompted some to dismiss the concept of cyberspace. But others have taken the term and the idea seriously, one of the first being architect Michael Benedikt, editor of *Cyberspace: First Steps* (1991). He argues that a "fully developed cyberspace does not yet exist outside of science fiction and the imagination of a few thousand people" (p. 123), but believes that "cyberspace is 'now under construction'" (p. 124). Offering proposals for the design of this cyberspace-to-come, Benedikt clearly has Gibson's matrix in mind, minus the dystopic elements. He describes his cyberspace as:

> a globally networked, computer-sustained, computer-accessed, and computer-generated, multidimensional, artificial, or "virtual" reality. In this reality, to which every computer is a window, seen or heard objects are neither physical nor, necessarily, representations of physical objects but are, rather, in form, character and action, made up of data, of pure information. This information derives in part from the operations of the natural, physical world, but for the most part it derives from the immense traffic of information that constitute human enterprise in science, art, business, and culture. (pp. 122-123)

Benedikt seeks to bridge the gap between science fiction and reality, but he situates his cyberspace in the future; therefore, his concept remains hypothetical, unrealized, and unreal. On the other hand, Michael Heim, in *The Metaphysics of Virtual Reality* (1993), connects Gibson's prophecies to today's technologies in the following definition:

> The juncture of digital information and human perception, the "matrix" of civilization where banks exchange money (credit) and information seekers navigate layers of data stored and represented in virtual space. Buildings in cyberspace may have more dimensions than physical buildings do, and cyberspace may reflect different laws of existence. It has been said that cyberspace is where you are when you are having a phone conversation or where your ATM money exists. It is where electronic mail travels, and it resembles the Toontown in the movie *Roger Rabbit.* (p. 150)

Here, Heim implies that we have already entered the cyberspace age; his description brings together Gibson's notion of the visualization of abstract data with more common conceptions of virtual reality. For many (including Benedikt), the terms *virtual reality* and *cyberspace* are more or less interchangeable, although Heim also refers to the electronic storage and transmission of spoken and written language and numeric data in his definition of cyberspace. Others, however, use the term in conjunction with *computer-mediated communication* and communications through computer networks. For example, in the following passage from *Cyberpunk: Outlaws and Hackers on the Computer Frontier* (1992), Katie Hafner and John Markoff introduce the word in their description of the experiences of a young hacker accessing mainframe computers through his personal computer and modem:

> Being inside a global computer network gave Pengo the same adrenaline rush that playing a video game did, magnified many times over. Once he had entered a computer network, he was no longer playing a game; he was master of real machines performing real tasks. He could be nowhere and everywhere at the same time. From in front of a computer screen, he could open doors and solve problems. He was able to get things. The stuff on the screen wasn't anything more than electrons hitting phosphor, but it was nice to imagine that there really was something there, around the back somewhere. The networks—unconstrained by conventional geographic boundaries—had become a self-contained universe known to a growing number of computer researchers as cyberspace. (p. 150)

Clearly, virtual reality technology is not a factor in this version of cyberspace. This usage, to describe a contemporary communications phenomenon, is attributed to John Perry Barlow, a Grateful Dead lyricist who went on to become a cyberspace pioneer and co-founder (with Mitchell Kapor) of the Electronic Frontier Foundation:

> Barlow was the first commentator to adopt novelist William Gibson's striking science-fictional term "cyberspace" as a synonym for the present-day nexus of computer and telecommunications networks. Barlow was insistent that cyberspace should be regarded as a qualitatively new world, a "frontier." According to Barlow, the world of electronic communications, now made visible through the computer screen, could no longer be usefully regarded as just a tangle of high-tech wiring. Instead, it had become a *place*, cyberspace, which

> demanded a new set of metaphors, a new set of rules and behaviors. The term, as Barlow employed it, struck a useful chord, and the concept of cyberspace was picked up by *Time, Scientific American*, computer police, hackers, and even constitutional scholars. "Cyberspace" now seems likely to become a permanent fixture of the language. (Sterling, 1992, p. 236)

A similar emphasis is found in Howard Rheingold's definition in *The Virtual Community: Homesteading on the Electronic Frontier* (1993): "the conceptual space where words, human relationships, data, wealth, and power are manifested by people using CMC [computer mediated communications] technology" (p. 5). In this sense, cyberspace is not identical with communication through computer media, but rather is the context in which such communication occurs; nor is it the same as the computer network, but instead is the sense of place created through such networks. From this perspective, cyberspace may be understood as a form of social space, as Allucquere Rosanne Stone (1991) states in her discussion of the term:

> Electronic networks in their myriad kinds, and the mode of interpersonal interaction that they foster, are a new manifestation of a social space that has been better known in its older and more familiar forms in conference calls, communities of letters, and FDR's fireside chats. It can be characterized as "virtual" space—an imaginary locus of interaction created by communal agreement. In its most recent form, concepts like distance, inside/outside, and even the physical body take on new and frequently disturbing meanings. (pp. 83-84)

Stone also suggests here that cyberspace exists only through social interaction; her emphasis on "communal agreement" is reminiscent of Gibson's (1984) reference to cyberspace as a "consensual hallucination." This perspective seems to rule out the more basic idea of cyberspace as the "place" where information is "located," as well as the possibilities for intrapersonal communication presented by virtual reality technology.

In sum, we have many different definitions of cyberspace, some viewing it as a fictional construct, others as imaginary but in development, others as real and present. Some equate cyberspace with virtual reality, others with the electronic storage and transmission of information, or with computer-mediated communication, or with communication over computer networks. Some see cyberspace as an individual conceptual space, others as a product of social interaction. Part of the ambiguity surrounding this word may be related to its novelty, but it is also true that the term acts as a nexus for a variety of different phenomena, such as telecommunications, cybernetics and computer technology, computer-mediated communication, virtual reality and telepresence, hypertext and hypermedia, and cyberculture. It is therefore useful to consider each of these phenomena in turn.

TELECOMMUNICATIONS

Throughout the history of our species, human beings have sought to conquer time and space through speech, art, and architecture; writing and printing; and various forms of transportation (Innis, 1951). It was not until the mid-19th-century invention of the telegraph, however, that we gained the ability to communicate instantaneously through electronic data transmission. *Telecommunications* continued to evolve and grow with the development of the telephone, radio, and television, and innovations such as cable television, satellite communications, and fax machines. Beyond the development of individual technologies, the most striking trend in contemporary telecommunications is the tendency toward convergence among the various media, a convergence that encompasses the computer as well. Thus, the term *telematics* (from the French *télématique*) was coined to refer to "the merging of computers and microcomputers with major data banks and transmission systems" (Provenzo, 1986, p. 28); whereas George Gilder (1994) offers *telecomputer* or *teleputer* to refer to the combination of computing, telephone, and television. More recently, the term *cyberspace* has been adopted within telecommunications to emphasize those technologies clustered around computers (and sometimes simply the telephone), and the phrase *information superhighway* or *infobahn* has become a popular way to refer to the continuing convergence of these technologies. The use of cyberspace emphasizes the social and cultural aspects of telecommunications, whereas the highway metaphor favors the commercial and otherwise utilitarian functions of computer-mediated communication (Gozzi, 1994a, 1994b; Rheingold, 1993). A somewhat more neutral term, *information infrastructure* (both national and global), is also used in this context.

Merged with telecommunications technologies, computing facilitates the transmission and storage of large amounts of data, in a variety of formats. Computerized telecommunications made possible experiments in teletext and videotex, the creation of online newspapers and other forms of electronic publishing, and ultimately bulletin board systems and commercial online services. The convergence of the computer with telephone and television technologies has led to new communication environments, from distance learning programs in penal institutions to home shopping networks. Often emphasized is computing's potential to bestow the quality of *interactivity* on mass media previously limited to one-way communication (Brand, 1987; Gilder, 1994; Woolley, 1992). Also highly significant is the computer's ability to store and transmit information in binary code, as a sequence of numbers, making possible *digital media* such as the compact disc; digitized images, sounds, and so on are easier to store, transmit, and edit than analogic versions, opening the door to new forms of expression and manipulation of content (Binkley, 1993; Kroker, 1993; Lanham, 1993; Ritchin, 1990; Woolley, 1992). Moreover, computer technology's ability to control and digitize a variety of forms makes it central to any discussion of *multimedia*, the combination and blending of otherwise discrete media and forms such as still images, video, and text (Pimentel & Teixeira, 1993; Rickett, 1993; Wachtel, 1978).

Most if not all the questions and problems that have been associated with telecommunications in the past also apply to cyberspace. For example, economic questions include who pays for and who owns cyberspace, the Internet, or the information superhighway? Should it be a public trust or privatized and commercialized; a monopoly, heavily regulated, or open to competition? Who benefits from the technology, and who has access to it? Will diverse degrees of access create differently advantaged cyber-classes—the information rich and the information poor, the virtual and nonvirtual? What are the effects of replacing an industrial economy with one based on information? Political and legal questions include who regulates cyberspace and who patrols the information superhighway? How will privacy, property rights, and freedom of speech be protected? How will laws be enforced and cybercrime punished? Could cyberspace be used to foster democratic participation through teledemocracy? Social questions include to what degree will cyberspace substitute for transportation, for example, home shopping, telework, and teleconferencing. What happens to communities and public places as more and more people go online, and what is the nature of the new forms of community formed? Is cyberspace creating a global community? These are just some of the issues currently being debated (Branscomb, 1994; Critical Arts Ensemble, 1994; Gandy, 1993; Gilder, 1994; Hafner & Markoff, 1992; Kroker & Weinstein, 1994; Rheingold, 1993; Ross, 1991; Smith, 1993; Sterling, 1992).

CYBERNETICS AND COMPUTER TECHNOLOGY

The term *cyberspace* is clearly based on Norbert Wiener's (1967) neologism, *cybernetics*. Referring to the function of information to control or govern environments, cybernetics is most closely associated with computer technology, but is meant to be applied to a variety of technological, biological, and social systems. Certainly, as James Beniger (1986) has made clear, the development of technologies of control predates the modern computer and the contemporary information society. The computer itself, as a technology for performing numerical calculation, can be traced back to such ancient devices as the abacus, as Janet Sternberg (1991) makes clear, and has a long history of technological development leading up to the advent of the electronic digital computer following World War II (Bolter, 1984; Kidwell & Ceruzzi, 1994; Lubar, 1993). Programming through direct manipulation of the computer's wiring, via plugboards and by batch processing of punched computer cards ("do not bend, fold, spindle, or mutilate"), gave way to computer terminals that include video monitors in the 1960s, around the same time that minicomputers were introduced. Further developments during the 1970s include early versions of menu-based graphic user interfaces (GUIs) and point-and-click input devices (e.g., "the mouse"), and the marketing of handheld calculators, videogames, and microcomputers. The 1980s were characterized by the rapid expansion of computer-related industries, with increasing emphasis on networks, supercomputers, and workstations (Kidwell & Ceruzzi, 1994). Halfway through the 1990s, there has been tremendous growth in all areas of computer-mediated communication and cyberspace, and great interest in virtual reality technologies. Furthermore, the quality of portability has become particularly popular, for example, laptop or notebook personal computers, personal digital assistants (PDAs), as well as beepers, cellular telephones, and fax machines.

As computing technologies have developed, so has interest in examining their nature, role in society, and relationship to human beings and culture (see, e.g., Bolter, 1984; Perkinson, 1995; Roszak, 1994; Turkle, 1984; Weizenbaum, 1976). Along with general studies of computers and society, more specific social and cultural aspects of computing being studied include artificial intelligence (Dreyfus, 1979; Dreyfus & Dreyfus, 1986; Hofstadter, 1980; Hofstadter & Dennett, 1981; Penrose, 1989), artificial life (Levy, 1992), education (Papert, 1980), the arts and entertainment (Peterson, 1983), word processing (Heim, 1987), and videogames (Provenzo, 1991; Sudnow, 1983). Critics and proponents of the computer may differ on the positive or negative effects of the technologies and debate the purposes for which they are or ought to be used. But by and large they agree that as a machine that is both virtual and universal, there seem to be few limits to the computer's applications and little that is unaffected by it. And projections for the future have just about every sector of human activity revolutionized by computing (Pickover, 1994). This, of course, includes and has included human communication.

COMPUTER-MEDIATED COMMUNICATION

Although most often viewed as a tool for performing calculations, processing data, and manipulating symbols, the computer is also an information technology and a medium of communication (see, e.g., Lubar, 1993; Provenzo, 1986). And any form of human-computer interaction can be seen as a form of communication, varying in the degree to which the computer or the user is in control (Chesebro & Bonsall, 1989). Thus, such interactions would include both humans programming computers and computers programming humans (e.g., through educational software, videogames, etc.), as well as using computer programs to input, store, search for, manipulate, output, and transmit information. The qualities most closely connected to contemporary computer-mediated communication, interactive computing, and direct human-to-human communication are dependent on the addition of video technology as a way to display information graphically and allow for much faster feedback than waiting for mechanically produced printouts and the addition of sufficient computing power and programming to handle multiple users simultaneously:

> The invention of time-sharing computers in the 1960s not only enabled many people to use the same central computer by exchanging commands and results with the computer interactively, it also provided a channel of communication between humans and humans—people on the earliest time-sharing systems built electronic mail systems for sending each other messages. As the time-sharing systems evolved, so did the mail systems. Eventually, what we will send one another over the telecommunication lines will not be restricted to text, but will include voice, images, gestures, facial expressions, virtual objects, cybernetic architectures—everything that contributes to a sense of presence. We will be sending worlds and ways to be in them. The advent of interactive computing and e-mail in the late 1960s was a twin milestone in the making of the Matrix, the network of networks where future cyberspaces will evolve. (Rheingold, 1991, p. 88)

Along with *electronic mail* (e-mail), which is asynchronous (messages are stored and need not be read at the time of receipt), early forms of computer-mediated communication include synchronous *chat* (text exchanged "live" as in a telephone conversation), and computer *bulletin boards* that allow for interchanges among many different users (later variations include the computer conference, the mailing list, discussion list or listserv, and the newsgroup). Pioneered through time-sharing computers with multiple terminals linked to one mainframe computer, itself a network of sorts, these forms of communication were extended as different computers were linked locally or over distance (e.g., by telephone lines or cable); furthermore, microcomputers could be linked directly to each other in a closed-circuit network or through modem and telephone services to other microcomputers or more powerful mainframe and minicomputers. Thus, the development of the personal computer in the late 1970s has led to a revolution in interpersonal computing, leading researchers to study computer-mediated communication on the interpersonal, group, and organizational communication levels (Chesebro & Bonsall, 1989; Sproull & Kiesler, 1991; see also Gumpert & Cathcart, 1986).

Cyberspace is most often associated with the interconnections among different computers, computer networks, and further interconnections among different networks. The sum total of this network of networks has been referred to as the matrix, the the Internet or Net, and the Worldnet. The Internet also refers to the specific network that has been supported by the U.S. government (although current plans are to privatize it, and it may well give way to newer networks in the near future), as opposed to other networks such as Bitnet, Usenet, and Fidonet. Many of the nodes or cyberplaces that make up these networks are computers owned by educational institutions, governments, and corporations. Another significant presence consists of tens of thousands of hobbyists who have set up Bulletin Board Systems (BBSs), some of which have turned commercial. There are also larger commercial services, including Compuserve, American Online, Prodigy, GEnie, and Delphi, that offer home shopping, entertainment, and online reference libraries and news services in addition to computer-mediated communications. Increasingly, both BBSs and commercial services offer access to the Internet as well as their own features.

Beyond e-mail, the current cyberscape includes Usenet newsgroups, the Internet Relay Chat (IRC), and connections to remote computers through Telnet. Also accessible are Multi-User Dungeons or Multi-User Dimensions (MUDs), that is, programs or nodes that allow many people to participate in role-playing games or simply interact in a computer-simulated environment. Moreover, many cyberspace nodes include databases of information that can be accessed and downloaded through File Transfer Protocol (FTP), Gopher, Wide Area Information Servers (WAIS), or the World-Wide Web (WWW). As Anthony Smith (1993) points out, cyberspace retrieves the ancient idea of the Alexandrian library as a storehouse to which people come, reversing the Gutenbergian principle of mass production and distribution (but not necessarily mass communication). Software that aids in the finding and retrieving of data, such as Archie (used with FTP) and Veronica (used with Gopher), are attempts to construct electronic librarians or navigators native to cyberspace, whereas many e-mail systems include a software "Postmaster." The projection of agentic status onto these programs is more than anthropomorphism; rather, it reflects ongoing efforts to develop (or evolve; see Levy, 1992) software capable of independent action in the cyberspace environment, software to search and retrieve, perform surveillance, and act as a surrogate for us, as well as perform maintenance functions. This effort may well reinvigorate the somewhat moribund state of artificial intelligence and expert systems research. Thus, we may anticipate a near-future cyberspace populated by projected "entities" variously known as intelligent agents, software agents, knowbots, or electronic personas or epers (Gelernter, 1991; Heim, 1993; Pickover, 1994; Rheingold, 1993).

VIRTUAL REALITY AND TELEPRESENCE

Of the terms associated with cyberspace, *virtual reality* (VR) has been one of the most compelling (e.g., Biocca, 1992; Hayward & Wollen, 1993; Heim, 1993; Laurel, 1993; Pimentel & Teixeira, 1993; Rheingold, 1991; Woolley, 1992). According to Pimentel and Teixeira (1993) the term virtual, in computing "refers to the essence or effect of something, not the fact. IBM started using the word in the late 1960s to refer to any nonphysical link between processes or machines, such as virtual memory (random-access memory being simulated using disk drives)" (p. 288).

Virtual reality, then, is not true, factual reality, but a simulation that gives the effect and essence of reality. The illusion of reality is generated through the computer's interface with its user; computer screens generate an artificial reality, so that we may imagine we are reading an electronic book when in fact we are viewing a video image, and we may feel a sense of presence when communicating over a network or playing a videogame and using a joystick or mouse. Virtual reality is generally associated with such interface devices as goggles, data gloves, and body stockings that in theory could both relay information about the individual's movements and position and convey realistic visual, auditory, and even tactile information to the user; the goal is to create the illusion of immersion in a virtual environment or virtual world. Through virtual reality technology, we would be able to enter into a video game, participate in a film or television program, go to work in a virtual office (Pruitt & Barrett, 1991), take a virtual vacation, and engage in virtual sex. Virtual reality can also serve as a blueprint or prototype (Benedikt, 1991), a real-time map or "mirror world" of actual reality (Gelernter, 1991), or a way to concretize abstract data as in Gibson's (1984) speculative fiction (see also Benedikt, 1991). Projections of virtual reality technologies include simulations produced at a particular site, and *televirtuality*, the transmission of a virtual reality from a distance through convergence with other forms of telecommunications.

Telepresence, the lesser known counterpart of virtual reality, refers to the transmission of the user's "presence" to another location, allowing the user to act from a distance. Anyone issuing commands to a computer system from a remote location may experience a sense of telepresence—related terms include *teleoperation* and *tele-existence*. Telepresence is particularly associated with the remote operation of machines or robots, *telerobotics*, and coupled with virtual reality technology it would give the user the illusion of actually being present. Through telepresence, individuals may safely engage in high-risk activities in outer space or in nuclear facilities, as well as in otherwise impossible situations, such as performing microsurgery through miniature robotics. Telepresence may also allow for new forms of safe sex, such as *telesex* or *teledildonics*.

HYPERTEXT AND HYPERMEDIA

Whether the virtual reality is a three-dimensional environment or an electronic book, cyberspace transcends conventional notions of dimension, connection, and navigation. The term hypertext, alluding to the higher dimensionality of hyperspace, was coined by programmer Ted Nelson (1987, 1990), although the original vision for this medium is credited to Vannevar Bush (1945). It refers to nonlinear documents, in which text nodes are linked to other relevant pieces of text, forming a textual network (Berk & Devlin, 1991; Bolter, 1991; Delany & Landow, 1991; Hawisher & Selfe, 1991; Landow, 1992). A node can include any type of text—words, graphics, moving images, sound, or any combination of these—making hypertext a form of multimedia or *hypermedia*. The manner in which hypertext is navigated is by linking text nodes to one or more other text nodes; for instance, a photograph of a Grecian urn can be linked to a paragraph of printed text describing that urn and to a map showing where it was recovered during an archeological dig. Also used as a compositional tool, much has been written about hypertext's impact on theories of writing and on the writing classroom. In its use as a "writing space," as Jay David Bolter (1991) puts it, a number of hypertext novels have been authored, and new forms of fiction and criticism are being created and legitimized. Ultimately, hypertext and hypermedia dissolve the differences between texts, book series, or encyclopedias, even libraries; between fiction and gaming (an intermediate form is known as *interactive fiction*); and between texts as objects to be read and as environments to navigate through (thus, virtual reality can also be viewed as a form of hypermedia).

One of the key aspects of hypermediated communication has been the development of useful navigational systems or *cybernautics*. Without ways to determine how to travel from one text node to another, hypertext can be viewed as a disorganized jumble: a pile of book pages without any sort of organizing pattern. Hypertext authors and programmers have been working to design creative and helpful systems that show relationships among text nodes. The basic goals of navigational systems have been to give readers a way of moving seamlessly through the text without getting lost in hyperspace. This has been accomplished through several navigational devices: leaving a trail showing where the reader has been, showing some paths to other relevant nodes, allowing only readers who have completed certain parts of a text to move on to other parts, and highlighting places where links are available instead of making links invisible. The Internet itself can be seen as one vast hypertextual network, but it is largely without the type of navigational links normally built into hypertexts; this is one reason why thus far communication in cyberspace has been something less than user friendly. Hypermedia, then, can provide cyberspace with navigational order, albeit one that transcends traditional conceptions of linear direction and the limitations of three dimensions. Services and interfaces modeled after hypertext, such as the World-Wide Web, Mosaic, and Netscape, have brought some coherence and clarity to the contemporary cyberscape, and many commercial services have also adopted hypermediated interfaces.

CYBERCULTURE

Through social interaction in the electronic environment of cyberspace, a new kind of culture has developed, referred to as *cyberculture* (Dery, 1993). Included under this heading are the various hacker subcultures, such as the original hardware hackers: unstructured programmers who see programming as an end in itself (Turkle, 1984). According to Steven Levy (1984), the first group of hackers formed in MIT circa 1959 and developed a "hacker ethic" that emphasized complete freedom of information and access to computers, decentralization and antiauthoritarianism, and better living through computing. Much of this was consistent with the counterculture of the 1960s, although the hacker's apolitical tendencies were not (see Roszak, 1994, for further criticism of their "cult of information"). Younger hackers, during the 1970s and 1980s, turned to programming for microcomputers (Levy, 1984), but the label "hacker" has come to be more closely tied with individuals who explore and break into computers and networks, generally through personal computers and modems. Both a counterculture and an underground, sometimes outlaw culture, contemporary hacker culture is seen by some as criminal and by others as unduly persecuted (Hafner & Markoff, 1992; Ross, 1991; Sterling, 1992).

The concept of cyberculture transcends the hacker phenomenon, however, and refers to the unique culture associated with computer-mediated communication (CMC) and online interaction. This includes the emergence of special forms of language and symbols; the development of rituals, conventions, norms, and rules of conduct for CMC; and phenomena such as *flaming* (hostile communication), *spamming* (messages that are too long or verbose), and less offensive forms of ranting (Benedikt, 1991; Dery, 1993; Jones, 1995; Rheingold, 1993). Over time a sense of social ties may develop, resulting in what Howard Rheingold (1993) refers to as a *virtual community*, also known as an *electronic village* (Dery, 1993) or *cybersociety* (Jones, 1995). Cyberculture is also linked to other forms of counterculture; thus, Douglas Rushkoff (1994) uses the term *cyberia* as a variation of cyberspace, but also to point to the associations among hackers, virtual reality pioneers, and members of virtual communities on the one hand, and the various contemporary subcultures associated with smart drugs and psychedelics, New Age mysticism and neopaganism, and raving and other forms of popular music and dance on the other.

There is, of course, a significant connection between cyberculture and the genre of science fiction, in which the term *cyberspace* originated. The style of science fiction produced by William Gibson, Bruce Sterling, and others is referred to as *cyberpunk*, which generally includes an emphasis on electronic technologies, urban decay, and underclass characters (Bukatman, 1993; McCaffery, 1991; Sterling, 1986). More than a literary genre, cyberpunk may also be applied to other forms and media, including film, comics, music, and fashion; it has also been used in conjunction with actual hackers (Hafner & Markoff, 1992). Sometimes interpreted as a critique of capitalism and an oppositional ideological stance, cyberpunk also may be seen as hacker chic or as a disembodied style that best fits social interaction in cyberspace. Donna Haraway (1991) appropriates the related science fiction concept of the *cyborg*, the cybernetic organism that is half human and half machine, to discuss our relationships to technology. It should be noted that not all forms of science fiction that deal with cyberspace are considered forms of cyberpunk (e.g., Disney's science fiction film TRON, 1982). Cyberpunk itself can be seen as a manifestation of postmodern culture.

The term *postmodern* refers to our own time period and is generally said to begin sometime after the end of World War II. Postmodern culture is the culture of the age of television and computers, and postmodernist theorists often make direct references to computer technology: Jean-François Lyotard (1979/1984) attributes the postmodern condition in part to computer science; Jean Baudrillard (1983) writes of our present "digitality," whereas his concepts of simulation and hyperreality seem to correspond to virtual reality (Woolley, 1992); Arthur Kroker (1993; Kroker & Weinstein, 1994) follows up on many of Baudrillard's insights, making their connection to the cyberspace phenomenon more explicit, if no less opaque. Fredric Jameson (1991) sees a correspondence between his notion of postmodernism as the culture of late capitalism and William Gibson's cyberpunk vision of cyberspace (see also Critical Arts Ensemble, 1994). Poster (1990) relates various forms of computing to the poststructuralist notion of the decentering of the self, whereas Gergen (1991) describes a saturated self in relation to symbolic communities such as those formed through computer networks. Moreover, hypertext theorists see in that form of computer media the concrete realization of much of postmodern, poststructuralist, and critical literary theory (Bolter, 1991; Landow, 1992). Along the same lines, Lanham (1993) connects computer mediated art to contemporary rhetorical theory (as well as the history of rhetoric), and Heim (1987) argues for the relationship between word processing and Heideggerian phenomenology (see also the somewhat self-indulgent "media philosophy" of Taylor & Saarinen, 1994). Although rooted in the tradition of continental philosophy and critical theory, postmodernism, as Strate (1994) points out, is also derived from the media ecology perspective.

Media ecology refers to the perspective of theorists such as Marshall McLuhan (1962, 1964; McLuhan & Powers, 1989), Harold Innis (1951), Walter Ong (1982), Neil Postman (1979, 1985, 1992), and Joshua Meyrowitz (1985). In many ways, cyberspace represents the culmination of McLuhan's arguments about electronic media: that through this extension of our nervous systems we become members of a global village, that we replace individual identity with role playing, and that our forms of perception and our sense of our own bodies are altered (see also Provenzo, 1986; Smith, 1993). Similarly, Ong suggests that electronic media continue to transform and technologize the word, continuing the process begun with writing and printing; he refers to our present postliterate stage as one of secondary orality. In this respect, we might consider the uses of computer technology for voice transmission, recognition, and synthesis, and the ways in which electronic writing retrieves characteristics of scribal and oral communication and culture (Bolter, 1984, 1991; Heim, 1987; Lanham, 1993; Woolley, 1992). Flaming may therefore be compared to oral culture's agonistic tendencies (Dery, 1993, insightfully compares it to "the dozens") and spamming to orality's bias toward copiousness and verbosity. Cyberspace also represents an unprecedented integration of analogic (i.e., audiovisual) and digital (i.e., verbal and numeric) forms of communication (Strate, 1994). Meyrowitz's (1985) sociological elaborations of media ecology theory are especially significant here, as cyberspace technologies further contribute to the fact that we have "no sense of place," increase the general accessibility of information, and alter the way in which we play our roles. Thus, Meyrowitz's theory coincides with the arguments of postmodernists such as Poster (1990) and Gergen (1991) concerning the decentering of the self. In general, the media ecology perspective suggests that cyberspace technologies not only constitute a site for new cultural formations, but also affect pre-existing elements of culture, situated in other kinds of spaces; more and more we may find mainstream culture mimicking cyberculture in a variety of ways.

Thus far, we have considered both communication and communication technology. We have examined the *cyber*, but not the *space*. It is easy to take the notion of space for granted, but in fact much of the confusion surrounding the meaning of cyberspace is connected to the ambiguity surrounding the idea of space itself.

THE SPACES

The concept of space is actually quite complex, and the notion that there is no one single, uniform "thing" called space can be traced back to the late 19th century (Kern, 1983). We are better off, then, making reference to the variety of spaces that can be encountered, beginning with *physical space*, the space that (theoretically) exists independently of human beings (itself no longer seen as uniform). Physical space is often confused with *perceptual space*, the impression of space that we obtain through one or a combination of our senses. At best, perceptual space can only correspond to a portion of physical space and is always subject to error. Also, we tend to equate perceptual space with visual space, but we also experience auditory space; tactile, thermal, and kinesthetic space; and even olfactory space—generally, our perceptual space is based on the interactions of all these senses (Hall, 1966). Another distinction that often goes unacknowledged is that between perceptual space and *conceptual space*, the sense of space generated within our minds. Conceptual space may include memories of perceptual space, as well as imagined and fictional spaces that have never been perceived. It is the space where plans are made and future actions visualized. It is the realm of the mind's eye and the place where we look when we turn inward in thought. The relationships among physical, perceptual, and conceptual spaces have been the subject of much debate throughout the centuries, and it is not our intention to enter into that discussion here, merely to note the distinctions. Suffice it to say that these three types form the basis for all other forms of space that we experience.

Edward T. Hall's (1966) investigations into proxemics teach us that human beings have further senses of space based on our interactions with others. There is, for example, a sense of a *personal space*, the individual's own sense of territoriality, and a sense of a *social space*, the area that is shared with others; pioneering research on the relationships between communication and social space has been conducted by Gary Gumpert and Susan Drucker (Drucker & Gumpert, 1991; Gumpert, 1987; Gumpert & Drucker, 1992). Our spaces are further defined through verbal designations such as public or private, sacred or profane, and through physical modifications, such as architecture. There are also forms of *aesthetic space* created through media, including the physical space occupied by an object, the relational space between the item and its audience, the illusionary perceptual space suggested by items such as visual images, and the conceptual space activated in the minds of audience members (Gumpert, 1987; Meyrowitz, 1986; Zettl, 1990). A book, for example, occupies space as a physical object, enters into a spatial relationship with its reader, displays information as words laid out on a page (much as objects may be arranged in a given physical area), and may produce a further experience of space in readers' imaginations through their decoding of its content.

Historically, new media have introduced new notions of space such as *writing space* and *typographic space* (Bolter, 1991; Ong, 1982), but never so radically as with the introduction of the electronic media, which eliminate both the need for human presence and for physical transportation. Thus, they create new forms of spatial relationships; for example, it is not entirely clear where your voice is when you talk on the telephone (at your end, at the receiving end, or somewhere in between), and therefore it is not entirely clear where you are (perceptually or conceptually). We might conclude that there is a whole new sense of space created in a telephone conversation, an *electronic space* (not cyberspace, as some suggest, but a closely related form—telephonic space). Electronic space, then, is divorced from any idea of physical location, which is why Meyrowitz (1985) characterizes it as providing "no sense of place." He goes on to suggest that both spatial situations and media are information systems that provide variable possibilities for transmitting and receiving information, that vary in the accessibility of and barriers to information. In other words, according to Meyrowitz, all forms of space are cybernetic, and therefore all might be referred to as cyberspace. Although we support this theoretical position, for reasons of precision we favor limiting the use of the term *cyberspace* to those forms of electronic space associated with computer technologies.

Furthermore, based on the preceding breakdown of the varieties of space, we might well refer to different types of cyberspace. There is the *physical cyberspace* of the computer itself, the structure of its chips and circuits, its "architecture." This physical structure determines the possible patterns of electronic flow and therefore the basic operations of the computer. But there is also a *logical cyberspace*, including the address space of the computer: "the range of numbers that can be invoked in fetching and storing data" (Bolter, 1984, p. 83). Logical cyberspace includes the locations where information is stored and processed in memory and the sectors where it is saved on magnetic and optical media. Physical cyberspace is almost never directly accessed or even conceptualized by programmers, as Bolter (1984) explains:

> This logical space exists in the programmer's mind. . . . The programmer ignores those qualities that have no bearing on his problem (such as the pattern of wires and transistors forming the memory) and is left with the fundamental qualities of electronic space. Logical space is not computer memory freed of its physical limitations, for the corporeality of information in the computer imposes restrictions and offers possibilities that the programmer cannot ignore—rather, it is computer memory reduced to its essence. (p. 84)

Bolter's (1984) description of logical space as "an abstract, geometrical, and mathematical field in which the programmer can build his data structures" (p. 243) has much in common with Gibson's (1984) description of a fictional cyberspace based on the visualization of abstract data.

As Rheingold (1991) notes, the evolution of computer technology has been toward putting greater and greater distance between the user and the hardware, thereby reducing or eliminating access to physical cyberspace. Instead, through the development of various interfaces, computers create a *perceptual cyberspace*, which would include the visual space of the computer monitor, graphic user interfaces, and tactile input devices such as the keyboard, joystick, and mouse. At the same time, our ability to go beyond our perceptions, particularly through computer-mediated verbal communication, results in a form of *conceptual cyberspace*. Cyberspace is also conceptualized through a variety of metaphors: The *electronic frontier* conceptualizes cyberspace in terms of the natural environment, whereas *information infrastructure* implies a human construction. *Information superhighway* and *infobahn* conceptualize cyberspace as a conduit, a place to pass through, whereas *virtual community* instead emphasizes the idea of an electronic landscape filled with relatively small, stable dwellings. *Electropolis* (Reid, 1992) and *netropolis* (Taylor & Saarinen, 1994) frame cyberspace as a more cosmopolitan locus of human activity. Liquid metaphors are also quite popular, as they emphasize the fact that cyberspace is not physical space, certainly not solid space—it is both liquefied and liquidated space. This metaphor is present throughout Benedikt's (1991) *Cyberspace* anthology, especially in Marcos Novak's (1991) discussion of "liquid architectures" (pp. 225-254), and in Rheingold's (1991) use of the term *cybernautics*. It is also implicit in the popular phrase "surfing the Internet," as well as the related notion of "channel surfing" through cable and broadcast television.

Together our perceptions and conceptions make up our experience of cyberspace, and through human-computer interaction or through the use of computing for intrapersonal communication, we generate a kind of *personal cyberspace* which includes our sense of territoriality directed at our computer's "desktops" and arrangements of files and directories, our working spaces on mainframe computers, and our senses of self as we "move" through the levels of our computers (and others we may connect to). Through our sense of personal cyberspace, we may be said to merge with the computer and become cyborgs.

We also may enter into a shared *social cyberspace* such as a bulletin board; generally, those that gain a sense of group membership in a virtual community also develop a sense of responsibility toward the social cyberspace in which it is situated, much as residents of a neighborhood may take responsibility for the area's cleanliness and safety (Rheingold, 1993). Finally, we may further consider *aesthetic cyberspace* and the design of human-computer interfaces, an area of particular interest to programmer Brenda Laurel (1990, 1993), who advocates the theater as an aesthetic model. These, then, are the cyberspaces.

ABOUT THIS BOOK

It has long been a typographic cliché to inform readers that they can read the chapters in an anthology in any order they please, and it is certainly in keeping with our topic that we welcome you to treat this collection as a database, randomly access its contents, and forge your own hypertextual links. Each medium has its own bias, however, and a printed book works best with a good measure of linearity. We therefore have put a great deal of thought and effort into the structure of this book and the sequence of the contributions, so that those in search of a traditional cover-to-cover reading will be rewarded. To this end we have divided the book into four sections, the first of which is devoted to essays that provide theoretical contexts, broad overviews, and general criticism of computing and cyberspace as communication phenomena. The purpose of Section One, therefore, is to provide perspectives that allow us to *place* cyberspace. The following three sections are based on the three-part conceptual structure used by architects and designers: form, function, and meaning.

Section Two, based on the idea of function, consists of discussion and research on cybernetworks (e.g., the Internet and the information superhighway) and cyberplaces (e.g., nodes, multiuser dungeons, virtual organizations). Of concern here are the ways in which cyberspace functions as an alternative for traditional locations and forms of transportation, and the consequences of such substitutions; also of interest are the ways in which cyberplaces and cybernetworks differ from their physical counterparts, and how such differences affect cyberspatial interactions. Section Three, based on the idea of form, brings together studies of new senses of space and navigation, or cybernautics. This includes examinations of the idea of virtual reality and the perception of immersion generated by cyberspace technologies, as well as hypertext and hypermedia as new forms of nonlinear space and new methods of steering through the electronic landscape. Section Four, based on the idea of meaning, consists of examinations of cybercommunication and cyberculture. Among the topics covered are the codes and modes of communication associated with communication in cyberspace and the new cultural formations, including altered notions of self, the body, and sexuality; relationships, community, and affiliation; and space, time, and reality that arise in this new communication environment.

Each section begins with a brief introduction that helps to identify the relationships among the section's chapters; each chapter has its own introduction, which also points to relationships with chapters in other sections. And we have given the last word, in the form of an epilogue, to Neil Postman, who raises the most basic question of all: Do we really need a cyberspace in the first place? His critical essay challenges us to justify cyberspace on the basis of genuine human needs.

Finally, we invite and encourage your responses and feedback. Let us know what you think of the book, and what the book made you think of.

REFERENCES

Baudrillard, J. (1983). *Simulations* (P. Foss, P. Patton & P. Beitchman, Trans.). New York: Semiotext(e).

Benedikt, M. (Ed.). (1991). *Cyberspace: First steps*. Cambridge, MA: MIT Press.

Beniger, J.R. (1986). *The control revolution: Technological and economic origins of the information society*. Cambridge, MA: Harvard University Press.

Berk, E., & Devlin, J. (Eds.). (1991). *Hypertext/hypermedia handbook*. New York: McGraw-Hill.

Binkley, T. (1993). Refiguring culture. In P. Hayward & T. Wollen (Eds.), *Future visions: New technologies of the screen* (pp. 92-122). London: British Film Institute.

Biocca, F. (Ed.). (1992). Virtual reality: A communication perspective [Special issue]. *Journal of Communication, 42*(4).

Bolter, J.D. (1984). *Turing's man: Western culture in the computer age*. Chapel Hill: University of North Carolina Press.

Bolter, J.D. (1991). *Writing space: The computer, hypertext, and the history of writing*. Hillsdale, NJ: Erlbaum.

Brand, S. (1987). *The media lab: Inventing the future at MIT*. New York: Viking.

Branscomb, A.W. (1994). *Who owns information? From privacy to public access*. New York: Basic Books.

Bukatman, S. (1993). *Terminal identity: The virtual subject in postmodern science fiction*. Durham, NC: Duke University Press.

Bush, V. (1945, July). As we may think. *Atlantic Monthly*, pp. 106-107.

Chesebro, J.W., & Bonsall, D.G. (1989). *Computer-mediated communication: Human relationships in a computerized world*. Tuscaloosa: University of Alabama Press.

Critical Arts Ensemble. (1994). *The electronic disturbance*. Brooklyn, NY: Autonomedia.

Delany, P., & Landow, G.P. (Eds.). (1991). *Hypermedia and literacy studies*. Cambridge: MIT Press.

Dery, M. (Ed.). (1993). Flame wars: The discourse of cyberculture [Special issue]. *The South Atlantic Quarterly, 92*(4).

Dreyfus, H.L. (1979). *What computers can't do: The limits of artificial intelligence* (rev. ed.). New York: Harper Colophon Books.
Dreyfus, H.L., & Dreyfus, S.E. (1986). *Mind over machine.* New York: The Free Press.
Drucker, S.J., & Gumpert, G. (1991). Public space and communication: The zoning of public interaction. *Communication Theory, 1*(4), 294-310.
Gandy, O.H., Jr. (1993). *The panoptic sort: A political economy of personal information.* Boulder, CO: Westview.
Gelernter, D. (1991). *Mirror worlds or the day software puts the universe in a shoebox . . . How it will happen and what it will mean.* New York: Oxford University Press.
Gergen, K.J. (1991). *The saturated self.* New York: Basic Books.
Gibson, W. (1984). *Neuromancer.* New York: Ace Books.
Gilder, G. (1994). *Life after television: The coming transformation of media and American life* (rev. ed.). New York: Norton.
Gozzi, R., Jr. (1994a). The cyberspace metaphor. *Etc.: A Review of General Semantics, 51*(2), 218-223.
Gozzi, R., Jr. (1994b). The information superhighway as metaphor. *Etc.: A Review of General Semantics, 51*(3), 321-327.
Gumpert, G. (1987). *Talking tombstones and other tales of the media age.* New York: Oxford University Press.
Gumpert, G., & Cathcart, R. (1986). *Inter/media: Interpersonal communication in a media world* (3rd ed.). New York: Oxford University Press.
Gumpert, G., & Drucker, S.J. (1992). From the agora to the electronic shopping mall. *Critical Studies in Mass Communication, 9*(2), 186-200.
Hafner, K., & Markoff, J. (1992). *Cyberpunk: Outlaws and hackers on the computer frontier.* New York: Touchstone.
Hall, E.T. (1966). *The hidden dimension.* Garden City, NY: Anchor.
Haraway, D.J. (1991). *Simians, cyborgs, and women: The reinvention of nature.* New York: Routledge.
Hawisher, G.E., & Selfe, C.L. (Eds.). (1991). *Evolving perspectives on computers and composition studies.* Urbana, IL: National Council of Teachers of English Press
Hayward, P., & Wollen, T. (Eds.). (1993). *Future visions: New technologies of the screen.* London: British Film Institute.
Heim, M. (1987). *Electric language: A philosophical study of word processing.* New Haven, CT: Yale University Press.
Heim, M. (1993). *The metaphysics of virtual reality.* New York: Oxford University Press.
Hofstadter, D.R. (1980). *Gödel, Escher, Bach: An eternal golden braid.* New York: Vintage Books.
Hofstadter, D.R., & Dennett, D.C. (Eds.). (1981). *The minds I.* New York: Basic Books.
Innis, H.A. (1951). *The bias of communication.* Toronto: University of Toronto Press.

Jameson, F. (1991). *Postmodernism, Or, The cultural logic of late capitalism.* Durham, NC: Duke University Press.

Jones, S.G. (Ed.). (1995). *Cybersociety: Computer-mediated communication and community.* Thousand Oaks, CA: Sage.

Kern, S. (1983). *The culture of time and space, 1880-1918.* Cambridge, MA: Harvard University Press.

Kidwell, P.A., & Ceruzzi, P.E. (1994). *Landmarks in digital computing.* Washington, DC: Smithsonian Institution Press.

Kroker, A. (1993). *Spasm: Virtual reality, android music, and electric flesh.* New York: St. Martin's Press.

Kroker, A., & Weinstein, M.A. (1994). *Data trash: The theory of the virtual class.* New York: St. Martin's Press.

Landow, G.P. (1992). *Hypertext: The convergence of contemporary critical theory and technology.* Baltimore: John Hopkins University Press.

Lanham, R.A. (1993). *The electronic word: Democracy, technology, and the arts.* Chicago: University of Chicago Press.

Laurel, B. (Ed.). (1990). *The art of human-computer interface.* Reading, MA: Addison-Wesley.

Laurel, B. (1993). *Computers as theatre.* Reading, MA: Addison-Wesley.

Levy, S. (1984). *Hackers: Heroes of the computer revolution.* New York: Dell.

Levy, S. (1992). *Artificial life: A report from the frontier where computers meet biology.* New York: Random House.

Lubar, S. (1993). *Infoculture: The Smithsonian book of information age inventions.* Boston: Houghton Mifflin.

Lyotard, J.-F. (1984). *The postmodern condition: A report on knowledge* (G. Bennington & B. Massumi, Trans.). Minneapolis: University of Minnesota Press. (Original work published 1979)

McCaffery, L. (Ed.). (1991). *Storming the reality studio: A casebook of cyberpunk and postmodern fiction.* Durham, NC: Duke University Press.

McLuhan, M. (1962). *The Gutenberg galaxy.* Toronto: University of Toronto Press.

McLuhan, M. (1964). *Understanding media: The extensions of man.* New York: Mentor Books.

McLuhan, M., & Powers, B.R. (1989). *The global village.* New York: Oxford University Press.

Meyrowitz, J. (1985). *No sense of place.* New York: Oxford University Press.

Meyrowitz, J. (1986). Television and interpersonal behavior: Codes of perception and response. In G. Gumpert & R. Cathcart (Eds.), *Inter/media: Interpersonal communication in a media world* (3rd ed., pp. 253-272). New York: Oxford University Press.

Nelson, T.H. (1987). *Computer lib/Dream machines.* Redmond, WA: Tempus Books.

Nelson, T.H. (1990). *Literary machines.* Sausalito, CA: Mindful.

Novak, M. (1991). Liquid architectures in cyberspace. In M. Benedikt (Ed.),

Cyberspace: First steps (pp. 225-254). Cambridge, MA: MIT Press.

Ong, W.J. (1982). *Orality and literacy: The technologizing of the word.* New York: Methuen.

Papert, S. (1980). *Mindstorms: Children, computers, and powerful ideas.* New York: Basic Books.

Penrose, R. (1989). *The emperor's new mind: Concerning computers, minds, and the laws of physics.* New York: Oxford University Press.

Perkinson, H. (1995). *No safety in numbers: How the computer quantified everything and made people risk-aversive.* Cresskill, NJ: Hampton Press.

Peterson, D. (1983). *Genesis II: Creation and recreation with computers.* Reston, VA: Reston.

Pickover, C.A. (Ed.). (1994). *Visions of the future: Art, technology and computing in the twenty-first century.* New York: St. Martin's Press.

Pimentel, K., & Teixeira, K. (1993). *Virtual reality: Through the new looking glass.* New York: Intel/Windcrest/McGraw-Hill.

Poster, M. (1990). *The mode of information.* Chicago: University of Chicago Press.

Postman, N. (1979). *Teaching as a conserving activity.* New York: Delacorte.

Postman, N. (1985). *Amusing ourselves to death.* New York: Viking.

Postman, N. (1992). *Technopoly: The surrender of culture to technology.* New York: Knopf.

Provenzo, E.F., Jr. (1986). *Beyond the Gutenberg galaxy.* New York: Teachers College Press.

Provenzo, E.F., Jr. (1991). *Video kids: Making sense of Nintendo.* Cambridge, MA: Harvard University Press.

Pruitt, S., & Barrett, T. (1991). Corporate virtual workspace. In M. Benedikt (Ed.), *Cyberspace: First steps* (pp. 383-409). Cambridge, MA: MIT Press.

Reid, E.M. (1992, Winter). Electropolis: Communication and community on internet relay chat. *Intertek, 3*(3), 7-13.

Rheingold, H. (1991). *Virtual reality.* New York: Touchstone.

Rheingold, H. (1993). *The virtual community: Homesteading on the electronic frontier.* Reading, MA: Addison Wesley.

Rickett, F. (1993). Multimedia. In P. Hayward & T. Wollen (Eds.), *Future visions: New technologies of the screen* (pp. 72-91). London: British Film Institute.

Ritchin, F. (1990). *In our own image: The coming revolution in photography.* New York: Aperture.

Ross, A. (1991). Hacking away at the counterculture. In C. Penley & A. Ross (Eds.), *Technoculture* (pp. 107-134). Minneapolis: University of Minnesota Press.

Roszak, T. (1994). *The cult of information: A neo-Luddite treatise on high-tech, artificial intelligence, and the true art of thinking* (2nd ed.). Berkeley: The University of California Press.

Rushkoff, D. (1994). *Cyberia: Life in the trenches of hyperspace.* New York: HarperCollins.

Smith, A. (1993). *Books to bytes: Knowledge and information in the postmodern era.* London: British Film Institute.

Sproull, L., & Kiesler, S. (1991). *Connections: New ways of working in the networked organization.* Cambridge, MA: MIT Press.

Sterling, B. (Ed.). (1986). *Mirrorshades: The cyberpunk anthology.* New York: Arbor House.

Sterling, B. (1992). *The hacker crackdown: Law and disorder on the electronic frontier.* New York: Arbor House.

Sternberg, J. (1991). The abacus: The earliest digital computer and its cultural implications. *New Dimensions in Communications: Proceedings of the 48th Annual New York State Speech Communication Association Convention, 4,* 69-71.

Stone, A.R. (1991). Will the real body please stand up? Boundary stories about virtual cultures. In M. Benedikt (Ed.), *Cyberspace: First steps* (pp. 81-118). Cambridge, MA: MIT Press.

Strate, L. (1994). Post(modern)man, Or Neil Postman as a postmodernist. *Etc.: A Review of General Semantics, 51*(2), 159-170.

Sudnow, D. (1983). *Pilgrim in the microworld.* New York: Warner.

Taylor, M.C., & Saarinen, E. (1994). *Imagologies: Media philosophy.* London: Routledge.

Turkle, S. (1984). *The second self: Computers and the human spirit.* New York: Simon and Schuster.

Wachtel, E. (1978). Technological cubism: The presentation of space and time in multi-image. *Etc.: A Review of General Semantics, 35*(4), 376-382.

Weizenbaum, J. (1976). *Computer power and human reason.* San Francisco: Freeman.

Wiener, N. (1967). *The human use of human beings: Cybernetics and society.* Boston, MA: Avon.

Woolley, B. (1992). *Virtual worlds: A journey in hype and hyperreality.* Oxford: Blackwell.

Zettl, H. (1990). *Sight sound motion: Applied media aesthetics* (2nd ed.). Belmont, CA: Wadsworth.

SECTION 1

CYBERSPACE IN PERSPECTIVE: THE THEORETICAL CONTEXT

On one side there is the hype, hoopla, and how-to-oriented discourse of the popular media, the communications industry, and computer hobbyists and professionals. On the other, there is denial, dismissal, and silence. Between the two lies the path we must follow if we are to take cyberspace seriously, to study it as a communication phenomenon. To do so properly requires a grounding of the electronic environment, a framework for contextualizing the topic, a way of providing even cyberspace with a sense of place—placing cyberspace and, possibly, putting it in its place. Thus, the purpose of this section is to provide theoretical and philosophical bases for more specific analyses of cyberspace and to provide links to larger issues in the field of communication.

This section begins with Gary Gumpert and Susan Drucker's exploration of the electronic landscape from the communication and social space perspective. Noting how cyberspace functions as a substitute for public places, they raise questions concerning cyberspace's impact on privacy and law and on social interaction and overall quality of life. Following with a strong critique of the Internet environment, John M. Phelan takes on the utopian fantasies of cyberspace boosters, discussing the social, political, economic, and religious implications of the digital world and the rhetoric that surrounds it. The third chapter by James R. Beniger is concerned with the present and future ownership, control, and exploitation of cyberspace. Arguing that the Internet will probably not continue in its present form indefinitely, he outlines the vulnerabilities of cyberspace to commercialization and outside political control. Whereas Beniger's focus is on control of cyberspace, the very concept of ownership is destabilized in an electronic environment, as Neil Kleinman explains in Chapter 4. Presenting a history of intellectual property rights and copyright law, he emphasizes the problems posed by cyberspace's immaterial nature and its lack of barriers to the flow of information.

The idea of virtual reality is one of the most evocative concepts related to cyberspace. In the section's fifth chapter, Herbert Zettl examines virtual reality (VR) technologies as a medium and art form, discussing the aesthetic, metaphysical, and ethical issues involved in implementing VR systems. Charles U. Larson, in the following chapter, explores virtual reality from a rhetorical perspective. Employing Burke's dramatistic model, he focuses on virtual reality as a virtual scene in which virtual acts are performed. The virtual environments described by Zettl and Larson are a far cry from today's primarily text-based forms of computer-mediated communication, networking, and hypermedia. In Chapter 7, Jay David Bolter considers the conflict between audiovisual modes of communication, such as VR, with their emphasis on sensory experience, and those based on electronic writing and print, which stress rational discourse. Providing a historical and philosophical context, he makes clear the relationship between multimedia and virtual reality and what has been described as the decentering of the subject, the dissolution of the Cartesian ego, or simply changes in the concept of the self.

However much these authors differ in their outlook and method, they all help to clarify the concept of cyberspace, and they all provide theoretical contexts for its study based on communication and related disciplines.

◇◇◇◇ 1

From Locomotion to Telecommunication, or Paths of Safety, Streets of Gore

Gary Gumpert
Susan J. Drucker

As innovations, the technologies of electronic space are intended to function as alternatives to physical location and transportation. In actual use, however, they also function as social environments, as human beings adapt the technologies to fulfill their own needs and desires. Thus cyberspace becomes the setting for social life in which we meet others, form relationships, even hold funerals. Gary Gumpert and Susan J. Drucker take the measure of cyberspace as a social environment, exploring its range and peculiarities. They take the position that, although we may use cyberspace as a substitute for the physical environment, the two are by no means equivalent. Thus laws that are drafted to deal with physical objects and real persons in actual locations may not quite work when applied to the unstable world of electronic transmissions over shifting networks. Common-sense notions such as the distinction between public and private may no longer apply in the microworld of computer-mediated communication. Ultimately, the most important difference between the two environments, according to Gumpert and Drucker, is quality of life; they are concerned not just with what computers and telecommunications can do, but with what they undo. Outside of Section I, further examinations of cyberspace as social and public space can be found in Michael Beaubien's study of gaming and community-building in Chapter 12, Elizabeth Weiss's essay on the cybergym in Chapter 14, and Mark Lipton's research on cybersex in Chapter 22; related views on social interaction and relationships are present in Philip Thompsen's research on flaming in Chapter 20, and Richard Cutler's exploration of self-concept in cyberspace in Chapter 21. Additional discussion of legal issues can be found in Ronald Jacobson's piece on cyberspace policy in Chapter 9; see also Sue Barnes's exploration of virtual environments in Chapter 13.

PROLOGUE

Probe I

This co-authoring relationship of scholarship is fragile. It has withstood crises and attack. It survives on productivity and originality. It has an intellectual foundation grounded in the study of the Canons of Communication. But it's time to confess. It is also a research relationship firmly rooted in conspicuous consumption and the psychological reverberation that derives from a deep-seated computer neurosis. It has come to this. We define ourselves by the size of our RAM, the number of megs, the compatibility of our machines and programs, the speed of our trusty steeds, and our concern with the quality of our CD-ROM. It innocently began with a nonthreatening frolick with computer #1, now sitting unused and unwanted in one corner of the memorial library, with a hard card (rather than disk) and its two yawning 5 1/4-inch floppy drives. It sits there alone, unwanted, an outmoded, impotent, former friend, a steady companion who was at our creating, soothing, and offending side for a long period of time. But relationships are ephemeral and we must move on to new friends. Remember bigger and faster is better.

We graduated to a 386 33-meg machine with a 2400-Baud Hayes modem, but it's too slow for the Windows environment in which we now work, and we were about to order a new Pentium 586 machine with a built-in fax/modem (it's awfully inconvenient working with the separate fax machine), CD-ROM (with quality speakers), and tape backup. We were about to order, but became concerned that our high-powered communication research might be threatened by the high-powered divisional flaw of the Pentium chip.

It's media central, the nerve center of the radiating scholarly empire that links us to the riches of the Internet, the chat rooms of America Online, to the Chase Manhattan bank for high-finance transactions, to the local library to check on whether they have a copy of Gumpert's *Talking to Strangers* or Drucker's *American Heroes in a Media Age,* to Prodigy and Zagat's listing and ranking of restaurants around the globe, to Compuserve and Eaasy Sabre for airline schedules and rates, and to the keyboard through which ideas flow and are processed. *But neither of us have ever been in a neighbor's house.*

Probe II

It was almost the deadline for submitting panels to the Environmental Design conference being held in Boston in Spring 1995. We had four days to get the panel together and send it to the conference organizer. A call to Boston. A friend advised us that the Dean of Architecture would be a good person to have on the panel and sent us his e-mail address. We quickly drafted a letter, and uploaded it to the College computer center. Two days later, in checking on the latest e-mail, we received a reply from the Dean who indicated that the e-mail sent to Boston two days before had caught up with him in Australia. The Dean agreed to participate in the panel—if he were free—and asked us to e-mail his assistant at MIT to check on his commitments. Everything was fine and we sent out the proposal on time, with an exciting group of scholars around the United States—and beyond—who have agreed to participate. *But we don't know our neighbors' names. Sometimes we wish someone were outside so we could talk away our loneliness.*

Probe III

A working relationship is predicated on ritual. It is influenced by where we work ("Your place or mine?"). Physically we are separated by 2.4 miles—miles that easily dissolve under the circumstances of electronic geography. The internalized path leads from the kitchen, where a pot of tea is delicately brewed, later to be replaced with coffee, to an amble down the steps into the basement corridor, which leads to the study, an environment of books, papers, photographs, collected memorabilia, and a soft black chair from which we enter the rest of the world. The early morning radio companion substantiates that there is an outside, and we sit surrounded by answering machine, facsimile, computer and modem, laser jet printer, and cordless telephone. A right foot hits the switch and our electronics center lights up and, unlike those ancient relatives of old with whom we shared the simple act of locomotion, we cavort and connect as travelers in electronic space. We check the answering machine, which was turned on as we left to run compulsory errands. It's only a matter of 15 minutes, but someone might be crazy enough to call this early. The idea of missing a call is a perverse and alien notion. (More sophisticated, perhaps more important, scholars have trained themselves to screen calls.) The Crosstalk Icon is selected, and the ceremonial sound of computer coupling (do they have sex?) is heard and eventually the necessary passwords are negotiated so that electronic mail that has reached our computer accounts through enigmatic nodes, paths, gateways, and bridges can be processed and figuratively fondled. We reject, reply, forward, upload, download—in a strange boundless environment that is often only located in our imagination and that is described by some as *cyberspace.*

SPACELESS SPACE AND VIRTUAL ROADS

The term *cyberspace* is attributed to science fiction author William Gibson, who coined the term in his novel *Neuromancer*, "where it names a 21st century virtual dimension, entered into via a neuro-electronic interface, in which the world's data networks unfold before the user as a sensually vivid geography" (Dibbell, 1993, p.13). It is described by Compuserve as "that nowhere space in the telephone line between you and where all things on-line happen, but it's also the 'room' or other expanse you're not really in when you're visiting any form of virtual reality" ("Cyberspace," 1994, p. 12). The telephone call is a ticket of entrance.

Cyberspace, although not limited to the Internet, is often associated with its most well-known and largest expanse. The Internet is an unbelievably dense global matrix of 46,000 computer networks, 3.2 million host computers, woven together by telephone lines, undersea cables, microwave links, and gigabit fiber-optic pipes. Touching down in 146 countries, linking 25 million to 30 million people and growing by a million users each month, it's doubling in size each year (Internet Society, 1994; Lewis, 1994b). It's a super data highway that carries the freight of the information age—electronic mail, digital video and sound, computer viruses, and more (Markoff, 1993a). There are an estimated 3.2 million computers around the globe today with predictions that the Internet will grow to more than 100 million computers in 5 years (Internet Society, 1994; Lewis, 1994b). There are 21,700 commercial "domains" (the Internet equivalent of storefront addresses) officially registered (Verity & Hof, 1994): "Some companies are . . . laying the groundwork for entirely new ways of doing business—dealing directly with suppliers, industrial customers, and potentially millions of on-line shoppers" (p. 39).

The Internet began in the 1970s as a U.S. Defense Department network called ARPAnet. Slowly, corporations, universities, and information providers phased and dovetailed their networks into the system, agreeing on compatible connecting software (McNichol, 1994). Furthermore, it is the Internet that is a focal point of the electronic data highway featured as a high priority in the Clinton-Gore Administration. Such a system includes digital libraries (making libraries accessible to everyone), database publishing, electronic mail, electronic communities (virtual or nonplace communities that link people with similar interests), software access, weather information, entertainment, and data exchange (Markoff, 1993b).

Progress and technological developments can be terribly exciting. Being able to connect with the outside world from our intellectual dungeon is amazing and helpful, but it is much more difficult to forecast the impact of such developments. It is not our intention to examine the intricacies of the electronic data highway. We are probably not capable of that task, and there are Internet experts who perform such functions well. What we are concerned with is the impact and relationship of such developments with concurrent situations and institutions.

Langdon Winner (1993) wrote an article for the *Chronicle of Higher Education* in which the problem is succinctly stated:

> What most conventional ideas about technology lack is any notion of technological development as a dynamic social and cultural phenomenon. This is not an arcane topic. Every thorough-going history of the building of technological systems points to the same conclusion: Substantial technological innovation involves a reweaving of the fabric of society—a reshaping of some of the roles, rules, relationships, and institutions that make up our ways of living together. (p. B1)

The preceding analysis stresses the complex interrelationships of innovation and states that "the technology is never the sole cause of the changes one sees. But it is often the occasion and catalyst for a thorough redefinition of the operating structures of society and of the daily experiences of people in their work, family, life, and communities" (p. B1). Winner, a professor of political science at Rensselaer Polytechnic Institute, quite astutely uses as an analogy the construction of the national interstate highway system after the Second World War. The system was inspired by a wish to improve commerce, foster social mobility, and bolster national defense. In actual usage, its grid of arteries and ring of roads permanently changed the American social landscape. Among other consequences, the interstate highways amplified a growing split between urban centers and outlying communities, a serious and troublesome split characterized by today's suburbia as compared with the inner cities. As it built physical boundaries between neighborhoods, the highway system modified not only the nation's economy, but our personal relations as well.

With the development of all communication systems prior to the telegraph, the stress was placed on place rather than on the movement of data. The early development of telegraphy was linked to transportation and speed of transmission, but the economic structure of even the telegraph had extraordinary implications. Anthony Rutkowski, executive director of the Internet Society, points out that "at the very earliest telegraph conferences of 1850, there were issues about the additional cost necessary to reach remote places and who should pay. The iteration of the debate is about the information superhighway" (quoted in Gerwig, 1994, p. 23). Thus, geographic implosion further redefines rural and urban divisions. About 20% of Americans must pay long distance rates to get on the electronic highway. Although the concept of rural may be defined by the expense of access to the highway, rather than by expanse of land, even some suburban and urban dwellers may find themselves distanced by cost as well.

The spatial relationship of radio was between listener and station, of television between viewer and channel. But the virtual community is a construction existing in our vision and imagination, and it is significant that geographical and architectural terms are the primary metaphors used to describe the emerging electronic environment in which place and location are deemphasized in favor of speed of transmission.

It begins as soon as we turn on the computer. We enter the graphical environment of Windows through which we can access software and connections to data and others. The screen of the computer is converted from an opaque frame to a transparent conduit that leads bits of data out to an amorphous electronic environment. We are linked to bulletin boards, malls, and rooms through ports, highways, exits, gateways, bridges, routers, and nodes.

SOCIAL LIFE AND SPACELESS RELATIONSHIPS

David Alsberg was a 42-year-old computer programmer. He was standing in a Times Square store when a stray bullet from a nearby robbery attempt instantly killed him. *The New York Times* account does not focus on the all-too-common circumstances of Mr. Alsberg's death, but on the grieving that followed (Lewis, 1994a). The story states that Mr. Alsberg lived in two communities, one being his Astoria neighborhood, where his wife, son, and hundreds of friends came together to mourn his death. The other community in which he lived was "the electric community called Cyberspace" (p. A1). Mr. Alsberg's personal computer friends came together in an online wake in an electronic forum.

In a world where physical contact is impossible, Mr. Alsberg's cyberspace neighbors consoled each other over the senseless loss of a mutual friend. And in their collective grieving, they demonstrated an impulse for togetherness that is as modern as the digital age and as old as humankind. For as more people become citizens of cyberspace, they are forging relationships that many describe as being as rewarding as their face-to-face-friendships (Lewis, 1994a, p. D2)

It is estimated that the population of cyberspace consists of between 30 to 35 million people. *The New York Times* reports that what some might call "artificial intimacy is catching the interest of psychologists and sociologists" (Lewis, 1994a, p. D2). The Alsberg incident links the hostile world of the street with the more secure, nonthreatening, electronic Internet highway of cyberspace. Safety seems to be the primary defining criterion by which individuals choose the spaces in which they work, play, live, and interact.

Not so very long ago our social lives were divided between public and private spaces. (We define such spaces on the basis of access rather than ownership.) We maintained our private relationships in the home, but activities outside the home were important. We learned about events and people. We played and watched others play. We escaped the tyranny of those we love for a moment or two by watching others whom we had not yet met. We conversed with strangers we might not meet again and old companions who were recurring supporting characters in our lives.

Social interaction of both a private and a public nature has entered the realm of electronic space, interaction located in a placeless vacuum in which two or more people can link via telephone or where one or more persons can become involved with the program of a distanced computer (Gumpert & Drucker, 1992). Face-to-face communication in physical space and mediated communication may serve the same purposes but are experienced in very different ways. Every media development alters the availability and nature of traditional private and public places. The newspaper influenced and defined, in part, the barbershop, the village green, and the cafe. The telephone shaped the nature of courtship. Radio altered the experiences of the living room, the car, and the doctor's office. The computer keyboard opens up distant retrievable vistas.

For some, cyberspace alternatives for social interaction are limited by lack of access to electronic connection because of cost, technophobia and/or lack of technical virtuosity. Street life which once beckoned and called has been swept away by the realities of fear and risk. Those who are afraid to go out instead sit alone in rooms, often disconnected from the environment in which they sit.

REGULATING METAPHORS

It is significant that at a time when we seek refuge from the street, when the highway has been reduced to a connection between hostile zones, as we continue down the path of interiorizing and privatization, that the nomenclature of urban planning and architecture has been transformed into metaphors of cyberspace. Thus, there is a reason for the subtitle of this chapter—"Paths of Safety, Streets of Gore."

The vocabulary surrounding new technologies, new uses for old technologies, and the joinder of multiple media is significant as it not only allows us to talk about a phenomenon, but also shapes the perception of the reality being named. In fact, the words created and metaphors employed function persuasively: "Kenneth Burke has argued that 'naming' is an interpretive act which functions as a guide to action toward that which is named" (Blankenship, 1980, p. 321). Therefore, "the command that one act one way rather than another is 'implicit' in the name" (Burke, 1950, p. 41).

Approached from a dramatistic perspective, we may see these clusters of metaphors as a symbolic reaction to an environment that involves "the use of words by human agents to form attitudes or to induce action in other human agents" (Burke, 1950, p. 41). The adoption of spatial terminology may appear a ready and useful mechanism for making the revolutionary changes of the information age less strange, intimidating, and boundless. Thus, for example, the concept of "broadcasting" can be traced to somewhere between 1760 and 1770, and it originally was an agricultural term used to describe the spreading or the sowing of seeds. To cast the seed broadly became a suitable metaphor to portray the transmission of sound in a manner quite distinct from the prior notion of point-to-point transmission. We now use the term not only to describe a medium of communication, but also the act of making something generally widely known, and sometimes it refers to the indiscriminate act of spreading lies. In this case, we begin to think, perceive, and reshape the world with an agriculturally based, technologically transformed metaphor. Although a few of us may throw seeds into the wind as a romantic gesture, the art of agriculture has also been redefined, and broadcasting is seldom performed by hand in an industry that has left the confines of the small farm for large conglomerate-run outfits. Furthermore, how do you keep them down on the farm when broadcasts have revealed that there are other and more varied fields to sow?

Words are what we make them, but they also make us over. In the case of cyberspace and electronic communication, the matter of metaphor is more than a simplistic linguistic exercise created to keep academics off the street. Very early in the primordial arcane days when strange people plotted the computer future of the world, decisions were made linking our metaphysical souls to the evolving communication philosophy that would emerge out of that mass of blinking, winking, and groaning set of tubes, lights, and valves. When the International Standards Organization adopted an Open System Interconnect reference model (somehow also linked with IBM's Systems Network Architecture) in order to assure compatibility among users, the language of architecture and urban planning had already provided a metaphorical lexicon to guide future development and usage.

Words are what we make them, but they (and what they represent) evolve, dynamically change, and reflect back on their origins. The significance of the landscape orientation of cyberspace is not only that a prior spatial identity has been applied to a nonterritorially defined medium, but that the very process of naming redefines the earlier application. The nomenclature of space, urban planning, and architecture has been transformed into metaphors of cyberspace. Metaphors shape perceptions, expectations, and psychological assumptions, which drive the relationships formed with that which has been named. Spatial metaphors have been transposed from the physical world in which property and ownership are defining principles to the electronic realm of connection. Through application of this metaphor the implications emerge as spatial metaphors become not merely useful tools for making the revolutionary changes of the information age less strange and unsettling, but a ready mechanism through which to manage and regulate the alien phenomenon. So, for instance, the technologies of communications challenge developments in applicable laws governing rights of free expression in such areas as libel,[1] hate speech,[2] and

---

[1] *Cubby v. CompuServe Incorporated*, (1991) is the sole case to date in which a libel action was reportedly brought against an information service provider. In this case a plaintiff sued CompuServe on the basis of allegedly false and defamatory statements contained in an electronic newsletter available in CompuServe's Journalism Forum; the newsletter was not published by CompuServe, however, but rather by a third party. The court granted CompuServe's motion for summary judgment relying upon CompuServe's actions as distributor, exercising no editorial control and acting as an electronic library.

[2] Hate speech has confronted information providers as an issue which requires attention. The Anti-Defamation League of B'nai B'rith cited anti-Semitic notes sent via e-mail but

obscenity,[3] as well as rights of privacy and related issues of sexual harassment,[4] and jurisdictional questions. In attempting to keep pace with technological growth, developments in "cyberlaw" have been handled through the application of preexisting legal doctrines, some taken from the pages of property law.

From a legal perspective real property, or physical space, is distinguished by possession and use and enjoyment. The laws of real property and access to that property in order to communicate produce distinct issues determined by whether the public space is publicly or privately owned. Although title to real property is easily identifiable, who owns cyberspace? Bulletin boards have been called the computer-age equivalent of a public forum (Naughton, 1993), but approximately 90% are operated by private individuals or organizations on privately owned computers (Feder, 1991). Many bulletin boards (particularly commercial ventures) are governed by subscription agreements that generally expressly reserve the right to reject messages deemed inappropriate or to terminate the user's privilege to use the board. For example, America Online's Subscriber Agreement "reserves the right, at its sole discretion, to immediately, without Notice, suspend or terminate a Member's access to and use of America Online upon any breach of the Terms of Service."

The laws of privacy represent an area of law that has been more fully developed with regard to electronic, nonphysical spaces of interaction. The evolution of the right to be let alone, or the right to privacy and reasonable expectations of privacy, has regularly been rooted in the nature of a particular geographic location. Fourth and Fifth Amendment rights are involved when considering search and seizure and freedom from self-incrimination associated with places in which there is a reasonable expectation of privacy. Courts have explored these expectations in physical spaces ranging from homes and offices to cars and school lockers (Kamisar, LaFave, & Israel, 1986). It is clear that reasonable expectations of privacy are no longer restricted to the physical spatial realm. Dating back to 1967, the Supreme Court enunciated this point in *Katz v.*

---

rejected for public posting by Prodigy as an example of electronically networked hate speech (Miller, 1991; for further discussion see Leroux, 1991).

[3]Obscenity has received a good deal of attention within the context of cyberspace (Jackson, 1994). One of the most widely noted cases involved the operators of "Amateur Action" electronic bulletin board service who were convicted under the federal law criminalizing transmitting obscene images electronically from California to Tennessee (Landis, 1994).

[4]Santa Rosa Junior College in California was the site of a case in which three students were offended by sexual comments on a computer bulletin board run through the school. Separate male and female bulletin boards were operated prompting the students to allege sexual discrimination. The students brought charges under Title IX of the Civil Rights Act which prohibits sexual discrimination in schools. Further it was found that one female student, Jennifer Branham, had been subjected to sexual harassment in that a hostile educational environment had been created with regard to the posting of the messages. A settlement was reached between the students and the college in the amount of $15,000. The case against the Education Department under Title IX remains open (Lewis, 1994b).

United States, at which time the Court found "the emphasis on the nature of a particular targeted area deflected attention from the issue of Fourth Amendment infringement" (p. 351). Justice Steward wrote:

> For the Fourth Amendment protects people not places. What a person knowingly exposes to the public, even in his own home or office, is not a subject of Fourth Amendment protection. . . . But what he seeks to preserve as private even in an area accessible to the public, may be constitutionally protected. (Katz v. United States, 1967, p. 351).

One of the most popular types of communication in electronic space is electronic mail, a nearly instantaneous means of exchanging written messages and documents. Is the electronic space involved private? Can one assume no one would open e-mail? The answer to this may be addressed in service agreements with commercial service providers, but additional issues are raised in the university or business setting. Employers often monitor employee's job performance, but the latest twist is to do this via access to employee e-mail. Employers claim they do this for reasons ranging from system maintenance, message routing, and trouble shooting to protection of trade secrets and quality control (Kelly, 1994). According to Joel P. Kelly, writing in the February 1994 *Employment Law Strategist:*

> The tremendous rise in the number of employees who now use this technology, and the increasing ability of management to monitor such use, raise novel legal and ethical issues including: Do employees have a privacy right in their electronic mail communications? Under what circumstances can managers lawfully monitor employees' electronic mail? Is the employees' consent necessary? What facts are necessary to show consent? (p. 831)

Answers? The Electronic Communications Privacy Act of 1986 (ECPA) generally protects e-mail from illegal monitoring and makes it a federal crime to intercept and disclose electronic communications (18 U.S.C. 2510, 1988) punishable by imprisonment for up to five years or a fine of up to $250,000 for an individual and $500,000 for an organization. Individuals who show communications have been intercepted or used in violation of statute can claim actual and punitive damages of up to $100 per day of violation. But the ECPA does not protect privacy of messages sent on internal company electronic mail systems. The law treats such messages as interoffice memos that can be read by authorized employees, supervisors, or systems managers without violating the law. One party to the communication must consent to the monitoring, but the employees' consent can be implied from the circumstances of employment. Employees claim this violates their privacy rights, particularly if the intercepted communication is of a personal nature, but to date the courts have not addressed the right of privacy in the context of employers' monitoring of employee e-mail for legitimate business reasons. Under the Fourth Amendment, courts have even upheld an employer's right to engage in workplace surveillance for legitimate business reasons (O'Connor v. Ortega, 1987). There is a developing policy regarding employee expectations of privacy that seems to indicate there is not a reasonable expectation of privacy for company files and business correspondence generated by employees during work time, using company equipment. This extends from physical files and offices to electronic space on e-mail and computer files.

THE REPERCUSSIONS OF CYBERSPACE ON PHYSICAL SPACE

Each medium leaves its mark by altering our institutions and personal attitudes and values, a concept eloquently embodied in Victor Hugo's *The Hunchback of Notre-Dame.* In that marvelous work the character of the archdeacon boldly states that "the book will kill the church":

> Omitting the detailing of a thousand proofs, and thousand objections to what has been said, we may sum the matter up as follows: That architecture, up to the fifteenth century, was as the chief register of humanity; that during this interval, no thought of any complexity appeared in the world that was not built as every religious commandment has its monument; that human nature, in short, had not thought of importance that it did not write in stone. And why? Because every idea, whether religious or philosophic, is concerned in being perpetuated. The idea that has stirred the emotions of one generation desires to affect others, and to leave its trace behind. . . .
>
> In the fifteenth century, everything underwent a change. Humanity discovered a means of perpetuating thought more lasting and durable than architecture, and even simpler and easier. Architecture was dethroned. To the stone letters of Orpheus are to succeed Gutenberg's letters of lead.
> *The book will destroy the church.*

The book unchained the worshiper from dependence on the institution of the church and created the individual supplicant. Similarly, the computer, at the apex of media technology, as the trigger of interactivity combining other media, will redefine not only other and previous media, but the structural metaphor it has borrowed in order to function. Victor Hugo understood the power of print to delineate the new spiritual relationship to be found in the church. Few of us comprehend that the electronic highway is not just an extension of the turnpike, that it not only co-opts but devalues the domain of public space.

In *Progressive Architecture*, Thomas Fisher (1988), discussing the new urban design, says: "The city of today is primarily a private city. Most of its open space, most of its transportation, most of its buildings, indeed most of the forces that shape it are private" (p. 7). In *The Conscience of the Eye,* sociologist Richard Sennett (1990) states:

> What is characteristic of our city building is to wall off the differences between people, assuming that these differences are more likely to be mutually threatening than mutually stimulating. What we make in the urban realm are therefore bland neutralizing spaces, spaces which remove the threat of social contact. (p. xiii).

It takes little acumen to understand that our cities are self-destructing. Suburbia dominates while urban life deteriorates to such an extent that we seek refuge from the street. Our highways separate rather than connect while transporting folks from place of work to place of residence, from home to mall, from outside threat to inside safety.

Although fear and decay threaten and alter the quality of urban life, there are those of us who continue the quest to rejuvenate the public place, sharing a romantic notion that there is a need for the opportunity to talk to and touch each other away from the obligations of office, home, and predetermined programmed responsibilities, and that the shopping mall does not provide the answer to isolation. But there is something seductive about electronic communication with others, and we in the United States have begun to rely on mediated communication and even to prefer that mode to the old, particularly because it is safe, forgetting that there are qualitative differences between the two. The mediated functional alternatives that we choose generally occur inside controlled private space.

So we retreat inward where we can control at least some of the threats. No one wants to hand in their facsimile machine, answering machine, telephone, television, CD-ROM, cassette player, radio, beeper, video games, cellular phone, laser discs, VCR, and walkman. No one, in their right mind, seeks to dismantle the electronic highway and its potential store of activities. Ironically, it is the electronic highway (and what it symbolizes) that threatens to dismantle the traditional streets, squares, highways, and communities that once were so important to us.

EPILOGUE

Once upon a time, not so many years ago, people could go out into the city lights when the fancy struck them, when they had nothing better to do, when it occurred to them that it might be fun to be with others. Sometimes it was necessary to walk into the street to find out what was happening in the world. They wandered out to the square to talk, to the cafe to contemplate their lives over a cup of coffee, to the park to stroll among others, to the pub to flirt with those who were there to rush the blood, to the bench where ancient memories reside, to the chess tables to advise and criticize, to the public realm to vanquish loneliness, discuss politics, or simply talk. But it is no longer that time past, and the old and familiar have often become hostile and menacing. We sadly step back and find other possibilities and less-threatening opportunities to play and frolic—safely, often alone.

REFERENCES

Blankenship, J. (1980). The Search for the 1972 Democratic nomination: A metaphorical perspective. In B. Brock & R. Scott (Eds.), *Methods of rhetorical criticism: A twentieth century perspective* (2nd ed., pp. 321-345). Detroit, MI: Wayne State University Press.

Burke, K. (1950). A *rhetoric of motives.* New York: George Brazeller

Cubby v. CompuServe Incorporated, 776 F. Supp. 135 (S.D.N.Y, 1991).

Cyberspace. (1994, March). *Compuserve Magazine,* p.12.

Dibbell, J. (1993, March). Let's get digital: The writer à la modem. *The Voice Literary Supplement,* pp. 13-14.

Feder, B.J. (1991, November 3). Toward defining free speech in the computer age. *The New York Times,* p. D5.

Fisher, T. (1988, March). Editorial. *Progressive Architecture,* p. 7.

Gerwig, K. (1994, November 28). Dealing with the price of rural access to the Internet. *Interactive Age,* pp. 22-23.

Gumpert, G., & Drucker, S.J. (1992). From the agora to the electronic shopping mall. *Critical Studies in Mass Communication, 9*(2), 186-200.

Internet Society. (1994, August 4). *Latest Internet measurements reveal dramatic growth in 1994* [press release].

Jackson, D.S. (1994, July 25). Battle for the soul of Internet. *Time,* pp. 50, 56.

Kamisar, Y., LaFave, W.R., & Israel, J.H. (1986). *Modern criminal procedure* (6th ed.). St. Paul, MN: West.

Katz v. United States, 389 U.S. 347 (1967).

Kelly, J.P. (1994, February). Whose e-mail is it anyway? In E. Kirsh, L. Rose, & S. Steele (Eds.), *Business and legal aspects of the Internet and online services* (pp. 831-834). New York: Law Journal Seminars Press.

Landis, D. (1994, August 9). Regulating porn: Does it compute? *USA Today,* p. D1.

Leroux, C. (1991, October 27). Hate speech enters computer age. *Chicago Tribune,* p. C4.

Lewis, P. (1994a, March, 8). Strangers, not their computers, build a network in a time of grief. *The New York Times,* pp. A1, D2.

Lewis, P. (1994b, June 19). Getting down to business on the Net. *The New York Times,* p. C1.

Markoff, J. (1993a, September 5). The Internet. *The New York Times,* p. 11.

Markoff, J. (1993b, January 24). A key project of Clinton and Gore raises a debate: Public or private? *The New York Times,* pp. 1,6.

McNichol, T. (1994, January 21). Fellow travelers on the info highway. *U.S.A. Weekend,* p. 4.

Miller, M.W. (1991, October 22). Prodigy network defends display of anti-Semitic notes. *Wall Street Journal,* p. B1.

Naughton, E.J. (1993). Is cyberspace a public forum? Computer bulletin boards, free speech, and state action. *The Georgetown Law Journal, 81*, 409-441.
O'Connor v. Ortega, 480 U.S. 709 (1987).
Sennett, R. (1990). *The conscience of the eye*. New York: Knopf.
Verity, J.W., & Hof, R.D. (1994, November 14). The Internet: How it will change the way you do business. *Business Week*, pp. 38-46.
Winner, L. (1993, August 4). How technology weaves the fabric of society. *The Chronicle of Higher Education*, pp. B1-B3.
18 U.S.C. Sections 2510-2520 (1988).

◊◊◊◊ 2

CyberWalden: The Inner Face of Interface

John M. Phelan

That cyberspace, virtual reality, the Internet, and the like are hot topics at present is quite clear. Newspapers and magazines now devote special columns and sections to these aspects of computer media and telecommunications; new books promising quick and easy access to the electronic environment abound, commercial services such as Prodigy, America Online, and CompuServe are flooded with new members. The hype surrounding cyberspace seems to draw on the self-help genre by promising better living through computing. In this wide-ranging essay, John M. Phelan deflates the utopian fantasies of cyberspace enthusiasts, arguing that the rhetoric of cyberculture misleads us about our own real-world efficacy. As a long-time cybernaut, he sees the Internet as an efficient research tool, but not a substitute for public life and political participation. Placing cyberspace in the larger contexts of cybernetics and broadcasting, he discusses its relationship to secondary orality and the retrieval of religious worldviews. Outside of this section of the book, additional research on the Internet appears in Mark Giese's historical overview in Chapter 8, and Ronald Jacobson's discussion of contemporary policy issues in Chapter 9; related critiques of Net culture and politics can be found in Michael P. Beaubien's exploration of the linguistic construction of community in Chapter 12 and Paul Lippert's examination of the political implications of cyberspace metaphors in Chapter 18; Richard Cutler's arguments concerning Net culture in Chapter 21 offer an alternate point of view.

new field for old dreams. It is the latest meeting place for both ıether and trying to figure out, as we never cease to do, where we ɾe the word comes from will help us to understand where we might be going with it.

Norbert Wiener, the child prodigy and mathematical wizard who formulated the basis for the engineering of "feedback" into so many of the devices we associate with computer-assisted living, from cruise control to the "smart house," gave his pathfinding book, *The Human Use of Human Beings*, the prescient subtitle of *Cybernetics and Society* (1954). Wiener, who had wanted to become a medical doctor, found he was unable to properly slice sections for up-to-standard microscopic slides (an essential task for all medical students in those days). He could not do so, not because he had unsteady hands, but because his vision was very poor. His eureka was to realize that his hand and eye formed a loop of control and adjustment; a feedback loop, he called it, realizing it was an essential component of all activity, because all activity is interactivity (Wiener, 1954). Feedback then began to be consciously engineered into all sorts of devices and was used metaphorically in the social sciences and group psychology. But it is important to note that the essential note of feedback is one of control effect, hence, the term *cybernetics*. The Greek root, guber-, also forms the gov- in government. *Cyber* indicates control effect through interactivity.

This is the essential note of cyberspace: people controlling devices through computers that give them the feeling of feedback as if the devices were parts of their own bodies. The defining characteristic of the later notion of virtual reality is not its visual verisimilitude, but its feedback and its acceptance of our manipulations. We can see a brilliantly realistic HDTV rendering of rainbow populated coral reefs, but we can have the illusion of swimming and catching fish inside the rather crude representations of much lower bit renderings of Virtual Surfing. We just don't witness it, we live in it. That's what makes it more "real" than the admitted greater vividness of HDTV.

Projection of our own body parts into inanimate tools and devices is an essential human experience of feedback because our senses always strive to be transparent. Anyone who drives knows that a sedan "feels" different from a hot sports car because it "responds" more sensitively to our control. The gears translate gas pedal pressure more immediately and delicately to engine rpm's. Transparent tight feedback is a sign of control. The machine is part of us. So, too, in sports: the better the athlete, the less mental distance between her and racquet or golf club. The best athletes transparently project their intentions to the flying tennis or golf ball after they have lost any "real" contact with it. It is like breathing or walking for them. Likewise, great performers so project personality out from the stage that they devour the audience.

Once computers, through video screens, began to give real-time feedback to operators, this sense of feel, of self-projection, inevitably followed. That's one of the main reasons we demand so much more speed from our chips than we need (for most of the programs actually used): the immediacy of the response makes it more transparent, more like a bit of ourselves, and thus greatly enhances our own interior neural net's natural tendency to integrate with the machine. Anne McCaffrey (1969), over 25 years ago, wrote of immense space ships that had handicapped and otherwise helpless human beings hardwired into their central computer control so that the ships could be seen as either enormously bionic humans or wetware-operated hardware.

This neural integration is getting tighter and tighter in cyberspace. Although most of the Net was first accessed through a kind of super DOS hell of maddeningly slow menu selections, arcane command strings, and absurdly unmemorable e-mail addresses, three developments have changed it. First is the growth of friendly GUI (graphic user interfaces) started at Xerox Parc 20 years ago, used by Apple for the past decade, and now coming to the PC world through NT Windows and its successor—Windows 95. The exponential explosion of microchip speed and sophistication (Pentium™, Power PC™, and beyond) gives enough speed and power to enhance these GUIs from sort of primitive kindergarten sketches to the more sophisticated graphics of full-motion video and superpaint toolbox stations. Finally, the building of the so-called Information Superhighway is providing sufficient bandwidth on most links to accommodate such heavy signal loads. Once the interface philosophy of America Online, Mosaic, and Netscape is teamed up with full access to the Net denied on most commercial services and humanizes the nerdland of TCP/IP and other gateway software, the illusion of being plugged into some kind of world will be hard to resist.

These technologies then enable us to experience control ("cyber-") as a projection of self out of our center, from our wills, into something else. That something else, that field of activity, is space. It is real because it is independent of us, but paradoxically more real because it also responds to us. It has dimensions that are real only because they can be probed. There is no perfect tee-shot without a green to go to.

The sense of projected bodily power onto a field, so readily grasped in sports, is thus naturally best and most easily translated into a game on a screen. From there it is a short reach to make the screen the world or environment for all action. This feature was one of the first to be exploited after video games—the adventure or story world in which the reader became a participant. The game player becomes the role player—but an active one whose moves, as in a game, will certainly affect the outcome of the story. And so the real-time responding screen becomes a field where one's actions produce outcomes and further enhance the metaphor and illusion of control through or in a space—cyberspace. The wedding of two old activities—game playing and vicarious living through fiction—transforms each. Fiction not only becomes interactive, it becomes collaborative, a kind of team sport.

The word *cyberspace* in its roots thus well describes any space that is a field for human effects through environmental interaction. But it has in fact been restricted to a certain type of human effect field—that of computer-mediated electronic tele-effects, most of them in the form of symbol exchange. *Cyberspace* is not unlike *technology* in that respect. Technology properly refers to any human organization of tool use, from chipping flints in the cave to cadcaming microchips in Silicon Valley. But it is almost always presumed to mean high technology of recent vintage. Also like *technology*, *cyberspace* evokes a shared space of common goals, for the human world requires both witness and collaboration, surveillance and competition.

Some years ago, commenting on the seminal work of Innis, McLuhan, Havelock, Ong, and others, I suggested that television and radio, by communicating through what Ong called Secondary Orality, had created a world of Secondary Tribalism (Phelan, 1980). That is, observers and call-ins on broadcast material participated without really being present and had the illusion of social interaction while remaining alone and, in any true political sense, impotent. My point at the time was that what was being touted as a brave new world of possibilities was in many ways a reduction of social life and real political participation to a pale substitute. What was a public, I said in the 1970s, was becoming an audience (Phelan, 1977).

Subsequent studies have borne out this view (Abramson, Arterton, & Orren, 1988; Barnet & Cavanagh, 1994; Chomsky, 1991; Dahlgren & Sparks, 1991; Entman, 1989; Greider, 1992; Herman & Chomsky, 1988; Krugman, 1994). From 1972 to 1992, there has been a steeply rising curve of money and time spent on political campaign media, especially television, and it has directly matched a descending curve of actual political participation (Phelan, 1995). Granted the hopeful presence of PeaceNet, EcoNet, the Electronic Frontier Foundation, and the alleged role of the Internet in getting news out of Iraq, Iran, China, Russia, and Mexico during recent crises, there is overwhelmingly greater evidence of big players and governments gaining Net control the old-fashioned way: by buying it and licensing it. Governments have more direct methods of control: the Clinton Administration has proposed the Clipper chip—a preinstalled opening for the U.S. Feds to tap all communications, however encrypted. The Saudis, more traditionally, have already outlawed all private satellite downlinks and are putting their oceans of cash into a totally government-controlled wired Islam.

This dramatic conflict of empowerment hope in the face of disenfranchising reality is being played again, it seems, by telecomputed MUDs (Multi-User Dungeons[= fantasies]/Dimensions) and MUSES (Multi-User Simulated Environments). Imaginatively, the Markle Foundation has funded Maxis to develop *SimHealth* as a device to educate the masses about the complexities of national healthcare policy; let's hope it helps. But we already have the dispiriting paradox of our real inner cities and suburbs sinking into a Grimpen Mire (the grim foggy bog haunted by the Baskervilles' hound) of actual ungovernability, as more and more bright people score brilliantly on *SimCity*. If real politics has degenerated into image management, who needs to bother with the real thing?

So we see the paradox of cyberspace, which enhances the illusion of images as reality because we can move and change the images and thus are deluded into thinking we are effective in the real world (Phelan 1984, 1988).

CYBERCELLS

In his trademark bizarre irony, Franz Kafka (1987) once wrote a letter to his betrothed imploring her to give up such obsessive correspondence with him, referring to a previous request in his last letter sent two hours earlier. I note that the ever-resourceful cyberworld has an online self-help usergroup for those who feel they are addicted to being online.

So a few fall a bit too deeply into the WELL, as one pioneering gathering place of disembodied scripts substituting for living presences is called. It affords not only a shared place of imagined story, as in MUDs, but an ongoing real-time conversation with a large number of globally scattered participants (IRC—Interactive Relay Chat).

What accounts for the stunning popularity of going online?

There is the magic of mysterious connection with the enchanted distant—something felt by youngsters in the 1920s (like young Richard Feynman in Brooklyn), who manipulated the old crystal sets under the blankets when they were supposed to be asleep, pulling in signals from ships at sea and from dance bands in Cleveland. There is the desperate need for contact among the marooned, like ham radio operators in snowbound Alaska or isolated islanders in the Pacific. Some of those obsessively hooked by Electropolis, as it has been called, are undoubtedly of this stripe. But there are not enough socially uneasy adolescents or cutoff adults to account for the wild popularity of Internetting on Usenet, IRC, MUDs and other variants.

Not ignoring that over one-fourth of all American households have but a single occupant (not a misprint!), and taking due account that more and more people flit from one workplace to another because there are far fewer long-term employments, I think a catalytic ingredient in the online explosion is the growing number of adults who, either in an office or increasingly at home, work in front of a monitor screen all day. Like it or not, it is their workplace: a relentlessly no-nonsense workplace with no water cooler, no stair landings, no snack room, no commuting buddies in car pools, trains, or even elevators.

Just as those glued to their television sets for six or seven hours a night reasonably prefer sets with PIP (picture in picture), which lets one see the action of more than one channel at once to enhance surfing (at the loss of coherence, if you value *that*), so, too, do workers chained to computer monitors for eight or more hours a day naturally prefer to have a large screen with 16 million possible shades and hues of color, with a number of programs opened at once. This affords the equivalent of a room with a view, a corner office, lots of windows to look through with all sorts of action going on. If one can wave to friends out the window, even talk to them and get answers back, so much the better. That the window can see as far as Japan or Tahiti is a thrilling bonus. Distance apart, cyberspace is a humanizing device for creating a kind of ersatz office/pub/common room/public square area for those deprived, rather cruelly, of one or more versions of the real thing. There are friendly conversations in bars, and then there are those who observe scripted conversations at Cheers. If you can't get to the former, you can at least, as it were, enter the set and talk back: CyberCheers.

A poignant note sounded by those engrossed in threading through cybertalk is how they are forced to use words to substitute for all the other physical cues of face-to-face conversations and IRL (in real life) settings—no mood music, no roaring sports fans, no candlelight, nor disco strobes. They thus have resorted to typographic signals such as :-) (a smiley, look at it sideways). This is seen as an achievement, and in a way of course it is. But it is stated in a context of reinventing the wheel. Shakespeare, who didn't have special effects to create battle scenes or regal pageantry or mysterious moors to put on high-tech stages, instead put words in auditing ears, the listeners, the *audi*ence.

All creative writers are liberated as well as confined by words. Joyce managed to create an entire inner world as well as to evoke everyday Dublin only with words. Using words to create worlds is what literature does: It requires great skill, it has standards, it is richly varied, it is available without a connect fee, it can be taught; with great effort and talent you can learn to do it, or at least appreciate it. Like reading a musical score, reading literature requires not only education, but some sensitivity training, a developed sense of nuance. These powers must be brought to the keyboard. However long one's days and nights in the blue glare of the screen, one cannot reach in and pull them out.

None of these rejections of thoughtless infomania and Net nuttiness is meant or felt to come from any Olympian height. Because the schools have imitated the old media in embracing marketing—reaching the most at the lowest cost for the highest possible price—one can see that young people, desperate for stimulation, gladly flee from the therapy-over-learning classroom to happily cruise on the Net, in the not unreasonable hope they might meet somebody more interesting.

I am on the Net, and I have been using various parts of it for the last seven years. It is a remarkably efficient tool for tracking down bibliographic references and vetted research citations (Knowledge Index is one of the best). When I can get an on-the-spot report of a riot in *The* [Johannesberg] *Star* over the Net, it sure does beat driving two hours to the Sterling Memorial Library at Yale to get a day-old copy of the paper at best. But, like Samuel Florman (1994), who fears that "flights through cyberspace, however energizing they may be for the imagination, may weaken the objective rationality needed to do good engineering," I agree with Alan Cromer that the formal linear thinking needed to do science "goes against the grain of traditional human thinking, which is associative and subjective" (p. 65).

Not just science, but literary and other studies, assuredly associative and serendipitous, are also largely linear. Literature is linear. We are led down a path by a master, a wizard, a sorcerer. He leads us to a wider world than we might ever know otherwise, and we are permanently changed. One used to hear that Vietnam was still awaiting its novelist; meaning that the tangled confused hypertext of millions of disparate defeats and small victories, lies, and photo-ops and press conferences make no emotional sense until some Tolstoy can lead us through the emotional and factual jungle to a deeper truth.

In this broader cultural context, cyberspace can in some ways be a step backwards. True, it enables us to do some things better than we can do in libraries; it can substitute for a laboratory if we don't have one; it can get us to resources we might not otherwise find. But it is no substitute for guided linear thinking, friendship, travel, or learning the craft of writing or the equally daunting task of critical reading of demanding texts. Although cyberspace can be a place to go and get things to use, a place to ask questions and give answers, it is not a world of primary experience.

From this perspective, the tendency of some observers to reify an immense collection of unevenly useful databases and switched telecommunications links into a world where one "navigates" suggests a return to an earlier worldview long associated with primary orality and its well-attested affinity for religion.

BACK TO THE FUTURE

Over the centuries there has been a basic human desire for some kind of invisible mental or spiritual atmosphere that connects in some mystic way all the minds and hearts of mankind. Although often allied with religion (Christianity's "Mystical Body"), this yearning goes back at least as far as the pre-Socratics and their preoccupation with the One and the Many. For the medieval schoolmen mining the classic philosophers (not the Bible), there was the Agent Intellect, that part of the mind that enabled it to apprehend essences. A power within each individual mind, it nevertheless existed by sharing in one Great Agent Intellect, that was a kind of animating soul of the world. Hegel, much later, spoke of the *Geist,* not only of the *Zeit* but of the Welt (Kaufmann, 1966; Olson, 1992). In post-war France and later the rest of Europe and America, Teilhard de Chardin brought these ideas back for a while by resurrecting the Greek notion of *nous* (the conceiving and communicating mind—opposed to *pneuma*, the animating spirit) and speaking of the global *noosphere* (Teilhard, 1959). In more recent years we have the newly fashionable "Gaia hypothesis" that the planet Earth has a kind of intrinsic ecosystem soul that keeps it in balance.

More than a decade after Teilhard's phrase "everything that rises must converge" had been on English-speaking lips, the debut of Telstar, the first of a shining silver constellation of communications satellites, established a quotidian engineering footing of sorts for the grand mystic vision. Further developments in the real world of affairs increasingly bolstered this originally airy notion of "convergence." The space program and the stunning pictures of Earth, at first grainy black-and-white shadows of the great shapes familiar from maps, gave further impetus to the idea of convergence, of one world.

In less exalted terms, international trade and marketing abetted a growing trend toward a common popular culture of advertising, film, blockbuster books, and top tunes. The World's Fairs in Brussels, New York, Osaka, and Seattle, marching with the development of mass jet travel the world over, accelerated the internationalization of leisure pursuits and fashion through the 1960s and 1970s. Finally, the explosion to satellite communications in the 1980s matched in the most recent years with fiber-optic switching systems and computer processing of cash, words, images, and data—the internetting of global consciousness—has swept up most human endeavors from local names and habitations into the global context of international trademarks, common credit cards, shared diets, world-class athletics, and intercontinental rock concert tours.

Nowhere is this more true than in the spectacularly converging field of communications technologies, communications corporations, software standards, and their correlative hardware open architectures. In technology, we have phones that show pictures, computers that listen, keyboards that paint. We have books on tape and on disc, movies zipping along not only close to the speed of light, but encoded in the form of light. Not only do Japanese manufacturers of TV sets and VCR's own rock stars and movie vaults, but Apple and IBM have collaborated with Motorola in creating a new generation of microchip. Microsoft, still firmly on the desktop, is moving into the cable boxes atop televisions. Mainframes, long identified with monolithic, isolated, and hierarchical megacorporations, have given way to PCs, which in turn have formed local area networks, patched into wide area networks, using netware newly rendered interchangeable. The new arrangements have forced smart work on both management and labor. Editors have access to little more information that lights up the screens of the rest of the newsroom. The shopfloors of Toyota and Chrysler alike bristle with interfaces demanding decisions, once reserved for supervisors, from line workers.

In fact, the ubiquity of by now well-established world pop culture, world finance, world trade, and world tourism into one headless network has made the very idea of convergence so commonplace that we cannot see clearly the microstitching in the seemingly seamless garment. Like a Mandlebrot set, the picture of the whole diverges from the tiny iterations of detail, but yet depends on them. If we miss the trees, we will be lost in the forest.

So a paradoxical merging of quite old and hoary concepts with modern industrial developments have informed the current enthusiasms and misconceptions about cyberspace (defined by Gibson with unconscious irony as "consensual hallucination"). These influences are nowhere more evident than in the tendency of many otherwise hardheaded writers to describe cyberspace as "nonphysical." Everyone is aware that without computers, silicon, copper, plastic, fossil fuel for energy production, and many other humbly tangible physical things, the Net could not be constituted nor even exist. But many forget that those magnetic or photonic ons and offs are physical, just as the electromagnetic waveforms of analog broadcasting are physical, although it must be granted their physicality is tenuous relative to the colossal freight of meaning they incrementally embody.

So deeming the content of cyberspace "nonphysical" presumably is thought to indicate that messages, designs, or commands—in short, language itself and the entire symbol world—are meaningless without the interpretations of minds "plugged in" to the Net. But in this sense, of course, all human action is "nonphysical," from sex and singing to tea parties and rock concerts. Flesh, soundwaves, tea sets, and megaboom boxes are all just substrates that permit cultural and symbolic nets to have somewhere to land. But somehow many take typing on a screen as less material than whispering in a lover's ear. There is an irony here in that many take the headless mass of interconnected computer neurons as some sort of world soul and personify "it," just when many scientists (Crick, 1994) and philosophers (Dennett, 1992) forthrightly pronounce that there is no mind, no soul, only neurons within each individual. Neurons may be organized in the brain, but there is no organization ordering the brain.

Are the positivist scientists out of sync with the latest intellectual fashion? Do all those formerly hard heads, once wired, go soft? Have the souls of Christianity and the tutelary spirits of wind, water, and sacred grove once invoked by pagan Greece and Rome come back as software and information, which never diminish however often they are used?

Stay tuned.

REFERENCES

Abramson, J.B., Arterton, F.C., & Orren, G.R. (1988). *The electronic commonwealth: The impact of new media technologies on democratic politics.* New York: Basic Books.

Barnet, R.J., & Cavanagh, J. (1994). *Global dreams: Imperial corporations and the new world order.* New York: Simon & Shuster.

Chomsky, N. (1991). *Deterring democracy.* London: Verso.

Crick, F. (1994). *The astonishing hypothesis: The scientific search for the soul.* New York: Macmillan.

Dahlgren, P., & Sparks, C. (1991). *Communication and citizenship: Journalism and the public sphere.* London: Routledge.

Dennett, D. (1992). *Consciousness explained.* Boston: Little, Brown.

Entman, R.M. (1989). *Democracy without citizens: Media and the decay of American politics.* New York: Oxford University Press.

Florman, S.C. (1994). The humane engineer. *Technology Review, 97,* 65.

Greider, W. (1992). *Who will tell the people? The betrayal of American democracy.* New York: Simon & Shuster.

Herman, E.S., & Chomsky, N. (1988). *Manufacturing consent: The political economy of the mass media.* New York: Pantheon.

Kafka, F. (1987). *Letters to Felice Bauer* (E. Heller & J. Born, Eds.). New York: Schocken.

Kaufmann, W. (1966). *Hegel: Reinterpretation, texts and commentary.* London: Weidenfeld & Nicolson.

Krugman, P. (1994). *Peddling prosperity: Economic sense and nonsense in an age of diminished expectations.* New York: Norton.

McCaffrey, A. (1969). *The ship that sang.* New York: Walker.

Olson, A.M. (1992). *Hegel and the spirit: Philosophy as pneumatology.* Princeton, NJ: Princeton University Press.

Phelan, J.M. (1977). *Mediaworld: Programming the public.* New York: Continuum Books.

Phelan, J.M. (1980). *Disenchantment: Meaning and morality in the media.* New York: Hastings House.

Phelan, J.M. (1984). Surfaces in the mediaworld of political fashion. *Media Development, 31*, 12-13.

Phelan, J.M. (1988). Communing in isolation. *Critical Studies in Mass Communication, 5*, 347-351.

Phelan, J.M. (1995). "Media". In P.A.B. Clarke & A. Linzey (Eds.), *Dictionary of ethics, theology and society* (pp. 150-155). London: Routledge.

Teilhard de Chardin, P. (1959). *The phenomenon of man.* New York: Harper & Brothers.

Wiener, N. (1954). *The human use of human beings: Cybernetics and society.* Boston: Houghton Mifflin.

✧✧✧✧ 3

Who Shall Control Cyberspace?

James R. Beniger

The "cyber" in cyberspace would seem to imply a controlled space, and yet the contemporary Internet-dominated electronic landscape is commonly characterized as decentralized, bottom-up, and anarchistic. Pioneers and homesteaders on the electronic frontier take pride in the egalitarian nature of cyberculture and seek to preserve the delicate balance of this technological ecosystem. It is not a closed system, however, as James R. Beniger makes clear in this essay. Situating cyberculture firmly within our larger social system, and using the impact of the computer on the U.S. Postal Service as an analogy, he argues that the cyberspace environment is an attractive and relatively easy target for commercial and political exploitation. As cyberspace becomes an increasingly contested terrain, Beniger foresees continuing change and rationalization of the Internet and its successors. In other sections of this book, further discussion of the sociological, political, and economic context of cyberspace can be found in Mark Giese's history of the Internet in Chapter 8, Ronald Jacobson's discussion of contemporary policy issues in Chapter 9, and Joseph Barrett's examination of cybercapitalism in Chapter 10. Additional consideration of the topic of control appears in Michael P. Beaubien's study of MUDs in Chapter 12 and Lance Strate's exploration of cybertime in Chapter 23.

Harvard Yard, like many American campuses, is crisscrossed by a web of concrete walks and asphalt paths. As new buildings open, both on campus and off, and popular courses move from one part of the university to another, the resulting shifts in Harvard's pedestrian traffic are recorded in new footpaths cutting across the various lawns of the Yard. Even after winter snows have covered the grass, the new paths endure as narrow trails of slush or ice. Each spring, as the melting snows give way to now muddy trails, where grass is unlikely to return without help, Harvard does not attempt to reseed—it simply paves over all the new paths chosen by sufficient pluralities of feet (so that we might imagine Harvard Yard approaching an entirely paved lot as time approaches infinity). In choosing to act in this way, Harvard has eschewed top-down control in favor of a bottom-up variety, forsaking the centralized control of the landscape architect in favor of decentralized control by emergent popular habits.

Cyberspace, born in the late 1970s on the world's first computer network, the U.S. Defense Department's ARPAnet, has grown much like the network of paved walks and paths in Harvard Yard. Despite initial attempts by the Defense Department to suppress what began as a virtual community of science fiction fans, the voices for bottom-up control eventually prevailed. The first citizens of cyberspace were allowed to make and enforce their own rules, bottom up, with relatively little centralized control. Two decades later, cyberspace continues to flourish in this way, not by design but by accretion—more like a coral reef than a product of RAND Corporation engineering. As Howard Rheingold (1993) describes the process:

> Biological imagery is often more appropriate [than are spatial imagery and a sense of place] to describe the way cyberculture changes. In terms of the way the whole system is propagating and evolving, think of cyberspace as a social petri dish, the Net as the agar medium, and virtual communities, in all their diversity, as the colonies of microorganisms that grow in petri dishes. Each of the small colonies of microorganisms—the communities on the Net—is a social experiment that nobody planned but that is happening nevertheless. (p. 6)

A similar view, although one closer to the level of human experience, is that of Michael Benedikt (1991), who characterizes cyberspace as "a common mental geography, built, in turn, by consensus and revolution, canon and experiment" (p. 2). As such, cyberspace continues to emerge, bottom up, its control also largely emergent from the social interactions of millions of independent individuals. This is much as the paved network of Harvard Yard emerges, from many individual and independent actions—in reaction to top-down, centrally controlled physical changes—as recorded by countless independent actors.

CONCEPTUAL SPACE

Unlike Harvard Yard's web of paths, cyberspace is not only a physical space. Although it is easy to see the entire network of paths in the Yard, it would be impossible ever to see cyberspace. The point is made by James Gleick (1994), who describes the Net as in no sense a physical entity: "It isn't a thing; it isn't an entity; it isn't an organization. No one owns it; no one runs it. It is simply Everyone's Computers, Connected" (p. 57).

In other words, cyberspace consists not only of material things like people and their artifacts (computers, modems, telephone lines, etc.); it also has two major nonmaterial components: relationships among individuals, and the cybercultural contents of their heads—the sense of belonging to cyberspace, and of what that might mean. Taken together, these three components—material, relational, and cognitive—constitute not only cyberspace itself, but what is often called "culture" more generally. In at least the ethnographic sense, that is, all human cultures can be seen as consisting of a material culture (tangible artifacts), a symbolic or relational culture (widely shared information), and a cognitive culture (less widely shared meanings that more directly influence the behavior of a particular individual). To make such distinctions is not to deny, of course, that all three components or levels must ultimately be manifest in some material form. For information, however, the material component is usually irrelevant to cultural control; for cognitive culture, the material level is entirely transparent.

That cyberspace might be subsumed by precisely these three levels of culture is echoed by Rheingold (1993), who formally defines *cyberspace* as "the conceptual space where words, human relationships, data, wealth, and power are manifested by people using CMC [computer-mediated communications] technology" (p. 5). As such, cyberspace is not a society unto itself as much as a proper subset of the larger society, a socioconceptual space that is shared—in greater or lesser degree—by all members of that subset and space. This does make cyberspace a true and distinct human culture, however, in that—as a conceptual space—it tends to organize the social production and reproduction of sense, consciousness, and meaning among its members.

In the foreseeable future, at least, the culture of cyberspace will remain a subculture of various more traditional human cultures. As its continuing development approaches the unreachable physical boundary of all information in all places at all times, however, cyberspace will become a more embracing culture, less a semiconscious artifact opposed to nature and more like nature itself—an entirely unconscious, virtual world that might eventually begin to constitute its own reality. Therefore cyberspace would approach Benedikt's (1991) description of "a place, one place, limitless; entered equally from a basement in Vancouver, a boat in Port-au-Prince, a cab in New York, a garage in Texas City, an apartment in Rome, an office in Hong Kong, a bar in Kyoto, a cafe in Kinshasa, a laboratory on the Moon" (p. 1).

CONTROL

Of all the known means for controlling human societies, none has proved more effective—in the long run—than the least centralized means of all: face-to-face communication in small, persisting, and intimate groups. Human societies first emerged, throughout the world, by just such means of distributed control. Such control still characterizes the societies least touched by or most resistant to change; it accounts for the common modern perception of small towns and tightly knit social groups as stultifying (whatever their other advantages).

If these earliest of social structures, still the vast majority of all those in recorded history, can be taken as prototypical, nothing has had a greater impact on human societies than the various technological innovations—beginning with the earliest infrastructures of transportation and communication—for increasingly centralized and mass social control. Viewed in modern terms of information processing and communication, the major result of such innovations has been a shift in control from individual programming (socialization) and interpersonal communication to more centralized processing and mass communication. Centralized information processing began with hierarchy, formal organization, and bureaucracy; centralized control developed with road systems and technologies for navigation (Beniger, 1986).

From these anthropological and historical perspectives, the emergence of cyberspace, in only the past 20 years, might be seen as the single greatest reversal in human history of the trend to centralized social control. Cyberspace's unrivaled impact stems more from the relative suddenness of its appearance, however, than from the nature of control on the Net. Throughout history, the trend to more centralized means of mass control has been continually countered by innovations—analogous in form to the infrastructure of cyberspace—to technologize and rationalize interpersonal communication and distributed control: the postal system, an infrastructure for personal world travel, the telegraph and telephone systems, two-way radio, and facsimile (fax) transmission, among many others. Cyberspace, at least to the extent that it depends on point-to-point communication among individuals, is only the latest in this succession of innovations that have countered the larger historical trend to mass communication and centralized control.

For those who would control vast populations, if only in relatively small ways, the growth of cyberspace does present an immediate setback, as well as the promise of even greater control in the near future. For those of you who might want to preserve the decentralized and interpersonal nature of cyberspace, consider: No such infrastructure or medium has ever resisted application to mass persuasion and control. Point-to-point telegraphic communication almost immediately produced the world's first mass newspapers. Radio is not only two-way, but used to reach audiences of millions around the world. Postal systems built to support the interpersonal exchange of letters have now been largely given over to mass mailings. Computers have begun to replace boiler room operations as the chief means of transforming the American telephone system into a mass medium, as have 800 and 900 numbers. New technologies now enable the mass production of personalized fax communication. Even face-to-face conversation can give way to shouting to crowds.

What might keep cyberspace, as we know it today, from a similar fate? Probably nothing. Struggles for centralized control of cyberspace, and between those who would centralize or decentralize its control, have already begun. The rest of this chapter attempts—based on the histories of the other innovations most similar to cyberspace—to outline some of what is likely to come.

VULNERABILITIES

For those who seek to advertise, politic, persuade, or otherwise control large populations, cyberspace presents two attractive features: First, because cyberspace has the feel (and currently the tradition) of interpersonal communication, it would well serve to conceal the inherently impersonal (and thus less persuasive) aspects of mass communication. Second, because almost all of its communication is inherently accessible, retrievable, and machine readable by virtually anyone, cyberspace would itself foster unprecedented mass processing to support centralized control.

Underlying these two vulnerabilities to centralized control is the essential tradeoff between the range and effectiveness of control of human behavior through persuasion, whether rational or irrational, conscious or unconscious. Our behavior is most affected by those we care most about or see most often: loved ones, friends, coworkers, neighbors—the same people whose behavior most affects us. Seeing and caring about are inherently limited activities; however, we simply cannot personally care about, or regularly visit with, the vast multitudes. To affect the behavior of thousands or even millions of people, we might, for example, publish a letter in a newspaper, but its effects—because the communication is obviously not personal—will usually be slight. Hence the tradeoff: We might have great range or great effectiveness of communication, but very rarely both, at least not with the same message.

Another reason why mass communication is limited in its effects, apart from this tradeoff, is that mass communication is usually one-way. Even the most powerful weapon will be useless in attempting to control someone to whom we cannot communicate, or whose behavior we cannot monitor; two-way communication will prove no less essential for control than the weapon itself. The only reason why mass communication can control human behavior at all is that the sheer numbers of targets can compensate for even the slightest probabilities of success: We know some small percentage will be affected by our message, but not which individuals will be, nor why. Two-way communication is much better than one-way, at least for controlling human behavior, because the effect of any one message can be monitored and responded to in a subsequent message.

A third reason why mass communication is limited in its effects is that it is neither interactive nor purposively iterative. The potential for any means of communication to control increases with the number of iterations of messages sent and responses monitored; however, a reasonable substitute for the monitoring of individual behavior is prior knowledge relevant to predicting that behavior. One reason why our loved ones and friends can so readily affect our behavior, for example, is that they know us so well. Among those who would control large populations, a large databank of prior knowledge, plus the capability to compare current behavior to the desired one and to respond accordingly, through many iterations, are both highly prized.

It ought to be clear by now why someone might want to hijack cyberspace for purposes of mass persuasion and control. Cyberspace presents the possibility, unprecedented in past technologies, to transcend the tradeoff between range and effectiveness in control of human behavior. Because the new technology is inherently interactive, and the tradition of its use still largely interpersonal, the very context of cyberspace would help to conceal the impersonal nature of mass communication, much as, for example, the interactive nature of Joseph Weizenbaum's (1976) ELIZA psychotherapy program helped to obscure its own impersonal nature. Mass communication to cyberspace could also be two-way, not only because each individual might respond to a given message, but also because the Net behavior of all individuals—following any given message or iteration—could be monitored and responded to, individually, toward a particular goal.

In short, mass communication to cyberspace might be based on large databases of the prior Net activity of each individual, driven by massive processing power, and even guided by artificial intelligence systems for persuasive behavior, now well understood by social psychologists. For all these reasons, as well as those mentioned earlier, the possibilities for effective control of a large population via cyberspace appear unmatched by those of any other existing means (at least of comparably large-scale and minimal coercion). Even without its considerable vulnerabilities to mass control, however, the cyberspace population, because of its demographics of age, education, and income (among others), would still rank among the most attractive to advertisers, marketers, and politicians alike, mostly because of the considerable influence this population has over others not yet part of cyberspace.

Discouraging as this assessment might seem, for those who would wish to preserve cyberspace as we find it today, the more important point is not that mass control via cyberspace will succeed, but that it will be tried. The attempts alone, successful or not, will greatly alter—probably irretrievably—the nature of life in cyberspace.

THE POSTAL MODEL

Lest this seem like so much science fictional extrapolation, if not outright paranoia, a real-life case study appears to be in order. None seems more applicable to cyberspace than that of the U.S. Postal Service, an ancient and for centuries highly interpersonal messaging network that—over roughly the period of cyberspace's existence—has been largely transformed into a computer-processable mass medium for advertisers, politicians, and other mass mailers.

The U.S. Postal Service remained a 19th-century bureaucracy, one that relied on antiquated mail-processing methods such as "pigeonhole" sorting, as late as 1957, when it installed its first automatic letter sorter—a five-position Dutch machine that could sort mail to only 300 different destinations. Today, 40 years later, after adopting optical character readers (1965), bar-code sorters (1982), and the 9-digit ZIP code (1983), the Postal System has become a computerized, highly targetable channel into every American household. In parallel to these developments, a major database marketing industry, which includes geodemographic targeting of mass mailings using census block statistics, ZIP codes, and postal carrier routes, has sprung up around the Postal System.

The Claritas company of Alexandria, VA, for example, links national address and telephone lists to neighborhood units with an average size of only 340 households. By means of the growing wealth of information collected on these units (Claritas routinely links to more than two dozen different databases), mass mailing and telephoning can be highly personalized, not only by name but by housing value, social status and mobility, purchase and credit behavior, and media preferences, among many other variables.

A fleeting hint of what might await cyberspace arrived in the mailbox at my house as early as 1986. I had then just moved from the East Coast to the West and did not yet know any of my new neighbors. The outside of the envelope, obviously a mass mailing promoting some contest, read "One in six will win," along with the computer-printed names of my family and the five other families who then lived on either side of us and across the street. So welcome did I feel, suddenly learning the names of my new neighbors, that I actually forgot—for just an instant—that this highly personalized communal intelligence had come not from a new acquaintance on my block, but from a machine several thousand miles away. It is by elaborating on just such impulses that mass communication masks itself as interpersonal.

Despite the sophistication of such highly computerized marketing applications, however, they exploit a messaging system that—like cyberspace—did not develop with them in mind. ZIP codes, for example, owe their origin to the postal zoning system (for which ZIP represented a "Zoning Improvement Plan") begun in 124 major city post offices in 1943 to save labor in letter sorting under wartime shortages. Only through modern computing power, unanticipated even when five-digit ZIP codes were adopted in 1963, could the database marketing industry have begun to transform the Postal System into the processable and targetable mass medium that it is today. With the data banks and processing power of the modern marketing industry, any informational system—including cyberspace—would seem grist for its mill. If this industry can so effectively exploit the U.S. Postal System, which ultimately still relies on hand-delivered pieces of paper, think of what designs it might have—and intelligently so—on cyberspace.

WHAT LIES AHEAD

What lies ahead for cyberspace? If the recent examples of the American postal and telephone systems can serve as models, cyberspace—a rather disorganized if not chaotic phenomenon by modern standards of communication, marketing, and control—is overdue to be rationalized. Although rationalization has a variety of meanings in such contexts, the essential idea is that control of anything can be increased by decreasing the amount of its information that requires processing (Beniger, 1976, chap. 1). Cyberspace, it would seem, is about to experience rationalization of its content if not its organization, from without if not from within.

Because this chapter has now reached the point of speculation about the future, always a hazardous enterprise, let me simply list (in no particular order) some of the things that others, judging by their past behavior, might have in store for cyberspace.

1. Massive operations for downloading and mining the cyberslush and reorganizing it according to user IDs. Nothing can be sold to cyberspace as a whole, nor much to the various universities and commercial gateway systems that make up the Net. Although many of the virtual communities found in cyberspace might well present commercial possibilities, the real gold lies at the lowest hierarchical level: the millions of individual citizens of cyberspace. Each one's immediately processable record of past behavior on the Net will afford unprecedented support for efforts to persuade, influence, and control her or him.

2. High-speed, programmable mailers to individual accounts on the Net. Rather than merely posting messages to listservers, newsgroups, or other mass media already part of cyberspace, with all of the limitations inherent in any such form of mass communication, marketers will exploit programmable technologies capable of delivering unique messages, personalized by means of already existing data sets, to each individual account—and at rapid rates.

3. New database marketing industries based on various data sets linked by inference to individual accounts. From my own user ID, it is easy to infer both my last name and my university. Using only these two data points, there is virtually no limit to the data that might be linked to my individual account and, via that, to my past and future activity on the Net.

4. Greater standardization of Net account formats. Although this is hardly necessary, and indeed would take much of the fun out of record linking, such fun costs both time and money—hence, a likely push for greater standardization.

5. Trafficking in specialized lists of user IDs. These would certainly include lists of the most affluent and the most gullible, and those most likely to purchase certain products or to support certain causes. Such lists are highly prized for marketing in other media; why should it be any different in cyberspace?

6. Detailed psychological profiles of individuals based on their past inputs to the Net. Only processing and storage capabilities will limit the extent to which marketers can dredge the cybersludge and sort by individual accounts. Imagine how much easier it would be to influence the behavior of individuals whose total activity in cyberspace you had analyzed, via artificial intelligence, to produce their psychological profiles (and perhaps also to tailor messages of maximum likely effectiveness for each of them as individuals).

7. Word-of-mouth campaigns via individuals determined, based on their past Net behavior, to be most likely to spread rumors and gossip. Anyone with experience in cyberspace could undoubtedly nominate a few likely candidates, marketers' algorithms will find those most likely to be effective. Word-of-mouth campaigns, positive as well as negative, have long proven effective, especially for particular types of products (e.g., political candidates as affected by the "dirty tricks" of whispering campaigns).

8. Individual accounts run by software "persuaders" that are the modern natural-language processing equivalent of the ELIZA system. Weizenbaum (1976) reported that even his secretary, who had watched him work on ELIZA for many months, and surely knew it to be merely a computer program, became hooked on it "after only a few interchanges." Are the citizens of cyberspace likely to find a modern version of ELIZA any less convincing as a personal pen pal on the Net?

WHO WILL PREVAIL?

Already the memories of what cyberspace once was, in its earliest days, have begun to fade. The vast majority of those in cyberspace today have no personal knowledge of these early times. If some of the changes forecast here seem incredible to imagine in cyberspace today, this may be—at least in part—because they will come about in a future in which memories of today's cyberspace have also faded.

Increasingly cyberspace has become polarized into two distinct classes: those who value the experience of cyberspace as inherently good, as an end in itself; and those who see cyberspace as merely one means to other quite specific ends, which might range from the making of an honest profit to various types of criminal behavior. A growing problem of cyberspace, one that afflicts all human societies that transcend face-to-face communication in small, persisting, and intimate groups, is the need to accommodate both those who value sociality as an end itself, and those who see it as but a means to other more personal ends—ends about which they might also disagree among themselves. In this way modernism has brought a certain loss to our collective innocence.

Recent battles over the control of cyberspace have centered on the protection of free expression, something that certainly cannot be overvalued. Completely free expression, however, includes the expression of those who value cyberspace as only a means and those whose expression might be in the feverish pursuit of ends radically different from our own. Free expression might also include expression by a few individuals backed by many employees, much computing power and expertise, and the unabashed intention to turn cyberspace to their own profit.

To preserve cyberspace as it is today is vastly easier than to preserve the basic freedoms of every one of its citizens equally. To do otherwise might be to provoke a cybernetic version of a civil war, not at all far-fetched if cyberspace is indeed a true subculture of human society. Seen in this way, the answer to our initial question becomes clear: Who will control cyberspace? Most likely those who will control society at large.

REFERENCES

Benedikt, M. (1991). Introduction. In M. Benedikt (Ed.), *Cyberspace: First steps* (pp. 1-25). Cambridge, MA: MIT Press.

Beniger, J. R. (1986). *The control revolution: Technological and economic origins of the information society.* Cambridge, MA: Harvard University Press.

Gleick, J. (1994, May 1). The information future: Out of control. *New York Times Magazine*, pp. 54-57.

Rheingold, H. (1993). *The virtual community: Homesteading on the electronic frontier.* Reading, MA: Addison-Wesley.

Weizenbaum, J. (1976). *Computer power and human reason: From judgment to calculation.* San Francisco: Freeman.

 4

Don't Fence Me In: Copyright, Property, and Technology

Neil Kleinman

Cyberspace is clearly a contested terrain, as early hacker subcultures emphasized complete freedom of information, whereas entrepreneurs and capitalists are increasingly seeking to colonize and capitalize on cyberspace through the extension of preexisting notions of property. But how can anyone own anything in an environment characterized by electronic flux? The notion of intellectual property provides a precedent, but as Neil Kleinman argues here, it is based on the physicality and fixity of the printed text. Providing a broad historical overview of the development of the concepts of ownership, property rights, and copyright, he discusses the complex economic, political, and legal factors that have resulted in our current notions of intellectual property, and the ways in which cyberspatial phenomena such as electronic publishing are undermining them. The conclusion, with an eye toward the brewing storm, offers suggestions for managing the approaching chaos brought about by the new digital mode of access. Aside from this section of the book, further study of the legal, regulatory, and economic issues of cyberspace appear in Ronald Jacobson's discussion of the information superhighway in Chapter 9 and Joseph Barrett's examination of money and markets in cyberspace in Chapter 10. Other views on electronic publishing and related forms can be found in Margaret Cassidy's essay on digital reproduction in Chapter 15, Stuart Moulthrop's exploration of the future of the book in Chapter 16, and Stephanie Gibson's overview of hypertext in Chapter 17.

"Who's going to own the new electronic frontier?" asked the squatter.
"Who owned the last frontier?" replied the cattle baron.

There's land, lots of land. We are told that the digital revolution is going to open up a lot of territory. Money's to be made by using it, subdividing it, selling it, farming it, and by setting up service stations and rest stops along the interstate. Public lands are going to become private lands, and the "new" West is going to be taken over, once again, so we are told, by the cattle barons (Barlow, 1994a; Kapor, 1993).

The opposite may, of course, be equally true. There are those who believe that the digital revolution is not going to create new baronies. It will "destroy" private property. Owners of large information estates like Time-Warner and TCI will soon find themselves pushed out of their protective enclosures. They will be forced to live in a new electronic wilderness, where hacker and director of information systems are equal, and victory goes to the fleet and wily (Peters, 1987). In this future, private property is free, public, and open. Although these metaphors are sketched out in terms of "real property" (public and private lands, property lines and highways), the battle is being fought in a much less "real" space, the space reserved for creations of the imagination—the legal terrain of intellectual property and the rules developed to protect it, those incorporated into copyright law.

Intellectual property is not a self-evident proposition. Its history is short. It began slightly more than 500 years ago with the advent of printing and continues until now (Kaplan, 1967; Katsh, 1989; Lanham, 1993; Patterson, 1968). This is not a long history, as histories go, and it may be coming to an abrupt end. What worked for print is probably not going to work for digital communications—not unless we are willing to engage in a great deal of stretching and straining. Still many are willing to try to make it all fit—the idea of intellectual property and copyright has become so appealing. On the other side, many are on the attack, looking for weak spots in the system—in its policy, its logic, or simply by showing why there are practical reasons it cannot work. The debate should remind us, if nothing else, that we are at a classic point in the evolution of technology and ideas when old models do not quite apply and new models have not yet been constructed. It is a good time to think about the models we are using. So much is in bold relief, and so little is self-evident. By taking a look at copyright, we can see the impact a technology has on the way we construct economic and legal systems. At the same time, we can see why some of our ideas about the economy led technologies such as printing or computers to succeed.

If we can understand how we got here, perhaps we will understand where we are going. At minimum, we will understand why we are approaching an intersection where a collision between copyright law and digital technology is inevitable (Lanham, 1993). For this reason, the strategy of this chapter is to look backward in order to look forward: to explain the relationship of intellectual property to print technology so we can look forward to the relationship between intellectual property and digital technology. I want to show that intellectual property, along with a number of other values we cherish in Western democratic societies, grew out of economic theory about property, commodities, and the marketplace that evolved toward the end of the Middle Ages. What should become evident is that the printing press was the "natural" machine needed in a society moving toward commercialism and the values encoded in ownership and property rights (Ong, 1971). If the printing press had not existed, we might conclude that the new commercialism might well have "demanded" that one be invented.

We need to remember that the thread of "property," woven throughout both liberal and conservative thought, is now characteristic of our "modern" sensibility. Since the late Middle Ages, ownership has become the defining issue—what can we own?—that decides the argument. All that is required is that we are able to make our "property" tangible. Within that tangible, fixed space, we gain a great deal of control and a number of rights. Rights we take to be fundamental—for instance, freedom of speech (First Amendment) and the right of privacy (Fourth Amendment)—are often explained in property terms based on the kind of control we have over the object we claim as our own.

"The dichotomy between personal liberties and property rights is a false one," wrote Justice Stewart. "Property does not have rights. People have rights. . . . In fact, a fundamental interdependence exists between the personal right to liberty and the personal right in property. Neither could have meaning without the other. That rights in property are basic civil rights has long been recognized" (*Lynch v. Household Finance Corp.*, 1972, p. 552). It does not require much embroidery to find in this language an argument for a woman's right to abortion—the right to control one's body as "property" that the State should have no ready access to (*Roe v. Wade*, 1973).

Similarly the notion of property rights serves to underpin some explanations for freedom of speech. In so much of our free speech discussions, we treat language and ideas as though they were commodities, to be traded and exchanged as property in a free market. Belief is best reached, wrote Justice Holmes, "by free trade in ideas . . . the best test of truth is the power of the thought to get itself accepted in the competition of the market" (*Abrams v. United States*, 1919, p. 630). What Justice Holmes describes is a marketplace in which fair competition takes responsibility out of the hands of the producer. The "buyers" decide what is of value. The "sellers" have only one responsibility: to produce. It is a powerful and appealing metaphor. But it does change our relation to both language and ideas. Language is shorn of responsibility. (I'm free to say what I want.) It does not define the speaker. (I can say something different tomorrow. I can become something different tomorrow through the "new" language I use to present my self.) Language *and* ideas become one of several objects—all of which can be exchanged and compared with similar objects presented in the public debate.

As free speech and privacy grow out of our commitments to property, so too does copyright law. The same elements are in play—ownership, property, and marketplace—and, in large measure, they define the way copyright law, property law, and the law defining individual rights has been constructed.

GETTING CONTROL OF THE IDEA

First Principles

The idea of intellectual property is a product of the imagination. It exists only after we determine the boundaries of something we have made and then find a way to point to it—so we can hold on to the thing itself. For the last 500 years, it did not seem particularly hard to find these boundaries and to make ideas into things. The advent of print as a dominant technology in the late 15th century allowed us to see these boundaries and created a consumer market based on an interesting theory: that ideas could be sold as though they were commodities (Ong, 1971).

"Typography," wrote McLuhan, "tended to alter language from a means of perception and exploration to a portable commodity" (1962, p. 161). He was right. The effect was to manufacture a visual and spacial domain for ideas. In this space, we became peddlers carrying "objects of art" on our backs, trading and selling ideas as we found buyers for them. We called this space the marketplace of ideas and adopted economic regulations like those embodied in copyright law to protect what was being sold. Ownership of real property is a curious concept in its own right. It was not always self-evident.

BEFORE FENCES: THE FOREST AND THE OPEN RANGE

The Forest—Efficiency and Protection

Before the field is the forest. Those who use it wander freely, hunting and trapping as they wish. This is the land of the Iroquois or the Algonquins. It is neither owned nor sold. It belongs in common to all. Then comes the European, hunting to make profit by selling and trading pelts. The land is not valuable in its own right, but because of the pelts that can be harvested. To preserve the harvest, the land is divided and partitioned. Each hunter controls the hunt on his property. He knows the harvest he can expect and the profit he can make. This is the beginning of ownership and private property (Demsetz, 1967). To divide and control is the way we turn nature into a commodity—a commodity we can shape and then exchange for other values.

Whoever Thought of the Idea of "Real Property"? One economist reminds us that property rights even for "real property" is not a natural and self-evident bundle of rights. Property rights did not, in fact, exist among American Indians until the development of the fur trade and a growing concern that overhunting of game would destroy both game and whatever profit there was to be made in selling pelts:

> Because of the lack of control over hunting by others, it is in no person's interest to invest in increasing or maintaining the stock of game. Overly intensive hunting takes place. Thus a successful hunt is viewed as imposing external costs on subsequent hunters—costs that are not taken into account fully in the determination of the extent of hunting and of animal husbandry. (Demsetz, 1967, p. 351)

If everyone is able to hunt a forest, who will take responsibility for animal husbandry? Too many hunters, unregulated, will leave nothing to hunt. The Indians, we are told, moved to the principal of property rights—control over a portion of the woods—as an economic necessity. *Even those who believe in a common land that none can own believe first in survival.* The same instinct informs the development of copyright protection. If anyone can publish a work, who will take responsibility for keeping the work uncorrupted? Who will invest money in promoting the book? In marketing and distributing it? In supporting the author in his or her next effort? Control means both profit and responsibility (Breyer, 1970).

If the idea of "real property" was not self-evident, the idea that we can own the "product" of our minds is even less obvious. To buy and sell the product of our minds! It was not always so. Some more examples follow.

The Lord and the Land—Efficiency and Use

Feudal property land was not owned. In the legal language of the time, "the grantee takes the land and holds it 'of' the grantor" (Tigar, 1977, p. 196). In fact, it could not be "owned" any more than the forest used by the Indian could be owned. It was held in trust (Lopez, 1976). If it could not be owned, it could not be sold, and it was not. Its value flowed from something other than that which a marketplace provides. The purpose of feudal property was to establish relationships among those who gave it, those who took it, and those who used it. It defined the society, the structure, the duties men owed each other, and the responsibilities they had to their superiors and inferiors. According to Tawney:

> [Property's] raison d'etre [in the feudal system] is not only income, but service. It is to secure its owner such means, and no more than such means, as may enable him to perform those duties whether labor on the land, or labor in government, which are involved in particular status which he holds in the system. (cited in Tigar, 1977, pp. 196-197)

The world—both social and economic—was well organized, and its organization was almost entirely based on the land one could claim as one's to inhabit. This system encouraged community. The land within each economic unit operated with the needs of the whole in mind. What was grown, used, and saved was very much the results of a delicate calculation of the interwoven mix of promises, responsibilities, and duties all the members of the community—from the top to the bottom—owed each other. As Tawney puts it: "He who exploits his property with a single eye to its economic possibilities at once perverts its very essence and destroys his own moral title, for he has 'every man's living and does no man's duty.'" (cited in Tigar, 1977, p. 197).

There are echoes here of the attitude medieval man had toward intellectual "property." Land and texts were both to be shared. Their value was determined by their ability to promote use and establish bonds of common belief. The rule appears to be: *In a precapital economy, efficiency is based on maximizing both the use of an object and the number of links between people it creates.*

The Commons—Efficiency and Control

Before the 16th century, much land in England was held in common. The nobility and the squires had their grand estates, but the English farmer had access to land too. He could use the land "owned" by his village. It was this right of *access* and *use* of the common land that gave many a servant the opportunity to improve his state. With access to common land, a man might do a bit of farming, hunting, and grazing of his few animals. His profits from that activity provided him with an opportunity to move one step up the social and economic ladder without the initial investment of capital required of an owner (Hammond & Hammond, 1966; Mingay, 1968).

Appealing as the idea of common land may be, the English had the same problem faced by the Indians, trappers, and settlers in the forests of North America. Land controlled by many is the responsibility of no one. The land was insufficiently productive because it was not being cared for in a regular and predictable fashion. Sheep left to graze devoured the countryside. Hunting, uncontrolled, threatened the stock. To protect the land, as well as to stabilize the economy and the social order, the English began to enclose the common lands. Land that had "belonged" to many became private property. The benefits of enclosure became apparent: "Fencing permitted controlled experimentation on improving yields of both crops and animals, as well as helping to limit the spread of disease by wandering animals" (Burke, 1985, p. 166).

The land became a factory for the efficient production of farm goods. Thus, a flock of sheep could be treated as nothing more than "raw" material—to be reared, tended, and sheared. The wool produced could then quite easily be gathered, sorted, and brought together to be made into cloth, all within the close confines of a well-defined and well-regulated enclosure: "The efficient exploitation of [common land] for mercantile purposes meant drawing together the production of raw wool and the manufacture of cloth" (Tigar, 1977, p. 205).

The formula seems clear: *In an early capital economy, efficiency and profit require that the way we produce and manufacture an item should be brought together under one roof—under which the thing being created can be controlled, organized, refined, and sold.* Early on, this same formula became clear to publishers. They pulled together writers, editors, and printers under one roof, giving them far more control over what was being produced and the time it was produced in than was possible under the scribal tradition (Eisenstein, 1983; Steinberg, 1974).

The Scribe and the Manuscript—Efficiency and Resource Development

Before Gutenberg, the rate of return was one man, one "book" at a time, and three months or more to make it (Eisenstein, 1983; Steinberg, 1974). There was no notion of "copyright," nor "plagiarism" (Eisenstein, 1983). Ownership was of little concern because the work at hand when completed had an immediate exchange value. The copyist made what he could out of his work and the "author," for his part, could not expect to make much out of such a limited production system.

Perhaps the reason there was so little concern for "ownership" is based on the limited role played by authorship. The principle of authorship was straightforward and based on the realities of scarcity and explained through religious doctrine. Anything could be used and incorporated into the manuscript; anything could be added, deleted, or changed. Here is the mirror image of what we have come to understand are the conventions of a digital culture. Again now, things can be added, deleted, or changed. We can write over the author's conclusions, add our own, and become the author too (Lanham, 1993). After all, it might be said that literature, in Drogin's words, "was a fund of man's knowledge, rather than belonging to its individual authors" (cited in Katsh, 1989, p. 172). In this light, knowledge was a common field, open to anyone who wished to use it. There was, in fact, a social need and a social incentive to use it, as Chaytor makes clear: "To copy and circulate another man's book [was] regarded as a meritorious action in the age of manuscript" (cited in McLuhan, 1962, p. 87). To copy was, without doubt, a blessed act.

There was also an economic value in copying, a reason to create no barriers to the act. Free use and the right to copy balanced the economies of scarcity. What little there was went further if shared. This is the communal economies of the poor, which we often find in those who have little and must share what they acquire merely to have enough. (It is odd but scarcity does not necessarily lead to the need for an economy structure based on barriers and enclosures. The have-nots have more to gain by sharing than by controlling their little pieces of property.) These principles made available a limited commodity to a wider audience. The fact that the commodity was often writing that set forth Church doctrine made it all the more easy to see as belonging to no one. The fact that often this was the work of scribes, who themselves had vowed poverty, made it even easier to subscribe to the principle that copying was a divine act, a work of mercy (Clark, cited in Katsh, 1989).

Second Principles

We can see why copyright did not exist before printing. It did not need to. It made no sense to protect work that was made by one craftsman for one buyer. (The cost of the print technology destroyed this simplicity.) Copyright, in fact, would have been destructive to the business of the copyist and would have restricted the growth of medieval culture.

What the age before printing demanded were incentives to stimulate copying. There was an audience of students, priests, teachers, and members of a growing bureaucracy who wanted to get their hands on a text (the works of the Church fathers, the writings of classical authors, the legal documents and analyses of the state or court authorities, medical tracts, etc.), but few copies were available. Scribes provided what was available. They were manufacturers and retailers of products that already had agreed-on buyers. And competition among scribes was all but nonexistent because each scribe was limited in what he could produce (Edmunds, 1991). He could not have taken on more business—sold more copies—because he could not have made more copies even if he had wanted to. The rule here is: *When we cannot get our hands on the information we need, we devise systems to promote copying or to make access to ideas and information easier.* A tax of the kind imposed by copyright on the dissemination of ideas would have limited the spread of information and the propagation of the faith. What was needed were more copies of Aquinas and Augustine, not fewer.

THE FIRST FRONTIER: PRINT SPACE

Print changed both the situation and attitudes toward authorship and ownership. Like those who argued for property rights to protect the quality and number of animals being hunted or those who argued for enclosures to make more efficient the production and manufacture of cloth, printers quickly understood that they too must assert their rights of ownership over what they were producing on their presses:

> By 1500, legal fictions were . . . being devised to accommodate the patenting of inventions and assignment of literary properties. Once the rights of an inventor could be legally fixed and the problem of preserving unwritten recipes intact was no longer posed, profits could be achieved by open publicity provided new restraints were not imposed. Individual initiative was released from reliance on guild protection, but at the same time new powers were lodged in the hands of a bureaucratic officialdom. Competition over the right to publish a given text also introduced controversy over new issues involving monopoly and piracy. Printing forced legal definition of what belonged in the public domain. *A literary*

> *"common" became subject to "enclosure movements," and possessive individualism began to characterize the attitude of writers to their work.* The "terms plagiarism and copyright did not exist for the minstrel. It was only after printing that they began to hold significance for the author." (Eisenstein, 1983, pp. 83-84; emphasis added)

Like any manufacturer, printers saw that they were producing products that were tangible, fixed forms of expression. Indeed, ideas once fixed were commodities, just like the press and the movable type used to produce books. And if they were commodities, they could be easily and cheaply manufactured and efficiently inventoried, displayed, and sold (Ong, 1971). As a result, printing first changed the business of collecting, producing, and circulating the new knowledge of the early Renaissance. Having begun that, it then changed the economics of production. What became clear was that a way had to be found to protect those investing in the wholesale production of ideas. Now there were many copies of the same work so there was no need to create an incentive that promoted copying. The opposite was true: *There was a need to end copying.*

The very fact that these printed products were mass produced made the potential of the enterprise attractive to want-to-be printers. They had not one buyer; they had the possibility of many. If a printer produced 100 copies of a book, he might just as easily produce 101 copies of the same book, do so for almost the same price it cost him to produce the first 100 books, and produce an extra copy in about the same amount of time. Unlike the scribe, the printer had the advantage of low marginal costs. Each new unit printed did not cost the same as the first one.

But these printers learned quickly that much more than mere printing skill was required. Those engaged in this new enterprise had to be ready to invest time and money for what was then an untried technology. What does one do with stacks of half printed books in one's storeroom? One must find ways to sell them. Printers were producing goods for an audience that was not yet proven (Morris, 1963), and they had to establish a means of promotion and distribution while they experimented with the technology. Many early printer/publishers were not able to carry it off. They could not invest in the technology, invest time and money in production, and also invest in a marketing plan, and then execute it. It was all too much.

Printers discovered the modern truism of capitalism: "Time is money." Put more exactly, time costs money. In publishing—although there is the promise of a good return—it takes time to get one's money back from the sale of books. One needs to invest in equipment, then in type, then in paper, and, of course, the clock keeps running. Printers also had to invest in people. They needed to hire people to edit, typeset, market, and distribute books. Authors had to be found; manuscripts translated and edited. Authors, editors, and journeyman printers had to be housed, fed, and taken care. Printers had to hire people to travel to sell these new products and discover new books worth publishing, and their houses became hostels and inns for those brought into the ventures (Eisenstein, 1983; Steinberg, 1974).

It took capital to get into the game and capital to cover the routine expenses of life and family while waiting for books to sell (Edmunds, 1991). And capital was something few early printer/publishers had (Tedeschi, 1991). Creditors were not patient, and many printers went broke early in their business careers. If it took money to get in, it also took stamina to stay. Early printer/publishers worked long hours well into the night, editing the work of others and composing their own material when they could (Febvre & Martin, 1958/1984).

Early printers faced problems similar to those confronting landholders in the feudal system. Both possessed something of value (books and land) but were not easily able to change it into capital. Until land could be traded, the "owner" could not attract investors, nor could he treat land as though it were currency or property that he could "mortgage." So too for the printer/publisher. Until he could control the number of copies that could be printed of any one text (until, that is, he had a copyright on the work), there was little reason for an investor to risk his money in the venture. The market value of the printed work was unpredictable because it might compete with any number of identical (and perhaps cheaper) editions of the same work. Copyright turned the book into a "safe" commodity, assuring a value for the item in the market and therefore making the production of books a somewhat more rational investment.

To summarize: Printing changed the economy of copying, the nature of the investment, the amount of time one needed to get one's investment back, and (perhaps most importantly) the requirements of what it meant to be a publisher. It was no longer a question of one copy made to be sold to a buyer already identified. Now, printer publishers had to have capital to invest and the wherewithal to develop a marketing, promotional, and distribution scheme (Morris, 1963). Printers and publishers found that they had invested much and were at great risk. They wanted a regulated marketplace in which they had some control.

The problem for the printer—unlike the other craftsmen of his time—was that he was producing multiples of the same item. It was the promise of this that attracted him to the trade in the first place. But it was also the ability to produce multiples that drove him to despair. If he could do it, his competitors might do so too (Morris, 1963). As Blagen argues, the printer needed to find a way to protect himself from others who might wish to flood the market with identical counterfeits: "To lie easy at night he wanted no reduplication of his book by another printer, no more hundreds of copies chasing an already limited number of customers" (cited in Morris, 1963, p. 229).

Copyright was the answer. It was an answer that could work because, by that time (the early 18th century), property itself was no longer inexorably linked to the people who were responsible for it. The idea of property had been transformed: It was not a means to confirm and bestow identities or a way to establish relationships; rather, it was a form of commodity, valued only as it could be sold in the open market.

The character of "real property" was almost entirely taken over as the underlying structure of "intellectual property." In a classic exposition of what "real property" looked like after the transition from the feudal economy, Renner wrote:

> The right of ownership . . . is a person's all-embracing legal power over a tangible object. As far as the object is concerned, ownership is a universal institution: all corporeal things, even, land, can be objects of ownership if they are recognized as such by the law and are not by special provision put [outside of commerce]. Ownership is equally universal with regard to the subject. Everybody has an equal capacity for ownership, and he may own property of every description. These are the norms which are characteristic of this institution. (cited in Tigar, 1977, p. 197)

What we might expect—and find—is that intellectual property is recast as a tangible object, packaged for sale, in which the owner's rights are stretched as much as the law will allow. Because items must be commodities before they can be traded in the marketplace, we extend copyright protection only after an expression becomes (or can be made to be) tangible property. Having accomplished that, we then locate authorship, almost as an afterthought, by bestowing ownership over this new made property. "Copyright protection subsists," the law states, "in original works of authorship fixed in any tangible medium of expression" (Copyright Act of 1976, 17 U.S.C. Sec 102a).

A legal historian, writing about the postfeudal reframing of property, paints a dark picture of the kind of marketplace this transformation created. When the law links people to things only for the purpose of sale and exchange through constructs of property or ownership, he said:

> Human society is dissolved into isolated individuals, and the world of goods split up into discrete items. One can no longer speak of a duty to use property or behave toward others in a certain way: all such duties as may be imposed by law are *prima facie* derogations from the fundamental "right of property." (Tigar, 1977, p. 197)

What is described here is a dramatic shift in perspective. Property became a "thing" (in law, *res*). One does not have duties when one owns a thing. Because property no longer defined the owner, it could be split off from him without changing his status. (This appears to be an earlier version of alienation but, in this instance, not alienation from self but from property.) The effect, as one might imagine, was equally dramatic. Land became capital, like any other form of currency. One could sell it and trade it. On the other side, anyone with the wit or luck could buy a feudal estate. With the bond cut between property and duty, ownership was a simple act of possession and control that stopped with the boundaries of the property (Tigar, 1977). When applied to intellectual property, this new idea made creative works—the product of one's mind—into something that could be more easily traded and sold. It turned language, expression, and personality itself into a commodity—with a market value and an exchange rate.

Practically speaking, what copyright gave the copyright holder was control over the territory he owned. It allowed him to regulate the market—decide the number available and the price at which each would be sold—while, at the same time, it gave him the right to police the "outlaw" printers who might try to copy his work (Patterson, 1968). Like the trapper, the merchant who bought the feudal estate, or the owner of newly enclosed land, the printer publisher now had control of the text—what it would look like, how it would enter the marketplace, and how many copies he would make available. The lesson to be drawn from these examples is clear: *The idea of property allows us to find ways to manage what is being produced—to control both quality and quantity and to set price.* Although the idea of property brings profit, it limits access. The result? The price of knowledge goes up. What had once been common property, open to anyone in the community who passed by, was now closed and cost something to use.

Still the copyright scheme serves a purpose. It does make investor money available to cover the cost of promotion, distribution, marketing, and sponsorship of new writings. But, at the same time, we need to remember, no matter how advantageous copyright was to the investor, it also created a monopoly. What's wrong with that? Prices are high. The owner can decide who gets to use it. Again, what's wrong with that? It wouldn't be a problem if we were talking about automobiles—one can always buy a different model, a cheaper model, a better model. But we are talking about access to information.

Such monopoly pricing creates problems for a democratic society constructed on the principle of market competition, the exchange of information, and the principles of an informed electorate. It creates problems for the poor, the young, and those not yet established. By protecting already established "authors," business, and corporations, we fix the economic game. The price of admission for the next generation may become too high for some to pay (Landes & Posner, 1989). This brings us to what one commentator called an "uneasy case" for copyright (Breyer, 1970) and the balance the authors of the Constitution tried to strike.

Copyright is an economic idea that puts two absolutes into conflict. The idea of property carries with it the idea of control, absolute control unregulated by the interests of the State. The idea of a State-defined regulatory system, like copyright, means that the State tinkers (from the beginning) with the idea of a "free" marketplace. The effect is the "uneasy case" for copyright. We preserve the property interests of one group by limiting the property interests of others, for example, the public's right to buy and sell intellectual commodities in the open market. In making the "uneasy case" for copyright, the authors of the Constitution tried to balance these interests (those of the individual producer and those of the public). Electronic publishing and the technology that surrounds it now damage this balance and weaken marketplace competition.

MAKING LAW: BALANCING BENEFITS

Principles

The key to appreciating copyright is that it is given grudgingly. There is something in the free enterprise system in a democracy that does not like a monopoly, and the authors of the Constitution seemed to share that view. They allowed for monopolies in intellectual property but limited their duration (U.S. Const., Art. I., Sec. 8, Cl. 8). The Constitution is clear: "secure for limited Times to Authors and Inventors the exclusive Right to their respective Writings and Discoveries." If they had a mind to, the authors of the Constitution need not have limited the duration of copyright. They could have made it continuous and without limit, but they did not. They recognized that broad and continuous copyrights vest absolute control over intellectual material in copyright holders, allowing them to set price and the terms for access. On the face of it, that does not seem terribly dangerous. We allow those who own real property to set the price and terms for access. But there is a difference between the two.

Real property is *not* produced and sold in multiples. One of the first questions raised by a machine like the printing press is how far does the "property line" extend: Does it rest with the original, or does it extend to every copy (Morris, 1963)? When we sell a piece of real property, we lose our rights to it, for example, we can no longer decide how it will be used. (The link has been broken between the person and the thing.) When we buy a piece of intellectual property, we are often only buying a copy of the property: We are not buying the rights to reproduce or exploit that property; they remain with the original owner, and he or she retains the right to decide who can buy the next copy and for what purpose.

Intellectual property *cannot* be sold like real property or other ordinary goods. To show it to a potential buyer, as a means of persuading him or her to buy it, is to disclose the information or some portion of it, giving away that which one intended to sell. On the other hand, intellectual property *cannot* be depleted. Its use does not, by itself, use it up. In fact, information may become more valuable as it is used by others who add on to it in order to create a new product.

Given the essentially ephemeral nature of intellectual property, it has taken some ingenuity to protect it. In part, the answer came with a technology like printing that made the property tangible—something like a commodity that could be counted, inventoried, and traded. You know what you have got when you have got your hands on it. Another answer came by finding a way to construct "boundaries" for the intellectual property being protected. Two obvious ones came to mind: time and subject matter. How long should the copyright last? How much material (and what kind of material) should be covered?

Duration

How long should the original copyright holder be allowed to have control over his or her piece of intellectual property? Only so long as it takes to get one's investment back and to make a "fair" profit, but not so long that when property reenters a competitive market it has no value because no one wants it. How long is that? We can look at the extremes.

An author writes a book. Copyright is for one month, or one year. The work becomes public after that. The public would quickly get cheap and easy access to the work, and, all things being equal, the cheaper version would be available while there was still interest in reading it (Braunstein, 1981; Breslow, Ferguson, & Haverkamp, 1977; Breyer, 1970). The public would benefit, but the author and publisher would have little time to reap their rewards. As a result, there would be little incentive to publish "risky" books, and there would be little incentive to invest in good editing.

An author writes a book. Copyright runs without limit. The work never becomes public. This would certainly appeal to authors and publishers. It provides a maximum incentive to producers. They are guaranteed complete control over their work in any form, for as long as they wished. Under this system, the public would, of course, be denied access to copyrighted material in both the present and the future except on terms prescribed by the copyright holder.

Neither option was one the authors of the Constitution had in mind. But, the way copyright has evolved, the second option is very close to what we have. Copyright now lasts a lifetime plus 50 years if the copyright holder is a person and 75 years if the holder is a corporation (Copyright Act of 1976, 17 U.S.C. Sec. 302a-c). If we apply this duration to software, we find that the law provides no realistic limit to the term of the copyright. The average useful life of most software is less than three years, and the useful life of databased information is equivalently short (Kleinman, 1993; Gleick, 1993; Post, 1983). Who will want to buy software competitively priced a generation from now when its usefulness had long since ended? To extend the copyright beyond a useful term is to give the copyright holder a *de facto* monopoly over the information.

Scope

There is another dimension to the copyright calculus beside that of duration. It is one of scope—how much should be covered? "Scope" is a tricky concept to pin down. It can mean a new medium to which copyright is applied, for example, sound recordings, motion pictures, photographs. It can mean new types and forms of expression, for example, electronic music, computer programs, and so on. It can mean new ways of storing or displaying material, for example, CD-ROMs, ROM chips, or television monitors. It can also mean new means of distributing already copyrighted material, for example, the videocassette recorder, local area networks, the Internet (see Committee on the Judiciary, U.S. House of Representatives, 1976).

The important principle involved in the issue of "scope" is the way it extends the value of copyrighted material. It is for this reason that there is a concern about extending both the duration of copyright at the same time one extends the scope of what is covered under the law. In the extreme case of continuous duration and extensive scope, the copyright holder has absolute economic control of the work. He or she "owns" it in whatever form it is produced in, in whatever medium is used, in all forms of distribution and storage, and does so without term.

Once in the marketplace, with copyright in hand, these owners have pretty extensive powers: They have the power to reproduce copies, prepare derivative works, distribute copies, perform, and display material owned by the copyright holder (Copyright Act of 1976, 17 U.S.C. Sec 106). (They have equivalent restraining powers too. They have the power to restrict the reproduction of copies, limit the audience, set the price, and control access generally if they care to exercise it.) The effect of this extension of ownership in time and scope is to distort the marketplace, creating value not only today and tomorrow, but in any of a number of future tomorrows.

Although copyright originated with the print technology, its scope changed with each new advance in technology, creating a new commodity to be sold as there developed new means of distribution. Thus, new technologies, whether photography, audio recordings, photocopying, cable, video recordings, or computers, create both new ways of reproducing material and new markets for that material. The net effect is that technology changes the market potential of the product created, allowing producers to include as potential sales those that but for the technology could not be anticipated nor factored into the value of the product when it was first produced. (Disney, for example, had no idea when first producing *Snow White* that there would be a market for the film on television, VCRs, and perhaps now on the Internet.)

Copyright is given grudgingly then because it distorts the marketplace. Its existence means that intellectual commodities may not compete with each other at fair market prices based on market forces—demand and quality. It increases the price of the product and adds other transaction costs—the cost of policing the system and the cost of obtaining permissions. By its nature, it makes it more expensive for "new," less well-funded publishers to get into the field and promotes consolidation by those who are already there (Breyer, 1970).

Why then should there be this form of monopoly? Why should the public pay more when it could pay less? The easy answer is that copyright protection provides an incentive for others to produce. Some argue the "moral" rights that each author has over the work he or she has created (Breyer, 1970). I sweated to produce this. Why should others make money off of my labors? If I do not control my work, others will corrupt and misuse it. Some present an economic argument: "Publishers would not be willing to go into the market if they feared they would need to compete with pirated editions of their work." "Authors would not be able to bargain with publishers since nothing would preclude a publisher from stealing the work and printing it without a contract" (Breyer, 1970).

To meet these problems, U.S. copyright law constructs—at least in theory—a delicate balance between the interests of individual producers on the one side and the interests of the public on the other. In a structural sense, the law reflects an attempt to balance the need to keep the marketplace unencumbered by regulation, at the same time that it hopes to stimulate enterprise. As the authors of the House Report accompanying the 1909 Copyright Act explained:

> The enactment of copyright legislation by Congress under the terms of the Constitution is not based upon any natural right that the author has in his writings. . . . The policy is believed to be for the benefit of the great body of people, in that it will stimulate writing and invention to give some bonus to authors and inventors. . . . Congress must consider . . . two questions: First, how much will the legislation stimulate the producer and so benefit the public, and, second, how much will the monopoly granted be detrimental to the public? (Committee on the Judiciary, U.S. House of Representatives, 1909, pp. 10-11)

How to strike the right balance? The question cannot be answered in the abstract, nor does the same balance work for all works of intellectual property—as is currently assumed to be the case. We may want to set different terms for electronic databases, novels, movies, hypermedia, news reportage, and so on. The answer we are interested in is whether the copyright scheme assures a predictable net increase of information at a cost related to its social value or usefulness (see, e.g., Braunstein, 1981; Braunstein, Fischer, Ordover, & Baumol, 1977; Breslow et al., 1977; Demsetz, 1967, 1969; Hurt & Schuchman, 1966; Landes & Posner, 1989). The question, as economists have observed, is whether "each potential extension of copyright power contribute[s] more to consumer welfare by stimulating the production and dissemination of new information than it costs in terms of availability of the presently existing stock and in increasing the cost of creating more information for the future" (Breslow et al., 1977, p. 7).

There is a lesson in this juggling act of property rights, equities, public good, and private incentives that we would do well to keep in mind. The elements of the balance were constructed by understanding the special nature of intellectual property in a primarily print environment. At the core of the law is an understanding that "ideas" can be made tangible, can become commodities, or can be cordoned off and then later opened up for the public to use. These elements—tangibility, fixity in time, and scope—are among the very elements drained of meaning in digital systems. What now that the tension between access and control increases under the ambiguities of the digital medium? What now that the open market is at risk when the time value of information grows increasingly shorter? We have to understand that the special nature of intellectual property changes as the technological environment changes.

In working one's way through terms such as *authorship*, *fixity*, and *tangible medium*, one gets a quick glimpse of the problems brought on by digital technology: The law links ownership with the idea of "authorship," as though an author can still be clearly identified and his or her originality easily established. If the theorists about hypermedia are right, authorship and originality will become harder to locate; the link between the thing and the person will be broken (Bolter, 1991; Landow, 1992; Lanham, 1993).

We do not need to know much about the digital technology to see how it may weaken many of the basic property notions at the core of copyright law. *Fixity*, the other key element in the paradigm, will be no less clear when applied to a highly interactive medium. What does fixity mean (how can we determine it) when the very form of expression—the order and the content—varies with each new interchange between "text" and "reader"? By threatening the connection between authors and fixed works, digital technology threatens the concept of copyright itself, as well as the economic system it is meant to work within.

SPACE: THE NEXT GENERATION

As we exit the more material space created by print, we enter a space in which objects, as well as ideas, are no longer fixed in tangible forms. There are consequences in the marketplace. There are some tentative conclusions we can draw. Electronic publishing is changing the nature of the marketplace and will in turn change the nature of most of these elements—ownership, authorship, the value we give to structure and form, the price we set for access, and so on. In a digital universe, the tangible object disappears, and control of the means of production becomes far less important than control of the means of distribution. Put baldly, the current principles of copyright will not work in an electronic space of the kind we are creating.

1. *Copyright will not work for practical reasons.* It is simply too easy to copy, too difficult to police those who copy, and nearly impossible to detect when "old," already copyrighted material has been combined with "new" material to create another work (Brand, 1987).
2. *Copyright will not work for technical reasons.* The application of copyright law assumes that one can identify "authorship," establish "originality," determine when a work is "fixed in any tangible medium of expression," and agree on when a work has been "copied" (Copyright Act of 1976, 17 U.S.C. Sec. 102a). These are concepts that are beginning to make less and less sense in the context of digital expression and electronic publishing.
3. *Copyright will not work for economic reasons.* It distorts the marketplace because it leads to increased monopolization of information by fewer producers and distributors of information, and monopoly is at odds with our principled commitment to free marketplace competition.

4. *Copyright will not work for structural reasons.* In an electronic culture, it mitigates against a dynamic economy—one that is organized for "constant change," "innovation," and "creative destruction." As many economists now argue, in a world economy based on information as the primary resource, a dynamic economy is what we will require (Drucker, 1993). In the new economy, current copyright protection may be the anchor in the water that slows us down.

CONCLUSIONS

Now in the late 20th century, the spread of electronic publishing, multimedia, electronic networks, and the new electronic space changes the nature of intellectual property and the marketplace in which it is sold. Principles we have taken for granted—especially those that support the notion that ideas can be made into commodities—are threatened.

The logic of digital technology leads us in a new direction. Objects, as well as ideas, are no longer fixed, no longer tangible. In cyberspace, there is no weight, no dimension; structure is dynamic and changing; size is both infinite and immaterial. In this space, stories are written that change with each new reader; new material can be added, and old material deleted. Nothing is permanent.

If language and ideas, taken together, are not commodities, what are they? It is not clear how we will finally come to describe ideas in electronic space, but it is becoming clear what they are not: They are not finite, tangible, permanent, and immutable. Perhaps they are infinite, immaterial, impermanent, and mutable.

Where Are We?

In the next decade under pressure from the technology, copyright owners will want to be clear about what they own, the extent of their property rights, in order to determine more accurately their value and price. Users will need to know what it is they have in hand in order to establish their rights to access and their rights to use. The strain on the copyright law will be especially felt as the technology expands to include average consumers who, in the past, relied on print media or conventional television and radio broadcasting for their entertainment and information.

If we continue to use the current copyright structure, the price of information must increase. Access to information (for the public, the consumer, and those engaged in the creative process) will be more difficult, if not more expensive. The social, political, and economic price we pay may be higher than we can afford: We will have less access to the "old" so we will be less able to construct or imagine the new. The amount and quality of information will be reduced. The marketplace will be distorted and organized to take advantage of the efficiencies of a monopoly-run economy. (Copyright benefits already increasingly accrue to corporate copyright owners in their role as contractors of works for hire, rather than to the actual authors of the copyrighted works.)

In a society based on the principle of a "free marketplace of ideas," we have become accustomed to a political and economic model that is the exact opposite of that found in absolute control of information. We have gotten much from a competitive marketplace for ideas. Up until now, in the context of a print culture with the support structure of public libraries, that marketplace has stimulated access, diversity, and dissemination, and it has encouraged the growth of a rich environment for individual entrepreneurs, authors of information, creative artists, and the public at large. Can it be structured so that it provides the same kind of stimulus?

If We Are Going, How Would We Get There, and How Can We Protect Our Social Interests?

If we do wish to continue with a commodities market for property, ideas, and information (assuming, of course, that we can figure a way to get the technology to maintain it), we need to rework the copyright system, keeping the following principles in mind:

1. The primary purpose of copyright law is to benefit society, not to benefit the copyright owner. The constitutional grant of a "limited monopoly" must be taken to mean exactly that—a privilege bestowed out of social necessity to stimulate invention and creativity but granted somewhat grudgingly by society as a means to an end—the public welfare.
2. Decentralized access and decentralized personal use of information is critical to social interests. Intellectual property "rights" should be assessed on the basis of whether they produce more information in the hands of more people. When they do not, the "rights" should be curtailed.
3. The statutory monopoly created by the copyright law, especially as applied to electronic media, blesses an anticompetitive spirit that encourages inefficiency and engenders a concentration of economic power and social control.
4. Copyright protection should be for a limited duration or should require that the applicant satisfy more rigorous standards: that the work promotes a significant social purpose that justifies an extended monopoly.

The Tug of War

For those who wish protection, access that is too easy is an invitation to piracy. For those who wish easy access or, at least, inexpensive access, protection that is too strict raises the specter of monopoly and a restricted or expensive public dialogue. If we must pay each time we wish to read the news, study U.S. history, or read those basic primers that help us learn to read, write, and do math, we may find that some of us are excluded because we cannot come up with the price of admission. Who will pay for those too poor to pay for themselves?

Another Way of Framing Questions and Answers

From a merely technical point of view, it does look like a digital culture will force us to rethink what we mean by such commonplace concepts as ownership, originality, authorship, and a "free" access to ideas. But we cannot stop there. Those questions of definition are basically conservative ones: *How can we adapt present law and its principles to the new technology?* We must go further, trying to take control over the technology: *What kind of economy and workplace do we want?* This is a hard question because it assumes that we can control both the technology and the economy.

One way to figure out what is going on is to take some cues from the past. It is easy enough when talking about copyright and property to think only in material terms. What do I own? What will it cost me to get this material? These are useful questions, but they divert us from more interesting questions. Earlier, I argued that the principle of copyright is bound up in certain postmedieval notions about property that lead us to treat ideas as commodities. This was only possible when ideas and language (like land itself) had been shorn of self-defining roles. In a commodities marketplace, one no longer thinks of property or language as carrying duties, defining relationships, or expressing responsibilities. Rather they are items given value only because they can be traded, and, because of that, our current notions about copyright become plausible and self-evident. In the electronic space that we are entering, such transactions may be less evident. The question then should be what kind of system do we now need? Another way of saying this: What kinds of economic and social "values" do we want to create or preserve?

If we argue that we still wish to maintain a transactional marketplace in which commodities are sold, we will have to work out a strategy that makes more "permanent," "finite," and "tangible," electronic images that are now not permanent, finite, and tangible. Once we have concluded that that is the value system we want, we will, no doubt, find a strategy that works. We need to take some of our clues for a structure from the past—the way we divided up the trapper's territory to preserve the stock, enclosed the commons to enhance control and efficiency, and made feudal property into real estate to free up land so it could be invested like capital in an economic expansion.

We should remember that there are alternate schemes we might embrace. We might want a scheme based on access, similar to the open commons. We might want one based on the needs of a scarcity economy, like that of the copyists who were central to promotion and distribution of both the old and new learning of the late Middle Ages. Currently the structure of the Internet has many similarities to the open commons. It was designed to encourage access and promote sharing and the exchange of skills and ideas (Kapor, 1993). Or we might want a scheme like that found in the feudal system—one in which "property" was inextricably interwoven with ideas of service owed to those who use the land.

What might such an alternative scheme look like? If, for example, we wished to emphasize ideas of services and the relationships between intellectual property and those who use it, we might dramatically reduce the duration of the copyright. To stay in the market—ahead of competition—the publisher would need to provide incentives to potential buyers. Especially in the case of publishers of software or databases, the limited life of their product creates opportunity for the sale of revisions. Publishers have other ways of bonding their products to potential buyers. They can offer support (800 numbers, manuals, discounted upgrades) as ways of "selling" service and selling their product.

The economics of software publishing would support this shift. Service is a commodity that cannot be infringed on, and operating manuals and documentation are easily protected under conventional copyright principles. According to some calculations, only 6% to 13% of the price of software can be attributed to its manufacture and revision. On the other hand, documentation accounts for 35% to 40% of the price, and service accounts for 2% to 4%. About 50% of the price can be attributed to marketing, packaging, promotion, and advertising (Beyers & Halcrow, 1984; Garber, 1992).

How might we protect the author? First we should understand that copyright quite often creates an illusion that weakens the bargaining position of most authors—rather than strengthening it. Authors bargain for the sale of their manuscripts on the expectation of royalties received over their lifetime. It is a fantasy that authors have and that the publishing contract reinforces. The value of a book in the marketplace is determined almost completely by the publisher—by how much he or she is willing to invest in advertising, distribution, and by how long he or she is willing to keep the book in circulation. Quite possibly, authors would bargain more wisely and receive fairer payment if they directed their negotiations to a clear contract for labor done.

If we wish to stimulate more authors and more work, there are stratagems for doing so. To strengthen the hand of the author in negotiating with the publisher, we might require that copyright be granted only to human beings, thereby eliminating corporate copyright. We might rework the tax code so that authors are entitled to deductions and depreciations similar to those we give businesses and investors. We might take the approach of Ireland, which exempts the income from writing from taxation.

Our laws are not developed to protect authors nor to promote service, no matter what we say to rationalize it (Mobilio, 1994). We have not yet refashioned the property lines of intellectual property because we would still like to try to keep it a commodity. The point is that a discussion of copyright is not merely a legal argument, nor for that matter an economic one. It reflects a view of language, culture, and the relationships we mean to have with each other. It is this we have to work through.

What we know—or, at least, what we are beginning to feel—is that we have entered a new age in which most conventions (be they legal or economic) no longer seem to apply and are not easily rationalized. Still, most of us live and work in an industrial economy, and it is the metaphor of that economy and space that still applies and the one we must try to understand before we move on.

REFERENCES

Abrams v. United States, 250 U.S. 616 (1919).

Barlow, J.P. (1994a, March). The economics of ideas: A framework for rethinking patents and copyrights in the digital age. *Wired*, pp. 84-90, 126-29.

Beyers, C., & Halcrow, A. (1984, March). What's behind the price of software? *Interface Age*, pp. 59, 61-63.

Bolter, J.D. (1991). *Writing space: The computer, hypertext, and the history of writing*. Hillsdale, NJ: Erlbaum.

Brand, S. (1987). *The media lab: Inventing the future at MIT*. New York: Penguin Books.

Braunstein, Y.M. (1981). The functioning of information markets. In H.A. Shaw (Ed.), *Issues in information policy* (Rep. No. NTIA-SP-80-9; pp. 57-74). Washington, DC: National Telecommunications and Information Administration.

Braunstein, Y.M., Fischer, D.M., Ordover, J.A., & Baumol, W.J. (1977). *Economics of property rights as applied to computer software and data bases* (rev. ed.; Rep. No. CONTU 77-0005). Springfield, VA: National Technical Information Services.

Breslow, M., Ferguson, A.R., & Haverkamp, L. (1977). *An analysis of computer and photocopying copyright issues from the point of view of the general public and the ultimate consumer* (Rep. No. CONTU 77-0008). Springfield, VA: National Technical Information Services.

Breyer, S. (1970). The uneasy case for copyright: A study of copyright in books, photocopies, and computer programs. *Harvard Law Review, 84*, 281-351.

Burke, J. (1985). *The day the universe changed*. Boston: Little, Brown.

Committee on the Judiciary, U. S. House of Representatives. (1909). *Report on the Copyright Act of 1909* [60th Cong., 2nd Sess.] (House Rep. No. 2222). Washington, DC: U.S. Government Printing Office.

Committee on the Judiciary, U.S. House of Representatives (1976). *Copyright Law Revision* [94th Cong., 2nd Sess.] (House Rep. No. 94-1476). Washington, DC: U.S. Government Printing Office.

Copyright Act of 1976, 17 U.S.C. Sects. 102, 106, 302 (1976).

Demsetz, H. (1967). Toward a theory of property rights. *American Economic Review, 57,* 347-359.

Demsetz, H. (1969). Information and efficiency: Another viewpoint. *The Journal of Law and Economics, 12,* 1-22.

Drucker, P. (1993). *Post-capitalist society.* New York: HarperCollins

Edmunds, S. (1991). From Schoeffer to Verard: Concerning the scribes who became printers. In S.L. Hindman (Ed.), *Printing the written word: The social history of books, circa 1450-1520* (pp. 21-40). Ithaca, NY: Cornell University Press.

Eisenstein, E. (1983). *The printing revolution in early modern europe.* New York: Cambridge University Press.

Febvre, L., & Martin, H.-J. (1984). *The coming of the book: The impact of printing, 1450-1800* (D. Gerard, Trans.). London: Verso Editions. (Original work published 1958)

Garber, R. (1992, August 31). The end of the shoestring. *Forbes*, p. 74.

Gleick, J. (1993, May 16). The telephone transformed into almost everything. *New York Times Magazine*, pp. 26-29, 50, 53-56, 62, 64.

Hammond, J.L., & Hammond, B. (1948). *The village labourer.* London: Longmans, Green.

Hurt, R.M., & Schuchman, R.M. (1966). The economic rationale of copyright. *American Economic Review, 2,* 421-438.

Kaplan, B. (1967). *An unhurried view of copyright.* New York: Columbia University Press.

Kapor, M. (1993, July/August). Where is the digital highway really heading? *Wired*, pp. 53-59, 94.

Katsh, M.E. (1989). *The electronic media and the transformation of law.* New York: Oxford University Press.

Kleinman, N. (1993). Mr. Bloom meets an electronic fox—The canon in the age of a new technology. *Readerly/Writerly Texts, 1,* 15-38.

Landow, G.P. (1992). *Hypertext: The convergence of contemporary critical theory and technology.* Baltimore: Johns Hopkins University Press.

Landes, W.M., & Posner, R.A. (1989). An economic analysis of copyright law. *Journal of Legal Studies, 17,* 325-336.

Lanham, R A. (1993). *The electronic word.* Chicago: The University of Chicago Press.

Lopez, R.S. (1976). *The commercial revolution of the middle ages, 950-1350.* New York: Cambridge University Press.

Lynch v. Household Finance Corp., 405 U.S. 538 (1972).

McLuhan, M. (1962). *The Gutenberg galaxy.* Toronto: University of Toronto Press.

Mingay, G.E. (1968). *Enclosure and the small farmer in the age of the industrial revolution.* London: Macmillan.
Mobilio, A. (1994, October). Inside publishing—Publish and retain your copyright or perish. *Lingua Franca,* pp. 17-19.
Morris, T.B. (1963). The origins of the statute of Anne. ASCAP Copyright Law *Symposium, 12,* 222-260.
Ong, W J. (1971). *Rhetoric, romance, and technology.* Ithaca, NY: Cornell University Press.
Patterson, L.R. (1968). *Copyright in historical perspective.* Nashville: Vanderbilt University Press.
Peters, T. (1987). *Thriving on chaos: Handbook for a management revolution.* New York: Knopf.
Post, D.W. (1983, February). Data communications: Online information industry's influence begins to spread. *Interface Age,* pp. 22, 157.
Roe v. Wade, 410 U.S. 113 (1973).
Steinberg, S. H. (1974). *Five hundred years of printing* (3rd ed.). London: Penguin.
Tedeschi, M. (1991). Publish and perish: The career of Lienhart Holle in Ulm. In S.L. Hindman (Ed.), *Printing the written word: The social history of books, circa 1450-1520* (pp. 41-67). Ithaca, NY: Cornell Universiiy Press.
Tigar, M. (1977). *Law and the rise of capitalism.* New York: Monthly Review Press.

◇◇◇◇ 5

Back to Plato's Cave: Virtual Reality

Herbert Zettl

Virtual reality (VR) has been described as "postsymbolic," implying an experience that is virtually mediated. Herbert Zettl here provides a very different perspective on VR, viewing it as an art form that can be analyzed in terms of aesthetics and as a medium that can be compared and contrasted with other media such as the photograph, the motion picture, and television. He also considers the philosophical implications of VR and the ethical dimension of human action and interaction in cyberspace, an aspect of the electronic environment ignored by many. In other sections of this book, further discussion of VR can be found in Terri Toles Patkin's human factors approach to the virtual organization in Chapter 11, Sue Barnes's exploration of virtual ecology in Chapter 13, Elizabeth Weiss's essay on the cybergym in Chapter 14, Margaret Cassidy's examination of digital experience in Chapter 15, Paul Lippert's study of cyberspace and the cinema in Chapter 18, Mark Lipton's research on cybersex in Chapter 22, and Lance Strate's piece on cybertime in Chapter 23.

Insert the CD-ROM. Click on Plato. Choose "Republic" and double click on Book VII. A picture of Socrates appears, in the stereotypical Greek attire, commenting and, as usual, asking questions:[1]

---

[1]The quotes are taken from Allan Bloom's (1968) translation of Plato's *Republic.* Bloom entitles his translation "The Republic of Plato." I have documented Plato's quotes with the customary numbers and letters as they appear in Plato's text, followed by the page number of Bloom's translation.

"Next then," I said, "make an image of our nature in its education and want of education, likening it to a condition of the following kind. See human beings as though they were in an underground cave-like dwelling with its entrance, a long one, open to the light across the whole width of the cave. They are in it from childhood with their legs and necks in bonds so that they are fixed, seeing only the front of them, unable because of the bond to turn their heads all the way around. Their light is from a fire burning far above and behind them. Between the fire and the prisoners there is . . . a wall, built like the partitions [proscenium] puppet handlers set in front of the human beings [audience] and over which they show the puppets.". . . "Then also see along this wall human beings carrying all sorts of artifacts, which project above the wall, and statues of men and other animals wrought from stone, wood, and every kind of material; as is to be expected, some of the carriers utter sounds while others are silent." [514a-c; p. 193] . . . "They are like us," I said. "For in the first place, do you suppose such men would have seen anything of themselves and one another other than the shadows cast by the fire on the side of the cave facing them?" [515a, p. 193] . . . "And what about the things that are carried by? Isn't it the same with them? . . . "If they were able to discuss things with one another, don't you believe that they would hold that they are naming these things going by before them that they see?" . . . "And what if the prison also had an echo from the side facing them? Whenever one of the men passing by happens to utter a sound, do you suppose they would believe that anything other than the passing shadow was uttering the sound?"

"No, by Zeus . . ." [515b, p. 194]

"Then, most certainly," . . . "such men would hold that the truth is nothing but the truth of shadows of artificial things." [515c, p. 194]

Plato has Socrates explain what would happen if one of the men were finally released, asked to stand up and turn to look into the light. He—the prisoner—would be dazzled by the light and unable at first to make out the things that caused the shadows. Even when told and shown that the things that caused the shadows are "nearer to what *is*" [emphasis in original] and that the shadows were "silly nothings," "he'd be at a loss and believe that what was seen before was truer than what is now shown" [515d, p. 194]. Eventually, his eyes adjust to the bright light of enlightenment and he feels pity for his fellow prisoners. He intends to share his experiences with them and goes back to the cave "to sit in the same seat" [516e, p. 195]. But now, in the dim light, he has become inept in discerning the shadows as accurately as his fellow prisoners, who now bestow honors and prizes for those who "are sharpest in making out the things that go by" [516d, p. 195]. And "wouldn't he be the source of laughter, and wouldn't it be said that he went up and came back with his eyes corrupted, and that it's not even worth trying to go up?" [517a, p. 196].

Click on Exit. Socrates dissolves into some Greek columns.

Have we not picked the wrong CD-ROM? No, definitely not. Although Plato wrote his Republic quite some time ago—at about 380 B.C.—he is talking about virtual reality. His cave analogy could have been written today as an appropriate and penetrating discourse describing our new synthetic world of shadows, an artificial environment that we so proudly call virtual reality. In fact, we hail virtual reality as a supreme technical achievement without, perhaps, realizing that we are returning to Plato's cave in order to become perceptual prisoners. Just as the prisoners in Plato's cave, we willingly restrict our vision by putting on a helmet that displays only a world of shadows, and limit our motion by being tethered by a thick cable to the computer. Plato's analogy, which seems uncomfortably close to our immersion into virtual reality, also directs us to take a look at the prisoners, who, "like us" [515a, p. 193] are fascinated with the shadow world. What I would like to do, therefore, is to examine in some detail how we perceive the new world of shadows and why we seem to feel so comfortable in our high-tech cave.[2]

THE PROBLEM

The problem, then, is twofold: to examine the aesthetics of virtual reality's visual and aural images, and to comment on some of the major ethical issues of virtual reality. This is a tall order because both subject areas are as amorphous as they are complex. I feel a little like St. Augustine, who more than 1,500 years ago (397A.D.) wrestled in his *Confessions* with the definition of time: "What then is time? If no one asks me, I know: if I wish to explain it to one that asketh, I know not: yet I say boldly that I know" (397/1961, p. 194).

Specifically, the brief analysis of the aesthetics of virtual reality includes three approaches: (a) a media-aesthetic or phenomenological one, (b) an ontological one, and (c) an ethical one. In the media-aesthetic approach, which ordinarily includes the five fields of light and color, two-dimensional space, three-dimensional space, time motion, and sound (Zettl, 1990), I concentrate only on some three-dimensional points, the perception of motion, and the role of sound in virtual reality. In the ontological approach, I attempt to show how virtual reality images differ structurally from other forms of mediated reality, such as the lens-generated two-dimensional imagery of the common photographic arts: still photos, television, and film. Such structural differences have an important, though less than obvious, impact on how we can use the various media most effectively. In the ethical approach, I simply raise some questions about our potential behavior in a basically amoral computer-generated environment. I am especially concerned about the freedom of choice within the deterministic parameters of computer-programmed virtual reality and the potential existential

[2]There are, of course, other studies that use Plato's cave analogy to highlight modern media or media practices. For example, Jay Newman (1989) uses Plato's cave as the philosophical basis for defining the nature and value of journalism. F.M. Cornford (1941) mentions that a modern Plato would certainly compare the cave to the shadows of the cinema.

dilemma of decision making in an environment that offers a virtual sanctuary in which choices bear no consequences.

Even at the risk of offending some readers or appearing too pedantic, I would like to define some terms. I do so in order to avoid any misunderstandings of what I mean and to keep the discussion on track:

1. *Reality.* In the aesthetic discussion, I mean by reality simply the actual environment in which we operate and the actual events we experience. In the Kantian sense (Kant, 1787/1956) I refer to phenomena, not noumena (Ding an sich).
2. *Virtual reality.* A computer-generated three-dimensional image and stereo sound that displays events (objects and environments) and that is interactive with the user. In this case, interactivity means that we change from mere observers or viewers to event participants. As such, we exercise some control over the event display.
3. *Media Aesthetics.* By media aesthetics, I do not mean the traditional study of beauty, form, and emotional response, but rather the study of fundamental image elements (light, space, time-motion, and sound) and how a specific medium—in our case, the computer display—uses these elements to produce specific perceptual responses (Zettl, 1990). I do not include in this discussion the haptic one, which deals with the sense of touch, although there are various efforts underway to integrate tactile sensations in the virtual reality experience (Time, 1993; Vingelman, 1993).[3]
4. *Ontology.* I use ontology as the branch of metaphysics that deals with the study of the ultimate nature of things (O'Hear, 1985). My ontological efforts are limited to the description and thinking about the inherent structural properties of things and events, and how one thing is essentially different from another.

MEDIA AESTHETIC ANALYSIS

My media-aesthetic analysis is limited to some aspects of three-dimensional representation, the simulation of motion, and the spatial aspects of sound.

Three-Dimensional Representation

We can witness a dramatic development of representing three-dimensional space on a two-dimensional surface from the time the Greek painter Zeuxis began

---

[3]Time (February 8, 1993) reports on the possibility of virtual sex, during which we would wear a tight body suit that transmits the erotic tickles of a virtual interactive lover. Vingelman (1993) reports on a similar development.

adding attached shadows to his painting of grapes to when the Renaissance painters and architects perfected and applied sophisticated rules of linear perspective. But nothing much has happened since that time. There is relatively little difference between the three-dimensional techniques used by Leonardo da Vinci and those by Edward Hopper, such trompe l'oeil artists as William Harnell and Peto, or the three-dimensional renderings of computer graphics. All of them use such Renaissance techniques as overlapping planes, relative size, height in plane, linear and aerial perspective, and cast and attached shadows.[4] The only real difference is that today the painter's brush has been replaced by the programmer's algorithms, and that virtual reality relies more on the mimetic vocabulary of the photographic image than eye-perceived space.

New is the ease and speed with which we can change the image in light and color, contour, and topology. Depending on the sophistication of the taxonomy of geometric transformations, we can manipulate lens-generated images as well as synthesize a great many points of view and degrees of distortions with the computer's virtual camera (Mitchell, 1992). More so, contrary to film and television, in which the change of point of view has been decided a priori and fixed in the editing room, in virtual reality such shifts in point of view are, at least to a certain extent, in the control of the user. For example, when I tilt my head up, I may see in a virtual reality (VR) display a mountain from below, and when I tilt my head down, I see the mountain from above. By turning my head I can see the landscape next to the mountain. These shifts in point of view lead to a continuity that approximates our rapid, yet smooth, cutting when scanning the landscape with our eyes. Nevertheless, such viewpoints are still limited and determined by the relative sophistication of the computer program.

Motion

Regardless of whether the virtual reality display is nonimmersive or immersive, users do not normally move about in virtual space, but are activating the movement of the screen display through limited hand and head movements from a fixed place. When manipulating nonimmersive virtual environments, we usually watch a three-dimensional screen image, very much like a three-dimensional movie, and change the screen environment through a joystick or computer mouse. Immersive environments are watched and activated through stereo video monitors inside a helmet and a glove that contains various activating sensors. In both cases, we *watch* rather than enter the displayed environment. The problem is that our kinesthetic sensations and our automatic processing of the figure/ground relationships will not make us feel as though we were actually moving through space, but rather leads to our perceiving virtual space move past us.

---

[4]Paul Messaris (1994) makes a case for different depth cues, which, however, do not render the traditional ones (as developed by Renaissance artists and confirmed by perception psychologists) invalid.

Kinesthesia and the Figure/Ground Principle

The kinesthetic problem is that when I move through actual space, I am aware of my movement and my change of position relative to the environment. I am doing the moving, not the environment, barring earthquakes. In actual space, the environment is being moved through; it is not passing us by. This is why subjective camera scenes rarely, if ever, make us feel as though we are part of the action. Seeing the tips of skis on the bottom of the picture frame with snow rushing past and the horizonline tilting one way or the other does not even approximate the sensation of racing down a steep slope. Even a more gentle movement, such as walking through our living room, is hardly duplicated by the subjective camera that makes the same moves. All we really experience is to see the living room moving on the screen or, at best, a continuous change of points of view of the living room. Our control of viewpoint in interactive VR displays does not make us less aware of the sensation that it is the display that is doing the moving, and not we.

Why, then, are some of the VR displays more convincing than others? For example, the landing strip rushing by in a flight simulator, or the street curving and moving past us in a driving simulation seems to be much more "real" and convincing than the snow rushing by in the downhill skiing simulation. A closer look at the figure/ground principle will help to deal with this problem.

As we all know, the figure/ground principle basically states that we tend to perceive the figure as doing the moving against a more stable ground (Arnheim, 1974; Rock, 1984). Furthermore, we tend to organize the visual field and, in our case, motion, into hierarchic relationships of figure and ground. As Karl Duncker (1929) points out, we always seek as ground the most approximate framework surrounding the figure. When sitting in an airplane, we take the airplane as the more stable ground. We are the figure and the airplane the ground. We seem to hold on to this perceptual security blanket even if the airplane banks in a turn. We tend to perceive the earth as doing the tilting, rather than the plane. When watching the airplane from the ground, however, it becomes the figure and the earth the ground. We properly perceive, therefore, the airplane doing the tilting. This hierarchic figure/ground relationship is directly applicable to our participation in the VR display.

When we ski down a slope, we are in motion and kinesthetically aware of this motion. We are the figure and the slope the ground. We know and feel that we are skiing downhill and that the slope is not rushing uphill past us. However, when watching a subjective camera display of the downhill skiing, we are basically at rest, even if we can control the display speed and point of view through some computer sensor device. Our ground is not the computer display, but the chair or room in which we are sitting. Even if the complex visual display succeeds in temporarily reversing our figure/ground perception, kinesthetically we remain *in loco* and at rest. And we are very much aware of it.

What about the simulation of landing an airplane or driving a car? Even in a relatively unsophisticated video arcade display of a car race from the driver's point of view, we seem to be more immersed in the display and more ready to act as an event participant rather than observer. I think that the reason for this acceptance is that when piloting a plane or driving a car, we are at rest. We sit in the plane or car seat and literally see the runway or the street curves rushing toward us. Although in actuality we are still aware that it is the plane or car that is doing the moving rather than the runway or the street, we nevertheless are kinesthetically *in loco*, with the cockpit or car interior being the most approximate ground. Perceptually, therefore, we may more readily switch from the actual windshield display to the computer-generated display of the "moving street." In cases in which the immersive VR environment allows us to walk through it rather than merely observe it, the figure/ground relationship will probably approach more our normal experience. However, the problem remains that we still see the ground move even if we are aware of actually walking through the virtual environment.

Sound

As in movies and television, sound plays an important part in orienting and immersing us in the VR environment. As we remember, Plato's puppeteers also relied quite heavily on sound in order to make the prisoners believe they were witnessing the real world instead of shadows. In VR displays, we should expect an equally effective audio-video relationship, a picture-sound synergy whereby the three-dimensional visual fidelity is matched by an equally convincing three-dimensional sound environment.

At first glance, we should think that the visual stereo display may best be complemented by stereo sound. However, in practice, stereo sound discloses some serious shortcomings in being truly three-dimensional. The problem is that traditional stereo sound best defines the x-axis dimension, as evidenced by the traditional pan pots that move the sound laterally from left to right or vice versa. But stereo systems do not seem capable of making the sound zoom along the z-axis (the depth dimension), toward or away from the listener/participant. The very point of a visual stereo image is that it emphasizes the z-axis extension toward the viewer—a virtual depth illusion that seems to catapult the object not only up to the screen, but *through* it into the viewer's lap (Zettl, 1990). Traditional stereo sound simply cannot match such a visual z-axis extension.

Surround sound does not fare much better. It merely repeats x-axis articulation at the sides or behind the observer/listener, but fails to add a z-axis dimension to the sound. A better system seems to be binaural sound, which, if properly recorded and played back through headphones, is capable of defining with some degree of accuracy the lateral as well as the z-axis (depth) positions of the sound source relative to the observer/listener (Alten, 1994). For example, if in our driving simulation we see an oncoming car, we can greatly enhance virtual space by having the car's sound rather soft and "far" when it is seen in an extreme long shot, but having it get louder and "closer" as the car approaches (moves to a closeup), become loudest when it is just about to pass us (our z-axis position), then pass us and fade in back of us at the opposite end of the stereo z-axis projection. There are computer programs being developed that can model human localization of sound with fair accuracy (Alten, 1994). Such programs will, of course, facilitate greatly the perceptual illusion that the shadows are actually doing the talking.

ONTOLOGICAL ANALYSIS

I am sure that Plato would have preferred the VR display to his cave analogy in trying to explain the real, and that Kant (1787/1956) would have welcomed it in his efforts to explain his transcendental aesthetics and the difference between phenomena and noumena. But they would have certainly pointed out that even the term *virtual reality* presents an interesting metaphysical paradox. If we assume that all perception is basically virtual, that is, dependent on the conscious perception of objects, what then differentiates the real world from the VR display? Because this chapter is not intended as a platform for metaphysical debate, my "reality" comments are limited to a brief analysis of the structural differences between lens-generated and computer-generated space.

Analytic and Synthetic Images

There is a rather subtle, yet important structural difference between the lens-generated and computer-generated images. Whereas the lens-generated images are basically analytical, the computer-generated images are synthetic. This means that the lens-generated images are always reflective and interpretative of the segments of reality they select (Bazin, 1967; Kracauer, 1960; Savedoff, 1992), whereas the computer-generated images are always medium-manufactured. We could also say that the lens-generated image is basically deductive, in which optical portions are snatched from a larger landscape event, and computer images are basically inductive, that is, built up from a great variety of pixels as controlled by numbers. Compared to the linear, analog nature of lens-generated images, computer graphics are nonlinear and modular in nature. The lens produces an instant and faithful light image of the object or event it sees, regardless of what the event may be. The computer image, on the other hand, must build its world, painstakingly bit by bit, through a series of elaborate algorithms. In practice this means that although the whole world is instantly available to the lens, the computer images of virtual reality are severely limited by what object and event modules have been developed. As Lev Manovich (1992) points out: "the photographic simulation of 'real scenes' is impossible on a practical level as the techniques available to commercial animators only cover very particular phenomena of visual reality" (p. 14). Of course, the digitizing of lens-generated images can help us build a visual library whose only real limits are monetary. In this case, the computer image is no longer synthetic, but has become a transformation and manipulation device for the optical image.

Even then, the computerized images, especially in their various manifestations of the VR display, can be amazingly crude. They appear more than occasionally cartoon-like, and remind us of painting by numbers (which, indeed, they are). Only the most sophisticated systems produce images that go beyond the video-arcade variety. But here we probably need a reorientation of what computer-generated visual images ought to look like. So far, the ultimate goal of computer graphics is paradoxically not to simulate the real environment, but the lens-generated one. Many computer programs have various photographic distortions built into them, such as forced linear perspective (which imitates the perspective created by a wide-angle lens), aerial perspective (which drastically reduces the depth of field in order to show only a limited portion of the z-axis in focus), z-axis compression (which simulates the view through a telephoto lens), z-axis stretching (which simulates the view through a wide-angle lens), and zoom effects (which moves the event toward or away from the observer). Such distortions are definitely not part of our normal perception.

The ontological question here is not whether virtual reality should imitate the lens-generated or eye-perceived environment, but rather what aesthetic parameters and codes are structurally appropriate and unique to this new medium. After all, artificial realities need not, as Krueger (1990) mentions, "conform to physical reality any more than our homes mirror the outside environment" (p. 422). This is, I think, where HDTV (high-definition television) went wrong. Instead of capitalizing on its own unique attributes, such as the high-resolution image and real-time layering of effects, it tried to mimic the movies.

VIRTUAL REALITY AND ETHICS

One of Plato's main points in the cave analogy is the risk we take when being exposed to the real world, and whether we would not feel more comfortable remaining in the world of shadows, a world in which we can construct our own safe society with its own games, such as bestowing honors and prizes on the one who can best identify the shape of the shadows and recall the order of their appearance. Plato has the prisoners question the wisdom of leaving the cave only to have one's "eyes corrupted" [517a, p. 196]. In fact, there might be a strenuous objection to such exposure to the world of reality and freedom: "And if they [the prisoners] were somehow to get their hands on and kill the man who attempts to release and lead up [the prisoners to the sun-drenched entrance of the cave], wouldn't they kill him?" "No doubt about it" [517a, p. 196]. Even if we do not react quite so violently toward those who help us understand reality, enlightenment is always accompanied by anxiety and discomfort. The ethical question I would like to raise here is whether our desire to return to the cave of virtual reality is not motivated, at least to some extent, by a basic yearning for irresponsibility, a yearning for not being held accountable for our decisions. Such a morally neutral environment can have negative as well as positive perspectives.

One of the highly practical functions of virtual reality is that it can let us see things that are ordinarily hidden from our view. For instance, a sophisticated VR display can give a medical student an unprecedented view of various organs in a human body, and let the student see how they function under normal and pathological conditions. With the simple movement of the computer mouse, the student can shift them about and look inside them, and even operate on them without ever touching a human being, dead or alive. A mistake in operating procedures may, at most, cause an angry computer beep, but it will certainly not jeopardize anyone's life. Similarly, flying or driving simulators render even serious mistakes totally harmless. There is no risk of getting, or having anyone, hurt even when participating in rather aggressive VR games.

However, there is a darker side to such graphic and seemingly harmless VR displays. Today, we have games on the drawing board and already on the market that offer the participants the opportunity to engage in extreme human behavior, such as mutilation, rape, and even murder. In a way, virtual reality provides a perfect existential world, in which we can exercise free will and make any number of decisions, however extreme, without the Kierkegaardian "dizziness of freedom" and the underlying anxiety of accountability (Kaufmann, 1956, p. 17). In effect, we are operating in an amoral environment, an environment free of threats or reprisals, whose virtual character liberates us from feeling any form of existential angst when making choices. After all, we are no longer interacting with real people in a real world, but with synthetic objects and subjects in a virtual environment. Shapiro and McDonald (1992) are quite right when asking whether we should "feel guilty about committing adultery" (p. 106) in virtual reality. The synthetic world of virtual reality seems to promise us not so much how to exercise control over our environment, but rather how to escape from it (Pasqualoni, 1993).

There are other potential problems when we see virtual reality in a postmodern existentialist context. One is the matter of the extent, rather than the consequences, of free choice. Even if the various electronic sensors that extend our nervous system respond to our choices and make the environment change according to where we look and how we gesture, our choices are not free but essentially deterministic. They are, after all, decisively limited by the parameters and algorithms of the computer program, very much like the number and kind of objects that were used to create the shadows in Plato's cave. As such, our decisions will inevitably be based on pseudochoices.

Another area of concern is the experience of extreme human behavior. When Sophocles and Shakespeare show us the tragic consequences of making the wrong choices, we may experience some kind of catharsis (at least, so Aristotle tells us), because we, as an audience, remain firmly rooted in the traditions and mores of a regulated society. But when operating in the neutral asocial environment of virtual reality, we may quite willingly shed our conscience and reinforce basic instinct instead of seeking a liberating catharsis. We may ask whether, as Shapiro and McDonald (1992) claim, "the user's memory of entering the VR environment can serve as a cue that the VR experience is not real" (p. 106). Couldn't there be instances when we will get so caught up in the VR event that we do not remember switching from the real to the virtual world? In any case, will we be able to transfer with ease and without psychological difficulty our responsibility-free actions of the VR environment to the real world in which we are held accountable again for what we do? Or will we eventually suffer some kind of psychosis similar to that of war veterans who, for the act of killing, are declared heroes in one environment and murderers in another?

Finally, we might also ask if or for how long we may derive satisfaction and pleasure from eating fruit that is no longer forbidden. Will we be able to remain competitive in an environment that advocates total and angstless freedom of choice? Is there a danger, as Pasqualoni (1993) asks, that repressive political regimes may one day use virtual reality to silence dissidents by immersing them in this limitless world? Or will we, sooner or later, have to establish a new ethical framework for virtual reality with a new value system by which our choices can be scrutinized and judged as good or bad? Will we then have to establish a virtual police, a virtual court system, virtual jails, and perhaps even virtual executions?

CONCLUSION

I do not want to give the impression that I am pessimistic about virtual reality. On the contrary, I feel that this new cybernetic development is not just another information pollutant, but a significant step forward that gives us a chance to shake loose from our perceptual complacency, to see our world with new eyes, to seek the really real, and to rediscover the value of genuine human relationships. So far, the philosophers are of more help in understanding this new phenomenon than are the social scientists, who have done little to help us elucidate cyberspace or to show us its vast potential and liabilities. The burden is clearly on us, the communication scholars and media artists, to study virtual reality and to guide its course with intelligence, prudence, and sympathy.

REFERENCES

Alten, S.R. (1994). *Audio in media* (4th ed.). Belmont, CA: Wadsworth.

Arnheim, R. (1974). *Art and visual perception.* The new version. Berkeley: University of California Press.

Bazin, A. (1967). *What is cinema?* (H. Gray, Trans.). Berkeley: University of California Press.

Bloom, A. (1968). *The republic of Plato.* New York: Basic Books.

Duncker, K. (1929). Über induzierte Bewegung [About induced motion]. *Psychologische Forschung, 12,* 180-259.

Kant, I. (1956). *Kritik der reinen Vernunft.* [Critique of pure reason]. Hamburg: Felix Meiner Verlag. (Original work published 1787)

Kaufmann, W. (Ed.). (1956). *Existentialism from Dostoevsky to Sartre.* New York: Meridian Books.

Kracauer, S. (1960). *Theory of film: The redemption of physical reality.* New York: Oxford University Press.

Krueger, M.W. (1990). Videoplace and the interface of the future. In B. Laurel (Ed.), *The art of human-computer interface design* (pp. 417-422). Reading, MA: Addison-Wesley.

Manovich, L. (1992, September). Synthetic realism. *Afterimage,* pp. 12-16.

Messaris, P. (1994). *Visual literacy: Image, mind, and reality.* Boulder, CO: Westview Press.

Mitchell, W.J. (1992). *The reconfigured eye.* Cambridge, MA: MIT Press.

Newman, J. (1989). *The journalist in Plato's cave.* Cranbury, NJ: Associated University Presses.

O'Hear, A. (1985). *What philosophy is.* Highlands, NJ: Humanities Press International.

Pasqualoni, M. (1993, November). *Virtual reality review.* Paper presented at a seminar on media aesthetics and production theory at the Broadcast and Electronic Communication Arts Department, San Francisco State University.

Plato. (1941). *Republic* (R.M. Cornford, Trans.) London: Oxford University Press.

Plato. (1974). *Republic* (G.M.A. Grube, Trans.). Indianapolis: Hackett. (Original work published ca. 380 B.C.)

Rock, I. (1984). *Perception.* New York: Scientific American Library.

St. Augustine. (1961). *The confessions of Saint Augustine* (E.B. Pusey, Trans.). New York: Collier Books. (Original work published 397 A.D).

Savedoff, B.E. (1992). Transforming images: Photographs of representations. *The Journal of Aesthetics and Art Criticism, 50,* 93-106.

Shapiro, M.A., & McDonald, D.G. (1992). I'm not a real doctor, but I play one in virtual reality. *Journal of Communication, 42*(4), 94-114.

Time. (1993, February 8).

Vingelman, L. (1993, September-October). S.O.M.A. Sexual orientation manipulation application. *Virtual Reality News,* pp. 16-17.

Zettl, H. (1990). *Sight sound motion: Applied media aesthetics* (2nd ed.). Belmont, CA: Wadsworth.

◊◊◊◊ 6

Dramatism and Virtual Reality: Implications and Predictions

Charles U. Larson

When understood as an art form and as a medium, virtual reality (VR) also becomes open to rhetorical criticism. Thus, Charles U. Larson draws on Kenneth Burke's dramatistic method to better understand how virtual reality functions as a form of rhetoric; in this, his approach parallels software designer Brenda Laurel's use of Aristotle's Poetics *to argue for the theatrical nature of computing and VR programming. For Larson, the central characteristics of virtual reality are the virtual act as performed in the virtual scene; also of interest is his focus on intrapersonal communication. In addition to considering the rhetoric of virtuality, he argues that Burkean dramatism is itself affected by the new technologies of cyberspace. Apart from Section 1, other studies that utilize different approaches to virtual reality include Terri Toles Patkin's human factors perspective in Chapter 11, Sue Barnes's exploration of virtual ecology in Chapter 13, Elizabeth Weiss's essay on postmodernism and the virtual health club in Chapter 14, and Mark Lipton's research on cybersex in Chapter 22; additionally, a rhetorical analysis of e-mail by Judith Yaross Lee can be found in Chapter 21.*

VIRTUAL REALITY: THEN, NOW, AND WHEN

From a conceptual perspective, virtual reality (VR) was "invented" by Aldous Huxley in his classic *Brave New World*, in which the citizenry entertained itself by going to the "Feelies." Feelies were an advanced form of the movies except that they engaged all of the five senses, not just seeing and hearing. Viewers entered a booth, and after planting their hands and fingers on an electronic contact board, experienced sensations identical to whatever was being depicted—eating, fighting, or making love—as if it were "really" happening to them at that moment in the privacy of their individual feelie booth. It is difficult to imagine what a feelie experience would be like, but touchstones to help us imagine one might be the "wrap-around" films displayed in the China and Canada pavilions at Epcot/Disney World, the virtual reality walk down a French street now integrated with the France pavilion at Epcot, the "virtual haircut" one can get from Mickey Mouse at MGM studios, and Alfred Hitchcock's 3-D version of *The Birds* at Universal Studios in Orlando.

In 1984, William Gibson first used the term *cyberspace* in his best-selling science fiction novel, *Neuromancer*, and since then the concept has captured the interest of the electronic game industry, the Pentagon, the pornography industry, and others. Underwritten to varying degrees by all of them, the search began for the technologies to create cyberspace, or virtual reality (Levy, 1992). The concept has various labels including *cyberspace, virtual reality, virtual environment, fake-space*, and the oxymoronic *artificial reality*. One of the Pentagon's interests in virtual reality was trying to determine how it could be used in training pilots, much in the way the old "Link" trainers were used for flight training in the past, and indeed the Air Force used the technology in Operation Desert Storm to permit pilots to "rehearse" their sorties. The electronic game industry quickly saw the potential of the medium to augment video "battle" games. Most of the publicly known advances in developing the technologies that might interface to form virtual reality emerged in the game industry, including high-definition television, digital audio and video, CD-ROM, interactive television, computer graphics, holograms, and laser imaging to name a few. The pornography industry is already marketing CD-ROM materials that employ VR technology—interactive conversations, full-motion live actor video, and a variety of others to titillate porn users.

In his introduction to the special VR issue of *The Journal of Communication*, Frank Biocca (1992) noted that, in 1941, a new and fully functional medium was being introduced, but "few [could] predict the significant influence of this new gadget with the odd name 'television'" (p. 5). Its potential went largely unrecognized by the general public, merchandisers, or social critics until more than a decade later. Today, we understand the enormous potential of television to radically alter society, but, like people in the 1940s, we remain skeptical of the claims made by VR evangelists for various uses of the medium. They cite such uses as being employed to train surgeons who can "practice" operations on virtual reality, correcting "mistakes" as they go, and only then perform the resulting "perfect" operation using computerized laser "knives" and magnetic imaging. This raises interesting questions such as what would constitute "malpractice" in such a case. Another possible use of VR technology is "virtual retailing." Charles Madigan (1993) uses the clothing industry as an example. In this use, consumers discuss their clothing needs with a designer—Ralph Lauren, for example—via a lifesize, 3-D, high-definition television screen. Ralph then suggests that they try on "virtual clothing," seeing how it fits and feels, and then make a "virtual purchase" by placing an order via phone or interactive television. Other suggested uses include invisible "virtual" computer keyboards, "virtual driving lessons," "virtual vacations" around the world (what happens to the tourist industry around the world?), "virtual sex" alternately referred to as *cybersex, cyborgasm*, and *teledildonics* by VR advocates (will this reduce STDs, rape, abuse, etc.?), and "virtual community."

Critics of virtual reality warn of a potentially overwhelming information age, and they wonder how many hours of the day people will want to spend in virtual reality, on the computer, with television, on the phone, and using other technologies that are bound to emerge with the growth of the medium (Ditlea, 1990,1992; Madigan, 1993). A central concern here is that, whereas other media like television, film, or even the personal computer rely to some degree on interactivity and involve some sense of community (i.e., we watch films in audiences, we "cheer" for the home team on television, and we have begun to "link up" with others using computer networks), virtual reality almost by definition limits the sense of community that accompanied earlier media.

One could think of virtual reality as the ultimate in *intra*personal communication (i.e., the interaction occurs between person, machine image, and one's own central nervous system) and thus is potentially capable of driving Western humanity further inward in the 21st century. Additionally, virtual reality calls into question the very concept of authenticity and what is subjective, objective, social, individual, or personal reality. Virtual reality also raises serious issues regarding our social order such as concern over the degree to which humans might vegetate their lives away playing in a virtual amusement park, never engaging in productive efforts. Another concern is how virtual reality might displace workers who refuse to or cannot learn to use the new medium and its related technologies and "like farriers in towns where there are no longer any horses . . . [become] 'technopeasants' who cannot cope with change" (Madigan, 1993, p. 16).

Moral issues include the right to enslave robots, the use of virtual reality as a tool for propaganda, and whether individuals will be held accountable for the actions they engage in while experiencing the medium. For example, if one commits adultery, theft, assault, battery, or even murder while using virtual reality, under what laws or codes of conduct (if any) are their behaviors to be judged? As Frank Biocca (1992) also notes, the new technology has many implications for the nature of communication research, and he urges researchers to consider at least six general areas for VR communication research, including research on the diffusion of VR technology. For example, will it follow the traditional flow from innovator and early adopter on down to late adopters and laggards? And if so, will it create a "virtual class structure" (especially given its probable price as was the case with early television and personal computer technology)? Another question might relate to the degree to which VR technology will be diffused into varying applications such as medicine, engineering, sports, travel, marketing, and, of course, various forms of VR "entertainment" technologies. He also suggests that because of its three-dimensional feature, virtual reality will probably result in as immense alterations in human communication as did the shift from still to moving pictures and will likely yield its separate semiotics and semiotic codes if Eco is correct about all forms of communication being but separate semiotica (Biocca, 1992, p. 11). Another area for communication research to explore in the face of virtual reality is its likely effects on interpersonal communication and cooperation: What are the implications of VR networks, work spaces, bulletin boards, and education? With its easy access code, virtual reality has immense potential to impact these kinds of questions. Another research area for potential exploration that may be impacted by virtual reality and its implications is, as noted earlier, rhetorical criticism.

VIRTUAL REALITY AND THE PENTAD

It is possible, then, to speculate about how virtual reality can and does impact dramatistic theory and research, especially as articulated by Kenneth Burke (1969) in his "Terms of Dramatism." In his introduction to the five key terms in *A Grammar of Motives*, Burke noted,

> Any complete statement about motives will offer *some kind* of answers to these five questions: what was done (*act*) when or where it was done (*scene*), who did it (*agent*), how he did it (*agency*), and why (*purpose*) . . . in pondering matters of human motivation, one can simplify the subject by this pentad of key terms which are understandable almost at a glance. They need never to be abandoned since all statements that assign motives can be shown to arise out of them and to terminate in them. (pp. xv-xvi; emphasis in original)

Numerous pieces of insightful and valuable communication research have resulted from and validate Burke's confidence in his key terms and their ability to explain human motivation. As Gozzi and Haynes (1992; Gozzi, 1993) argue, television has significantly implanted the metaphor of the drama into everyday life—especially for those who cannot remember life without television. For these persons the dramatic metaphor and the terms of the pentad seem natural, logical, and obvious as Burke implies.

Enter virtual reality. It potentially alters the way we all think about, define, and apply these five key terms. *Act* becomes "virtual act" or an act that "almost" occurs. Likewise with the other terms of the pentad—*scene* becomes a "virtual scene" or an "almost" scene; *agent* loses some of its identity to "virtual agent," *purpose* is transformed into "virtual purpose," and *agency* to "virtual agency." Within the context of virtual reality, let us explore in more detailed analysis two of Burke's key terms—*act* and *scene*.

VIRTUAL ACT

The *act* that occurs in virtual reality is rarely shared or in Burke's (1969) words "'addressed' to some person or to some advantage" (p. xvii). The virtual act is a private affair, never externally enacted. Thus, in virtual reality, acts never "really" occur in the same way Burke envisioned—virtual acts are innately private and intrapersonal just as other nonoccurring acts (e.g., dreams and fantasies) never "really" occur and, for the most part, remain unaddressed to any audience other than the self. Instead, such nonoccurring acts become totally internalized, both within the VR device and within the brain of the virtual interactant. However, although virtual acts never really occur in the objective world (except in the computer print-outs that sometimes accompany virtual battle games), they surely seem to occur in the subjective "reality" of the VR user's central nervous system. In virtual reality, Burke's term *act* thus becomes "agentified" by the VR participants who act to turn their gaze and who use the glove or joystick to shoot enemies on the video screen. It is the agent's psyche, nerve endings, and past history that make any given virtual event possible. The relationship between act and agent in virtual reality mirrors the two paradoxical meanings for the word *cleave*. In one use *to cleave* means "to adhere closely; to stick; to cling" and in the alternate definition *to cleave* means "to split asunder; to divide." In virtual reality, act and agent are impossible to cleave, yet are always cloven.

Not to worry—in his discussion of the pentad and the ambiguity that arises out of distinctions (such as the terms of the pentad), Burke (1969) tells us that such distinctions:

> Arise out of a great central liquid where all is merged. . . . Let one of these distinctions return to its source, and in this alchemic center it may be remade . . . whereat it may be again thrown forth as a new crust, a different distinction. So that A may become non-A. . . . And so with our five terms. . . . Their participation in a common ground makes for transformability. (p. xix)

Because of the nature of the VR medium, what Burke calls "a merger" between act and agent is accomplished. But what about the scene in which this merger occurs?

VIRTUAL SCENE

Burke (1969) describes *scene* as the "setting" or "background" (including time place and occasion) and seems to take a proscenium perspective in most of his examples. The viewer always remains outside the scene looking in through the fourth wall. For example, he observed that:

> From the motivational point of view, there is implicit in the quality of the scene the quality of the action that is to take place within it. . . . Thus when the curtain rises to disclose a given stage-set, this stage-set contains, simultaneously implicitly all that the narrative is to draw out as a sequence explicitly. Or, if you will, the stage set contains the action *ambiguously* . . . and in the course of the play's development, this ambiguity is converted into a corresponding *articulasy*. (p. 7; emphasis in original)

In virtual reality, the scenes—video battles, airplane cockpits, hospital operating rooms, driving lessons, or love nests—never fully appear to VR interactants because the interactants are not on the outside looking in as in a proscenium theater—they are on the inside looking *around*. The interactants must turn their heads and gaze beyond the fourth wall and around its limits to observe not only the wings, but the entire theater, including the grand circle, the various balconies, the back of the house, and even the exits. By doing so, they locate places, enemies, lovers, events, occupations, and so on, and choose to interact with them or not. Thus, the scene in virtual reality is greatly expanded and always incomplete; it is a "virtual scene" or (like an inexpensive turkey)—a scene with "parts missing." The "virtual scene" also always remains in flux; it changes in the parts observed and their affects as well as in the parts unobserved and their implied but unrealized affects. Both sets of affects depend on where the interactants choose to turn their heads. In its present manifestations, the scene for virtual reality consists not only of the VR device being used or the settings depicted on the screen, in the cockpit, or via the viewing helmet, but as internally perceived by the interactant. In that sense, like the virtual act, the virtual scene becomes "agentified" or merged with the agent. As Burke (1969) observes: "It is a principle of drama that the nature of acts and agents should be consistent with the nature of the scene . . . [and that] . . . the scene is a fit 'container' for the act" (p. 3), and that "scene is to act as implicit is to explicit" (p.7).

To Burke, the scene implies motivation as well—the setting beckons the agent to action, inviting him or her to enter it and follow their own motivations and courses of action. Burke exemplifies this motivational aspect of the scene in a reference to Hamlet's temptation to follow the ghost of his murdered father. Horatio articulates that motivation when he warns Hamlet, using scenic motivations apparent in his words:

> What if it tempt you toward the flood my lord,
> Or to the dreadful summit of the cliff
> That beetles o'er his base into the sea,
> and there assume some other horrible form,
> Which might deprive your sovereignty of reason,
> And draw you into madness. Think of it;
> The very place puts toys of desperation
> Without more motive, into every brain
> That looks so many fathoms to the sea
> And hears it roar beneath. (p. 6)

Burke (1969) hypothesizes that Horatio fears that "the shear natural surroundings might be enough to provide a man with a motive for an act as desperate and absolute as suicide" (p. 6). However, motivation and action are not synonymous. In objective reality, the agent *must choose* to act and follow or not to follow the paths implicit in the scene. In virtual reality, the interactant *must decide* to look left, look right, zoom in, zoom out, or remain static, and the results of his or her decisions determine an infinite web of potential and subsequent paths to follow—any and all of them determined by their agentification for good or evil: "The agent is the author of his acts which are descended from him, being good progeny if he is good, or bad progeny if he is bad, wise progeny if he is wise, silly progeny if he is silly" (Burke, 1969, p. 16).

Unlike live theater or mediated dramas in print or on electronic media, the agentified scene in the mind of the of VR audience member takes at least partial control of the scene on the VR screen and manipulates it to some degree for his or her purposes using the agency of VR technology. Burke (1969) seems to have anticipated the quicksilver nature of virtual reality as transformed into individual sensation and experience to produce a "virtual drama." He reminds us that:

> There is of course, a circular possibility in the terms. If an agent acts in keeping with his nature as agent (act-agent ratio), he may change the nature of the scene accordingly (scene-act ratio), and thereby establish a state of unity between himself and his world (scene-agent ratio). Or the scene may call for a certain kind of act, which makes for a corresponding kind of agent, thereby likening agent to scene. Or our act may change us and our scene, producing a mutual conformity. Such would be the Edenic paradigm, applicable if we were capable of total acts that produce total transformations. In reality we are capable of but partial acts, acts that but partially represent us and that produce but partial transformations. Indeed, if all the ratios were adjusted to one another with perfect Edenic symmetry, they would be immutable in one unending "moment." (p. 19)

IMPLICATIONS AND PREDICTIONS

A number of implications emerge from this discussion of virtual reality and its potential effects on dramatism, especially as articulated by Kenneth Burke (1969) and elsewhere. For example, virtual reality transforms all of the elements of the pentad and their ratios to some degree. These transformations arise out of the fact that virtual reality is rarely "addressed" to an "audience" with the hope of gaining some "advantage." Instead, virtual reality, as presently envisioned, internalizes the concept of the audience; only one person experiences a given virtual event in a given one-time "program." In this sense, virtual reality is the ultimate in intrapersonal communication (i.e., the communication only occurs once and then only with oneself and using VR technology), and the "drama" only really occurs in the central nervous system of a single individual.

Another implication of virtual reality for dramatism is that it calls the concept of authenticity into question and merges subjective, objective, and social reality by redefining parts of the scene. For example, the definition of time and its passage are important elements of "scene." We might ask such questions as: Does the setting occur in your time? My time? In society's time? Or in Burke's unending moment—a scene that is always and never "really" occurring? We all experience Burke's unending moment or the phenomenon of having "time fly" at some time or another. Think about what happens to time when we are absorbed with composing and revising on a word processor. Hours slip by like minutes and minutes like seconds. The same compression of time occurs while reading a gripping novel or when one's vacation "suddenly slipped away." Contrast that sensation with what we experience while sitting through a boring lecture or working at a boring task. Here the time seems to drag out forever, and repeatedly looking at the clock only seems to slow its passage even further. What kind of sense of time flow will exist in future versions of virtual reality? The medium, when perfected, will probably resemble the computer experience more than the boring lecture or task. The medium will make "time fly" because it captivates its interactants by involving all five senses allowing the audience to engage in "virtual participation." Virtual participation resembles the interactive films where the audience chooses the direction of the story by selecting from among several "routes" or "paths" for the characters or plot to follow. Thus, it affects the pace of a particular drama's chronology, and depending on the path(s) selected, all five terms of dramatism become transformed in some way. One concern over the effects of virtual participation is that, like the computer, its elements are totally internal and intrapersonal. Virtual reality has the potential to further drive Western culture inward in ways similar to those wrought by both literacy and electronic technology. They forced us to internalize significant portions of daily life and resulted in the interiorization of self-perception.

Another implication, also pointed out by Gozzi (1993), is that virtual reality reinforces a powerful metaphor that has fascinated humans for millenia and that has served as an organizational device for explaining human actions—that drama resembles life. With increasing audience involvement with and within the dramas depicted via virtual reality, the already powerful metaphor of drama as life becomes even more central to our explanations of motivation. The distinction between fantasy and reality become mores blurred as VR interactants become scene, players, and audience in a "virtual drama " that results in captivating intrapersonal dramas reminiscent of Ionesco's "Six Characters in Search of an Author," except this time the plot is "in spades."

Biocca's analog of the impact of television technology on individual and social life provides us with a useful lodestone in anticipating the potential effects of virtual reality as presently envisioned. That analog taken together with the facts that the technologies needed to produce high fidelity, sophisticated, and multisensory versions of virtual reality already exist hints at much. As Madigan (1993) points out: "Information technology is moving so rapidly, developing so exponentially, that no one knows quite where it will lead" (p. 16). A major obstacle, however, lies in the development of high-definition television with enough lines of resolution and enough pixels per line to deliver multisensory information capable of producing not only a sophisticated film experiences, but realistic holograms, digital/dolby sound, as well as realistic odors, tastes, and feelings. And the solutions to these problems will necessitate more powerful and infinitely faster computers. We need to keep in mind though that the technology to produce the primitive versions of today's virtual reality appeared on the scene only a few years ago, and new and improved versions are being developed. Other technologies are also rapidly improving (e.g., hologramatic three-dimensional microchips capable of increasing storage, graphic fidelity, and speeding up the computing process by several factors). And we need to remember that the first international conference on virtual reality occurred only recently. Perhaps we should bear in mind the words of Neil Postman:

> We are a culture consuming itself with information and many of us do not even wonder how to control it. . . . We proceed under the assumption that information is our friend. . . . It is only now beginning to be understood that cultures may also suffer grievously from information glut, information without meaning and information without control mechanisms. (cited in Madigan, 1993, p. 30)

The probabilities are awesome; the possibilities mind-boggling.

REFERENCES

Arthur, C. (1992, May 23). Did reality move for you? *New Scientist*, pp. 22, 24-27.

Biocca, F. (1992). Communication within virtual reality: Creating a space for research. *Journal of Communication, 42,* 5-22.

Burke, K. (1969). *A grammar of motives*. Berkeley: University of California Press.

Ditlea, S. (1990, August 6). Grand illusion—coming soon, to your home . . . artificial reality. *New York Magazine*, pp. 27-34.

Ditlea, S. (1992, October). Virtual reality virtually here. *Hemisphere*, pp. 26-27.

Gozzi, R., Jr. (1993, November). *Ten propositions about dramatism in an age of electric drama.* Unpublished conference paper, Speech Communication Association Conference, Miami Beach, FL.

Gozzi, R., Jr., & Haynes, W.L. (1992). Electric media and electric epistemology: Empathy at a distance. *Critical Studies in Mass Communication, 9,* 217-228.

Levy, M.R. (1992). Editor's note. *Journal of Communication, 42*, 3-4.

Madigan, C.M. (1993, May 2). Going with the flow: It's sink or drown as computers overwhelm us with a rising tide of information. *Chicago Tribune Magazine*, pp. 14-16, 20, 30.

◇◇◇◇ 7

Virtual Reality and the Redefinition of Self

Jay David Bolter

The conflict between word and image is as old as the Ten Commandments of Moses, and is present in current discussions of cyberspace. On the one hand, computer programming, word processing, hypertext, and computer-mediated communication remains largely text-based; on the other hand, there is much interest in and anticipation concerning graphic user interfaces, sound synthesis and recognition, multimedia applications, and virtual reality. In this chapter, Jay David Bolter discusses this opposition as it exists in electronic environments and its connection to philosophical arguments concerning reasoning versus sensory experience. Noting that our conceptions of the self are related to our interactions with communications media, he examines the way in which multimedia and virtual reality technologies further the 20th-century tendency to repudiate Descartes's text-based notions of ego and body grounded in discursive reasoning, in favor of a new subjectivity based on nonlinguistic visual perception. In Sections II, III, and IV, further discussion of cyberspace and the self appears in Sue Barnes's ecological explorations in Chapter 1, Elizabeth Weiss's piece on the body and the cybergym in Chapter 14, Richard Cutler's examination of self and relationship in Chapter 21, Mark Lipton's essay on self, body, and cybersex in Chapter 22, and Lance Strate's piece on cybertime in Chapter 23. Notions of textuality are taken up again in Stuart Moulthrop's consideration of the future of the book in Chapter 16, Stephanie Gibson's profile of hypertext in the classroom in Chapter 17, and Judith Yaross Lee's research on the oral, literate, and iconic codes of e-mail in Chapter 19.

It seems clear that in the coming years two- and three-dimensional graphics will play an increasingly important role in electronic representation and communication. Cyberspace is a graphic space, and the role of prose, of discursive written communication, in cyberspace is problematic. It is not only that prose will have to share this new space with other modes of communication, but the legitimacy of prose is called into question. The growing cultural importance of graphics technology seems to be undermining the power of prose to convey and convince. Enthusiasts for cyberspace tend to subscribe to what Murray Krieger (1992) in another context has called the "desire for the natural sign." They believe that a virtual environment rendered in immersive, three-dimensional graphics makes possible unmediated (natural) communication. Written communication, which is mediated by arbitrary signs, then becomes unnecessary.

If our culture does move away from discursive communication into graphic electronic environments, our cultural definition of self will be affected. Writing in general and print technology in particular have contributed to a series of related definitions of self in the period from the Renaissance to the 20th century: The self has been regarded as an autonomous ego, as the author of the text that constitutes one's mental life. Virtual reality and cyberspace suggest a different definition. The self is no longer constructed as an autonomous, authorial voice; it becomes instead a wandering eye that occupies various perspectives, one after another. This virtual eye knows what it knows not through a capacity for abstract reasoning, but rather through empathy, through the sharing of the "point of view" of the object of knowledge.

TEXT IN MULTIMEDIA

Computer-controlled multimedia programs might be positioned at the near edge of cyberspace. The term multimedia is often eschewed both by computer scientists and by cybernauts because it smacks of kiosks and other business applications. Nevertheless, multimedia applications, especially information kiosks and training programs, are like other programs in cyberspace in the sense that they use text sparingly, if not grudgingly. A typical multimedia application relies for its rhetorical effect principally on video and graphics and secondarily on sound. Words are used most often as captions for graphics or to identify buttons. Like the label on an icon in a desktop interface, the text on a button is as much operational as referential. The words function as a magic formula: When the user clicks on the words, he or she calls forth some other graphic or video. In other cases, text in multimedia is confined to rectangles and used to communicate only what cannot be pictured easily. Multimedia designers consider it an admission of failure to clutter the screen with blocks of text. The worst criticism one can make of a multimedia system is to call it a mere "page turner," a set of texts that the user examines one after another—in other words, the electronic equivalent of a printed book.

Educational multimedia cannot dispense with text as easily as business applications, but even here the strategy is to displace and marginalize the text. A good example is provided by IBM's showcase hypermedia application called "Ulysses," produced in the late 1980s (AND Communication, 1990). The "Ulysses" in question is the poem by Tennyson, and the application is meant to demonstrate how point-and-click hypermedia can be used to teach English literature. The student can click on words and obtain a dictionary definition, an historical explanation, or a critical interpretation. Whenever possible, the linked material is delivered not as alphabetic text, but as video or audio. If the user asks for a critical explanation of a passage, he or she receives a videotaped interview with a literary critic. If he or she wants a summary of the Trojan War, the system presents a short and very well-produced video—the kind of production one sees on public television. A disembodied narrator explains the war while the screen shows mythological figures on Greek vases or in modern European paintings. The text of Tennyson's poem itself is always available in a window, but the user can also choose to have the poem read to him or her by one of a numbers of actors. In fact, the actors offer dramatic performances rather than mere readings. The user can elect to hear the actor's voice while still viewing Tennyson's text. In this case, a wire frame jumps from word to word as the actor declaims, presumably so that semiliterate users will know what word is being pronounced. The system also supplies video of some of the actors performing the poem as if it were a monologue in a play. In general, the goal of the "Ulysses" program seems to be to pull the user away from the text itself and to replace the text as a network of signs with visual or aural experiences.

What happens in the "Ulysses" program might be called the "breakout of the sensory." Images and sound jump out and displace the verbal text, as if the prose can no longer support the process of meaning by itself. This process of displacement is itself made visible: A video window opens up and competes with the text window for the reader's attention. Tennyson's poem is transformed into a series of video clips, as if these were its semiotic elements. The breakout of the sensory is characteristic of multimedia presentation systems in general, as static graphics and video muscle the verbal text into marginal positions on the screen.

TEXT AND THE INTERNET

For many enthusiasts, multimedia is not a legitimate prototype for cyberspace; they are more likely to regard the Internet as the prototype. In contrast to multimedia, on the Internet verbal text still plays an important role. Electronic mail and newsgroups remain the most widely used applications, and in their generic forms these applications are purely textual. However, it is not likely that they will remain so, as the technology improves for transmitting graphics and audio over the network. Furthermore, even in their purely textual form, e-mail and newsgroups are beginning to show signs of the breakout of the visual.

One of the peculiar characteristics of writing for e-mail and newsgroups is the use of ASCII characters to form iconic faces. For example, the sequence :-) represents a smiling face and adds some ironic nuance to the previous sentence or paragraph. Such icons, or emoticons, are meant to put the verbal text in context: The writer tries to enforce a univocal interpretation on prose that is otherwise open to many interpretations. The desire to contextualize in this way shows that the implicit model is not written or printed text at all, but face-to-face conversation or perhaps conversation on the telephone. Handwritten letters and especially printed prose have always faced the problem of decontextualization. However, at least in Western writing in the last several hundred years, these difficulties have not led to the development of icons designed to fix authorial intent. With a few important exceptions, such as Sterne, modern Western writers have depended entirely on the prose itself in order to manipulate their own and their readers' perspectives. Often, writers have exploited decontextualization to produce texts that are open to several interpretative strategies. The use of icons in e-mail and newsgroups suggests that contemporary electronic writers are not interested in the distancing and ambiguity that prose offers. Instead they want to give their prose a single voice and if possible a face.

As the Internet evolves, it seems likely that synchronous and asynchronous video will replace e-mail for many purposes, precisely because video offers the users the presence and the apparent univocality that prose cannot. The lure of presence will easily be strong enough to overcome the objection often made about videotelephones: that users do not always want to be seen. On the other hand, text need not vanish from electronic communication: Many kinds of documents may continue to be transmitted. Documents may be appended to and sent along with video messages, just as they are appended to ASCII electronic mail today.

Another important manifestation of text on the Internet is the text-based virtual environment called MUD (and its variations, MOO, MUSE, MUSH, and so on). It has often been noted that MUDs (Multi-User Dungeons) and their predecessors, the interactive adventure games, have much in common with hypertextual fiction. However, MUDs seldom employ the techniques of distancing and self-reference found in mature hypertextual fictions such as *afternoon* (Joyce, 1987) and *Victory Garden* (Moulthrop, 1992). But these fictions are interactive verbal texts, in which the reader follows electronic links from screen to screen and so constructs the text in the act of reading. In *afternoon, Victory Garden*, and other similar works, the reader is repeatedly made aware of the artificial character of reading and writing fiction. MUDs function more simply. They embody the naive assumption of perspicacity: that to read a descriptive or narrative text is to look through a window onto another world. With current network technology, a MUD is an example of the classical rhetorical device of *ekphrasis*, the elaborate description in prose or poetry of a striking object or scene. What is unusual is the collaborative character of the ekphrasis. Many writers may work together to create the world, often a building or built environment with a specialized area devoted to each activity. These same and other users then occupy the rooms synchronously and asynchronously, leaving behind their textual traces. In a typical MUD, a user adopts a persona, consisting of a name (say, Luke Skywalker or Madonna) and set of characteristics. He or she can then enter the MUD and travel from room to room. If the writer types a sentence in quotation marks, that sentence is broadcast as his or her utterance to the other characters in the same room. That is, every other user sees on his or her screen: "Luke Skywalker says: '. . .'" The user's typed sentence becomes dialogue in a collective fiction: Each user becomes a textually realized character, and the other characters respond to the text he or she generates.

To participate in a MUD is to accept the illusion of the natural sign, the notion that there can be a simple denotative relationship between a verbal text and a perceived world. Because they accept the illusion of the natural sign, MUDs may be stories, but they are not novels. In a novel, especially in a modern novel (e.g., Conrad, Woolf, Joyce), the reader moves back and forth between an awareness of the text as text and the forgetful act of losing him- or herself in the story. The text is not only a window onto another world; it is also a rhetorical structure of allusions and references. The reader oscillates between looking *at* the textual structure and looking *through* it. Most MUDs do not function in this way: They do not set up an oscillation between rhetorical awareness and forgetfulness. They do not ask their users to look *at* the text, but only to look *through* the text to the world that is being described. There are some notable exceptions—MUDs that do seek to set up this oscillatory relationship between the text and its apparent reference.

The typical MUD is an heroic attempt to recreate in prose what its users would prefer to be a sensory experience. For most users the words only get in the way. Anyone who watches participants in MUDs can see the intense involvement that such participation can require. Repetitive stress syndrome is a vocational hazard among MUD users, as they seek to sustain the rhythms of the visual and auditory illusion entirely in typed prose. So, like e-mail and newsgroups, MUDs seem destined to become video experiences, as soon as Internet technology can support this change. MUDs will then be multiuser, networked virtual realities. And just as with single-user virtual reality, textual communication may be more or less abandoned in this shift. (For a discussion of the distinction between looking at and looking through, see Lanham, 1993. For a further discussion of the illusion of the natural sign in electronic communication see Bolter, in press.)

TEXT IN VIRTUAL REALITY

Most virtual worlds consist almost entirely of graphic objects: Text is limited to a few words used as labels. In some more interesting cases, the software offers menus that float in virtual space. There is a technical reason for the absence of text. Many head-mounted displays (in which small display screens are mounted over the eyes) cannot make text legible. Users still complain about the readability of text on conventional CRTs, but conventional screens are much easier to read than the current generation of virtual reality (VR) displays. On the other hand, the resolution of head-mounted displays continues to improve. Ultimately, the problem of entering text may prove more intractable than the problem of reading it. Users can hardly be expected to type on a virtual keyboard while wearing one or more datagloves. Speech recognition would be an obvious solution: The user could then dictate into a microphone, and the computer would translate and display the text. However, speech recognition software will not apparently achieve the needed accuracy in the foreseeable future. (For a realistic assessment of speech recognition, see Rudnicky, Hauptman, & Lee, 1994.)

Part of the difficulty of representing text in virtual reality is that software developers have not concentrated on this problem. Instead, both the engineering research and the cultural promotion of virtual reality have focused on giving the user a sense of direct, perceptual (above all, visual) participation. Typical VR applications in telepresence and simulation require little or no verbal information. There is the tacit assumption that perceptual presence can replace words, or indeed symbolic representation altogether. The developer Jaron Lanier has made this assumption explicit. He claims that virtual reality can usher in an era of "postsymbolic" communication, an era in which people show each other what they mean through natural signs (Bolter, 1991). Explicitly for Lanier and tacitly for many others, virtual reality is the realm in which the arbitrariness of the sign can be eliminated. So, in virtual reality we do not see visual elements in the process of breaking out of the text, as we do in multimedia. The visual has already broken free and replaced text altogether. Text is not hiding behind the virtual scene. It is absent, and its absence does not leave behind even a poststructuralist trace.

THE ELECTRONIC REDEFINITION OF SELF

Our quick survey suggests that alphabetic text is not faring well in early manifestations of cyberspace. It is under challenge by graphic techniques in a way that was not true during the centuries of print. Graphics have played a role in printed books since the 15th century (see Eisenstein, 1979). But with some important exceptions, such as atlases, printed books have firmly asserted the primacy of alphabetic text. Printed books *contain* illustrations; they *are* texts. And they are texts of a certain kind: They define a writing space that is stable and monumental. As our culture moves toward a greater reliance on electronic graphic presentation, the qualities of printed prose are being displaced or marginalized. It seems very unlikely that alphabetic writing itself can be wholly replaced by graphics, but graphic presentation will clearly take over some of the cultural work that is still done by the alphabet. Above all, the graphic rendering of electronic space may well affect the definitions or constructions of self in our culture.

The importance of writing in the cultural definition of self has long been noted (see, e.g., Ong, 1982). In the past several hundred years, Western definitions have been influenced by alphabetic writing in general and by print technology in particular. The printed, prose self has been a complicated creature, modulated by many cultural currents and by various innovations in the technology of printing. For example, the invention of the stream-driven press and mechanical printing in the 19th century made possible the mass-circulation newspaper and the serialized novel with their new constructions of self. Two of the most influential constructions of self in the age of print have been the Cartesian ego and the Kantian subject. In both cases, there was an insistence on the autonomy of the individual and a radical separation between subject and object. In both, the visual and sensual aspects of human nature were subordinated to the faculty of reason. In Descartes's version the subordination was absolute, but even in Kant's version reason could reach beyond the human senses to understand the a priori conditions that made empirical knowledge possible. I concentrate on Descartes below because among the Anglo-American writers he seems to get more of the blame than Kant. (Kant has received more attention from continental writers, especially through Heidegger and those influenced by him, such as Derrida, and through the Frankfurt School and those in its tradition, such as Habermas.)

The Cartesian definition of self was by no means created by the technology of print. However, print technology did offer a writing space in which this definition could flourish. Print emphasized and rewarded the individuality and uniqueness of the author. And in subordinating images to words, print technology encouraged a rhetoric in which abstraction was privileged at the expense of the senses and sensory information. On the other hand, printed versions of the self have been under attack by philosophers and theorists for much of the 20th century, even while our culture was still in the industrial age of printing, although radio and television were already having an impact. The arrival of fully electronic technology does not alone explain the growing dissatisfaction with the notion of the enlightened, autonomous Cartesian ego. But once again this new technology of representation is playing a role in the redefinition of self: It reenforces other popular and elite pressures to replace the autonomous ego as a cultural ideal.

Electronic technology is helping to change the communicative balance between word and image in our media. It calls for a new relationship between (arbitrary) symbolic representation and perceptual presentation. Electronic technology fosters the return of iconic writing and the reemergence of the perceptual out of prose. It is the breakout of the visual that leads to new constructions of the self. In *The Electronic Word*, Richard Lanham (1993) analyzes the shifting balance between the verbal and visual in this period of computer-mediated communcation (see particularly Chap. 1 & 2). Lanham agrees with others that the computer disrupts and destabilizes linear text, but he points out that this destabilization has been a feature of the visual arts throughout the 20th century. The "digital aesthetic" predates the digital computer itself. I would add that this digital aesthetic and the destabilization of text make less attractive to our culture the self defined in printed prose from the Renaissance to the 20th century. Kenneth Gergen (1991) has argued that a "postmodern" definition of the self is emerging, a self that is fragmented, empathetic, and anti-Cartesian: "Technologies of social saturation" are responsible. Gergen includes electronic telecommunication as one technology that is dismantling the traditional (Romantic and modern) definitions of self. Some of Gergen's technologies (railroad, automobile, airplane) simply accelerate the pace in which we propel ourselves around the world. More important, I think, are such technologies as radio, television, print, and the computer, which are means of representation and self-presentation. They are media for presenting ourselves to ourselves and to others, and as such they invite a definition or redefinition of the self.

PERSPECTIVE AND THE SELF

Electronic technology offers two distinct sets of tools for presentation and representation: tools for writing, and tools for visualization and sensory presentation. The computer and attendant technologies call forth both a new writing space and a new perceptual space. (For more on this distinction and its consequences, see Bolter, 1993, 1994.) Each of these new spaces in turn fosters a different construction of self.

Word processing, numerical and textual databases, (verbal) electronic mail and newsgroups, and hypertext constitute a new writing space. Electronic writing, particularly hypertext, challenges some of the qualities of the printed or handwritten self. The self in electronic writing space is no longer the relatively permanent and univocal figure of the printed page. The electronic self is instead unstable and polyvocal. However, like all earlier writing technologies, electronic writing remains the manipulation of arbitrary networks of signs, so that the hypertextual self is still a written self (Bolter, 1991). The relationships among the author, text, and reader are more complex in hypertext, but the notions of author, reader, and textual mediation remain. Hypertexts are polyvocal, but the notion of voice remains (and can be exploited in hypertextual fictions such as *afternoon* and *Victory Garden*). Hypertext is the writing technology that best realizes the strategies of poststructural literary theory, and so, like poststructural literary theory, hypertext insists on retaining and exploiting the referential ambiguity of the sign. (For more on hypertext and literary theory, see Landow, 1992.)

Computer animation and video, particularly three-dimensional, immersive graphics or virtual reality, are not tools for writing because they are not tools for manipulating systems of arbitrary signs. Instead of a writing space, the computer as graphics engine constructs a new perceptual space. Virtual reality is the most impressive, although not the most practical or widely used, application of computer graphics, and it can serve as a paradigm for the electronic space of perception. Virtual reality belongs in the tradition that begins at least as early as perspective painting in the Italian Renaissance and includes photography, cinema, and television. Like these earlier examples, virtual reality is a technology of illusion, whose purpose is to convince the viewer that he or she is occupying the same visual space as the objects in view. The key innovation is that virtual reality gives the viewer control of his or her own spatial perspective. Illusionistic art since the Italian Renaissance often sought to provide a consistent, linear perspective, but that perspective was necessarily static, determined by the artist. The Italian Renaissance's definition of art depended on the artist's ability to manipulate the viewer's perspective for dramatic purposes (see the contrast between Dutch and Italian art in Albers, 1983) In conventional photography, the viewer's perspective is not as easily manipulated, but it is still constrained by the placement of the camera. Film and television set the perspective in motion; not only could images move in front of the camera, but the camera itself could move. But this motion is determined by the director and editor of the film or video. It is only with virtual reality that the user can have substantial visual control of the scene.

Anne Balsamo (1993) describes virtual reality as a new version of the filmic eye:

> In most programs, a user experiences VR through a disembodied gaze—a floating moving 'perspective'—that mimes the movement of a disembodied camera eye. This is a familiar aspect of what may be called a filmic phenomenology where the camera simulates the movement of a perspective that rarely includes a self-referential visual inspection of the body as the vehicle of that perspective. (p. 126)

An important difference between traditional cinema and virtual reality is that virtual reality enables the viewer to control the placement and duration of each "shot." Just as in electronic hypertext the reader becomes the author, in virtual reality the viewer becomes the painter or the film director. This shift of control enables the viewer to explore the virtual space as he or she will. The ability to change perspective becomes the way to learn about the space. As Balsamo (1993) puts it, in virtual reality the filmic "perspective" becomes the locus of sense knowledge. In fact, perspective becomes the locus of all knowledge because in a virtual world there is nothing to be known apart from the senses. With its filmic eye, virtual reality necessarily construes knowledge as sense perception, not as intelligence of the abstract or the a priori. The virtual traveler defines what he or she knows as what he or she can see and therefore "interact" with.

The eye can be construed as the most abstract and abstracting of the senses. It is so construed by many postmodern writers, as Martin Jay (1988) points out. This construction in fact associates Cartesian rationality with the Renaissance notion of perspective: Jay refers to "Cartesian perspectivalism" in which an "ahistorical, disinterested disembodied subject" claims to know the world by gazing at it from afar (p. 10). But this construction can be turned around. Vision can be construed as involving the viewer in the world and also as a means of reducing the abstract to the visible. For Descartes (as for Plato long before him), sight was ultimately tied to the body. We recall that in his *Meditations* Descartes considered the possibility that everything he saw (as well as heard or felt) was the product of an evil deceiver. To achieve real knowledge, he proposed to withdraw entirely from the realm of perception. He concluded that sense perception itself was derivative from reason rather than the reverse.

> I now know that even bodies are not strictly perceived by the sense or the faculty of imagination but by the intellect alone, and that this perception derives not from their being touched or seen but from their being understood; and in view of this I know plainly that I can achieve an easier and more evident perception of my own mind than of anything else. (Descartes, 1986, p. 22)

DENYING DESCARTES

No one in the VR community can share Descartes's distrust of the senses. The virtual traveler sees and interacts with bodies, not minds, and must be inclined to deny the traditional hierarchy in which we *are* minds and merely *have* bodies. (This was, by the way, an appropriate hierarchy in an age of printed texts, which are words and merely contain graphics.) Marcos Novak (1991), an architect and VR enthusiast writes:

> The trajectory of Western thought has been one moving from the concrete to the abstract, from the body to the mind; recent thought, however, has been pressing upon us the frailty of that Cartesian distinction. The mind is the property of the body, and lives and dies with it. Everywhere we turn we see signs of this recognition, and cyberspace, in its literal placement of the body in spaces invented by the mind, is located directly upon this blurring boundary, this fault. (p. 227)

This rhetoric places virtual reality in another important tradition: the 20th-century tradition of anti-Cartesianism that reaches from Wittgenstein and Heidegger through Ryle and Rorty to the poststructuralists and various postmodernists. All these have attacked the dichotomy of mind and body, the rigid division of subject and object. It is hard to find a trend of 20th-century thought that does not begin from a tacit or explicit denial of Cartesianism. In a recent article Katherine Hayles (1993) summarizes one important strategy for denial. She describes what Bourdieu and others advocate as "embodied knowledge":

> To look at thought in this way [as Bourdieu does] is to turn Descartes upside down. The central premise is not that the cogitating mind can be certain only of its ability to be present to itself, but rather that the body exists in space and time and through its interaction with the environment defines the parameters within which the cogitating mind can arrive at its "certainties," which not coincidentally almost never include the fundamental homologies generating the boundaries of thought. What counts as knowledge is also radically revised, for conscious thought becomes as it were the epiphenomenon corresponding to the phenomenal body the body provides. . . . Whereas causal thinking that Descartes admired in geometry and sought to emulate in philosophy erases context by abstracting experience into generalized patterns, embodiment and especially vision create context by forging connections between instantiated action and environmental conditions. Marking a turn from foundation to flux, embodiment redefines the role and importance of context to human cognition. (pp. 160-161)

This strategy certainly turns Descartes upside down. We have only to recall his famous rejection of the body to realize the gulf that separates Descartes from his modern and postmodern critics:

> I will now shut my eyes, stop my ears, and withdraw all my senses. I will eliminate from my thoughts all images of bodily things, or rather, since this is hardly possible, I will regard all such images as vacuous, false and worthless. I will converse with myself and scrutinize myself more deeply; and in this way I will attempt to achieve, little by little, a more intimate knowledge of myself. (Descartes, 1986, p. 24)

Now, if the Cartesian rejection of images were the path to true knowledge, then true knowledge could certainly not be found in the lenses of a head-mounted display. Virtual reality is the technology for turning Descartes upside down. Its wandering filmic eye reduces all abstraction to a series of visual perspectives. What it offers in place of causal thinking is precisely that faculty of imagination (making images) that Descartes disparages. The goal of virtual reality is not rational certainty; it is rather the ability of the individual to empathize through imagining. When Jaron Lanier was asked to characterize this new technology, he pointed to new possibilities for emotional involvement. Wearing a VR helmet, "You can visit the world of the dinosaur, then become a Tyrannosaurus. Not only can you see DNA, you can experience what it's like to be a molecule" (Ditlea, 1989, p. 92). So even a molecule can be known through empathy; the symbol systems of mathematics and physics can be left aside.

Knowledge is a matter of perspective, and so the virtual self is defined through perspective. VR specialist, Meredith Bricken (1991), elaborates on this theme:

> You don't need a body; you can be a floating point of view. You can be the mad hatter or you can be the teapot, you can move back and forth to the rhythm of a song. You can be a tiny droplet in the rain or in the river; you can be what you thought you ought to be all along. You can switch your point of view to an object or a process or another person's point of view in the other person's world. Assuming multiple perspectives is a powerful capacity; only after young children are developmentally ready to understand that each person sees from a different perspective can they learn to relate to others in an empathetic way. (p. 372)

Putting Novak, Lanier, and Bricken together, we can see the notion of self that virtual reality and cyberspace promote. The key is to experience the world as others do, not to retire from the distractions of the world to discover oneself as a thinking agent. And instead of asserting its identity over against the world, the virtual self repeatedly denies its own identity, its separateness from others and from the world. It does not learn by scientific study in a subject-object relationship, but by identification and empathy.

In all these ways, virtual reality seems to support the modern and postmodern rejection of Cartesian or Enlightened thought. However, Hayles herself remains suspicious. For her the proper alternative to Descartes's decontextualized reason is an embodied knowledge that virtual reality cannot achieve. Virtual reality threatens to detach the user from his or her body—as, for example, Bricken seems to suggest earlier—and such detachment sounds dangerously Cartesian. Allucquere Roseanne Stone (1991) shares this concern: "Cyberspace developers foresee a time when they will be able to forget about the body. But it is important to remember that virtual community originates in, and must return to, the physical. . . . Forgetting about the body is an old Cartesian trick" (p. 113). Balsamo (1993) too is troubled: "What is of interest to me in my encounter with virtual reality is the way that the repression of the body is technologically naturalized" (p. 126).

From various feminist perspectives, virtual reality is still too Cartesian. The sense of sight is not adequate to give the user a feeling of complete embodiment. On the other hand, such embodiment remains the ultimate goal for many VR specialists. They have designed entire body suits that will allow the user to manipulate an image of her whole body, not merely her hand. There has also been serious work on "haptic feedback," so that a joystick or eventually a glove can simulate the resistence appropriate to the object that the user is trying to move in virtual space. The fact that the typical virtual interface consists of a disembodied eye is in part an artifact of the current stage of technical development. Enthusiasts for virtual reality may sometimes sound, as Bricken does earlier, as if they wanted to get rid of the bodies. Yet theirs is still a rhetoric of the body; they do not really have an alternative to offer. Consider, for example, Randal Walser's prediction:

> More than any mechanism yet invented, [cyberspace] will change what humans perceive themselves to be, at a very fundamental and personal level. In

> cyberspace, there is no need to move about in a body like the one you possess in physical reality. You may feel more comfortable, at first, with a body like your "own" but as you conduct more of your life and affairs in cyberspace your conditioned notion of a unique and immutable body will give way to a far more liberated notion of "body" as something quite disposable and, generally, limited. You will find that some bodies work best in some situations while others work best in others. The ability to radically and compellingly change one's body-image is bound to have a deep psychological effect, calling into question just what you consider yourself to be. (cited in Rheingold, 1991, p. 191)

Walser is no Cartesian; he is not denying the importance of the body in defining the self. For him, the importance of the body is precisely the reason why virtual reality will have its great impact. Virtual reality will change our conception of our bodies. Our notion of self will change because we will now be dynamic or unstable bodies. The wandering perspective of virtual reality may not be sufficiently tactile for feminist theory, but it can only define itself in terms of visible bodies in visible space.

Contemporary theorists are diffident about virtual reality, yet they share important assumptions with the VR and computer graphics technologists. Both the assumptions and the diffidence can be found, for example, in the complex rhetoric of Donna Haraway (1991), in such influential essays on "A Manifesto for Cyborgs: Science, Technology and Socialist Feminism in the 1980s" and "The Biopolitics of Postmodern Bodies: Determinations of Self and Other in Immune System Discourse." Haraway's "cyborg" seems to be both a technological monster and a figure of revolutionary potential. Haraway's rhetoric, too, seems to be an ambivalent reaction to the breakout of the visual. Her prose is highly wrought and almost brutally sensual, but it is at the same time full of postmodern jargon and strategies of self-reference and abstraction. Haraway's neologism "cyborg," which derives from "cybernetic" and reminds us of "cyberspace," shows how contemporary theorists are in fact forging a common language with virtual reality enthusiasts.

In virtual reality, the Cartesian ego is dissipated as completely as any postmodern theorist could wish. In fact, if it ever reached the degree of perfection suggested by its proponents, virtual reality would be the perfect technological expression of Descartes's malicious deceiver. It would offer to Descartes's eyes a world that looked completely natural, responded to his movements, and yet bore no correspondence to nature. It was the possibility of a malicious deceiver that led Descartes to cut himself off from every source of sense evidence that might be contaminated. By contrast, virtual reality offers the user nowhere to withdraw to. This is no Cartesian center that is immune to perceptual context. The self in virtual reality is all context. And feminist theorists, poststructuralists, and it seems everyone else (except perhaps a few Thomists and the remaining followers of Ayn Rand) agree that any plausible definition of self must now deny Cartesian detachment and rely exclusively on knowledge obtained in context and through the senses.

VIRTUAL SILENCE

The self constructed in virtual reality differs in many ways from the constructions of writing or print. Perhaps the fundamental difference is the absence of voice in the virtual self. Like many others, I have referred to the "rhetoric" of electronic media, but this phrase is a catachresis, at least when applied to computer graphics technologies. Computer graphics may be understood as the denial of rhetoric, just as it may be the denial of discursive communication in general. "Rhetoric" comes from a Greek root that means to speak, and virtual reality is utterly silent. It has no rhetorical voice, nor does the addition of sound in virtual space give it one. It is not even silent in the way the printed prose is silent, for in print the silence is accompanied by the trace of the voice that was explored by Derrida and other poststructuralists. Virtual reality and other graphic manifestations of cyberspace substitute sight for sound. And for this reason, unlike MUDs, graphic virtual environments constitutes the inversion of the figure of ekphrasis. For ekphrasis subordinates perception to language; virtual reality subordinates language to visual perception.

Virtual reality denies any construction of self as a linguistic entity. In the space of virtual reality, the Enlightened ego, which was in large part a linguistic entity, is destabilized and ultimately dissolves. The dissolution is more complete and less ambiguous than that accomplished by Derrida, or for that matter by Heidegger and Wittgenstein. Those philosophers were still working inside the textual tradition, ultimately within the same writing space as Descartes. They are all philosophers of print. Virtual space is the abnegation of the space of personal cognition that Descartes envisioned. That space was pure ego, abstracted from the visual and the sensual. Virtual space, cyberspace, is one of pure, if utterly artificial, sense perception.

REFERENCES

Albers, S. (1983). *The art of describing: Dutch art in the seventeenth century.* Chicago: University of Chicago Press.

AND Communication. (1990). Ulysses and beyond: Knowledge prototype system [computer software]. Presented by J.E. Dezell, "Restructuring Education Through Technology," at IBM Schools Executive Conference, February 2, 1990, Palm Springs CA [videotape].

Balsamo, A. (1993). The virtual body in cyberspace. In J. Rothschild (Ed.), *Research in philosophy and technology: Vol. 13: Technology and feminism* (pp. 119-139). Greenwich, CT: JAI Press.

Bolter, J.D. (1991). *Writing space: The computer, hypertext, and the history of writing.* Hillsdale, NJ: Erlbaum.

Bolter, J.D. (1993). *Writing on the world: The role of symbolic communication in graphic computer environments.* In Proceedings of SIGDOC '93. New York: ACM.

Bolter, J.D. (1994, April). Authors and readers in an age of electronic texts. In B. Sutton (Ed.), *Literary Texts in an Electronic Age: Scholarly Implications for Library Services: Proceedings of the 31st Annual Clinic on Library Applications of Data Processing.*

Bolter, J.D. (in press). Virtual reality, ekphrasis and the future of the book. In *Proceedings of "The Future of the Book" Conference* (pp. 7-19).

Bricken, M. (1991). Virtual worlds: No interface to design. In M. Benedikt (Ed.), *Cyberspace: First steps* (pp. 363-382). Cambridge, MA: MIT Press.

Descartes, R. (1986). *Meditations on first philosophy with selections from the objections and replies* (J. Cottingham, Trans.). Cambridge: Cambridge University Press.

Ditlea, S. (1989). Another world: Inside artificial reality. *PC Computing, 2*(11), 90-99, 102.

Eisenstein, E. (1979). *The printing press as an agent of change* (2 vols.). Cambridge: Cambridge University Press.

Gergen, K.J. (1991). *The saturated self: Dilemmas of identity in contemporary life.* New York: HarperCollins.

Haraway, D. (1991). *Simians, cyborgs, and women: The reinvention of nature.* New York: Routledge.

Hayles, N.K. (1993). The materiality of informatics. *Configurations, 1*(1), 147-170.

Jay, M. (1988). Scopic regimes of modernity. In H. Foster (Ed.), *Vision and visuality* (pp. 3-23). Seattle: Bay Press.

Joyce, M. (1987). *afternoon, a story* [computer software]. Watertown, MA: Eastgate Systems.

Krieger, M. (1992). *Ekphrasis: The illusion of the natural sign.* Baltimore: Johns Hopkins University Press.

Landow, G. (1992). *Hypertext: The convergence of contemporary critical theory and technology.* Baltimore: Johns Hopkins University Press.

Lanham, R. (1993). *The electronic word: Democracy, technology and the arts.* Chicago: University of Chicago Press.

Moulthrop, S. (1992). *Victory garden* [computer software]. Watertown, MA: Eastgate Systems.

Novak, M. (1991). Liquid architectures in cyberspace. In M. Benedikt (Ed.), *Cyberspace: First steps* (pp. 225-254). Cambridge, MA: MIT Press.

Ong, W.J. (1982). *Orality and literacy.* New York: Methuen.

Rheingold, H. (1991). *Virtual reality.* New York: Simon and Shuster.

Rudnicky, A.I., Hauptman A.G., & Lee, K.-F. (1994, March). Survey of current speech technology. *Communications of the ACM, 37*(3), 52-57.

Stone, A.R. (1991). Will the real body please stand up? In M. Benedikt (Ed.), *Cyberspace: First steps* (pp. 81-118). Cambridge, MA: MIT Press.

SECTION 2

FUNCTION: CYBERNETWORKS AND CYBERPLACES AS ALTERNATIVES TO PHYSICAL LOCATION AND TRANSPORTATION

Face-to-face interaction in real, physical space is the primary mode of human communication. The technologies of telecommunication and computer-mediated communication are meant to function as substitutes and extensions of the primary mode, providing new ways of disseminating information, sharing meaning, and congregating and communing. Used as a functional alternative to a place or a set of places, these technologies give rise to the electronic equivalent to space. This includes all computer networks, from local area networks to the Internet and the information superhighway. These cybernetworks are in turn made up of nodes, *cyberplaces*, such as virtual offices, schools and stores, and other electronic versions of traditional locations; computer conferences, discussion groups, and other electronic versions of face-to-face gatherings; electronic mailboxes, bulletin boards, and cyberspace versions of actual installations; and entirely new cybersites such as MUDs (Multi-User Dungeons).

This section begins with Mark Giese offering an overview of the history of the Internet, which is generally acknowledged as the "Main Street" of contemporary cyberspace. The chapter examines the technical innovations, institutional foundations, and cultures of the U.S. Department of Defense and the Academy that led to the configuration of the Internet today. Giese discusses the significant role of the Internet in framing the debate on the "information superhighway." Ronald Jacobson's piece picks up where Giese leaves off in the second chapter in this section, considering present and future plans and policy for the "infobahn." He critically explores corporate interests, the National Telecommunications and Information Administration proposal for an advanced National Information Infrastructure, and public interest concerns. Most significantly, Jacobson raises important questions concerning such issues as access and the impact on older forms of public institutional space.

Turning from the general notion of cyberspace networks to more specific cyberplaces, in this section's third chapter Joseph Barrett examines the new electronic marketplaces made possible by computer-mediated telecommunication, focusing on financial markets and the implications for the world's financial system. Tracing the history of money as it relates to communication systems, he shows how media alter monetary systems and markets. In the fourth chapter, Terri Toles Patkin focuses on the virtual organization, reviewing research related to human factors in developing virtual reality simulations. Emphasizing its educational function, she describes a desktop virtual environment and identifies elements important for a successful implementation of the simulation. In the final article of this section, Michael P. Beaubien focuses on MUDs, which are text-based environments for role-playing games accessed online via computer. Beaubien reviews research on gaming as he explores this new space for interaction created by cyberspace MUDs and their implications in terms of language, power, and the social construction of community.

Cybernetworks and cyberplaces vary in the degree to which they differ from actual locations and physical structures, from entirely abstract nonplaces that bear little or no resemblance to the physical realm, to attempts to construct virtual worlds indistinguishable from reality. However close the simulation the functional alternatives made available through cyberspace cannot help but differ from their real-world counterparts, in turn changing the way in which the functions are performed, their effects, and the purposes for which they are performed; in the end, they cannot help but change us too.

✧✧✧✧ 8

From ARPAnet to the Internet: A Cultural Clash and Its Implications in Framing the Debate on the Information Superhighway

Mark Giese

Guides to the Internet abound, but few offer more than a cursory sense of its history. In this chapter, Mark Giese discusses its origins in the Department of Defenses's ARPAnet (Advanced Research Projects Agency network), and the subsequent creation by computer scientists of the tangential USENET NEWS. The chapter covers both the technical innovations and the institutional foundations of the Department of Defense and the Academy that led to the configuration the Internet has today. Giese explores the consequences of the inevitable cultural clash between the Department of Defense, guided by it sense of mission in the name of national security, and university computer scientists, influenced by the hacker ethic of the free flow of information. He argues that this prehistory of the Internet and its evolution is important to understanding the current discourse that is framing the debate on the national information infrastructure, also known as the "information superhighway." Additional discussion of the Internet and its political context in other sections of this book can be found in Gary Gumpert and Susan J. Drucker's overview of cyberspace as social space in Chapter 1, John M. Phelan's critical essay in Chapter 2, and James R. Beniger's exploration of the issue of control in Chapter 3; see also Paul Lippert's comments on cyberspace metaphors in Chapter 18.

The concept of a national information superhighway has been around for at least a decade, but with the installation of the Clinton Administration, the rhetoric on the subject seems to have exploded. There are several reasons for this, some of a technical nature and some of a social one. On the technical side, what is known as the convergence of computer, telecommunication, and broadcast technologies has much to do with this increased awareness of the topic. These technologies are converging into a single integrated complex that will allow access to a wide range of information in as many formats as exist today. This means that, according to the rhetoric, an individual will be able to access anything from online databases to the latest movie from his or her couch. Television will be interactive. The viewer may be able to pick from several different camera angles of a sporting event, or, upon seeing a commercial for a product of interest, be able to query the universal box in the living room for more information. According to television ads by the phone companies and cable networks, a brave new world of communications is dawning.

The dawn of this new communications age is made possible by several technical innovations in the still separate communications and computer industries. Among them are fiber-optic cables that afford a quantum leap in capacity over traditional copper and coaxial cables, new compression algorithms that make it possible to squeeze ever more data into the existing copper and coaxial networks, and software packages that make navigating through this sea of data intuitive and natural.

On the social side, there is a growing national feeling that the postindustrial age of information has arrived at last and the fear that failure to foster the technologies that make it possible may accelerate the United States' decline in the global trading arena. There are also speculations that this convergence of technologies will lead to a more participatory democracy. Balancing that optimistic view are those who predict that these technologies will make corporate and governmental agencies more prone to invade the private lives of their employees and citizens, thus violating tenets of freedom of speech and the rights of privacy. There are also those who ask questions about the quality of content typified by the question: "500 channels of what?" echoing Bruce Springsteen's lament—"57 channels and nuthin's on."

The metaphor of the superhighway is apropos on three levels. First, it is appropriate on the level of technical achievement in which the building of the information infrastructure is in many ways analogous in cost and engineering to the construction of the Interstate highway system. Second, it also may be analogous in that the construction of the information superhighway has the same potential for social transformation that the Interstate highway system had. And third, its original impetus was provided by the military for reasons of national security. In addition, just as the Interstate system was looked on as a more efficient replacement to the network of state highways and two-lane back roads, the information superhighway is looked on as a major improvement on an already existing web of computer networks. That web of networks is known commonly as the Internet. The purpose of this chapter is to examine what the Internet is and how it came into being. What was its intended use? How did it grow, and how is it used now? The answers to these questions might be useful in understanding how the information superhighway should be structured and how it might be used.

THE INTERNET TODAY

What is the Internet? Briefly, it is a network of computer networks that connects over 5,000 smaller networks, almost 1.5 million host computers, and 21 million users worldwide (Rutkowski et al., 1993). During a 2-week period in late April 1993, "87,000 people at 30,000 different USENET sites[1] posted about 26,000 articles per day to 4902 groups" (Hauben, 1993, p. 17). Traffic during this 2-week period totaled 65 megabytes. Over 364,000 individual articles were posted" (Hauben, 1993, p. 17). USENET comprises only the social aspect of the Internet. It is composed of thousands of topic-oriented "conversations" ranging from electronic want ads to discussions of sex, Star Trek, or recovery from child abuse. Total traffic is much higher: "3.4 gigabits per second, or, in the popularized measurement, more than three encyclopedias' worth of text a second" (Stix, 1993, p. 102). These statistics are all from mid- to late 1993, but tracking the traffic volume of the Internet is complicated by the fact that it has and continues to have an annual growth rate of 124% (Rutkowski et al., 1993), and all indications are that this rate is accelerating.

This swelling stream of electronic data accommodates not only the relatively minuscule trickle of social conversations—less than 20% of the traffic (Rutkowski et al., 1993)—but also an enormous amount of information related to the original purpose of the network—the facilitation of research, commerce, and governance. William Gibson (1984) coined the term cyberspace and described it as a "consensual hallucination" (p. 5). In the decade since the publication of *Neuromancer*, Gibson's vision of a tech noire future, a global network of computers, linked co-equally, has begun to take shape. The emergence of this global information network has gradually taken shape over the past 30 years and holds both the promise of McLuhan's "global village" and the threat of Gibson's darker vision of transnational capitalism run amok.

---

[1] *USENET sites* refers, in geographical terms that are typical of discussions of the Internet, to the topic-specific discussion groups that can be accessed via the computer network. A specific site refers to a specific topic rather than an actual place. These spatial terms are common in discussion about the Internet despite the fact that space and distance, in the traditional sense, are not particularly relevant.

GENESIS: THE EARLY RATIONALE AND CONCEPTUALIZATION OF ARPANET

The first wide area network (WAN) was developed under the direction of the Department of Defense Advanced Research Projects Agency (ARPA). The rationale behind the development of the ARPAnet (Advanced Research Projects Agency network) was the Defense Department's concern for maintaining the military's ability to communicate in the face of the destruction of one or more key links in the chain of command that might happen during a nuclear engagement. The major design constraint in the face of this threat was to create a communications system that was nonhierarchical and geographically dispersed. The rationale underpinning the research and its connection with the military was stated in 1962, in the report "On Distributed Communications" by Paul Baran:

> The report proposes a communication system where there would be no obvious central command and control point, but all surviving points would be able to reestablish contact in the event of an attack on any one point. Thus damage to a part would not destroy the whole and its effect on the whole would be minimized. (cited in Hauben, 1993, p. 3).

It is interesting to note here that the driving rationale behind the initial work on the construction of a redundant and highly connective computer network was essentially the same as the one behind the construction of the interstate highway system—national security. Unlike the interstate system, however, the engineering problem was fundamentally different. The interstate highway system was fundamentally a hardware problem—one of building physical structures. The construction of ARPAnet was essentially a software problem—how to connect and get different kinds of computers to "talk" to one another.

The key technical solution that made the Internet possible was derived independently by several researchers: Baran at Rand, Donald Davies in the United Kingdom, and Larry Roberts at MIT. The concept was called *packet switching.* Packet switching entails breaking a message up into several equally sized "packets," with each packet containing the address of the recipient. The packets could be sent separately and reassembled at their destination. The breakthrough concept in this idea was that each packet could be routed independently of the other packets. In this manner each packet could be sent along the most efficient route available at the moment and reassembled when all had reached their destination (Hart, Reed, & Bar, 1992).

Packet switching was easy to implement on a network that was composed of terminals made by the same manufacturer. The problem was that the Department of Defense wanted to implement the concept on a network composed of widely dissimilar computers and terminals. Getting different kinds of computers to "talk" to one another was a thornier problem. It was solved by Vinton Cerf and Robert Kahn, who together came up with the "gateway" concept.

This concept allowed packet switching to be accomplished between different networks despite the fact that they used different-sized packets and worked at different speeds. This gateway concept led to a software package known as TCP/IP (Transmission Control Protocol/Interconnection Protocol). Hart et al. (1992) explain the benefits of this software package:

> Thanks to its robustness, adaptability and relative simplicity TCP/IP has become the *de facto* world standard for interconnecting networks. The gateway concept makes TCP/IP particularly useful for people who wanted to interconnect computers and networks manufactured by different companies. Thus TCP/IP pioneered what is now called the "open systems" approach (p. 671).

The TCP/IP suite of protocols solved one of the technical problems that stood in the way of constructing wide area networks (WANs), and in 1969 ARPAnet was launched with four nodes. A node on this network was a mainframe computer, typically at a university computer science department, that was capable of addressing, sending, and receiving the electronic packets. Each node might have several "dumb" terminals connected to it capable of displaying output or sending input to the mainframe. By 1971, the network had expanded to 23 nodes and by 1977 grew to 111 nodes (Hart et al., 1992). Almost from the very beginning ARPAnet began to grow geometrically. Demand seems to always have exceeded capacity in the case of first ARPAnet and then the Internet. Unlike the "if we build it, they will come" rhetoric that has dominated the cable and telephone industries' responses to questions about who and how broadband networks will be used, the question for the builders and operators of WANs from ARPAnet to the Internet as it is today has been how to meet traffic demands that seem to have always exceeded capacity despite heroic efforts to increase it. The question has always been: "How can we make the pipe bigger?" not "How will we fill this pipe?" or "Who will use it?" This exponential growth in demand is ironic given the fact that originally the ARPAnet was intended to be restricted exclusively to defense agencies and defense contractors.

Another interesting irony in this open systems approach to the problem of maintaining the military communications system is that an organization known for its rigid centralized, hierarchical organization and its dependency on secrecy was forced into a solution that ultimately went against the ingrained nature of that organization. Despite the Department of Defense's institutional imperative to restrict access, the original ARPAnet grew. There were several factors that contributed to this phenomenal growth. The first, already discussed, was the simplicity and elegance of the technical solution: the TCP/IP protocol suite. It should be noted here that, whereas the protocols were flexible and simple, the arrival at this solution was a time-consuming process that took several years. The problem of getting computers from the same manufacturer to talk to one another was relatively simple. This involved the production of interface message processors (IMPs). IMPs were built for the first nodes by Bolt, Beranek, and

Newman under a contract awarded by ARPA in 1969. These specialized processors served well during the period when the number of nodes on the network was relatively small. However, as the ARPAnet grew, it became increasingly difficult and expensive to supply specialized hardware to each node. In addition, the Department of Defense wanted to incorporate satellite and packet radio transmission, as well as dedicated telephone lines, in the delivery system. It was under this new impetus that Vinton Cerf and Robert Kahn developed the gateway concept.

Concurrently with the development and implementation of this gateway concept, the process of debugging the protocol suite took place as a collaborative process among the scientists working at each of the nodes (Hart et al., 1992). This debugging process could only be done on an actual network (Hauben, 1993). Two important factors worked to foster the early growth of the ARPAnet. The first was that an actual network was needed in order to perfect the TCP/IP protocol suite, as well as a cooperative effort by researchers at different nodes in order to successfully debug the system. This cooperative effort fostered discussion of problems and solutions on the network and gave rise to online discussion groups. These discussion groups, in the form of the thousands of topic-specific USENET newsgroups, have become a permanent feature of the Internet.

A second factor that contributed to the growth of the Internet had little to do with finding solutions to the technical problems for the Department of Defense. This second factor can only be described as a clash of cultures. This clash of cultures was between the defense establishment—centralized, hierarchical, rigid, and secretive by nature—and the members of the academic community the Defense Department called on to find solutions to the problem. As already discussed, the design conceptualization of the computer network was one that was, at its very roots, antithetical to the organization it was to be built for and used by. "Open systems" architecture by its very nature goes against the organizational imperatives of the Defense Department. The threat to this institution from the enormous destructive power of nuclear weapons demanded precautions to protect its strategic secrets, its centralized command and control system, and its hierarchical organization. Paradoxically, the only precaution that could be effective called for a nonhierarchical, decentralized, and essentially egalitarian solution.

The computer network, much like the interstate highway system, was to be constructed and maintained by the government. Unlike the interstate highway system though, in the beginning it was never intended for public use. Use was to be subsidized and restricted to an elite group: "Access to the ARPAnet was limited to defense agencies and defense contractors. Within that group the heaviest use of the ARPAnet was by computer scientists" (Hart et al., 1992, p. 670). The question begged by the original conception of the network is: How did the network escape the umbrella of its highly secretive and powerful progenitor—the Defense Department?

The answer resides in a combination of factors that involve the interaction of large social institutions in a given historical context. One factor that played a very important role in this "coming out" is the rather odd coalition of two institutions that had very different internal social tenets—the defense establishment and the academic research community. This cultural clash is made explicit by Steven Levy in *Hackers* (1984), a book that documents the early days of computer programming and the now-stereotypical image of computer "geeks." A basic tenet of the hacker ethic was the free flow of information. A corollary to that axiom was a basic distrust of bureaucracy:

> The best way to promote a free flow of information is to have an open system. Bureaucracies, whether corporate, government or university, are flawed systems, dangerous in that they cannot accommodate the exploratory impulse of true hackers. Bureaucrats hide behind arbitrary rules: they invoke those rules to consolidate power, and perceive the constructive impulse of hackers as a threat. (p. 41).

These basic conflicts in worldviews were resolved, at least on the side of those involved in the early development of computer science and the network, by what Levy terms "willful blindness." This blindness was difficult to maintain in the milieu of the late 1960s. The antiwar movement worked to point out these conflicts, but largely failed.

One can imagine that the military might have viewed the conflict somewhat differently. The task must have seemed much like trying to direct the efforts of a group of deliberately willful but extremely bright children. In the end, the military lost this contest of wills. Perhaps a contest of wills is a less accurate description than one of a gradual subversion of the intended purpose of the network. Taylor has admitted diverting Defense Department funds from "mission-oriented" projects to more "pure science" and research-oriented efforts during those years (Levy, 1984, p. 131). Here cultural tenets of a particular institution are reflected and reproduced through a particular individual's action in an institution and cultural setting that held contradictory tenets and institutional imperatives. These particular actions set the stage for the way the culture of the Internet developed.

ESCAPE: THE DEMILITARIZATION OF THE INTERNET

ARPAnet could not survive what might be called an almost genetic ideological tenet of the "hacker ethic": the free flow of information. "The challenge which ARPAnet could not handle, and which led to its demise, was to expand access beyond the community of defense agencies and defense contractors" (Hart et al., 1992, p. 671). The turning point in the growth of the Internet was the advent of

USENET NEWS in 1979—a "poor man's ARPAnet" (Hauben, 1993, p. 14). USENET NEWS was the result of the effort of computer scientists that were excluded from ARPAnet to provide themselves with a similar computer network. Beginning in Berkeley, they constructed a network that was separate but touched the ARPAnet tangentially. USENET NEWS was the beginning of what is now known as the Internet, and its birth can be traced to the cultural conflicts between the Department of Defense and the community of computer scientists that was responsible for the construction of the ARPAnet.

One symptom of these cultural conflicts was the proliferation of discussion groups. This was due, in part, to the fact that those responsible for the construction of the network initially did not look at it as a medium of communication specifically, but rather conceptualized it as a "tool." During this 1960s period in the development of computer technology, mainframe computers were the only type available. Microcomputers, minicomputers, and desktops were not available, and mainframes were extremely expensive and difficult to acquire. They were used for solving intractable mathematical problems—number crunching. The network was seen as a way to share scarce and expensive resources. However, it was the interconnection, the communication aspect of the network, coupled with the collegial culture of the research community that soon made the network something more than a research tool.

Two major factors played a large role in the expansion of the closely held military network, ARPAnet, as a command and control tool for the military to what has been described as an ad-hoc network (Stix, 1993), commonly known as the Internet. The first is the cultural tenets held by the people who built the network, indicated by Levy (1984) in *Hackers*. The second is the nature of the economic forces that provided the initial funding for ARPAnet. These two factors combined to produce some unanticipated results. One of those results was evident almost from the beginning: "The two most widely used applications on the ARPAnet were electronic mail and remote login services" (Hart et al., 1992, p. 670).

The speed and reliability of e-mail soon spawned what could only be termed "unauthorized communication" on the network. This was made possible by software that made "mailing lists" possible. Mailing lists were a convenient way for researchers to have an ongoing conversation with many people. Essentially a mailing list sends a note to everyone on the list so that one can easily make comments and review feedback from everyone on the list. The original purpose of these mailing lists was to facilitate communication about specific research projects, but tangential conversations quickly sprang up. One was a mailing list with the title "sf-lovers"; it discussed a topic near and dear to many of the researchers' hearts—science fiction. These tangential conversations were tolerated as part of the accommodations that were made between the institutional cultures of the military "clients" and the computer scientist "suppliers." Although documentation is lacking, it is easy to speculate that from the military point of view they were harmless, used few resources, and provided a way to let their unpredictable charges blow off steam. From the other side of the cultural divide they were probably looked at in much the same way: It was easy, it was fun, and it was free—a well-deserved perk.

The clash of the two cultures was directly responsible for the expansion of the network. On one side there was the cultural imperative of the military to hold its assets closely. On the other side, researchers began to resent the exclusivity of access that prevented them from participating. USENET NEWS was the response:

> Usenet News was available to all who were interested as long as they had access to the Unix operating system. And posting and participating in the network was available at no cost besides what the college paid for equipment and the telephone calls to receive or send Netnews. Therefore, the joys and challenge of being a participant in the creation of the ever-expanding network was available via Usenet News to those without political or financial connections—to the common folk of the computer science community. (Hauben, 1993, p. 15).

Like the interstate highway system, ARPAnet's primary purpose was to strengthen national security; however, unlike the highway system, ARPAnet had never been intended to provide access to the general public. Computer scientists not connected to the defense establishment must have felt like eager motorists denied access to a new freeway. USENET NEWS was an end-run around that kind of military exclusivity. In essence, they built their own freeway parallel to the one reserved for military use. Interconnection of the two networks began in 1979. Berkeley had acquired an ARPA contract to supply the Unix operating system to ARPAnet. Already on the ARPAnet, Berkeley joined USENET. This initial joint connection brought into stark relief the sense of exclusion among the non-defense-connected members of the computer science community—between the "haves" of the ARPAnet and the "have-nots" of the USENET. Stephen Daniel notes this division: "It was initially very hard to contribute to those [ARPAnet] lists, and when you did you were more likely to get a response to your return address than to the content of your letter. It definitely felt second-class to be in read-only mode unable to post comments to the mailing list on human-nets and sf-lovers" (cited in Hauben, 1993, p. 15). This shows the sense of resentment felt by those excluded from ARPAnet, but also documents the peripheral and unauthorized nature of some of the mailing lists that had sprung up on ARPAnet. This began the transformation of the conceptualization of the network from a "tool" to a medium for social interaction.

A second major factor in the growth of the Internet had to do with the economics of the network. From the beginning, demand for access to the network and actual traffic has outpaced the network's ability to handle the load. A major reason for this is that users almost never pay for access nor do they pay the cost of their individual messages on the network. Eugene Miya recalls what can only be called the emotional aspect of this method of financing the network and lends credibility to the sense of resentment and exclusion felt by the founders of USENET NEWS that was fostered by the way it was financed:

> ARPA was the sugardaddy of computer science. Some very bright people were given some money, freedom, and had a lot of vision. I think the early ARPAnet was kind of a wondrous neat place, sort of a golden era. You could get into other people's machines with a minimum of hassle (someone else paid the bills). (cited in Hauben, 1993, p. 9).

This points not only to the impact of the government's subsidization of the network on the user, but also provides an implicit view of the clash between the cultural imperatives of the two institutional forces most responsible for the implementation of the early network. An interesting point to note about the advent of USENET NEWS is that its founders were able to maintain, at least from the end-users' standpoint, a financing structure that shielded them from the direct costs of the expansion of the network. These costs were borne by their institutions rather than the individuals using the network.

Despite the fact that ARPAnet was not decommissioned until 1990, replaced by the National Science Foundation Network (NSFNET), the advent of USENET marked the beginning of the end of the military's control of the computer network that was to grow into the Internet. The Internet continues to grow at an exponential pace. This phenomenal growth has been and continues to be fueled by the "free" nature of the original ARPAnet and its first successor, USENET. The Internet is free both in the intellectual sense, because it fosters a diversity of communication among a wide variety of users, and in the financial sense because the vast majority of users are shielded from the direct cost of implementing and maintaining the network. The Internet's intellectual freedom stems from the legacy of the hacker ethic—the free flow of information—the major cultural tenet of the builders of the network. The financial "freedom" stems from the legacy of subsidization of the original ARPAnet by the Defense establishment and the ability of those involved in wresting control of the network away from the military to transfer the ongoing costs of implementation and maintenance to the institutions (largely academic) they worked for rather than to the individuals who use Internet. These twin legacies of freedom have the potential to play a large role in shaping the national information infrastructure.

EXPANSION: THE ROLE OF THE INTERNET IN FRAMING THE DEBATE ON THE INFORMATION SUPERHIGHWAY

The cultural and economic factors that engendered the original construction of what has now grown to a worldwide computer network are changing again. The advent of USENET NEWS was the beginning of a rapid and exponential growth in the life of the computer network. Rapid expansion has brought the attention of private enterprise, notably the telecommunications industry, and has awakened the realization of the industry to a potentially huge new market. The cultural clash between the military and the academic community, surprisingly, has been resolved in favor of the academic community. This is, in part, due to both the fact that the network was built by the academic community and subverted almost from the very beginning from the purposes of its commissioners—the military. The subversion and victory coupled with new technological developments and the popularity of this new medium of communication has set the stage for another clash of institutional cultures whose outcome is by no means obvious.

This debate has been framed in economic terms that stem directly from the cultural imperatives of both institutions and can be seen in a brief comparison. The telephone network because of the historical moment of its advent and the social institution of private enterprise within which it grew in its early days has always been perceived as a pay-as-you-go and for-profit enterprise by its users. On the other hand, and also stemming from a particular historical moment, users of the Internet have always been shielded from the costs of using it. In the beginning they were paid for directly by the military establishment, now, while construction costs are still largely financed by the government, user costs such as processing costs, data storage costs, and connect charges are still subsidized by the institutions that the users are members of, principally institutions for research and higher education.

It is almost inevitable that within the next decade there will be a trend toward commercialization and privatization of the Internet: "Most of the registered internets today already are commercial entities. And most of the growth today of internets and the Internet is dramatically commercial" (Rutkowski et al., 1993, p. 20.). How far this trend will go and what effect it has on the shape of the national information infrastructure remains to be seen. However, there are factors in play that give rise to the hope that the chaotic diversity of the Internet as it is today will not be completely obscured by the profit motives of the large commercial interests who are the most vociferous proponents of the information superhighway. One of the biggest factors may simply be the existence of the Internet and its present constituency. Bruce Sterling (1992) makes a strong argument for this in the last chapter of his book, *The Hacker Crackdown*, citing the organization of the Electronic Frontier Foundation as an exemplar.

A comparison of the computer network as it exists today (essentially in its infancy) and the rise of the telephone network may be useful in understanding how the debate on the information superhighway is being framed. There are several interesting parallels as well as some interesting divergences. In the beginning, both the phone network and the computer network were restricted to social elites. In the case of the telephone network that elite was the economically privileged. Use was restricted to businesses and the rich upper class. This was due, in large part, to the cost of the technology and the commercial nature of the enterprise. Because the telephone company had an organizational imperative to acquire capital—make a profit—it catered to those users who could afford to finance its technological innovation. In the case of the computer network, as we have seen, the elite class that was cultivated was intellectual rather than economic. Once again this was due in large part to the nature of the way the construction of the network was financed. Because the organizational imperative was different—in this case, national security rather than profit—the cost of development was directed by the military and financed by the taxing authority of the national government.

At the social level, the uses the two networks were put to were originally restricted as well. The diffusion of telephone technology and its use in a social and communal mode was surprising to its enabling institution. Sidney Aronson (1977) noted that "company officials were still somewhat influenced by the concepts that governed the telegraph industry; they saw that medium primarily as an aid to commerce and had given little priority to social telegraphy" (p. 26). The same is true about the advent of discussion groups not related to computer science problems or the construction of the computer network. Both the telephone company and the Defense Department envisioned communication networks that were "strictly business," when in reality both networks were put to more communal and social uses. Although the move to more social uses was unanticipated to both institutions, the motivating forces for that move were different. In the case of the telephone, it was the need by the phone company to expand a market and increase profits. In the case of the computer network, it was largely driven by the users themselves.

From a technical standpoint, the initial conceptualizations of the two networks were driven by differing institutional economic imperatives. The technologies that engendered the telephone network were originally thought of as having no particular use. It was looked on as a novelty. William Orton, head of Western Union, dismissed the new invention as an "electrical toy" when presented with the opportunity to buy the patent for a mere $100,000 (Aronson, 1977).

Conversely the initial conceptualization of the computer network was closely envisioned and narrowly defined to solve a specific strategic military problem. Although Bell and his financial backers searched for a commercial use for an invention whose use was not immediately obvious, the Defense Department had no intention of putting the technical innovations that made the computer network possible to commercial use. In fact, that possible option was probably one that was actively discouraged in Defense circles due to security considerations. Yet, despite this lack of vision on the parts of both establishing institutions, the social uses of both networks have come to play a large role in the constitution of these networks.

It is perhaps this common convergence to a set of social rather than business uses of the two networks that sets the stage for the coming debate about the nature of the information superhighway, despite the fact that this point of convergence was arrived at from two different directions. Any complex social agglomeration is composed of many specialized subgroupings of people and institutions. These internal constituencies may have competing and conflicting purposes over particular issues and resources as well as across differing political milieu and time. Alfonso Molina (1989) notes how these internal institutional conflicts play out in the definition of what he calls institutional raison d'être:

> Ways and means vary not only for different social forces and historical periods, but also for different institutions within the same social force. This flexibility implies the existence of particular interests which constitute the practical expression of social forces' overriding interests. Particular interests thus relate to the more ordinary, daily activities of institutions and people. They are informed by the overriding interests of social forces, but also by other factors such as economic and political pressures, organizational traditions of institutions, and also the personalities, ambitions and visions of individuals working and making decisions in the particular institutions. (pp. 3-4).

Examples abound in the world of communications—the battle over Paramount Communications has been characterized as a battle of egos between the two principles, Sumner Redstone and Barry Diller. This is an example of the bitter competition that may arise within a particular social institution. During ARPAnet's formative years, Robert Taylor redirected funds from mission-oriented projects to pure research projects. Both examples point to the interplay between institutional imperatives and the institutional social constraints operating on individuals and, conversely, how particular individuals may affect the social milieu and raison d'être of the institutions they work within. The cultural clash between the defense establishment and the academy is an example of inter-institutional competition. In the case of ARPAnet and the early development of the Internet, this competition seems to have been resolved more or less in favor of the more libertarian conceptual model of the academy. However, the very success of the Internet and its phenomenal growth has brought the social institution of private enterprise into this institutional social dynamic. The way individuals within particular institutions articulate the institution's raison d'être plays an important role in how issues are framed. Although the raison d'être of the business community is not the same as that of the defense establishment, it still has many points of possible conflict and competition with the academy. In the case of the debate on the information superhighway, both cable baron, John Malone, and key executives in the telephone industry, notably Ray Smith of Bell Atlantic, tend to frame the debate in narrow, self-serving economic terms centering on what applications to provide and how much the public will pay for particular applications.

This narrow economic view was the one used for both the telephone network and the cable networks. It worked well because, in both cases, neither technology had developed a constituency. In the case of the Internet, a large and growing constituency already exists and, more importantly, this constituency's cultural tenets are in direct conflict with those of the business interests intent on developing the information superhighway. With the rise of the debate on the information superhighway, there will be a continued debate on who will control the highway and access to it. The outcome of this debate may hinge directly on and determine the very existence of the Internet.

The key difference in the historical moment of the rise of the telephone network and that of the rise of the Internet is that, in the early days of the developing telephone system, there were no institutions that could compete with the private enterprise model of that development. In the case of the Internet, it was allowed to develop a substantial constituency before the private sector challenged the economic model it has been based on. That constituency, as has been noted, has grown accustomed to the "freedom" of the Internet in both the economic and intellectual sense. In addition, that constituency is growing at a phenomenal pace and has well-known and powerful advocates such as Mitch Kapor, founder of both Lotus Software and the Electronic Frontier Foundation, which provides a powerful public voice for the cultural tenets of the Internet with its legacy in the hacker ethic. This provides a base for strong opposition to the commercialization of cyberspace.

Despite this cultural legacy of freedom, the phenomenal growth of the Internet has brought to the forefront even in academic circles the realization that there are substantial economic costs associated with maintaining the computer web that has grown up over the past 30 years. David Wilson (1993) notes that the way Internet services and connections are paid for have much to do with the freedom, in the intellectual sense, that is a hallmark of the Internet:

> One of the keys to understanding why colleges and universities make their computers available to the public is the fact that it doesn't really cost them anything. The computer servers are always on. Cycles can be thought of as amount of time a computer is on. "You've got all these clock cycles on a computer, and once they're gone they're gone forever, so you might as well have somebody get some good out of them," says John P. Doyle, assistant law librarian at Washington and Lee University Library. (p. A18)

This indicates that, even at the institutional level, the costs associated with the growth and maintenance of the Internet are diffused and indirect. Once the investment in computer hardware is made, there is little additional cost associated with making access to the Internet available to a wide range of people. However, with the explosive growth of the Internet, new investments in infrastructure will be needed, and it is unclear whether institutions of higher education will be either willing or fiscally capable of subsidizing the construction and maintenance of additional infrastructure. This opens the door for the private sector to impose a direct pricing structure that does not hide the cost of network usage from the end-user.

If the information superhighway is based, as many of the commercial interests involved want it to be, on a model similar to the telephone system, the costs associated with access to the data stream that is the Internet would skyrocket. This usage-based rate structure is one that is widely accepted in many areas of the telecommunications industry, most prominently the telephone and the cable sectors. A key component to this pricing strategy is what Vincent Mosco (1989) calls "the commodification of information" and is a key step in the construction of an economic model that allows the commercialization of a product that is intangible and has been traditionally hard to measure: "According to this view, information possesses unique characteristics that distinguish it from other resources, preeminently, that information is non-depletable. It can be used, but not used up" (p. 23). This conceptualization of information as a resource puts it in the same realm as minerals or other natural resources and like other resources open to development and exploitation. Mosco notes that in an electronic age information has been increasingly commodified. This comodification has and will continue to be problematic because of the nondepletable nature of information and because there is a fundamental difference between *information* as a resource, whose value is variable to different people and over time, and *data*, which are measured in volume and can therefore be priced based on usage. This commodification is not new but has accelerated with the advent of electronic telecommunications technologies that allow precise and quantified measurements of a commodity that traditionally has been difficult to measure in terms of value. What these electronic technologies have done is to make data measurable in terms of volume and time—bits, bytes, and minutes. This makes information as a resource subject to rate making on the same basis as other raw materials. This sets up a conflict between the giants of the telecommunications industry and the primary users. In effect the industry wants to have the privilege of charging for a commodity that to this point has been free. Given the exisisting Internet community's strong affinity for the cultural tenets of the hacker ethic, epitomized by the phrase, "information wants to be free," and the indirect finacing method that has been employed for infrastructure construction to this point, this is somewhat akin to telling them that there are plans to charge them for the air they breathe.

Another powerful model private enterprise is using as a template for the construction of the information superhighway is a "free" system as well. It is the broadcast or mass media model. Over-the-air broadcasting in America is also based on a method of paying for the products and services available that shields the end-users from direct costs. This method of financing the system is directly connected to the nature of the technology. Broadcasting lends itself to a top-down, one-to-many method of operation. Advertising pays for the content directly, but the end-users ultimately pay for the system through higher prices added to products and services due to the cost of advertising.

Two factors here may work to subvert the kind of culture that has grown up on the network. The first is the way commercial interests in the information superhighway are using the broadcast business model as a template. This model has a very restricted conceptualization of the interactive features of the superhighway. Commercial interests tend to visualize interactivity as a way for couch potatoes to order up movies on a pay-per-view basis or to inquire further about products they might see advertised by requesting a brochure or a more elaborate video description of a product through their remote control. One of the most interesting facets of the Internet has been the way individuals have used it to make connections with other like-minded individuals or groups rather than restricting their communication to "authorized" uses. A major concern in this area is that commercial interests may attempt to restrict the interactivity of the superhighway to a passive consummerist mode that is much like the broadcast model. Although this may seem difficult or a remote possibility, Howard Rheingold (1993) documents how one of the most high-profile commercial services, Prodigy, attempted to do this. As a commercial business, Prodigy began their service to sell information services such as banking, stock transactions, and airline reservations, but offered e-mail for free as an added benefit. The commercial services languished while the e-mail service flourished. And, like its much larger cousin, the Internet, free-ranging discussions sprang up, some of which involved topics and comments (specifically antisemitic comments) that Prodigy deemed harmful to its commercial services. Prodigy responded first by monitoring and then censoring customers' e-mail; and then, when the users made an end-run on this tactic by turning provisions of the Electronic Communications Privacy Act of 1986 to their advantage by forming mailing lists, Prodigy retaliated by curtailing e-mail privileges and increasing fees (Rheingold, 1993).

The second, and perhaps more ominous, factor is the way commercial interests intend to use the two-way flow of information to perform what Oscar Gandy (1993) has called the "panoptic sort." This is the practice of commercial interests gathering, collating, and processing information about individuals in order to target markets more precisely. Many businesses already routinely gather and sort information about their customer's lives and buying habits by monitoring credit card purchases and other electronic trails of information that individuals leave in the course of leading their lives in the age of information. The technology of the information superhighway provides a quantum leap in the ability of large commercial interests to invade the privacy of individuals surreptitiously. But this information gathering is more complex than described because it encompasses a struggle by commercial interests to restrict individual access to particular types of information that they can be charged for while, at the same time, increasing their ability to control their use of personal information incidentally gathered in these commercial transactions for additional commercial purposes. In effect, the thrust of these maneuvers is an attempt to narrow individuals' uses of the Internet to consumerist purposes rather than social or political purposes. Both these factors can be connected to Molina's (1989) articulation of organizational raison d'être and have historical precedents. Witness Aronson's documentation of Bell executives' failure to envision the social use of the telephone that developed because they were tied to the conceptual template of the way telegraphy was already being used as a model for the telephone business.

This points to the importance of how the debate on the National Information Infrastructure should be framed. There are good arguments on both sides of this conflict. An important ideological tenet of our society has been the importance of the freedom of expression and a lively and free "marketplace of ideas." Equally important has been the commercial and capitalistic nature of our economic structure. The resolution of these institutional contradictions and conflicts will have an important impact on the nature of our culture and social institutions as we move into the next century and the rhetoric about the information society becomes social reality. Important social issues and concerns that are most often expressed in the phrase "information rich" and "information poor" need to be resolved in an equitable manner that preserves both the economic vitality of the society and the intellectual diversity. Issues that revolve around intellectual property rights, copyright, and universal access need to be resolved in a way that protects economic interests without jeopardizing freedom of expression and access to information that is not based strictly on an ability to pay.

There seems little doubt that metering of information on the computer network will become a reality. What remains to be seen is to what extent this privatization and metering will be allowed to go. There is some hope that there will be an effort to limit this trend. The first indicator of hope is the very explosiveness of the growth of use on the Internet. To this point, the Internet has been self-regulating and egalitarian within the limits of the technological access. The cultural legacy of the hacker ethic—the free flow of information—is promulgated to new members of the electronic community as they enter. This will provide, at least for a time, an ever-growing base of opposition to the kind of commodification that Mosco (1989) fears. Many members of the Internet community share his fears. The second indicator of hope is the military's historic failure to contain and control the use of ARPAnet. This stems from two factors: the technological simplicity of the TCP/IP suite of communication protocols, and the network's initial conceptualization as a decentralized and flexible communication tool. Marvin (1988) seems to feel that the very nature of communication may have a causal relationship to this institutional failure to maintain control by one of our society's most powerful social institutions: "New media embody the possibility that accustomed orders are in jeopardy, since communication is a particular kind of interaction that actively seeks variety. No matter how firmly custom or instrumentality may appear to organize or contain it, it carries the seeds of its own subversion" (p. 8). The historical precedent of the way the social use of the telephone developed coupled with its parallel in the Internet may provide a reminder to those who wish to force computer-mediated communication into a commercial mold based on a mass media model. The examples of both the telephone and the Internet seem to indicate that, if given an opportunity, people will choose to communicate interactively with each other, rather than attend exclusively mass-mediated, one-to-many products as commercial interests might prefer.

It is perhaps fitting that the term *cyberspace* is a geographic or topographic metaphor. This geographic element seems to capture many of the issues inherent in Mosco's (1989) sense of information as a resource. It also harks back to the days of the Wild West in that many of the issues at the forefront of the debate about the information superhighway seem to echo the issues those early settlers faced. David Ronfeldt (1991) makes this geographical notion of colonization explicit:

> Still another analogy views it [cyberspace] as a frontier that virtually exists and beckons for exploration, colonization and development. In this view, different "cyberspace colonies" will be (indeed, they already are being) carved out by many different kinds of actors, many of them initially misfits and adventurers from ordinary society. As colonies get established and grow, they may be expected to develop different forms of government, citizenship, and property rights. (pp. 35-36)

Ronfeldt's geographical conceptualization of cyberspace shares something in common with Mosco's (1989) definition of information as a resource. Virtual real estate, unlike its physical counterpart, seems to have the ability to expand. Like the nondepletable nature of information, cyberspace has no known natural limits—cyberspace expands as information grows. This will be important to remember as players square off in what might constitute a virtual range war between the "mountain men" and "prospectors" of the Internet and the "sodbusters" and "railroaders" of the telecommunications industry who want to fence the frontier in. There should be room in cyberspace for an unprecedented range of diversity. The cultural legacy of the Internet has established both a precedent for that diversity and a large number of proponents. However, the rhetoric of the information superhighway threatens to reframe the debate into a more constricted and limited vision. The outcome of the debate is still in doubt. Will cyberspace indeed become a "pay-per society" as Mosco suggests? There is hope that the raucous and colorful diversity that is the Internet today will continue to grow and provide a model for future development.

REFERENCES

Aronson, S.H. (1977). Bell's electrical toy: What's the use? The sociology of early telephone useage. In I. de Sola Pool (Ed.), *The social impact of the telephone* (pp. 15-39). Cambridge, MA: The MIT Press.

Gandy, O.H., Jr. (1993). *The panoptic sort: A political economy of personal information*. Boulder, CO: Westview Press.

Gibson, W. (1984). *Neuromancer*. New York: Ace Books.

Hart, J.A., Reed, R.E., & Bar, F. (1992, November). The building of the Internet: Implications for the future of broadband networks. *Telecommunications Policy, 16*(8), 666-689.

Hauben, R. (1993, June). *The development of the international computer network: From ARPAnet to Usenet News (On the nourishment or impediment of the NET.Commonwealth)*. Paper presented at "Europe in Turmoil: Communication and Democracy in Civil Society," a conference of the International Association for Mass Communication Research, Dublin, Ireland.

Levy, S. (1984). *Hackers: The heroes of the computer revolution.* New York: Bantam.

Marvin, C. (1988). *When old technologies were new: Thinking about electric communication in the late nineteenth century.* New York: Oxford University Press.

Molina, A.H. (1989). *The social bias of the microelectronic revolution.* Edinburgh: Edinburgh University Press.

Mosco, V. (1989). *The pay-per society: Computers and communication in the age of information.* Toronto: Garamond Press.

Rheingold, H. (1993). *The virtual community: Homesteading on the electronic frontier.* Reading, MA: Addison-Wesley.

Ronfeldt, D. (1991). *Cyberocracy, cyberspace, and cyberology: Political effects of the information revolution.* Santa Monica, CA: RAND Corporation.

Rutkowski, A. M., et al. (1993). Who's "on line" with whom: The new global internetworking business, from computer bulletin boards to national infostructure. In C.S. Gregory (Ed.), *Telegeography: Global telecommunications traffic statistics & commentary* (pp. 8-17). Washington, DC: Telegeography Inc.

Sterling, B. (1992). *The hacker crackdown: Law and disorder on the electronic frontier.* New York: Bantam.

Stix, G. (1993, August). Domesticating cyberspace. *Scientific American, 269*(2), 100-110.

Wilson, D.L. (1993, July 28). Electronic riches are free on the Internet, but some worry about the consequences. *The Chronicle of Higher Education*, pp. A18-A21.

◇◇◇◇ 9

"Are They Building an Off-Ramp in My Neighborhood?" and Other Questions Concerning Public Interest in and Access to the Information Superhighway

Ronald Jacobson

Cyberspace is a contested site, and different segments of society are staking their claims in what may well be the greatest "land grab" since the closing of the frontier. The competing interests include big business; local, state, and national governments; institutions such as universities and hospitals; computer professionals and hobbyists; and the general public. In this chapter, Ron Jacobson discusses competing visions and concerns about the emerging National Information Infrastructure, juxtaposing corporate commercial interests in the information superhighway with the National Telecommunications and Information Administration (NTIA) proposal for an advanced National Information Infrastructure. Several public interest questions are posed, including: Who will benefit most from the proposed telecommunications infrastructure, and what will constitute basic service on this information highway? In raising these and other questions, the author calls for a wider public debate to consider the political, economic, social, cultural, and ethical implications of our changing communications infrastructure. Beyond Section II, additional examination of issues, policy, and law can be found Gary Gumpert and Susan J. Drucker's comments on cyberlaw in Chapter 1, John M. Phelan's critique of Internet hype in Chapter 2, James R. Beniger's essay on the control of cyberspace in Chapter 3, and Neil Kleinman's exploration of property rights in Chapter 4; see also Paul Lippert's arguments concerning social class in Chapter 18.

The convergence of the computer with telephone and television technologies is frequently conceptualized today as the *information superhighway*, a popular metaphor for the building of a National Information Infrastructure (NII) made up of seamless communications networks, databases, and consumer electronics. Stand-up comedian Paul Rodriquez tells his audience that he's heard all this great talk about an information superhighway, but he's pretty sure "they're not building an off-ramp in *my neighborhood*." The information highway, Rodriquez continues, is "just another place where I can get pulled off and frisked." Rodriquez's humor is entertaining, but, more than that, it is social commentary that critically points to the inevitable human gap between our aims and achievements, our ideals and performance. Rodriquez raises significant public access and privacy concerns about emerging electronic forms of social interaction as he implicitly poses a key question: "In which directions will the much-heralded information superhighway go?"

The answer to this question depends on whom you are asking. Individuals and groups, often with divergent interests and purposes, envision different social worlds evolving from new interactive, multimedia environments. These groups include, among others, the telecommunications companies, federal government, public interest groups, and current users on today's "cyberlanes" (the precursors of the great highway). The purpose of this chapter is to explore corporate, government, and public interest visions and concerns about the emerging telecommunications environments, and to raise questions for further discussion and debate. This is a critical period in government policy concerning the evolution of converging technologies and their applications. Industry structure and practices, guided by regulation influenced in part by the public interest, will influence this evolution.

CORPORATE VISIONS

The public is being sold idealized images of the future, as some corporate visionaries speak of the information superhighway almost as if it were the way to enlightenment. Corporate interests would have us believe that the knowledge of the world will soon be available at our fingertips and that the consequences of this information revolution will be wholly positive, as if an injection of new technology is the panacea for our social problems. Corporate interests are largely to blame for the hype about the information superhighway (or "hypeway" as some critics have appropriately termed it), as they take their own goals, embellish them, and promote them as the aims of the whole society.

Corporate America is constantly sharing with the public its "exciting" vision of a future characterized by the magic of technology. In an AT&T brochure, *Connections: AT&T's Vision of the Future*, video compression technology is described this way:

> Think of it as the high-tech equivalent of concentrated orange juice. With orange juice, the manufacturer takes out the water at one end, ships the juice to you in a smaller package, and then you bring the juice back to its original form by adding water at the other end. And in the case of video compression, AT&T does all the work for you—you don't even have to add water.

The corporate message is that rapidly advancing technology will soon be bringing the information superhighway to our doors: Ready or not, here it comes. A NYNEX advertisement, publicizing the company's technical involvement in interactive education projects, reads: "We're Teaching Driver's Ed for the Information Superhighway." Although new interactive educational services will certainly evolve, the corporate sector expects most profits to come from what is sometimes referred to in the industry as the *killer applications*—movies-on-demand, games, and, someday, gambling. Therefore, for many people, the information highway to the home is likely to be experienced initially as an alternative to getting in the car and driving to the video store or the casino. If the past (e.g., broadcast teletext services) provides any indication for the future, other more information-intensive applications of new interactive technologies will be relatively slower to evolve. Perceptions and the realization of greater convenience, efficiency, and economy will no doubt be significant factors in growth of new services along the information superhighway.

Contrary to the seemingly incessant telecommunications industry chatter, history suggests that the information superhighway will not be curbside nationwide and popularly accepted by the general public anytime soon. Cambridge Associates, a consulting firm, predicts that by 2004, 55% of U.S. households will be wired for two-way electronic delivery services, but only 50% of those households will subscribe to the new systems ("Fate of videotape," 1994). The fact is that new technologies tend to be adopted gradually by the public. Take, for example, personal computers, which have been around for a couple decades but are found in just over one-third of the nation's households. This bodes well for, among other predigital media, the newspaper and the VCR. No doubt significant changes will occur, but they most likely will come in decades, not years, and be evolutionary rather than revolutionary (Wade, 1994).

Undaunted by skepticism, criticism, and regulatory uncertainty, businesses forge ahead, experimenting with ways to attract the masses to get on and navigate the highway once it is built. For example, Bell Atlantic's Stargazer project proposes the shopping mall metaphor as the menu program through which consumers might navigate on their system. Once on the highway, you enter the mall, where you might go to the movie store to order a movie-on-demand, enter the bank to pay your bills, or visit the food court to order a pizza for home delivery. The mall metaphor is a telling one about the direction most corporate builders would like the superhighway to take. Like its real-world counterpart, the simulated mall might offer a sense of community within an ahistorical yet highly valued context of consumption. It should be noted that libraries, museums, schools, and churches do not exist in our current notion of malls. If the future even remotely resembles the past, we can be assured that this mall will be strewn with commercial enticements every click-step of the way. We already see the trend toward commercialization on the Internet. *Adweek* columnist Michael Schrage (1993) believes:

> Internet is a medium just aching for its own Bill Paley—some aspiring mogul who can redefine this hodgepodge of globally interconnected machine intelligences into a formidable commercial medium that commands premium prices from traditional advertisers and unconventional advertisers alike. Once advertisers come onto the network, internet usage (already growing 20% a month compounded) will skyrocket even faster, because more consumers will come on board. Of course, advertising will subsidize network growth for computers just as it did for radio and television. (p. 26)

What the information superhighway is really about is the transformation of information and knowledge rather than its growth. The public sphere is shrinking as indicated by signs such as libraries losing their funding; more information, including government data, being distributed through private commercial vendors; and blatantly commercial services like Channel One in the public schools. Herb Schiller (cited in Ruggiero & Sahulka, 1994, p. 2) suggests, "Things that are fundamentally changing for the worse. Limiting access to information and the commercialization of public space are being presented as wonderful benefits in the offing. It's a sickening con game."

The information superhighway metaphor itself is a popular but inappropriate one in significant ways. As Browning (1994) aptly points out, the government built our federal highway system, but it will not be building the information superhighway. Similar to railways, information networks are being constructed by people who stand to profit from them. Dordick (Freedom Forum, 1993) suggests that the building of the asphalt interstate highway system also had its drawbacks, as "it served large companies, bypassed many small communities, and essentially blocked investments for public transportation for many years" (p. 25). Today, although we talk about an information superhighway, the reality is that most large corporate interests would prefer to be building private toll roads.

A major question for these highway builders is whether the personal computer (a decentralized model with the Internet as a prototype) or the curent television system (a centralized model) will be the principal gateway to the information highway for the masses. Tele-Communications Inc. (TCI), the nation's largest multiple-system cable operator, and others are busy building centralized 500-television channel universes. TCI's National Digital Television Center, established in 1994, will convert and digitally compress television signals from program suppliers, as well as serve as a "birthing center" for new programs and services. The TCI project represents one example of an ongoing strategy by corporate giants in the telecommunications industries to vertically integrate through content creation, packaging and marketing of content and services, and physical distribution of the packaged product.

Of course, this emerging 500-channel universe is not without it critics. Jeffrey Chester and Kathryn Montgomery (1993), co-directors of the Center for Media Education, envision such a universe as a "vaster wasteland" in which advertising-created programming flourishes, prohibitive rate structures make it difficult for nonprofit groups and small independent producers to gain system access, and consumers pay higher fees to obtain programming. With the onset of the 500-channel universe, they see the decline of "free" broadcast television, local news and public affairs programming, and public television as we know it today. Nancy Kranich (1994), a member of the American Library Association's Subcommittee on Telecommunications, fears that "if not controlled, industry giants will transmit 500 or more channels of highly profitable vaporware that will fall far short of serving the full spectrum of society's needs" (p. 35).

Important questions about the information superhighway, inclusive of the 500-channel universe, are not widely debated today outside of the Internet and the academic community because of corporate zeal complemented by mainstream news media behavior that more frequently resembles a corporate public relations campaign than any social watchdog function. As Schiller (cited in Ruggiero & Sahulka, 1994) suggests, "Once corporate control is given, it is alienated from the public arena and we lose rights to discuss its disposition." But all is not lost. Corporate visions of the information superhighway have been slowed by uncertainty about government policy. (For example, in 1994, TCI and Bell Atlantic called off their $33 billion merger at least partly because Congress passed a bill that forced the cable industry to roll back subscription rates.)

GOVERNMENT VISIONS

Vice President Al Gore is the Clinton Administration's most ardent supporter of national telecommunications reform. His vision is to bring the economic, health, and educational benefits of the information revolution to more Americans, and he has publicly challenged private industry to connect every hospital, classroom, and library to the information highway by the end of this century. To that end, in 1993, the National Telecommunications and Information Administration (NTIA) in the

U.S. Department of Commerce, under the Clinton Administration, proposed a plan for a National Information Infrastructure (NII) that would be built by private-sector investment; promote interactive, user-driven operation; and ensure universal basic service to all at affordable costs. In fact, Gore and the NTIA's version of the proposed information superhighway features miles and miles of promise and potential. The Information Infrastructure Task Force Report (1993) claims:

> People could live almost anywhere they wanted, without foregoing opportunities for useful and fulfilling employment, by "telecommuting" to their offices through an electronic highway;
>
> The best schools, teachers, and courses would be available to all students, without regard to geography, distances, resources, or disability;
>
> Services that improve America's health care system and respond to other important social needs could be available on-line, without waiting in line, when and where you need them. (p. 3)

In February 1996, President Clinton signed a major telecommunications bill that removed legislative and judicial restrictions on telecommunications companies so that the "paving" of the highway can begin. With deregulation, telephone, broadcast and cable, and computer companies are forming manufacturing and marketing agreements. All of this seems to spell out a continuation of national communications policy largely guided by private commercial interests in the marketplace, tempered by federal regulation for the "public interest" in areas such as technical standards, concentration of ownership, consumer pricing, and access to both users and content providers. For example, of the latter, Gore (1994) asks, "How can you sell your ideas, your information, your programs, if an intermediary who is also your competitor has the means to unfairly block your access to customers? We can't subject the free flow of content to artificial constraints at the hands of either government regulators or would-be monopolists" (p. 6).

The President and Congress realized that the proposed NII plan required major regulatory reform because assymetrical regulatory models existed for the converging technologies and industries. For example, broadcasting regulation, under the Communications Act of 1934, was regulated following a public interest model. However, spectrum scarcity, the driving force behind broadcast regulation, is no longer the dominant paradigm. Once considered almost a natural resource, parts of the electromagnetic spectrum have recently been auctioned off to the highest corporate bidders. Cable was regulated principally as a local franchisee under federal guidelines, and telephone companies historically were regulated as public utility common carriers. These differing regulatory models could not simply be combined in creating new policy concerning the information superhighway (Geller, 1991). The NII plan recognizes that the new regulatory policy needs to be flexible, adaptable, and fair in dealing with changing and emerging technologies and their applications, with business structures, and with public interest concerns that will affect distributors, content providers, and consumer users along the information superhighway. Important questions and problems about issues such as First Amendment rights, privacy, security, and intellectual property rights will continue to be worked out through practice, the courts, legislation, and policy decisions.

PUBLIC INTEREST CONCERNS

While the NTIA paints a pretty picture of future possibilities, some fear the future will widen the gap between the information haves and have-nots. There already is evidence of the direction toward greater inequities. In 1994, five consumer and civil rights groups, including the NAACP and the National Council of La Raza, charged that regional telcos were practicing "electronic redlining," excluding poor and minority communities from plans of upgrading infrastructure and offering new information services (Wiseman, 1994). (Maybe Rodriquez wasn't joking about the absence of an information superhighway "off-ramp" in his neighborhood.) Of course, Bell Atlantic and the other "Baby Bells" deny the accusation, so who is to be believed? Richard Mandelbaum (1992) places this early conflict into perspective:

> When the American Telephone and Telegraph company ran the telephone system, it was bound by the principles of universal service and equal access for all. But since 1984, when the regional operating companies were divested, their primary obligation has been to their stockholders, not to society. So it is no surprise that the wiring plans for the new network technologies favor large financial institutions, Fortune 500 corporations and others that can generate the greatest revenue for the phone companies. Those not on the path of money and power will have to wait in line for the information age. (p. 13)

Countering the corporate lobbies, public interest groups, including the Electronic Frontier Foundation, are calling for universal low-cost access to public information. These groups argue for a public information carrier model that would reserve "electronic space free from corporate control and censorship" (Ouelette, 1993, p. 24). Geller (1991) believes this can be accomplished through a fiber-based integrated switched broadband telecommunications structure, with at least one line separating the conduit from the content. This means that at least one line into the home would be solely that of a common carrier with no control over content, similar to our traditional telephone system. Public interest groups see such structural regulation as key to preventing monopolistic or oligopolistic constraints that would limit diversity of expression and marginalize alternative views.

Reuben-Cooke (1993) proposes that government take a stronger public interest, access-based policy approach to regulation, considering factors such as audience receipt of ideas (e.g., the public's right to information), quantity of services (e.g., guaranteed access for content providers), cost (e.g., greater affordability through subsidies), and literacy (e.g., ability to operate hardware and use software intelligently). Although all these factors are important, it is the last factor, literacy, that often fails to be included in public interest discussions. Those who gain access to the information superhighway must not only learn how to navigate but also to critically discern the quality of content in cyberspace. That is to say, whereas the future promises a diminished role for professional mass media gatekeepers and fewer controls on content, such a future also suggests the possibility of an increasing burden on individual users who will take on greater gatekeeping responsibilities (conjuring up the oxymoron of the "empowered couch potato"). As technology progresses, audience control increases, but are individuals ready to assume control, including scanning and filtering their own information (Neuman, 1993)?

It is not difficult to envision a scenario in which some form of universal service exists, but social stratification is still clearly delineated by the ability to afford knowledge of and access to quality gatekeepers (software, people, and services that evaluate, select, sort, and package customized information). It is a scenario in which the poor and uneducated have fewer "maps" for use on the superhighway and are more likely to get lost on detours or stuck at commercial roadside attractions selling entertainment and/or information in the guise of knowledge. It is all too easy to forget that information is not knowledge. Knowledge is gained by making evaluative judgments on the quality of information, which in turn is achieved through the cognitive skill of separating the significant from the irrelevant. Therefore, Reuben-Cooke (1993) and others realize that the push for low-cost, universal access to the information superhighway must be accompanied by a push for more media literacy education.

Literacy is indeed a pertinent issue and one implicitly suggested in broader public interest concerns about the information superhighway. As I see it now, the principal public interest access questions are these:

- Who will benefit most from access to the emerging telecommunications infrastructure?
- Who gets what, where, when, how, and for what purpose?
- What are the social consequences of inequitable access to the information superhighway (e.g., even greater polarization along social class lines)?
- If access is deemed a right (some Republicans are already labeling universal access as another Democrat-concocted "entitlement"), what will constitute basic service?

In addition to such basic questions about access, there are many more public interest questions, including the following, that require greater thought, discussion, and debate concerning the future of telecommunications and cyberspace:

- How can our many significant educational, health, and cultural problems be better addressed by our new technologies? (Shouldn't a major driving force behind our national telecommunications policy be the explicit goal to equate technological progress with improvements in social welfare?)
- How will users navigate through, socially interact with others, and form new senses of shared community in cyberspace?
- Once access is achieved, how will privacy be protected?
- Will virtual communities lead to a further deterioration of our older communities, especially our cities?
- What will happen to other public institutional spaces, such as tax-supported libraries, in this new age of electronic information? (For example, will the libraries go the way of the downtown stores when the suburban malls moved in, or will they serve as hubs for universal access? See Roszak, 1986, for an excellent argument for the latter.)
- Will a 500-channel universe further isolate us from one another and "individualize our approach to and our knowledge of issues of public justice and of each other," as Janette Dates asks, and will there be "more avenues for individual speech but fewer for robust, wide-open debate," as Les Brown ponders (Center for Media Literacy, 1994, p. 11)?
- As the media become more decentralized and seemingly more democratized, will old and new media serve the needs of democracy or further solidify existing power structures? There are many questions about the future of the relationship between cyberspace and politics. For example, Lawrence Grossman asks, "How do we reconcile a representative political system that is based on, and defined by, geographical boundaries—districts, counties, cities and states—with the powerful new telecommunications media that obliterate political boundaries" (Center for Media Literacy, 1994, p. 12)?
- Finally, we must ask ourselves not only what the information superhighway will be like, but what will we be like; that is, how will we change through communication and evolving forms of social interactions in cyberspace?

CONCLUDING THOUGHTS

So far, I have been discussing the information superhighway on a national scale, but the issues are cross-cultural and international. The information superhighway yearns to be intercontinental and borderless, bringing us conceptually closer to McLuhan's notion of a global village transcending time and space. But it is a village still marked by ideological and cultural conflicts, and inhabited by haves and have-nots, with over half the world's population still lacking access to a telephone. Information technologies can contribute significantly to political and social change, as witnessed in Poland, the former Soviet Union, and South Africa; one can only hope that the emerging global information infrastructure will lead to environments that offer potential for leveling great socioeconomic inequities and for improving the quality of life for more humans.

We live during an exciting time of hype, promise and potential. Corporate ideology of the information age pervades our lives. With less powerful voices, federal and state governments and public interest groups outline their concerns, push their own agendas, and fight to keep powerful corporate entities from setting the parameters of the debate. Chester and Montgomery (1993) believe "the next few years create a unique opportunity—a narrow window of neccessity—for the public interest to be asserted, for the debate to be reframed in terms of the larger democratic and social consequences, and for legislators and the public to become centrally involved and ultimately decide the key questions of public policy" (p. 117).

No doubt, the 1990s is a crucial time during which telecommunications policy decisions will likely influence communication and interactions in cyberspace for decades to come. What is ultimately at stake is the very nature of communications institutions, audiences/users, and the forms of relationship between them. Borrowing from Raymond Williams's (1974) interpretation of Laswell's model, we must ask ourselves anew, "Who will be able to say what to whom for what purpose and with what effect?" For no matter what your view is on or from the information superhighway, you are part of a significant ideological struggle about power and control.

REFERENCES

Browning, J. (1994, February). Get on track: There will be no info highway. *Wired*, p. 65.

Center for Media Literacy. (1994). Visions of a brave new TV world. *Connect, 6*, 10-13.

Chester, J., & Montgomery, K.C. (1993). A public-interest perspective for the future U.S. telecommunications infrastructure. In C. Firestone (Ed.), *Television in the 21st century* (pp. 55-75). Queenstown, MD: The Aspen Institute.

Fate of Videotape. (1994, June 24). *The New York Times*, p. D20.

Freedom Forum Media Studies Center. (1993). *Media, democracy and the information highway: A conference report on the prospects for a national information service*. New York: Author.

Geller, H. (1991). *Fiber optics: An opportunity for a new policy.* Washington, DC: The Annenberg Washington Program in Communication Policy Studies of Northwestern University.

Gore, A. (1994, January 11). *Vice-president proposes national telecommunications reform.* Washington, DC: The White House Office of the Vice President.

Information Infrastructure Task Force. (1993, September 15). *The national information infrastructure: Agenda for action.* Washington, DC: U.S. Department of Commerce.

Kranich, N. (1994, November 15). Of cyberspace: Can libraries protect public access? *Library Journal,* p. 35.

Mandelbaum, R. (1992, December 20). Who benefits in the information age? *The New York Times,* 4, p. 13.

Neuman, W.R.. (1993). The psychology of the new media. In C. Firestone (Ed.), *Television in the 21st century* (pp. 35-54). Queenstown, MD: The Aspen Institute.

Ouelette, L. (1993, September/October). The information lockout: Is there a place for have-nots in cyberspace? *Utne Reader,* p. 24.

Reuben-Cooke, W.M. (1993). Rethinking legal and policy paradigms. In C. Firestone (Ed.), *Television in the 21st century* (pp. 55-75). Queenstown, MD: The Aspen Institute.

Roszak, T. (1986). *The cult of information: The folklore of computers and the true art of thinking.* New York: Pantheon Books.

Ruggiero, G., & Sahulka, S. (1994, March). The information superhighway: Paving over the public. *Z Magazine* [online]. Available on America Online.

Schrage, M. (1993, May 17). The ultimate network. *Adwcck,* p. 26.

Wade, N. (1994, January 16). Method and madness: Future non-shock. *The New York Times Magazine,* p. 14.

Williams, R. (1974). Communication as a cultural science. *Journal of Communication, 42,* 17-26.

Wiseman, P. (1994, May 24). FCC told poor left off info highway. *USA Today,* p. 1.

✧✧✧✧ 10

Killing Time: The New Frontier of Cyberspace Capitalism

Joseph Barrett

Over the past 25 years, money in our own country has changed from a relatively stable, gold-backed currency to a free-floating electronic abstraction. Joseph Barrett claims that this evolution of money, brought about by computer processing power and telecommunications, is yet another stage in the 10,000-year historical relationship between money and communication systems. In this study he traces that history and discusses how various communication technologies have destroyed one barrier after another in pursuit of profit—first volume, then mass, then space. Barrett argues that today, in the relatively new frontier of cyberspace capitalism, time is the target of the electronic market. Aside from this section of the book, other perspectives on the economics of cyberspace appear in Gary Gumpert and Susan Drucker's discussion of communication and social space in Chapter 1, James R. Beniger's essay on the control and commercialization of cyberspace in Chapter 3, and Neil Kleinman's historical research on property and copyrights in Chapter 4; additional discussion of the concept of time can be found in Lance Strate's exploration of cybertime in Chapter 23.

Money has been changing from a standard unit of value—a fixed and limited asset, a substantial and absolute "truth"—into something ethereal, volatile, and electronic. Over the last twenty-plus years it has been moving from a

> government mandated equivalency—$35 equals one ounce of gold—to a new electronic form. It has become nothing more than an assemblage of ones and zeros, representing money, that are piped through miles of wire, pumped over fiber-optic highways, bounced off satellites, and beamed from one microwave relay station to another. This new money is like a shadow. Its cool-gray shape can be seen but not touched. It has no tactile dimension, no heft or weight. . . . Money is now an image.
>
> —Joel Kurtzman, *The Death of Money* (1993, pp. 15-16)

Set free by a stroke of Richard Nixon's presidential pen and given flight by computer technology, money indeed seems to have changed from something concrete to something ineffable. Within the lifetime of most people reading this chapter, it has moved from green cash in the pocket to a piece of plastic that taps into checking accounts, buys gas and groceries, makes long distance calls, and pays the electric bill. Money is no longer invested with optimism in simple stocks, which represent ownership, or bonds, which represent loans, but is now often placed in such exotic financial instruments as collateralized mortgage-backed debentures, which represent pieces of pools of loans on homes. Money no longer simply changes hands on the floors of stock exchanges; it passes electronically from the floor of one exchange to another in pursuit of profit from even the smallest difference in the value of whatever is being traded. Money still does not grow on trees, but divorced from the real world of labor and production, it does give the illusion that it can reproduce itself; or, even more frighteningly, disappear.

Although money has undergone a radical change during the last 30 years, this period is certainly not the first time that such a change has occurred. This chapter explores some of the ways money has changed in an era of vast computing power and fiber-optic communication systems. It places those changes in the context of the longer term relationship between money and communication. While communication systems have moved from oral to written to print to electronic forms, money has changed from a barter system in which actual goods were exchanged for other goods, to a precious commodity currency in which the medium of exchange held an inherent value, to coins minted or bills printed by government, to stocks and bonds issued by companies, to financial futures issued by speculators, to its current electronic form. Each form of money attempted to solve a problem inherent in the communication system in which it operated; and each created its own set of new problems. Earlier forms of money were able to eliminate volume and mass by replacing physical commodities with smaller representations of them; others responded to the elimination of space by the telegraph and created a market for time. This chapter argues that today's electronic money combines the attributes of earlier forms of money and attacks a new problem with its own set of risks: the annihilation of time.

Much has been written about the effect of electronic communication on shopping, home entertainment, and the workplace. Gumpert and Drucker (1992) have explored the changing relationship between the consumer and citizen as shopping passed from the public world of the agora to the semiprivate world of the shopping mall and into the fully privatized world of the comfy sofa, the channel changer, and QVC. Pruitt and Barrett (1991) have envisioned a world in which the worker never leaves his or her home physically, but telecommutes through the virtual reality of cyberspace, a three-dimensional electronic world in which business meetings are conducted complete with full-color demonstrations and mind-bending new software tools. Even mainstream publications such as Businessweek ("'The office is a terrible place to work'," 1993) and The New York Times ("The virtual office," 1993) have begun to fret over the life of the isolated, virtual worker and offer a solution of sorts: the virtual watercooler.

A handful of recent books and articles ("The secret money machine," 1994) have attempted to bring attention to the changes taking place in today's financial system. Kurtzman (1993) locates the change in the loss of tangibility of money, eliding the fact that money has always been a somewhat ethereal concept. Gibson (1993) examines the changes legislation, technology, and increased competition have brought to Wall Street, creating a situation in which once sensible financial firms are increasingly desperate to find new ways to generate money, not out of simple greed but in order to survive. Drucker (1993) cites the growing importance of the institutional investor, and makes the case that the United States, through pension funds, is becoming a country truly owned by the worker. Blume, Siegel, and Rottenberg (1993) trace the history of the New York Stock Exchange (NYSE) and show how changing economic realities and the NYSE's own mistakes are helping to decrease its importance in the financial world.

Finally, there is an extensive literature from both the left and right on the nature of money. Marx launched the leftist critique with his description of money as a "radical leveler" destroying the uniqueness of whatever it touches and a "pimp" between man's desire and fulfillment (Tucker, 1978). Mosco and Wasko (1988) see today's electronic money in the "pay-per-society" threatening traditional liberty as each transaction we make adds to the databanks of the system. Ewen (1988) has described the system of differentiating between credit cards—green, gold, platinum, black—as a reflection of the style and mystique of money, tied up ultimately in money as power. On the right, or in America, the center, money is defended as one of society's "great rationalizing habits" (Mitchell, 1916/1950, p.170). In a more recent approach, Zelizer (1994) analyzes the ways individuals and groups give meaning to the standardized money printed by the government, designating it as gift money, lunch money, allowance, and pay checks—each donating and supporting a web of social relationships. But none of these works sees the current relationship between money and communication as a phase in a relationship that goes back more than 10,000 years.

HISTORICAL PERSPECTIVE

The origins of money are commonly said to be shrouded in the "mists" of antiquity. But the archeological record helps reveal a long and deeply rooted relationship between the need to store information in a form more permanent than spoken words and the need to control the economic world. Around 8,000 B.C., Sumerian farmers and traders began to develop a complex accounting system with as many as 200 three-dimensional tokens representing commodities such as wheat, cattle, or containers of olive oil. These symbols made it easier to keep track of one's possessions without relying on memory. This early symbolic system was an attempt to eliminate both mass and volume. One need not continually recount one's cattle, or carry all the cattle about, in order to know they exist. A token representing the commodity alone could do the job. The symbolic system became more abstract as tokens were grouped for convenience and placed inside clay containers. These containers were at first marked with actual tokens on the outside to represent those within. It was a rather large evolutionary step to replace the actual three-dimensional tokens on the outside with simple two-dimensional symbols engraved on the surface of the container. A more conclusive step occurred as marks alone were inscribed on clay tablets, eliminating the need for three-dimensional tokens altogether (Logan, 1986). These two-dimensional marks were even easier to manipulate than the three-dimensional signs they replaced. The marks made true writing and a true symbolic currency possible.

It is a short step from the use of symbols to represent commodities to a system of trade that uses those symbols. A true system of money develops when a standard value can be established for a currency—that is, some medium of exchange and stored value. Some of the earliest fragments of writing that have been preserved show this evolution. A stone tablet from 2,600 B.C. has been interpreted as a ledger sheet representing land purchases with barley used as payment. A later papyrus tablet written in cuneiform shows the official weights of silver to be used as legal tender (Cribb, 1986). Eventually, gold, silver, and salt, the preferred wage or salary for the Roman soldier, became the most common currencies.

As Western communication systems developed from writing to print to electronic forms, so money moved from concrete representations of value, what economists call commodity money, to money that was minted or printed by governments, or fiat money. Commodity money, of course, was subject to inflation if the amount of the commodity could not be controlled. Similarly, governments could overprint or mint their own currency. This has been one of the great advantages and dangers of government-backed currency. Revealing something of both the developing power of state governments and the technology of minting and printing, the very first coins, minted in Lydia according to Herodotus, soon took on a value greater than their value when melted into their constituent metal (Richardson, 1970,). By 700 B.C., money had already become an image.

Although communication systems had a great deal to do with the form of money, they also influenced the way money circulated within that system. Even in a system of commodity money, in which the value of the currency might be relatively stable, wild fluctuations in the value of other commodities could take place on the arrival of new information through the communication system. In Medieval and Renaissance Europe, for example, the arrival of a ship at port might cause the value of wheat or coffee to plunge as the added supply was absorbed by the local market. Similarly, news that a ship had been sunk or lost might cause prices to skyrocket. Soon news began to be seen as a commodity as valuable as the ships themselves. Thus, in 1663, Samuel Pepys learned at a coffeehouse—a major center for the exchange of information in his day—of the safe arrival of a ship he was about to insure, saving a considerable expense (Stephens, 1988, p. 178). And, in 1815, the banker Nathan Rothschild sent one of his own agents across the English Channel to learn the outcome of the Battle of Waterloo and turned the news to a profit on the London Stock Exchange. News itself was something to be hoarded and from which to turn a profit.

With the growth of a local bourgeois in Europe and advances in navigation and shipping, which extended Europe's trade and communication system, new forms of storing and investing money developed. The first companies to buy debt from the public were the great import/export, exploration and settlement ventures setting forth from Europe to the New World (Werner & Smith, 1991). Stocks and bonds became an essential part of the Western European financial system as markets expanded beyond countries and across oceans. Gold remained an international currency, but many a nascent capitalist placed money for the future in shares of ventures such as the East India Company. The first markets for shares were well established by the beginning of the 18th century.

Local markets remained essentially isolated until the telegraph. Speculators, technically called *arbitrageurs*, up to the first half of the 19th century might be able to profit by moving commodities from one market to another if the difference in price were greater than the cost of transportation. The telegraph radically changed the nature of markets as pricing information was available almost instantaneously across the country and eventually the world. With the telegraph, anyone could become an arbitrageur, and therefore prices stabilized from one market to the next. Or, as Carey (1988) explains, the telegraph, put "everyone in the same place" for the purposes of trade (p. 217). Space had been "annihilated." Although differences in prices between markets were reduced or eliminated, the telegraph created a new zone for speculation: the future. Instead of moving commodities across space to take advantange of price differences, the new speculation involved buying commodities before they were even planted and speculating on their future value. The futures contract represented the destruction of space as a barrier to money, but it left open the battle against time.

The worldwide Depression of the 1930s helped to reveal the

interrelationship among the world's financial systems aided substantially by the telegraph. After World War II, the industrialized nations recognized both the interrelationship of their economies and the need for a stable currency. With the memory of the runaway German inflation between the wars fresh in their minds, Western leaders meeting at Bretton Woods, NH, devised a remarkably durable new monetary system based on a dollar backed by gold. The United States promised not to increase the supply of dollars beyond the rate of growth in the economy, and to continue to tie the dollar, although somewhat indirectly, to the amount of gold in Fort Knox.

The Bretton Woods era in international finance is the era of civics book economics—a relatively stable period of international growth often used as a backdrop for writers detailing the horrors of the present financial moment. The United States led the world economy, and even as other countries began to catch up, the United States's own rate of growth was phenomenal, based on an ever-increasing rate of productivity (Levy, 1987). Investors in U.S. stocks and bonds could count on a steady march of profit as Wall Street brokers grew rich and faced little competition for investors' money. In 1972, two factors began to unravel the paradigm. Nixon took the United States off the gold standard, allowing the dollar to float freely against other currencies. And the National Association of Securities Dealers Automated Quotation System, or NASDAQ, flashed onto the financial scene. NASDAQ is not a traditional stock market, but an electronic computer system linking brokers' offices across the country. Brokers were no longer simply in the same place for purposes of trade, as the telegraph had allowed; they could now be anyplace.

With the free-floating dollar and the ability to trade it over computerized networks—Reuters introduced terminals with the ability to receive news and make trades in 1973—changes in the financial world began to accelerate. Automatic teller machines replaced real tellers in banks. NASDAQ slowly began catching up to the NYSE in terms of volume and the prestige of the companies whose shares it handled (Blume et al., 1993). Institutional investors, those representing pension funds, insurance companies, and mutual funds, muscled out the individual investor and even the big players on Wall Street as the real financial powerhouses in the U.S. economy (see Blume et al.,1993; Drucker, 1993). Wall Street slowly became one of the largest buyers of new computing power in the country, investing upwards of $19 billion on communication and computing equipment in the early 1990s alone (Gibson, 1993). The financial system was becoming more faceless, more dispersed, and faster.

Much attention has been focused on the elimination of physical space by cyberspace. But as already discussed, the elimination of physical space can be seen as the continuation of a process begun by the telegraph. Whereas today's fiber-optic cables allow simultaneous two-way transmission of large amounts of information compared with the humble telegraph, this change can be seen as a matter of degree. The ability of individuals to access cyberspace from remote locations is a continuation of a trend begun with the ham radio, continued with the introduction of the satellite, the beeper, the cellular phone, and the fax machine. The emergence of electronic trading systems such as NASDAQ simply fulfills the promise of the telegraph to bring all players together for purposes of trade. If there is truly something qualitatively different about the current state of money and communication, it is in the effort to set money free not only from a physical volume, mass, and space, but to also unchain it from time. The remainder of the chapter examines the implications of this effort.

"ELIMINATING" TIME

Although money once moved in a face-to-face exchange—a turning over of goods for currency, a signing of documents, the passing of a check—today's transactions occur at the click of a mouse, the swipe of a card, the dispatch of a computer program into cyberspace. Money today is not stored in Fort Knox or in the vaults of banks but in computer banks. The amount of cash bills and coins—in circulation is but a tiny fraction of the amount of money stored electronically. And with the advent of cash cards—cards that represent money in checking accounts that can be used directly to pay for goods and services without any cash ever changing hands—the trend can only be seen to accelerate. This electronic money is more often invested in the "financial" economy than the "real" economy. According to some estimates, the amount of money in the real economy—the economy of factories, restaurants, and stores in which labor is applied to raw materials to produce products—is 30 to 50 times smaller than the financial economy (Kurtzman, 1993). In the financial economy, money is not tied to assets so tangible as factories, farms, or homes; rather, it moves about from one financial instrument to the next in search of profit, with no regard for whether anything gets made, bought, or sold.

Each of these changes at heart is part of the effort to eliminate time. Money must always be working, not tied up in transfer from one bank to another, as when a check is written. There is no time to wait for a promising new company to eventually turn its potential into profits, or to wait 30 years for a homeowner to pay off his or her mortgage. The eventual profits must come now. The effort to eliminate time in today's financial system is examined at three levels: consumption, investing, and speculation.

It is no secret that credit card companies, cable shopping networks, online shopping services, and the purveyors of the new cash cards all make their pitch to consumers based on the saving of time. Why bother making a separate trip to the cash machine to get money to make purchases when those purchases can be made directly on cash cards—with the money automatically deducted from your account? Why go to the mall when you can shop at home? Why watch television when you can dispatch a program into cyberspace to make your purchase for you? The tradeoff in each of these time-saving transactions, as Gumpert and Drucker (1992) and Mosco and Wasko (1988) have shown, is in both a diminishing of human contact in day-to-day transactions as well as an ever-deepening knowledge gained by the system of our every action and purchase. Ironically, among the first places testing out the new cash cards are college campuses, where students use a single card for meals, to buy books at the book store, and for off-campus purchases. Green cash here and in other ways can be seen as an increasingly black market currency of exchange—traceless, laundered money for transactions outside the "official" economy; that is, outside the reach of Big Brother, as well as Mom and Dad.

Individual investors today are far more likely to place their money in mutual funds or other pools of money than in individual stocks. This practice too can be seen as an effort to escape time. Whereas buying an individual stock requires patience, study, and perseverance, mutual funds offer a statistically proven better rate of return. Computing power also helped this process along, as many critical steps in the proof that diversifying a portfolio—not putting all your eggs in one basket—required calculations not possible until the 1980s (Bernstein, 1992). Diversification spreads risk over the marketplace and attempts to escape the tyranny of time by creating a mathematical formula of investing. Investing becomes an average outcome rather than a time-testing strategy.

As has already been mentioned, the real players in today's financial system are not the individual investors, but institutions, such as pension funds, insurance companies, university endowments, and mutual fund companies. These big players have a variety of diversification strategies that are sometimes referred to as passive investing. This type of investing involves buying financial instruments that mirror assets as diverse as the entire S&P 500 stock index. While the S&P 500 has historically risen over time, only recently has it been possible to invest in the entire index without buying stock in each company. The new index options, which have only a tangential affect on the underlying assets they ostensibly represent, seek to eliminate time as a factor in investing, by essentially investing in everything. Passive investing assures that the fund manager will not get beat by the "market" because she "owns" the market. Her capital, however, is not actually invested in anything.

Speculators in today's electronic financial system aim to turn on its head the common-sense notion enshrined in the phrase, "Time is money." To program traders, "hedge fund" leaders and financial engineers dreaming up the next financial "derivative," time only eats money. They hope to use the power and speed of computer communications to destroy time.

Today's speculators view time as a boundary, just as pretelegraph speculators viewed space—on the other side lays profit. News that happens anywhere in the world is accessible on computer screens everywhere in the world. International news organizations such as Reuters and AP-Dow Jones have the capacity to send headlines electronically around the world within seconds. CNN can broadcast the events live. An OPEC meeting in Geneva, for instance, may rattle petroleum markets in New York. In a ripple effect, the same news can hit bond markets, affecting the government's ability to refinance its debt; stock markets, affecting individual companies ability to invest in new plants and equipment; and overseas stock markets. Fiber optics have also eased the transfer of funds between markets. In a very real sense, cyberspace is creating one interrelated world market, in which the fortunes of any one investor, any one market, are tied into the fortunes of all the others.

This is a world that is coming very close to what is termed a transparent market—one in which all the players share the same information, one that in other words eliminates the role of the speculator. In part to counter this transparency, speculators are forced to use ever-more bizarre trading strategies in order to attempt to beat the market. These strategies—program trading, hedge funds, and derivatives—represent the new logic of capitalism.

Program trading, at its simplest, involves the buying or selling of large blocks of stocks without human intervention. It can be used by large institutional investors as a convenience. But the more risky form, known as index arbitrage, involves the selling of one financial instrument on one trading floor and the simultaneous buying of another somewhere else. Aided by the type of computing power that only became practical in the 1980s, academic theorists developed ways to calculate the value of such complex trading instruments as futures and other, even more abstract instruments—asset-backed securities, asset-stripped securities, and index options futures (see Bernstein, 1992; for a more succinct handling, see Kurtzman, 1993). With the ability to calculate the values of these complex instruments, computer programs are able to compute the value differentials between financial instruments. Even if the difference in value is slight, the ability to shift large amounts of money with ease and speed makes the transactions lucrative. But in their wake, they can leave havoc on the floors of the exchanges that they invade.

During the "Black Monday" market crash of October 19, 1987, the programs all came to the same conclusion and flooded exchanges with shares for sale. With few buyers, the deluge of sell orders by the programs turned a market downturn based on a touch of bad economic news into a record drop in the value of stock worldwide. Individual investors, who attempted to get through to their brokers to place their orders on that day, often failed to receive a reply. The telephone proved itself an outdated technology compared with the computer. Brokers spent most of their day monitoring the flood of information on their computer screens rather than being tied up with a single client on a phone line (Kurtzman, 1993).

What programs buy and sell sometimes are not simple stocks, bonds, and futures, but derivatives—the newest, strangest creation of Wall Street. Derivatives are complex financial instruments whose value is based on, or derived from, some underlying asset. There are derivatives based on credit card payments, mortgage payments, even car loans. Derivatives allow buyers to acquire a financial instrument with a highly specific set of characteristics with little money actually invested up front. Through derivatives, it is possible to make a bet that interest rates will drop. For instance, the investor acquires the derivative that behaves like a real asset whose value increases when interest rates go down, without actually acquiring the underlying asset. If the bet works, the investor can make a large profit. If the bet goes awry, however, the manager can be left with a liability much greater than the original investment. The list of investors who have been burned by these complex instruments is slowly growing.

One group of funds that engages heavily in such bets are known as hedge funds. These funds operate in secrecy and are the domain of only the richest of investors. Their founding strategy—backed by massively complex computer programs—is to place bets that a given financial instrument will both rise and fall. They are able to make money off this seemingly paradoxical position by borrowing a great deal more than their original investment and placing this borrowed, or leveraged, money also on both sides of the market. If the market moves a small amount, a great deal of money can be made. If the market moves too much, fortunes can be wiped out.

The logic of all three of these strategies—program trading, derivatives, and hedge funds—is to attempt to break free of the tyranny the new instantaneous communications environment has created. There is literally too much information available to make speculators happy these days. What they aim to do—for a fraction of a second or less—is hold all things equal as they place their massive bets. What speculators and the wider world of cyberspace capitalism fail to take into account is their own effect on the market and the real world—remember the real world? Consumers seek convenience but leave an electronic trail that binds them ever more tightly into the state and the marketer's control. Investors seek to place their money in a safe place but forget to serve the underlying economy on which their ultimate fortune depends. And speculators, disregarding Heisenberg's uncertainty principle, take everything into account but themselves. All things do not remain equal for long, especially as technology makes trading ever faster and cyber-capitalists' own actions begin influencing others' and their own fortunes.

As this chapter has attempted to demonstrate, money is and always has been an image—a symbol circulating within a communication system. Over time, its shape and form have changed as the communication system in which it operates has changed. Speculators, always attempting to stay one step ahead of the herd, have been shown in different eras to reveal the inner logic of money's relationship to its communication system. In today's high-speed communication system, the speculator's latest challenge has been to escape the constraints of time. Money must move ever faster. Computer communication technology has made that possible. Although it is clear the financial system, along with money, is traveling at ever faster speeds, where it is heading remains a mystery.

REFERENCES

Bernstein, P.L. (1992). *Capital ideas: The improbable origins of modern Wall Street.* New York: Free Press.

Blume, M.E., Siegel, J.J., & Rottenberg, D. (1993). *Revolution on Wall Street: The rise and decline of the New York stock exchange.* New York: Norton.

Carey, J.W. (1988). *Communication as culture: Essays on media and society.* Boston: Unwin Hyman.

Cribb, J. (Ed.). (1986). *Money: From cowrie shells to credit cards.* London: British Museum Publication.

Drucker, P.F. (1993). *Post-capitalist society.* New York: HarperCollins.

Ewen, S. (1988). *All consuming images: The politics of style in contemporary culture.* New York: Basic Books.

Gibson, P. (1993). *Bear trap: Why Wall Street doesn't work.* New York: The Atlantic Monthly Press.

Gumpert, G., & Drucker, S.J. (1992). From the agora to the electronic shopping mall. *Critical Studies in Mass Communication, 9*(2), 186-200.

Kurtzman, J. (1993). *The death of money: How the electronic economy has destabilized the world's markets and created financial chaos.* New York: Simon & Schuster.

Levy, F. (1987). *Dollars and dreams: The changing American income distribution.* New York: Norton.

Logan, R.K. (1986). *The alphabet effect: The impact of the phonetic alphabet on the development of western civilization.* New York: St. Martin's Press.

Mitchell, W.C. (1950). *The role of money in economic theory. In The backward art of spending and other essays* (2nd ed., p. 170). New York: Augustus M. Keeley. (Original work published 1916)

Mosco, V., & Wasko, J. (Eds.). (1988). *The political economy of information.* Madison: University of Wisconsin Press.

"The office is a terrible place to work": Companies save and more work gets done when employees stay home. (1993, December 27). *Business Week*, p. 46.

Pruitt, S., & Barrett, T. (1991). Corporate virtual workspace. In M. Benedikt (Ed.), *Cyberspace: First steps* (pp. 81-118). Cambridge, MA.: MIT Press.

Richardson, D.W. (1970). *Electric money: Evolution of an electronic funds-transfer system.* Cambridge, MA: MIT Press.

The secret money machine. (1994, April 11). *Time,* pp. 28-35.

Stephens, M. (1988). *A history of news: From the drum to the satellite.* New York: Penguin.

Tucker, R.C. (Ed.). (1978). *The Marx-Engels reader* (2nd ed.). New York: Norton.

The virtual office becomes reality. (1993, October 28). *New York Times*, p. 1.

Werner, W., & Smith, S T. (1991). *Wall Street.* New York: Columbia University Press.

Zelizer, V.A. (1994). *The social meaning of money.* New York: Basic Books.

◇◇◇◇ 11

Constructing the Virtual Organization: Using a Multimedia Simulation for Communication Education

Terri Toles Patkin

There has been a great deal of speculation and fantasizing over virtual reality technologies, but what are the practical applications of virtual worlds? In this chapter, Terri Toles Patkin focuses on the technical and psychological challenges of constructing a simulation to aid in teaching organizational communication. Emphasizing a human factors (e.g., cognitive, instrumental, normative) approach to the design of human-computer interfaces, she explores the many features of multimedia and virtual reality that may contribute to the process of education, and profiles current work relating to the development of a "virtual organization" as a learning tool/environment. In Sections II, III, and IV, additional discussion on virtual reality appears in Herbert Zettl's aesthetic study in Chapter 5, Charles U. Larson's rhetorical analysis in Chapter 6, Sue Barnes's ecological analysis in Chapter 13, and Elizabeth Weiss's essay on virtual reality in the health club in Chapter 14; other research on education can be found in Stephanie Gibson's examination of the pedagogy of hypertext in Chapter 17; research also relevant to organizational communication includes Philip Thompsen's theoretical study of flaming in Chapter 20.

Virtual Reality (VR) has been in the headlines often recently, usually in juxtaposition with some exotic entertainment with a futuristic twist. Media personalities appear decked out in the requisite high-tech bodysuit as they try their hand at a new game, compare the results to Star Trek's holodeck, and snicker nervously about the possibility of teledildonics replacing the real thing. But is virtual reality simply the newest whiz-bang toy, or might it be used for serious applications in education? Certainly, with its ability to provide realism in an immersive computer simulation, virtual reality has the potential to alter the meaning of "experiential learning" significantly. This chapter reviews the current literature on virtual reality's human factors, particularly in relation to education, and describes the potential construction of one prototype education oriented virtual reality, the Virtual Organization, which uses a standard desktop PC.

WHY A VIRTUAL ORGANIZATION?

The advantages to students participating in a Virtual Organization go well beyond simple participation in a classroom exercise. Properly developed, the Virtual Organization will allow communication students to hone communication skills at their own pace and to focus on weaknesses. If needed, basic drill-and-practice exercises in grammar and punctuation could be incorporated for some students, whereas others could be challenged with more advanced techniques.

More significant than such short-term gains, however, would be the opportunity for students to wear a number of virtual hats. Communication students who get the chance to intern in organizations today generally report dissatisfaction with the tasks they are assigned. Dreams of creative fulfillment tend to be misplaced among the filing, telephone duty, and fact checking that typically constitute the intern's job description. Often the experience of a corporate environment and the chance to "network" provide more valuable experiences for the student than the substance of the assigned tasks.

The Virtual Organization would complement such internship experiences by providing students with a substantive example of organizational communication. As students progress through the simulation, they will be able to build on their knowledge and test their ability to perform new and interesting tasks. Although the real intern might prepare a mailing list, the virtual intern could also design the entire advertising campaign and test its effectiveness.

Different types of organizations, with differing cultures and unique communication needs, could also be developed. Students could try working in a small family business or a Fortune 500 headquarters during a single semester. They could then select the type of organization they would prefer to concentrate their efforts on in the future. The Virtual Organization simulation would supplement, not replace, current classroom and internship experiences.

VIRTUAL TECHNOLOGY AND REALITY

Virtual reality is a computer interface that enables people to participate directly in real-time three-dimensional environments created from computer-generated simulated environments, digitized images of people and objects, or imported video. Most inclusive are full-immersion systems that provide first-person interaction within the computer-generated world via head-mounted stereoscopic displays, gloves, bodysuits, and audio systems, in which computers generate images on goggles with liquid crystal displays, offering the user the sensation of being in a different place. Less-immersive environments include "through-the-window" approaches, in which the user sees a 3D world through the computer screen and steers via a spaceball or flying-mouse, and video-projected worlds that provide a second-person experience where the viewer stands outside the imaginary world but communicates with characters or entities inside it.

The origins of virtual reality include computer graphics, computer-aided design and drafting (CADD), auditory interfaces, military research (especially flight simulators), video games, mediated entertainments (such as the 1950s Sensorama depicting a motorcycle ride through New York City), video art exhibits (such as Videoplace, Video Living Rooms etc.), literature and film (especially science fiction and cyberpunk, particularly Gibson's *Neuromancer,* 1984), and entrepreneurial firms that produce hardware such as the dataglove for use with virtual reality. Applications can be found in CADD, computer games, the military, museums, theme parks, training and education, medicine, and manufacturing, to name just a few. Other application possibilities include remote performance of dangerous industrial tasks (e.g., nuclear disaster cleanup) or repairing spaceships or satellites from earth. Architects design buildings, tennis games are simulated, and surgeons practice delicate techniques (Krueger, 1991; Rheingold, 1991; Woolley, 1992).

Many of the current developments in virtual reality focus on entertainment, such as the Battletech Multiplayer Simulators that allow users to suit up in camouflage gear and practice driving a virtual tank, or amusement park games and rides that offer particularly realistic sensations. Of course, military applications have played a crucial role in the development of VR technology, and the military has sponsored the largest networked virtual simulation to date. The Department of Defense's SIMNET project has linked as many as 250 tank and helicopter simulators at multiple U.S. and European sites, allowing soldiers to practice on a virtual battlefield.

Virtual teleconferencing, manipulation of graphically rendered objects, telepresence surgery, architectural design, and vehicle movement are only a few examples of current civilian projects using VR techniques. Most work in this area is theoretical at present; few completed projects are on the market or even available as demonstrations. The most common projects include architectural walkthroughs that allow students to test design modifications, flight simulators, biological visualizations, and telepresence surgery.

Most of the VR projects described are simply too expensive, both financially and computationally, for widespread public use. However, low-end virtual reality is possible today. Price-competitive, 16-bit game machines targeted at the home market are driven primarily by the entertainment aspects associated with virtual reality rather than the simulated reality function. Because games and animated cartoons do not strive to duplicate the real world, they can create an internally consistent artificial world that provides an enjoyable and cost-effective experience. Important parameters for VR game displays include local pixel quality (smooth), global display appearance (fast response, readable text), global economic specifications (perception of telepresence even in a relatively narrow field of view, color, resolution), and unit manufacturing cost (low) (Becker, 1991).

At present, there seem to be more social prognostications regarding the effects of virtual reality than there are working VR environments. Technical barriers to development of virtual environments include tactile feedback, a slow frame rate, flat appearance of three-dimensional scenery, user resistance to the goggles and gloves required for sustained high-end applications, a lack of network support for multiple players, and the high cost of fully immersive environments. The literature seems split between highly technical data and social forecasts, but some work has been done on specific human factors relating to virtual reality.

Human Factors

Human factors refers to aspects of human performance, behavior, and desire that must be considered when designing any machine or information system, including issues relating to sensation, perception, participation, and experience. Some of what we know from experimental psychology about the basics of sensation may be applied to virtual reality, especially questions regarding perceptions of depth, shape, motion, texture, flavor, and localization. Making the experience of being in the virtual world as transparent as possible to the user is a primary goal of VR developers.

Some examples of human factors that must be considered in designing communication and human-computer interfaces include cognitive, instrumental, normative, expressive, and somatic factors. Cognitive factors include perception and psychophysics, attention, motivation, decision making and judgment, procedural memory, and semantic memory factors. Instrumental factors include individual, social, and organizational communication goals and the relationship to other communication instruments. Normative factors include cultural variation in communication expectation, performance or norms, contextual and environmental factors, and ethical considerations. Expressive factors include code usage and message variability, and somatic factors include anthropometry and biomechanics (Biocca, 1993).

Visual Factors

Current human factors research in virutal reality is preliminary and concentrates on visual and psychomotor testing, including vision testing (people are functionally nearsighted in the virtual world), color blindness, subject recognition, turning ability, search-and-locate tests, and manipulation tests. The battery of tests takes about two hours. Many of the tests are being done specifically for military applications and have predictable difficulties with generalizability beyond those scenarios (Morie, 1992). One test, for instance, involves recognizing a soldier as "ours" or "other" based on his uniform and weaponry.

It takes some practice to get used to navigating in a virtual environment. Game players at *Virtuality,* a chain of VR arcades, report that they need to play the game three or four times in order to feel comfortable with basic maneuvers, even after a brief video training session and assistance from the game attendant. Similarly, many VR users find it difficult to differentiate a virtual painting from simulated reality and tend to bump into the "wall" on which it is displayed (Latta, 1992).

Auditory Cues

One of the most overlooked aspects of the VR experience has been the rhythmic nature of visual, auditory, and kinesthetic experience. Poetic meter, musical beat, and behavioral cadence all have been shown to affect humans at primal levels, as the Muzak Corporation has so profitably shown. The most popular commercial video games are not necessarily those with the flashiest graphics or the most interesting storyline; they are the ones that start off at about 70 beats per minute and steadily increase in speed. Incorporating audio cues is an important feature contributing to the participant's perception of "realness" in a virtual environment and costs are relatively low (Jones, 1993; Orr, 1992).

Social Factors

Early research into virtual reality has suggested that the emotional state experience of being in the virtual world is almost equivalent with that of being in the "real world," as measured by semantic differential scores of an architectural space. Certainly, experimental and field research in computer-mediated interaction indicates that despite the lack of nonverbal cues, low social presence, low media richness, and lack of social context cues, social bonds form and communities emerge (Walther, 1992).

In over 2,500 demos completed at the University of Washington's Human Interface Technology Laboratory, researchers have found that a large proportion of people do not even think to turn around with the VR helmet on because they simply are not used to the hardware. Users wearing headsets found it almost impossible to point to a physical object, whereas locating objects within the virtual world was easy. It may be that we can carry only one cognitive map in our head at a time (Weghorst, 1992). Novice users in particular require the support of another person familiar with the technology.

Despite some critiques of virtual reality as yet another solitary, mediated activity contributing to individual isolation, most people today participate in virtual environments as part of a social event. In public demonstrations or video arcades, it is necessary to have a monitor on during the demo because people get lost, run into walls, forget how to maneuver, and so on (McLeod, 1992). Players at Virtuality arcade centers pay about $4 for 4 minutes of play, at which they have the opportunity to drive a virtual race car or tank, or shoot at an animated pterodactyl. Other arcade visitors can watch their progress on a television screen and freely offer advice to the participants. This phenomenon may, of course, diminish over time as VR technology becomes more widely available in inexpensive home formats, in much the same way that the introduction of the personal computer into the nation's family rooms has encouraged computing as a solitary activity.

Philosophical Issues

Cyberphilosophers warn about the importance of integrating the real body with the virtual body. The emotional attachment that a player holds for his or her computer construct can be intense, as evidenced by the strong bonding made by players in text-based virtual realities (MUDS; Multi-User Dungeons). Players in these virtual communities evince a close affective bond with their online personae and can experience very real distress when their "cyberalter ego" suffers a setback.

The human cost of VR use can include some significant psychological and physiological symptoms, including brain-body lag, self-identity split, and a split between primary body and cyberbody (Heim, 1993), particularly for heavy users of the technology. Health issues may include headaches from spending too much time in a virtual environment, disease transmission from the equipment, pain, fatigue, disorientation, motion sickness, and trauma (Latta, 1992). Some have raised concerns about the potential for addictive or abusive behavior via VR technology, but the question of ethics remains largely unexplored.

Rather than the traditional view of the computer as rival (a chess partner or artificial intelligence adversary), virtual reality's conception of the computer is paradigmatically different: The computer functions as a contact lens—transparent but still affecting what and how the user sees. Cyberspace weaves together language, technology, architecture, and mathematics to create a place where mind and machine merge (Benedikt, 1991). Unlike previous computer interfaces, virtual reality includes the viewer inside the message; the medium is not only the message, it is also the viewer.

EDUCATION AND VIRTUAL REALITY

The use of virtual reality in educational settings is based on the assumption that active learning provides a superior experience to passive learning, a notion that can be traced back at least as far as Dewey. Students who participate in responsive learning environments in which they become engaged in full body-mind kinesthetic learning not only retain more information but also manifest a fuller understanding of the information presented.

One of the key assumptions of VR work is that the brain can process information better when it is presented through sight, sound, and touch instead of just text and numbers. Putting a virtual environment at the disposal of teachers could allow students not only to observe, for example, daily life in ancient Greece, but also allow them to participate in interactive discussions of philosophy with Socrates or science with Aristotle. Alternate paths could be explored; students might restage the Civil War or experiment with a variety of physical or historical concepts.

Computer-based instructional simulations allow learners to practice the skills needed for real-life situations without the risks of injury or equipment damage that actual practice might involve. Flight simulators, space station operations, nuclear reactor repair, and police work have all successfully provided scenarios for virtual practice grounds. One distinct advantage of the virtual environment lies in its ability to present a simplified reality to the beginner, with complicating factors stripped out of the scenario until the student is ready to handle more complexity. First the pilot learns to land the plane, then he or she can try it in a crosswind.

Virtual learning environments promise to be more active than traditional classrooms, less formal, perhaps more fun, and provide a greater range of experiences. The attributes of virtual reality that make it potentially useful for education include flexibility in the creation of virtual worlds, ability to support a feeling of presence, the ability of the user to control and interact with objects and characters within the virtual world, and physical feedback from the virtual world. Whether original source materials (videos or documents) or simulated environments (computer generations) are used, users may participate in problem solving, concept development, and creative expression. Three primary applications exist: visualization (seeing connections and relationships that would otherwise be difficult to comprehend, such as architectural structure), simulation (synthetic replication of some real-life experience, such as flying a plane), and constructing participatory virtual environments (such as a rainforest or the Lascaux caves; (Ferrington & Loge, 1992; Middleton, 1992; Randall, 1992).

Although most projects have to date simulated physical actions (behavior of water, wind, molecules, etc.), there is no reason that virtual reality might not be used for more abstract skills as well, although graphical representation will be more challenging. Virtual reality might, for example, be applied to the training of people in cross-cultural communication; for instance, an American business traveler could practice appropriate negotiation skills with a virtual Japanese client. Portions of the scenario could be practiced as many times as necessary for comprehension or success, and continual feedback can focus the student's efforts on weak areas (Meyer & Dunn-Roberts, 1992).

Early work has shown that students can effectively learn new tasks such as spatial navigational skills in virtual reality, and students report that it is possible to interact with the illusory world as if it were real (Regian, Shebilske, & Monk, 1992). Such simulations effectively train students to apply specific knowledge to new situations. When students play a role (such as tank commander in a military simulation), their newly acquired knowledge can be effectively translated into a field setting (Shlecter, Bessemer, & Kolosh, 1992).

CONSTRUCTING THE VIRTUAL ORGANIZATION

The Virtual Organization represents an electronic case study approach in which the communication student is given the opportunity to solve a variety of problems in a simulated organizational setting. The immersive graphical interface allows for interactive exercises in organizational communication to take place. Simulations can be created using any of the desktop VR toolkits, including Virtual Reality Studio, Virtus VR, or VREAM, all object-oriented VR development systems that allow the user to design, build, enter, and interact with virtual worlds using a windowed, mouse-driven graphical user interface on a desktop PC. Higher end VR hardware such as head-mounted displays, three-dimensional tracking systems, and gloves may also be incorporated. The prototype described here simply utilizes a through-the-window approach with a 486 PC and a standard mouse.

The structure of the simulation somewhat resembles a game. A game requires that users be given a goal, most often through providing an increase in a "score" following the performance of a series of actions. In an entertainment setting, this could include finding a treasure, solving a puzzle, or winning a battle against an object or another player. In the organizational setting, points can be earned for such activities as correctly proofing a press release, following guidelines for scheduling a press conference, planning a crisis response, or resolving a conflict.

The student begins the game as a part-time intern assigned the most routine tasks, such as editing an already prepared press release. When a certain number of tasks have been completed, the student is offered a summer job, in which more complicated problems are presented, such as writing a press release from already assembled facts. Successful completion of this level earns the player a full-time job offer in the Virtual Organization at the level of Communication Assistant. Here the tasks become more complex again and require a greater level of independent thought until the student progresses through a number of ranks and finally is promoted to Vice President for Corporate Communication. The tasks become progressively less reactive (in-basket exercises, decision making, negotiation tactics), and students must ultimately plan a long-term communication strategy for the organization.

A good game must have both breadth and depth. Breadth is the extent to which the simulation is able to deal with things the players want to do. If there is water, the players may want to swim; if there are trees, players may want to climb them. Depth expresses a sense of the level of detail provided. Games with good depth generally model the real world to some extent. For example, a glass object will break when dropped on a hard surface, but not if it is dropped on a soft surface. Although this can become computationally expensive, its judicious use enriches the player's experience of the "reality" of the illusion. In the Virtual Organization, the illusion is enhanced by the graphical interface that permits visualization of an office space, ranging from a cubicle for the Assistant to a spacious corner office for the Vice President, as well as cartoon-like representations of coworkers, clients, and supervisors.

Text can also contribute to the sense of reality. Interactions can be simulated through careful compilations of text that guide the player through the scenario at hand. For example, dialogue in a software code inspection simulation is dynamically constructed using the history of the current game, simulated situation, and character definitions given by the player as guidelines (Christel, 1992).

Interactivity provides perhaps the most sophisticated sense of reality for the user. Interactivity is built through software links, in which certain conditions (pushing a button on a radio) will cause certain responses (music is played). Links may be triggered by actions of the viewer (touching or moving an object, entering a room) or actions of objects within the world (a thrown object collides with a wall and bounces accordingly). The simulation will utilize text windows as one linked response. For example, students who take initiative beyond the minimum requirements of the simulation may enable a link to a window in which a glowing letter appears in their virtual personnel file. Links can also be performed with external calls to a program, batch file, or DOS command. Students who touch the virtual in-basket could be transported to a word processing program, CD-ROM, spreadsheet, or database, and then returned to the virtual office once they have completed the assigned task.

Later versions of the simulation will additionally incorporate complete multimedia capabilities, including full-motion video, audio, and hypertext links. Students may be able to interview characters online through careful editing of stock phrases uttered in response to some keyword (Summitt, 1993, offers a parallel structure for creating a virtual newsroom). Eventually, the scenario could even be distributed on CD-ROM, which would increase the flexibility and portability of the simulation (Smith, 1992). In later versions, the student's response will influence the scenario itself. A poorly prepared press release could lead to negative news coverage, which might in turn influence sales, thus necessitating a series of follow-up actions by the student.

The ultimate interactivity, of course, comes from human interaction. It is hoped that later versions of the Virtual Organization will incorporate multiple players, perhaps an entire class, with full electronic mail and interactive chat capabilities added to the scenario. Interactivity is the critical element in computer media, and the interactivity of multiple users within virtual reality potentially creates the most interesting experience. In a study of a text-based "virtual classroom" setting, no significant differences in mastery of course material occurred between the virtual and traditional classrooms, but the majority of students reported that the virtual classroom improved the quality of the learning experience, particularly when "group learning" was experienced (Hiltz, 1993).

Interestingly, the Virtual Organization concept has already been introduced by some not-at-all-virtual organizations through the introduction of computer-mediated communication at all levels of the workforce. For example, the Social Virtual Reality project at Xerox PARC is extending MUD technology into nonrecreational settings, particularly in the scientific community. A social virtual reality is a software system that allows several people to interact in pseudo-spatial settings that are text based. Real-time audio and video as well as window-based graphical user interfaces complement the text base to make the computer-mediated experience competitive with face-to-face communication in the workplace (Curtis & Nichols, 1993). The Virtual Organization simulation could one day be a student's first experience with an organizational media environment that will later be encountered on the job.

REFERENCES

Becker, A. (1991, July). *Virtual reality for home game machines.* Paper presented at the Virtual Reality Symposium, Tokyo.

Benedikt, M. (Ed.). (1991). *Cyberspace: First steps.* Cambridge: MIT Press.

Biocca, F. (1993). Communication research in the design of communication interfaces and systems. *Journal of Communication, 43*(4), 59-68.

Christel, M. (1992). Virtual reality today on a PC. *Instruction Delivery Systems, 6*(4), 6-9.

Curtis, P., & Nichols, D.A. (1993). *MUDs grow up: Social virtual reality in the real world.* Palo Alto, CA: Xerox PARC.

Ferrington, G., & Loge, K. (1992). Virtual reality: A new learning environment. *The Computing Teacher, 19*(7), 16-19.

Gibson, W. (1984). *Neuromancer.* New York: Ace Books.

Heim, M. (1993). *The metaphysics of virtual reality.* New York: Oxford University Press.

Hiltz, S.R. (1993). Correlates of learning in a virtual classroom. *International Journal of Man-Machine Studies, 39,* 71-98.

Jones, S. (1993). A sense of space: Virtual reality, authenticity and the aural. *Critical Studies in Mass Communication, 10*(3), 238-252.

Krueger, M. (1991). *Artificial reality II.* Reading MA: Addison Wesley.

Latta, J.N. (1992). The quest for virtual reality applications. In *Proceedings, DPMA Virtual Reality Conference.* Washington, DC.

McLeod, D. (1992). Art and virtual environments. In *Proceedings, DPMA Virtual Reality Conference.* Washington, DC.

Meyer, C., & Dunn-Roberts, R. (1992). Virtual reality: A strategy for training in cross-cultural communication. *Educational Media International, 29*(3), 175-180.

Middleton, T. (1992). Applications of virtual reality to learning. *Interactive Learning International, 8*(4), 253-257.

Morie, J.F. (1992). Multi-disciplinary history of VR and IST in VR research. In *Proceedings, DPMA Virtual Reality Conference.* Washington, DC.

Orr, J.N. (1992). Anthropocybersynchronicity: Rhythm and intimacy in VR. In *Proceedings, DPMA Virtual Reality Conference.* Washington, DC.

Randall, J.P. (1992). The emerging potential of virtual reality in postsecondary education. *New Directions for Teaching and Learning, 51,* 77-01.

Regian, J.W., Shebilske, W.L., & Monk, J.M. (1992). Virtual reality: An instructional medium for visual-spatial tasks. *Journal of Communication, 42*(2), 136-149.

Rheingold, H. (1991). *Virtual reality.* New York: Summit Books.

Smith, D. (1992). VR and multimedia: An evolutionary approach. In *Proceedings, DPMA Virtual Reality Conference.* Washington, DC.

Shlecter, T.M., Bessemer, D.W., & Kolosh, K.P. (1992). Computer-based simulation systems and role-playing: An effective combination for fostering conditional knowledge. *Journal of Computer-Based Instruction, 19*(4), 110-114.

Summitt, P.M. (1993). *News, information and knowledge in cyberspace.* Unpublished manuscript.

Walther, J.B. (1992). Interpersonal effects in computer-mediated interaction. *Communication Research, 19*(1), 52-90.

Weghorst, S. (1992). Human factors in virtual reality design. In *Proceedings, DPMA Virtual Reality Conference.* Washington, DC.

Woolley, B. (1992). *Virtual worlds.* Cambridge: Blackwell.

◊◊◊◊ 12

Playing at Community: Multi-User Dungeons and Social Interaction in Cyberspace

Michael P. Beaubien

Of all the cyberplaces currently available online, none try harder to generate a sense of place than Multi-User Dungeons (MUDs). In this chapter, Michael P. Beaubien examines this cyberspace alternative to face-to-face gaming, explaining how they have evolved from fantasy board games into text-based, role-playing computer games. He makes it clear that MUDs, which are communities involving thousands of users from all over the world, have important lessons to teach us regarding free expression and social responsibility. In particular, he considers the linguistic and social implications of MUDs' promotion of uninhibited communications and the mutual construction of social space, arguing that the mastery of programming languages constitutes true power in cyberspace. Apart from Section II, related discussions of virtual community can be found in Gary Gumpert and Susan J. Drucker's examination of computer-mediated social space in Chapter 1, John M. Phelan's essay on cyberspace utopianism in Chapter 2, Richard Cutler's discussion of relationships in MUDs in Chapter 21, and Mark Lipton's exploration of cybersex in Chapter 22; an alternate view of cyberspace power appears in James R. Beniger's essay on the control of cyberspace in Chapter 3.

Imagine standing on the moon chatting with an alien dressed in a blue leisure suit. Imagine building your dream home out of Cheerios. Imagine seducing a brown-eyed, brown-haired, four-legged raccoon-like creature of indiscriminate gender. This is just a sampling of what can and does happen everyday in the worlds of Multi-User Dungeons (MUDs).

Known originally as Multi-User Dungeons and now often referred to more generically as Multi-User Dimensions, Multi-User Simulated Environments (MUSE), or MUDs, Object Oriented (MOO); MUDs are computer-based, role-playing games that create social environments in cyberspace. Unlike other computer games where players are confronted with entirely preprogrammed environments, MUDs provide a multiuser space, where, through programming, players create and constantly redefine the fundamental reality in which they interact. In effect, MUDs serve as highly structured, programmable communications media. Currently, most MUDs rely on a text-based interface, in which whole worlds are defined solely through written descriptions and typed dialogue. However, as the creators of Lucasfilm's graphics-based Habitat MUD affirm, "cyberspace is defined more by the interactions among the actors within it than by the technology with which it is implemented" (Morningstar & Farmer, 1993, p. 274). Whether sitting at a keyboard or donning a headset and bodysuit, entering cyberspace is an involving experience.

Text-based MUDs, for instance, despite their "primitive" interface, have no shortage of immersive appeal. In most instances, a player can access a MUD 24 hours a day, 7 days a week, from almost anywhere in the world. Some players, usually students with free Internet accounts, log up to 80 hours a week in these alternate worlds. Because MUDs have proven to be so addictive, they have been banned not only from Amherst College, but from the entire continent of Australia, where data links to the rest of the world are few and precious (Kelly & Rheingold, 1993).

THE ORIGIN OF MUDS

Physically, MUDs exist as lines of code on computer hard drives and can be accessed via modem over the Internet or through private online services. Newcomers ("newbies" in MUD lingo) can log in, select a name for their character, provide a description, and wander off to explore. Players can move around by typing commands like "go east" or "climb stairs." Whenever they enter a room they are given a text description that mentions prominent features and obvious exits. When a player enters a room it is announced to the other players, so that the screen might read, "Matilda enters east." Most games allow players to "talk," which can be heard by everyone in the room, and to "whisper," so that two players can converse only with each other. More advanced players usually learn how to talk to players in a different room, or even to *teleport*, materializing in any room they choose.

There are currently in excess of 300 MUDs in the world, with a regular player base in the tens of thousands (Germain, 1993; Leslie, 1993). Although most early MUDs were designed around adventure themes, akin to *Dungeons and Dragons*, the diversification of the Internet has lead to a much greater variety of available themes for "MUDders." Players can participate in MUDs based on Star Trek or set in a postnuclear holocaust. One MUD, called LambdaMOO and created by Xerox computer scientist Pavel Curtis, is based on the floor plan of Curtis's house. Another MUD, called FurryMuck, is populated entirely by furry animals (Quittner, 1994). MicroMUSE, based at MIT's artificial intelligence lab, was designed to promote collaborative work between children and adults. Its centerpiece is Cyberion City, a space station orbiting the earth, where killing is outlawed and children as young as 6 years old log on to explore. The most recent trend in MUDs is toward creating nonfantasy environments for professionals, where shop talk and social interaction go hand in hand. MediaMOO, for instance, is a MUD intended to serve as a professional virtual community for media researchers. In January 1993, on the night of President Clinton's inaugural ball, MediaMOO held an inaugural ball of its own, complete with outrageous costumes and lavish accommodations. Another MUD, called the Jupiter Project, will include voice and image capabilities in creating a virtual research center for the international astronomy community. Despite these recent developments in "serious" MUDding, however, most MUDs remain committed to free-wheeling fantasy play. Where these are concerned, the possibilities are as limitless as language itself.

The appeal of MUDs as a form of entertainment and a forum for interaction can be traced to three mutually reinforcing characteristics: (a) the games involve multiple players who interact directly, (b) role playing promotes free and creative expression, and (c) MUDs are computer mediated, which creates a dynamic, responsive, and immersive space in which to play. Each of the various antecedents of MUDs exhibit some of these characteristics, but none provides such a powerful combination. Most games involve multiple players, such as basketball, chess, or Monopoly, but these usually require a player to adopt a narrow role and to perform fairly specific functions. MUDs, on the other hand, require deep personal involvement because open-ended role playing calls for a great breadth of possible roles and functions. Single-user computer games are another antecedent of MUDs. Some of these involved extended fantasy role playing, such as *Adventure* and *Zork*, but these were limited to whatever scenarios and options were programmed into the game, and only one player at a time could occupy the gaming space. Even the cleverest programming is no substitute for human spontaneity. Still other games, such as the MUD namesake *Dungeons and Dragons*, involve multiplayer role playing, but these are confined to game boards and neighborhood friends. They lack the urgency and sense of immersion provided by computers. Although MUDs have clearly benefited from these other forms of gaming, they have moved beyond them to create a new occasion for human interaction.

The first MUD to appear on the Internet, created in 1980 at the University of Essex (Kelly & Rheingold, 1993), was only intended to be an electronic version of *Dungeons and Dragons*, but with the leap into cyberspace, many things changed about the way the game was played. Rather than neighborhood friends gathered around a game board, MUDs are played only via networked computer. This seemingly slight change had a dynamic impact on the experience of gaming.

Most games create a symbolic space that serves to simplify and simulate some aspects of reality. These symbols are mapped out on a board, graph, or field so that their respective positioning creates the potential for certain types of meaningful interaction (the specific meanings are determined by the symbols involved and the moves of the players). Such designs are meant to simulate action that occurs, or could conceivably occur, in physical space. Monopoly, for instance, is based on a simple model of real estate development, whereas football reflects a pseudo-militaristic strategy of attack and defense. Similarly, some of the most elaborate gaming simulations came out of war games, which used octagonal graphs to map the action. It was experience with medieval war game simulations that lead Dave Arneson and E. Gary Gygax to develop the first versions of *Dungeons and Dragons* in the early 1970s (Fine, 1983). Rather than creating simple, conditional "if-then" contingencies, *Dungeons and Dragons* drew increasingly on a variety of computer-generated statistical manuals that allowed for a greater breadth of possible outcomes. As one young *Dungeons and Dragons* fan raved, "In D and D there is so much in the world. It's so big. There is an incredible amount of data" (Turkle, 1985, p. 80). Although not yet computer mediated, early *Dungeons and Dragons* clearly owed much of its richness and depth to the data processing power of the computer.

This more open-ended approach represented a more realistic, more complex attempt to simulate reality, to create a kind of virtual encounter. As comprehensive and spontaneous as these simulations became, however, they still lacked the immediate, immersive quality that is the mark of most computer games. As Sherry Turkle (1985) put it, "When you play a video game . . . [y]ou have to do more than identify with a character on the screen. You must act for it. Identification through action has a special kind of hold. . . . For many people, what is being pursued in the video game is not just a score, but an altered state of mind" (p. 83). The added element of role playing in MUDs means that, rather than acting for an object, players can act for themselves, or for the self that they create as their gaming persona. As computers can enhance the complexity of the gaming space, they can also accommodate complex gaming personas that simulate the self.

Another way of considering the notion of gaming space is as a matter of boundaries and of context. Edward T. Hall's (1989) discussions of high-and low-cultural contexts provides a useful framework. Most games are relatively "high-context" because the rules by which they are played are well established and the boundaries between the game and real life are clearly drawn. The reality represented by the gaming situation ends at the sidelines or at the edge of the game board. MUDs, however, represent a "low context" communications environment, where all interaction occurs within the simulated reality of the gaming space. Players cannot chat with each other across the game board because they are all *in the game*. Even when conversation does veer away from gaming, it is impossible to leave one's gaming persona completely behind because there is no clear way to distinguish it from the invisible, presumably "real" player sitting at a computer somewhere.

MUD players also have fewer communications options open to them than co-present gamers because most MUDs rely solely on text. This will change with time and increased processing power, but even multimedia communication lacks the range of communicational possibilities inherent in co-present interaction. Whereas *Dungeons and Dragons* players are usually gathered together in the same room, MUD players are often physically separated by hundreds and even thousands of miles. One important characteristic of such low-context environments, Hall points out, is that they are open to manipulation. Howard Rheingold (1993) tells the story of a MUDder who proposed marriage to a fellow player named Sue, only to find out that Sue was actually a married British man named Steve, who had recently been arrested for defrauding the Department of Transport. As Rheingold states, "the opportunity for deception . . . is designed into the medium. Cyberspace explorers ignore that fact at their peril" (p. 166).

The main difference between MUDs and their forerunner, *Dungeons & Dragons*, is the medium involved—the computer, and the cyberspace it establishes. To understand MUDs, one has to understand the crucial role that computer programming plays in the design and everyday functioning of MUDs. Currently, most MUDs allow some form of computer programming *within the game* so that players can actually change the game itself as they play. This is considerably different from a high-context gaming environment, in which rules can be changed only through consensual agreement, often requiring the approval of some organizational body. In MUDs, as in much of cyberspace, individual programmers can change the rules of the game on their own with very real consequences for the other players. Because of this, MUDs are often compared to lawless frontier towns where it is every player for him- or herself. Not surprisingly, this has led to groups of "cybercitizens" banding together in an attempt to gain more control over their virtual communities. MUDs are important to cyberspace as a whole because they provide testing grounds where these kinds of conflicts can be "played" out. Rheingold makes it clear that such issues have larger social implications:

> And our attempts to analyze the second-level impacts of phenomena like MUDs on our real-life relationships and communities lead to fundamental questions about social values in an age when so many of our human relationships are mediated by communications technology. (p. 146)

In a world in which computers are quickly becoming the most ubiquitous technology, the importance of understanding the implications of MUDdish interaction looms large. The following example illustrates some of these points.

A CYBERRAPE

In the December 21, 1993 issue of the *Village Voice*, Julian Dibbell wrote an article called "A Rape in Cyberspace," which recounted a virtual rape that had occurred in the previously mentioned LambdaMOO MUD in March 1993. Let us begin with the virtual narrative. The aggressor in the event was a character named Mr. Bungle, who began his assault in LambdaMOO's living room by using a voodoo doll to force Legba, one of the room's occupants, to have sex with him. Legba appropriately cursed Mr. Bungle out during the ordeal, and Bungle was ejected from the room. His voodoo doll worked at a distance, however, and he subsequently drew three other individuals into his atrocities, forcing them to violate themselves and each other in violent ways. Finally, an experienced player named Zippy arrived and fired a magic gun at Mr. Bungle, which created a cage that even the voodoo doll's powers could not penetrate. The episode was over.

Stripped of its colorful narrative trappings, this is what happened. Mr. Bungle, a student logging into LambdaMOO from New York University, wrote a subprogram (the voodoo doll) that allowed him to attribute actions to other players that they did not write. The entire encounter took place as lines of text scrolling slowly up the screens of those players who happened to be in the living room of LambdaMOO that evening. The gun was another subprogram that cut off Mr. Bungle's channel of communication. The substance of the attacks was a matter of some perverse creative writing on the part of Mr. Bungle. The victims were physically hundreds and even thousands of miles away.

The crime, however, was taken very seriously by the regular residents of LambdaMOO. The reason for this is that regular players put a lot of time into building their game characters, which means that along the way they put a lot of themselves into the characters as well. The more established and skilled they become, the larger the stake they have in maintaining the character and the world in which it moves, even if it is a world built from text. Other media have helped to bring us to this point, in which vicarious participation can at times seem more important than the physical circumstances in which we are immersed. Vicarious or not, the sense of participation is real. *Cyberspace*—the social space created by using computers as a communications medium—has proven to be a powerful and involving form of interaction. As the residents of LambdaMOO found out, deep involvement in the game only makes the situation that much more confusing when one is asked to draw boundaries between the game and reality.

This is clearly illustrated by what happened in LambdaMOO in the wake of Mr. Bungle's attack. The MUD's sense of communal identity was clearly in jeopardy, so the matter of what to do with Mr. Bungle was a cause for very serious discussion. The ensuing debate on bulletin boards and in LambdaMOO was intense, but when all was said and said, nothing definite had been done. This was not the end of the incident, however. JoeFeedback, a wizard (the highest level of player) who had followed the events with great concern, took it upon himself to resolve the situation in the absence of a consensus. So he eliminated Mr. Bungle from the database. The community had failed to arrive at a democratic resolution to the incident, so JoeFeedback acted alone.

Soon afterward the game's creator, Pavel Curtis, returned to find his virtual community fractured. To address the problem of self-governance he imposed universal suffrage on LambdaMOO by installing a system of petitions and ballots whereby anyone could lobby for a vote regarding any action that required a wizard's programming ability. In eight months, 11 ballot measures were passed, which created new commands to eject out-of-control characters and established an ad-hoc system of arbitration to settle player disputes. LambdaMOO even has an architectural review board that selects new additions to the MUD so that it does not grow out of control. All in all, participation has been robust, and Bungle-like dilemmas have been successfully avoided.

LESSONS AND CONCLUSIONS

There are lessons to be learned from this tale, lessons relating to the nature of computer-mediated interaction as exemplified by MUDs. In order to better understand this situation, it is useful to apply Jean-François Lyotard's (1991) arguments concerning language games to communication in MUDs. In *The Postmodern Condition*, Lyotard argues that meaning is created socially through participating in language games, in which the rules defining a game must be "agreed on by its present players and subject to eventual cancellation" (p. 61). MUDs, then, can be seen as social locations where these language games can be played with great vigor, owing to the freedom provided by virtual anonymity and the feeling of power and control that comes with computing. The incident at LambdaMOO exemplifies the kind of conflicts that can occur as these language games are played out. Ultimately, the problems experienced by the residents of LambdaMOO in their attempt to define their community can be traced to an insufficient understanding of how the computer medium affects language games. The electronic town halls of cyberspace, it turns out, are much different than the wood and stone town halls of our forebears.

After relating the case of the LambdaMOO rape, Dibbell (1993) proposed his explanation for the confusion that can accompany deep immersion in the virtual worlds of MUDs, offering his thoughts not as an argument, but "as a kind of prophecy":

> Anyone the least bit familiar with the workings of the new era's definitive technology, the computer, knows that it operates on a principle impracticably difficult to distinguish from the pre-Enlightenment principle of the magic word: the commands you type into a computer are a kind of speech that doesn't so much communicate as *make things happen*. . . . I can no longer convince myself

> that our wishful insulation of language from the realm of action has ever been anything but a valuable kludge, a philosophically damaged stopgap against oppression that would just have to do till something truer and more elegant came along. (p. 42; emphasis in original)

Here Dibbell is asserting that computer technology imbues language with new power. To a user immersed in this type of computer-mediated textual environment, language assumes the guise of action, because in MUDs words can make things happen. Because computers are the "era's definitive technology," Dibbell argues, the disintegration of the distinction between language and action is destined to become a broad social trend. By calling his musing a "prophecy," Dibbell lends a certain sense of the inevitable to this transformation.

Although this is indeed an intriguing observation, it has more to do with perception than with reality. By assuming that this trend is somehow inevitable, Dibbell is endorsing the confusion of language games that can occur with computer-mediated communication. Specifically, it is the language of computer programming that imbues the entire computing experience with special efficacy. As one of the many language games floating around in the low-context sprawl of cyberspace, computer programming tends to become mixed in with all the other functions of language. Simple commands are a part of the flow of conversation, a normal part of the linguistic terrain. This is especially true for MUDs, where learning the programming code is often built into the process of gaming. As players advance in a game they are given access to more programming information. This was a natural fit with the mythology of *Dungeons and Dragons*—the wizards know the most magical incantations.

The events in LambdaMOO were played out exactly according to this hierarchy. Mr. Bungle was capable enough to write a subprogram that gave him power over other players. Zippy was a skilled enough programmer to thwart him, and JoeFeedback was advanced enough to remove him from the database. Curtis, the ultimate source of the source code, clearly has god-like powers in controlling the realm he created. The fact that the wizards in LambdaMOO seem to be fairly beneficent is laudable, but this is historically not the case in most MUDs, in which wizards are generally free to be as capricious with their powers as Greek gods. The discussion about the Bungle affair in LambdaMOO seemed a model of democratic debate, with everyone having their say. This demonstrates quite clearly the difference between speech and action. The discussion was a wonderful example of free speech, but JoeFeedback demonstrated soon enough, through the activity of programming, where the real power in computer-mediated communities lies.

Programming, rather than being part of the flow of what is being communicated, allows players to *alter the environment in which the communication is taking place*. As much as it may blend into the linguistic terrain, programming must always be recognized as the privileged language game of cyberspace. As such, it is capable of purely constructing reality rather than in any sense reflecting it. It is the difference between creation and utilization. Through programming a person can create a MUD from scratch. Players who use the MUD to create a self are working from within a more basic construct supplied by the programmer. It is the tension between these two levels that is the root of many social problems in MUDs. The reason that the rape in LambdaMOO was taken so seriously is that, through programming, Mr. Bungle altered the rules of interaction. In doing so, he not only verbally raped his target characters, he raped the entire constructed reality and, by extension, the constructed selves of all the other players. Access to programming, to the fundamental reality of that virtual world, is what made the violation possible.

Any cyberspace community, then, must directly and self-consciously address the issue of what place programming will take in the societal structure. Turkle (1985) sees the inclusion or exclusion of programming from a game as the fundamental dividing line between future generations of video games. Habitat, for instance, was designed from the beginning to accommodate broad consumer usage—several thousand players at any given time. Like most commercial software, the basic code for the game was kept beyond the reach of the players so that there would be no "leakage" between the structural level that defines the reality of the virtual world and the experiential level of images and words (the interface) with which players interact. This was done to save players from the distraction of worrying about maintaining the game and to prevent players from cheating, which is defined as "gain[ing] an unfair advantage over the other players, an advantage moreover of which they may be unaware" (Morningstar & Farmer, 1993, p. 292). Such an approach would have prevented the rape in LambdaMOO because Mr. Bungle would not have been able to use his programming skills to an unfair advantage. In Habitat, system operators have learned to solve problems within the experiential level of the game. In one instance, a systems operator playing the role of Death lost his magic gun, which was picked up by a player. When the player refused to give the gun back, the operator threatened to cancel his account. The threat worked, but it also violated the experiential reality of the game. When this happened again, the operators maintained their role as Death and negotiated (quite flamboyantly) a deal in which they paid to get the gun back. They refused to use the real weapon in their possession, their programming, and thereby maintained the integrity of the world they created.

For all the richness of Habitat, however, it is MUDs like LambdaMOO that offer the most complex environments, specifically because they take the risk of allowing additional programming on the part of the players. The issues raised by these MUDs concerning freedom, programming, and power reflect questions being grappled with by the Net as a whole. Should the government have the key to all privacy codes so that they can monitor communication on the Net? Should corporations control the infrastructure of the Net to more readily serve the capitalistic ebb and flow of supply and demand? As the makers of Habitat suggest, we should not be distracted from these fundamental issues by the more colorful discussion of what type of interface will prevail when a person enters cyberspace.

Whether people peck away at keyboards or attach electrodes to their heads, questions concerning structure, access, and control in cyberspace will still apply.

Lyotard (1991) suggests that our goal as a society should be to foster a communications system of perfect information and complete freedom. If we are to approach this goal in the construction of cyberspace, we must deal self-consciously with questions about the power of programming and the involving, often bewildering nature of computer-mediated communication. This will require some attempt from each "cybercommunity," and from society at large, to define a set of common values and priorities. Will it be the prescriptions of government, the motives of business, or the collective actions of the community of participants that determine the dominant institutions of cyberspace? Whatever the future holds, the vitality of MUD life illustrates that there should always be room on the Net for people to participate in virtual communities controlled by the users themselves, with all the risks that entails. From programmers this will require the most basic social virtue—the responsible use of freedom.

REFERENCES

Dibbell, J. (1993, December 21). A rape in cyberspace. *Village Voice*, pp. 36-42.

Fine, G.A. (1983). *Shared fantasy: Role-playing games as social worlds.* Chicago: University of Chicago Press.

Germain, E. (1993, September 13). In the jungle of MUD. *Time*, p. 61.

Hall, E.T. (1989). *Beyond culture.* New York: Anchor Books.

Kelly, K., & Rheingold, H. (1993, July/August). "The dragon ate my homework . . . " *Wired*, pp. 68-73.

Leslie, J. (1993, September). MUDroom. *Atlantic*, pp. 28-34.

Lyotard, J.-F. (1991). *The postmodern condition: A report on knowledge.* Minneapolis: University of Minneapolis Press.

Morningstar, C., & Farmer, R.F. (1993). The lessons of Lucasfilm's Habitat. In M. Benedikt (Ed.), *Cyberspace: First steps* (pp. 273-301). Cambridge: MIT Press.

Quittner, J. (1994, March). Johnny Manhattan meets the furrymuckers. *Wired*, pp. 92-97, 138.

Rheingold, H. (1993). *The virtual community: Homesteading on the electronic frontier.* Reading, MA: Addison-Wesley.

Turkle, S. (1985). *The second self: Computers and the human* spirit. New York: Touchstone.

SECTION 3

FORM: VIRTUAL REALITY AND HYPERMEDIA AS NEW KINDS OF SPACE AND NAVIGATION

Cyberspace may be intended to perform the same functions as physical space, but it does so by introducing new forms that are intrinsically different from real space and from other forms of mediated space (e.g., books, film). Through virtual reality and hypermedia, new perceptions and conceptualizations of space, location, dimension, direction, travel, and navigation are created. Of course, we cannot actually step into the computer and slide along the neural pathways of the CPU as movie characters sometimes do. In fact, the point of cyberspace communication is that it all can take place from the comfort of a chair. The illusion of immersion in a virtual landscape is based on the interface between user and computer: the graphic user interface (GUI) such as Windows or the Macintosh desktop; the keyboard, mouse, or joystick; the hypermediated "page" and links; or virtual reality and telepresence interfaces. Out of this interface with the digital world, familiar environments and objects gain new forms, and the boundaries between forms dissolve. Navigation takes on new meaning as well, as travel in cyberspace can be accomplished with a single keystroke; we can "move" from northeastern United

States to southwestern Australia without having to get out of our chairs and without any sense of motion, so seamless is most electronic navigation; on the other hand, it is quite easy to become "lost" in dataspace.

Sue Barnes begins the section by examining several forms of cyberspace, including virtual reality, telepresence, and ubiquitous computing in real spaces. Surveying such phenomena as cyberpunk, cyborgs, artificial intelligence, and artificial life, she explores the ecological pressures of this new environment and the forms of life and consciousness adapted to it. In doing so, she argues that bodiless existence in cyberspace is characterized by a number of paradoxes. The second chapter in this section, by Lizzy Weiss, presents a case study of a combined form of virtual reality and ubiquitous computing: the cybergym. What could be a more paradoxical application for cyberspace technology than the body-oriented health club? Weiss examines the digital impetus to sculpt bodies into conceptual perfection, connecting this surreal combination of the virtual and the actual to postmodern culture and its reconfiguring of the mind-body relationship.

Peggy Cassidy, in this section's third chapter, shifts the focus from the virtual to the digital, in an essay that opens up such forms to critical inquiry. Revisiting Walter Benjamin's arguments concerning mechanical reproduction, she extends them to the digital reproduction of experience, also calling on Daniel Boorstin's concept of the pseudo-event, and Jean Baudrillard and Umberto Eco's notion of hyperreality. Cassidy suggests that the utterly protean nature of digital experience and travel forces a rethinking of values. Stuart Moulthrop concentrates on typographic form, as it makes the transition from paper to screen, in the next chapter, which takes its name from *Writing on the Edge* (an electronic journal also produced in traditional print). Moulthrop argues for taking the plunge into complete immersion in electronic texts; if Moulthrop had his way you would be reading this on your screen, not holding a traditional printed book in your hands. In this piece he examines some reasons why print remains a dominant medium and electronic text still struggles to get inside the gate of the academic castle.

Continuing, in the fifth chapter of this section, with an examination of hypertext and hypermedia forms, Stephanie Gibson gives a broad overview of the pedagogical issues surrounding hypertext in the classroom (and as a classroom). Examining both positive and negative possibilities, and providing a comparison with printed text books, Gibson considers the impact of this new, more open form of textuality on teacher-student relationships. She also discusses its paradigmatic implications for both curriculum and canon. Finally, in this section's sixth chapter, Paul Lippert steps inside traditional cinema to examine the new routes carved out by cyberspace technologies. In a thoughtful piece that discusses class implications of concrete and abstract symbolic forms, Lippert proposes that cyberspace is itself digital, and representations of it are unnecessarily analogic. Ultimately, he is critical of postmodern and cyberpunk attempts to reify virtual space.

Communications technologies have traditionally altered our relationships with space and navigation. The telephone, for instance, allowed our physical selves to be in one spot while our voice and ears traveled metaphorically to another. The places we went were real, and there was an exchange of actual sensory experience. Because of the telephone, the manner in which humans interact has been irrevocably altered. What impact will cyberspace technologies have on human understanding and interaction? Some surprising food for thought follows.

✧✧✧✧ 13

Cyberspace: Creating Paradoxes for the Ecology of Self

Sue Barnes

A recurring theme in this anthology is the impact of the cyberspace environment on conceptions of the self. In this chapter, Sue Barnes employs an ecological approach, taking the reader on a tour of artificial environments and the life forms that are or may be adapted to them. In doing so, she explains the trend-setting desire of cyberculture aficionados to create and maintain consciousness solely in cyberspace, and the resulting philosophical and social paradoxes. Covering topics as diverse as science fiction, cyberpunk style, artificial intelligence and artificial life, virtual reality, telepresence, and ubiquitous computing (in which computers are installed into physical environments, creating media spaces), she is concerned with all forms of digital incursion into everyday life and their impact on the delicate balance between self and environment. Aside from this section of the book, other perspectives on cyberspace and the self can be found in Jay David Bolter's essay in Chapter 7, Richard Cutler's research on relationships in Chapter 21, Mark Lipton's examination of cybersex in Chapter 22, and Lance Strate's discussion of cybertime in Chapter 23; an alternative to the environmental perspective appears in Gumpert and Drucker's piece on social space in Chapter 1.

By erasing the boundaries between what is real and artificial, cyberspace creates a series of paradoxical situations that undermine the natural balance of self. Paradoxes occur in cyberspace because it blurs the distinctions between living people and artificial environments. In traditional physical environments, a concept of self is developed through face-to-face encounters with other people and objects. In contrast, cyberspace interaction takes place symbolically in a media-generated space. Depending on the computer system, the individual interacts in a digital environment of written language, images, video, sounds, three-dimensional computer-generated objects, virtual people, and artificial life. Therefore, the perceptual experience of one's physical environment is replaced by the sensations of being in a symbolic or artificial environment. Moreover, the physical self is replaced by a digital representation of self. This digital self can be distributed throughout a network of cyberworlds to interact with other digital selves.

The concept of creating a digital self to exist in electronic media is a theme in the work of science fiction writers (Gibson, 1984, 1986, 1988; Stephenson,1992; Sterling, 1988), cyberpunk authors (Kroker, 1993; Sirus, 1992), and scientific researchers (Minsky, 1986; Rucker, 1982). Their writings reflect a shift in attitude about the relationship between living humans and digital technology. In contrast to early science fiction writings that viewed human nature as being more important than machines, these works remove the human from its privileged position and advocate human-machine equality. Human nature no longer controls the machine. In some cases, the machines and cyberspace are viewed as superior to natural existence. Human-machine equality is a cultural paradigm shift in thinking about human relationships to technology. This shift has profound implications for the natural ecology of self and the development of self in digital environments.

Currently, a new generation of computer technology is emerging that enables people to separate themselves from physical space and reality in order to enter the artificial worlds of cyberspace. These technologies include personal computers, computer networks, virtual reality, media spaces, teleconferencing, and ubiquitous computing. To enter cyberspace, people create a digital persona. The self that exists as a unified mind and body in a physical space becomes a separate and distributed digital self. This new digital self encounters paradoxical situations in cyberspace that could threaten the ecological self that inhabits a natural world.

DEFINITIONS OF CYBERSPACE

Cyberspace is a term that is used synonymously with other phrases such as cyberia, virtual space, virtual worlds, dataspace, the digital domain, the electronic realm, the information sphere, virtual reality, computer networking, and the Internet. The word was originally introduced by William Gibson (1984) in his science fiction novel Neuromancer to describe a futuristic computer network. However, Gibson (1991) states that he assembled the word *cyberspace* as an "act of pop poetics" to describe today's postmodern culture. Although Gibson's stories take place in the future, they are based on his observations about our present relationship to technology. For example, Gibson's inspiration for the term cyberspace came from watching kids playing video arcade games. In an interview, he described these games as "a feedback loop with photons coming off the screens into the kids' eyes, neurons moving through their bodies, and electrons moving through the video game. These kids clearly *believed* in the space games projected" (cited in McCaffery, 1992, p. 272). Gibson observed that video game kids and computer users seem "to develop a belief that there's some kind of *actual space* behind the screen, someplace you can't see but you know is there" (p. 272; emphasis in original). It is a "nonspace," a hyperdimensional realm that we enter through technology. Therefore, in his books, *cyberspace* became a term to denote the nonspaces created by futuristic electronic media.

However, Gibson's term takes on additional meanings when it is applied to current media such as personal computers (PCs) and computer networks. For example, "now that PCs are linked through networks that cover the globe and beyond, many people spend real time out there in 'cyberspace'—the territory of digital information. This apparently boundless universe of data breaks all the rules of physical reality" (Rushkoff, 1994, p. 2). From home, people can explore information in cyberspace stored at any geographic location. When the term *cyberspace* is applied to computer networks, it moves out of the realm of science fiction and into everyday life.

Gibson's original use of the word *space* in cyberspace relates to electronic spaces created by computer-based media. Today, it has been adapted by an emerging *cyberculture* as a general term for digital media space. Cyberculture represents the merging of the present and the future and the total encroachment of technology into human lives. *Cyber-* has become the prefix of the 1990s—cyberspace, cyberpunk, cybernaut, cyberart, cybergames, cybersex. It is derived from the word *cybernetics*, a term coined by Norbert Weiner (1954). Weiner applied it to an entire discipline of communication theory that studies the transmission of messages in animals, machines and society. Weiner (1954) states he derived cybernetics "from the Greek word Kubernetes, or 'steersman" (p. 7). In Gibson's (1984, 1986, 1988) science fiction novels, the term *cyberspace* encompasses the idea of people steering through a matrix of digital information.

CYBERPUNK COUNTERCULTURE

Since the publication of Gibson's books, an entire cybercounterculture has evolved. Science fiction writers Wilhelmina Baird (1993), Ben Bova (1989), Alan Dean Foster (1990), Neal Stephenson (1992), and Bruce Sterling (1988) have all written books using the concept of cyberspace. Magazines such as *Mondo 2000* and *Wired* feature articles describing cyberspace and its counterculture.

Additionally, the term *cyberpunk* has appeared to refer to its inhabitants. Cyberpunks are people who explore the digital landscapes of electronic space. It is a word that has "escaped from being a literary genre into cultural reality. People started calling themselves cyberpunks, or the media started calling people cyberpunks" (Sirius, 1992, p. 64).

For example, *Cyberpunk* is the title of Katie Hafner and John Markoff's (1991) book about the "outlaws and hackers on the computer frontier." They use the term to describe people who are involved in illegal computer activities, such as breaking into networks. In contrast, Bruce Sterling (1992) describes *cyberpunks* as "perhaps the first SF [science fiction] generation to grow up not only with the literary tradition of science fiction, but in a truly science-fictional world. For them, the techniques of classical "hard SF—extrapolation, technological literacy—are not just literary tools, but an aid to daily life" (p. 344). Computers that were once the tools of science fiction characters are now in the hands of the cyberpunk generation.

Cyberpunks have developed ideologies based on the work of Arthur Kroker (1993) and Jean Baudrillard (1983). These authors write about human relationships to technology. It is a relationship that blurs the boundaries between human and machine. Cyberpunks want the human nervous system to merge with the computer matrix by making reality and hallucinations collapse into each other in an electronic universe. Mind invasion is their technological theme. It includes: "brain-computer interfaces, artificial intelligence, neurochemistry—techniques radically redefining the nature of humanity, the nature of self" (Sterling, 1992, p. 346). Additionally, the cyberpunk perspective encompasses the idea of body invasion—implanted circuitry, cosmetic surgery, prosthetic limbs, and genetic alteration. These visions of mental invasion and biological alterations correspond to Gibson's imaginative writing.

Gibson's characters immerse themselves in information by entering "a new universe, a parallel universe created and sustained by the world's computers and communication lines" (Benedikt, 1991, p. 1); this universe generates "a three-dimensional field of action and interaction: with recorded and live data, with machines, sensors, and with other people" (p. 129). Cyberpunk fictional characters are fitted with surgical implants and "jack-in" to cyberspace directly through their brains. Software programs "create computerized virtual bodies to exist inside the computer matrix, the boundary between human and computer is erased and the nature of the human psyche is redefined in accordance with the computer paradigm" (Springer, 1993, p. 721).

Neal Stephenson (1992) describes this process in *Snow Crash*. His characters create a computer-generated "avatar" that dwells in a parallel world called the "Metaverse": "Your avatar can look any way you want it to, up to the limitations of your equipment. If you're ugly, you can made your avatar beautiful. . . . You can look like a gorilla or a dragon or a giant talking penis in the Metaverse" (p. 36). Your physical appearance is only limited by the hardware you possess. Human bodies become obsolete as the mind circulates through the software. In cyberjargon this is referred to as "getting rid of the meat." In the philosophy of cyberpunk, "the ultimate revenge of the information system comes when the system absorbs the very identity of the human personality, absorbing the opacity of the body, grinding the meat into information" (Heim, 1991, p. 66). The mind becomes immersed in the medium while the body is left behind in physical space.

THE PHILOSOPHICAL PARADOX

In an interview with Woolley (1992), Gibson states that the word cyberspace meant to suggest "the point at which media [flow] together and surround us. It's the ultimate extension of the exclusion of daily life. With cyberspace as I describe it you can literally wrap yourself in media and not have to see what's really going on around you" (p. 122). But Gibson is an usher rather than a participant in cyberspace. In reality, his books draw nihilistic conclusions about mankind's current relationship to technology and environment. Although traditional science fiction "frequently problematizes the oppositions between the natural and the artificial, the human and the machine, it generally sustains them in such a way that the human remains surely ensconced in its privileged place at the center of things. Cyberpunk, however, is about the breakdown of these oppositions" (Hollinger, 1992, pp. 204-205). Human nature is no longer superior to the machine. Cyberpunk "invokes a rhetoric of technology to express the natural world in a metaphor that blurs the distinctions between the organic and the artificial" (p. 205).

Cyberpunk is a philosophy whereby hyperreal or virtual icons of human simulations infiltrate reality. The physical environment is replaced with a symbolic media-generated landscape. Prosthetic devices "plug the human sensorium into interactive communion with the computer, so that the user transcends—and, all too often in this context, elides—not only his (or her) being in an imperfect human body, but also the imperfect world that we all 'really' materially create and physically inhabit" (Sobchack, 1993, p. 575). Cyberpunks contend that escape from the physical world into an artificial world is notable because the "earth is this incredibly boring place" (Turin, 1993, p. 48). By connecting ourselves to artificial worlds in cyberspace we not only leave our physical bodies, but also the physical world in which we live.

Immersion into this world of data distances the individual from physical culture. As a result, "lifestyle has fled its basis in the domain of personal ethics, becoming an empty floating sign-object—a cynical commodity—in the mediascape" (Kroker, 1993, p. 6). Cyberpunk becomes "a virtual theory of those organs without bodies that come to dominate the electronic landscape of digital culture" (p. 6). It is a virtual reality that escapes the vicissitudes of the physical body by replacing the natural with the artificial: "Virtual reality, the ideology of which could be triumphantly described by Marvin Minsky of MIT"s Multi-Media

Research Lab as the production of cyber-bodies with the soft matter of the brains scooped out, and skulls hard-wired to an indefinite flow of telemetry" (p. 7). Cyberpunk seeks to replace flesh and blood with silicon and chips. Human and machine merge together, and the machine takes control as the natural body is gradually eliminated.

For academics, cyberpunk ideology raises serious questions about human relationships to technology. Forgetting the body may be a Cartesian trick to place the mind in a different category than the body, but it has profound implications. Cyberpunk authors view the human body as "meat" and as being obsolete as soon as consciousness can be uploaded into a computer network. But the human body is a complex technical hardware device that must function properly to perform complex software operations, such as thinking. Its "software, human language, is dependent on the condition of the hardware [body]" (Lyotard, 1991, p. 13). Stone (1991) states: "Cyberspace developers foresee a time when they will be able to forget about the body. But it is important to remember that virtual community originates in, and must return to, the physical. No refigured virtual body, no matter how beautiful, will slow the death of a cyberpunk with AIDS. Even in the age of the technosocial subject, life is through bodies" (p.113). Human consciousness is rooted in the physical body and without the body, consciousness does not exist.

From an academic perspective, cyberpunk ideology demonstrates the frailty of Cartesian philosophy that separates the body from the mind or the concrete from the abstract: "The mind is a property of the body, and lives and dies with it. Everywhere we turn we see signs of this recognition, and cyberspace, in its literal placement of the body in spaces invented entirely by the mind, is located directly upon this blurring boundary, this fault" (Novak, 1991, p. 227). Thus, by grinding the meat to eliminate the physical body, cyberpunks would simultaneously be destroying the human hardware that is necessary for consciousness and thinking to exist. From a philosophical perspective, destroying the body paradoxically destroys consciousness or the thinking mind. Once the mind is destroyed, the self ceases to exist.

CYBERCULTURE AND SCIENCE

Getting rid of the meat to explore cyberworlds is an imaginative theme for science fiction books; however, it becomes an ominous vision when it crosses from the realm of fiction into the research of legitimate science. Sterling (1992) states: "Technical culture has gotten out of hand. The advances of sciences are so deeply radical, so disturbing, upsetting, and revolutionary, that they can no longer be contained" (p. 345). For example, John von Neumann introduced "The General and Logical Theory of Automata" in the late 1940s: "An automaton is a machine that processes information, proceeding logically, inexorably performing its next action after applying data received from outside itself in light of instructions programmed within itself" (Levy, 1992, p. 15). Simply stated, von Neumann argues that machines could be internally programmed to react to outside stimulus. This led to the idea of self-replicating machines and factories. Scientists during the 1950s considered the possibility of sending robots to the moon to design and build a self-growing lunar facility. The robots would be preprogrammed on earth to find the raw materials, manufacture the parts, and construct the factory. Once sent to the moon, the robots would self-replicate and build.

Von Neumann's theory was based on the mechanistic perspective that views life literally as an automation process. Scientists reasoned that if life is an automata, then machines could be designed to self-replicate and think. During the late 1960s and early 1970s, the discipline of artificial intelligence (AI) had high hopes of digitally duplicating the human thinking process: "Nearly all authorities agree that artificial intelligence seeks to produce on a computer, a pattern of output that would be considered intelligent if displayed by human beings" (Gardner, 1985, p. 11). AI researchers postulated that computers could behave like thinking minds. But their original approach to creating "thinking machines" was top-down. Structures were not encouraged to emerge, but imposed. Programs for AI were solution oriented: "They posed a question to the computer and tried to make the computer answer it in the way a human being would" (Levy, 1992, p. 158). Hubert L. Dreyfus (1979) in *What Computers Can't Do* explains why the original AI researchers failed. In the book, he argues that computers "can't think like people because there's no way to represent all the background knowledge of ordinary human life—the stuff we associate with common sense—in some form a computer can understand" (cited in Rose, 1984, p. 84).

With the failure of an imposed top-down approach to AI, these researchers started to explore other ways of creating artificial life. For example, Marvin Minsky (1986) in *The Society of Mind* argued that "nature's approach toward intelligence and behavior was decentralized" (cited in Levy, 1992, p. 285). Moreover, he states that computers can be designed to duplicate natural processes. From Minsky's (1986) perspective, the mind is a process or activity of the brain. Therefore, he argues that biological human brain cells could be replaced with computer chips. This replacement creates a substitute machine that "would reproduce the same processes as those within your brain" (p. 289). Minsky goes on to state: "There isn't any reason to doubt that the substitute machine would think and feel the same kinds of thoughts and feelings that you do—since it embodies all the same processes and memories" (p. 289). He then asks, "*Would that new machine be the same as you?*" Minsky believes microscopic differences would exist because "it would be impractical to duplicate, with absolute fidelity, all the interactions in the brain" (p. 289). These microscopic differences, he argues, do not matter because we are always changing as we age. Because people are never the same from one moment to the next, you cannot claim that your brain machine is not you. In essence, the artificial you is the same as the physical you. Therefore, from Minksy's view, there is no difference between the real you and your digital clone.

Minsky's concept of the possibility of digital duplication is supported by mathematician/cyberpunk writer Rudy Rucker. Rucker uses mathematical theory to claim that machine consciousness can exist. Rucker (1982) states: "If one gets an artificial leg, kidney, or heart, one is still the same person. I maintain that it is possible to envision a time when one could even get a new artificial brain" (p. 197). But, Rucker's perspective goes beyond the mechanistic view that argues "neither men nor robots are anything but machines, and there is no reason why [hu]man-like machines cannot exist" (p. 197). He states that "everything, whether man or machine, participates in the Absolute" (p. 197). Therefore, machines can have souls because they exist the same way that human beings exist. Rucker directly challenges the idea that human beings are superior to machines. According to his view, humans and machines are equal—both can exist with souls.

The work of von Neumann, Minsky, and Rucker reflect a paradigm shift in scientific thinking. The boundaries between real and artificial life are eliminated. The human being is no longer placed in its privileged position at the center of things, but is now on the same level as machines.

The work of these scientists has influenced the relatively newer discipline of artificial life (a-life). In contrast to AI research that focuses on the thinking mind, a-life looks at self-reproducing artificial organisms: "The premise being that the basis of life is information, steeped in a dynamical system complex enough to reproduce and to bear offspring more complex than the parent" (Levy, 1992, p. 22). A-life "studies ways of building systems that act as if they are alive. This broad area of study encompasses chemical attempts to synthesize self-replicating molecules, the linguistic analysis of self-perpetuating belief systems, robotics, and the design of computer programs capable of evolving into new forms" (Rucker, 1992, p. 30). Intrigued with the concept, Steven Levy (1992) in *Artificial Life* describes the work of a-life researchers to create and study lifelike organisms and computer systems that are built by humans. According to Levy, a-life research has two different points of view. The purpose of "weak" a-life research "is to illuminate and understand more clearly the life that exists on earth and possibly elsewhere" (p. 5), and this "weak" research tends to be conducted by biologists, astronomers, and physicists. Bolder practitioners engage in "strong" a-life research: "They look toward the long-term development of actual living organisms whose essence is information. These creatures may be embodied in corporeal form—a-life robots—or they may live within a computer" (Levy, 1992, p. 6). In general, a-life researchers replace organic molecules and chemical compounds as the essence of life with information.

THE "ARTIFICIAL VERSUS HUMAN" PARADOX

Currently, strong a-life researchers work with digital information instead of living compounds and organs (referred to as *wetware*). Despite the fact they work with digital software instead of living wetware, this research is still clouded by the legacy of Mary Shelly's *Frankenstein* (1963). In Shelley's story the monster destroys his creator. Upon meeting his creator the monster states: "Do your duty towards me, and I will do mine towards you and the rest of mankind. If you will comply with my conditions, I will leave them and you at peace; but if you refuse, I will glut the maw of death, until it be satiated with the blood of your remaining friends" (p. 95). This powerful image of a manmade creation gone awry raises moral questions about a-life research. For example, what will happen if these new life forms are unleashed on the world? Will they go out of control, and could they harm human life? Based on examples of existing software patterns, the answer is most likely yes.

In *Digital Woes*, Lauren Ruth Wiener (1993) argues that software is unreliable. In her book, she describes 13 tales of how software can go wrong. Some of the stories are comic, others are tragic, and sometimes both. For example, she describes how the AT&T telephone system went down on January 15, 1990 as the result of a common software error. Wiener states: "It isn't that the people who design, build, and program computers are any less careful, competent, or conscientious than the rest of us. But they're only human, and digital technology is unforgiving of human limitations" (pp. 3-4). The details that must be tracked in a software program are so enormous that the "job of testing a software program could take decades . . . centuries . . . sometimes even millennia" (p. 4). She argues that depending on software to run human-related systems is risky. Future system failures could result in injury or fatalities to plants, animals, owners, operators, users, future generations, and the life-sustaining qualities of the earth.

Another example of software failure that is more closely related to a-life is computer viruses: "The dangers of viruses are a vivid paradigm of the perils inherent in any realized form of a-life" (Levy, 1992, p. 333). Releasing uncontrolled viruses into the information ecosystem "can certainly reap unhappy results for those who depend on the stability of that system" (p. 333). For example, Robert Tapan Morris unleashed a computer virus that all but shut down the Internet. According to Hafner and Markoff (1991), Morris got one of the numbers wrong in his program. As a result, his virus went out of control and a major human communication system was affected. Currently, software unreliability creates a paradoxical situation in cyberspace. The more we depend on artificial software systems, the larger the risk to human systems of all kinds.

CYBORGS AND POPULAR CULTURE

In popular culture, the merging of people and artificial systems is the *cyborg*. Cyborgs are fictionalized in films, videos, books, computer games, and popular magazines (Jamison, 1994). "A cyborg is a cybernetic organism, a hybrid of machine and organism, a creature of social reality as well as a creature of fiction" (Haraway, 1991, p. 149). An examination of the fictional cyborg reveals social attitudes about the relationship of people to machines. For example, films such as *Robocop* and *Terminator* "embrace technology at the same time as they armor the human against the technological threat. There is, underlying these works, an uneasy but consistent sense of human obsolescence, and at stake is the very definition of the human" (Bukatman, 1993, p. 20). A cultural attitude in cyborg fiction begins to emerge that challenges our concept of what it means to be a human being rather than a machine.

The cyborg symbiosis of machine and human questions the very essence of human personality. For example, novelists Amy Thomson (1993) and Marge Piercy (1991) write about the process in which cyborgs develop a sense of self. In *Virtual Girl*, Thomson describes how a female cyborg named Maggie struggles to digitally develop her memory and sense of identity. Similarly, Piercy in *He, She and It* discusses the socialization process of a male cyborg and how he attempts to develop a personality and life separate from his creator. In both cases, the cyborg strives to be accepted as human. Through software manipulations and adjustments, the cyborg engages in interpersonal human relationships. By viewing human personality through the eyes of the cyborg, these authors begin to examine the idea of what it means to be human, machine, and a hybrid of both.

The cyborg is representative of a new type of human persona. It is a human personality that "is replaced by pure information whose configurations 'signify' disembodied human sensoria, personality constructs, and artificial intelligences" (Tomas, 1991, p. 35). Today, the cyborg is representative of two new cultural myths. First, digital cyborg personalities could be equal to human personalities. Second, the human personality could be duplicated in a digital format.

THE "HUMAN UNIQUENESS" PARADOX

Cyborg digital identities create a paradox. The cultural acceptance of digital personalities opens up the possibility of personality duplication and memory alteration. If memories are stored in a digital format, they can be enhanced, augmented, erased, or changed according to electronic models. The ability to alter memories has profound implications: "Since memories form the foundation of human identity, loss of memory is equivalent to loss of self. . . . Thus it suggests that advanced technologies can potentially be used to destroy human uniqueness" (Springer, 1993, p. 723). For example, Baudrillard (1983) states that the automation of the robot is "a perfect double for man, right up to the suppleness of his movements, the function of his organs and intelligence" (p. 93). The mechanical robot body can double for the human body, or eventually replace it. If this occurs, the original human presence would be replaced by a cyborg personality. This digital personality could be copied. A contradiction occurs when human identity is duplicated by computer technology. In the process of copying ourselves we destroy the very nature of what makes us individuals.

Social theorists argue the mind and body together are an integral part of our unique presence: "Our bodily existence stands at the forefront of personal identity and individuality" (Heim, 1991, p. 74). Replacing the physical body with a cyborg simultaneously eliminates oneself. Thus, the cyborg paradox occurs when digital duplication of body and mind destroys the essence of what it means to be a unique human being. Although the cyborg remains an imaginary creature, the cultural attitudes represented in its myth challenge our existing concepts of what it means to be a unique living person.

TRADITIONAL THEORIES OF SELF

Social theorists Mead (1959) and Berger and Luckmann (1966) argue the mind and body together are necessary to develop a sense of self. Writing from a monist perspective, they believe the mind is "inseparably associated with and dependent upon the physical organism known as body" (Hintz, 1960, p. 105). A person's "experience of himself [herself] always hovers in a balance between being and having a body" (Berger & Luckmann, 1966, p. 51). Without experiencing the physical body a person cannot develop a sense of self. For example, the work of Mead (1959, 1962) depicts how an individual self evolves through body interaction with objects and other people.

According to Mead (1959, 1962), in the first stage of self-development, the actions of physical objects become internalized within oneself. For example, taking hold of a hard object stimulates oneself to exert an inner mental effort. The individual begins to make a relationship between holding an object and the effort of pressure in the action of holding. When the individual takes the attitude of the object (holding), the object becomes a part of an individual's inner experience.

In the next stage, a transference takes place when the individual "in grasping and pushing things is identifying its own effort with the contact experience of the thing" (Mead, 1959, pp. 121-122). In other words, after making the relationship between the object and pressure, the individual must then realize that he or she is exerting the effort to hold the object. At this point, the individual now becomes aware of him- or herself as an object that exists with other objects in an environment. As surrounding colors, shapes, and objects come in contact with the body, they begin to occupy a defined place within an individual's world. The pressure of the body and grasping of the hands localizes objects from an inside attitude, and the individual becomes aware of him- or herself as an object through body interaction with other objects. Simultaneously, while the individual is becoming aware of him- or herself, he or she is also becoming aware of "other" individuals in addition to objects.

Mead (1959) stated: "The others and the self arise in the social act together" (p. 169). An individual self is established by organizing the attitudes of other individuals toward the self and toward one another through participation in social interaction. For example, a social act is playing the game of baseball. Each team member knows his or her role in the game as well as the roles of every other player. Because each player understands the role of the "other" players, each player can socially interact according to the game's rules. Every individual player takes on the roles of others and addresses themselves in their multiple roles as well as in their singular role. Simply stated, a person could not play the role of the batter, if he or she did not understand the roles of the pitcher and catcher. Thus, by understanding the role of others, we can develop our own individual roles and consequently a sense of self. Mead (1962) invents the term the *generalized other* to describe "the organized community or social group which gives to the individual his unity of self" (p. 154). The generalized other is the "attitude of the whole community" or, as described previously, the baseball team.

Summarizing Mead's view, the formation of self involves encounters with objects in the physical world and social interaction with other people: "The formation of the self, then, must also be understood in relation to both the on going organismic development and the social process in which the natural and the human environment are mediated through the significant others" (Berger & Luckmann, 1966, p. 50). An underlying concept is the idea that the self is formed through body interaction in a natural space. Monist theories of self argue that the physical body is an integral part of self-development. Touching, feeling, and having access to all five senses is essential to interacting with objects and people. According to this perspective, a separation of mind and body in cyberspace will inhibit self-growth. Therefore, integrating the physical body with the digital representation of self in cyberspace would be essential for developing self-identity.

THE INTEGRATION OF THE PHYSICAL BODY WITH THE DIGITAL SELF

Currently, a new generation of computer technologies are developing to integrate the physical body with a digital self. These technologies fall into two types of computer development. The first is virtual reality and the second ubiquitous computing. *Virtual reality* (VR) is essentially "the use of computers to create a simulated reality" (Zachmann, 1992, p. 107). It is immersing ourselves into a computer-generated world "to tighten the bond between humans and computers, and allows us to more directly enter those digital worlds that, until now, we could only passively observe through the window of the computer screen" (Porter, 1992, p. 43). The physical self wears goggles, gloves, and/or body suits to interact in computer generated space. In contrast, *ubiquitous computing* is a "computing environment in which each person is continually interacting with hundreds of nearby wireless interconnected computers" (Weiser, 1993, p. 7). Computers are invisibly woven "into the fabric of everyday life until they are indistinguishable from it" (p. 94). Virtual reality is immersing the self in cyberspace; in contrast, ubiquitous computing is transparently placing hundreds of computers within our real-world environments. However, by integrating computers with real space, the lines between reality and cyberspace are blurred. On the one hand, virtual reality and ubiquitous computing may appear to be different approaches. But on the other, they both have the same goal of integrating the physical body into virtual space. In the future, the information we receive in the virtual world may rival the information we receive in actual real-world face-to-face encounters.

William Gibson is "credited with inspiring the idea of virtual reality with his concept of cyberspace" (Woolley, 1992, p. 36). The goal of VR development is to integrate the physical senses into a computer-constructed environment and create experiences that are "life-like" interactions. This is accomplished through the use of peripheral devices that are connected to the body such as glasses, head-mounted displays, three-dimensional interactive sound, data gloves, tactile feedback controllers, and body suits. The body is integrated into cyberspace through peripheral attachments and clothing. Ideally, the entire body would become the *interface* or point of contact for computer interaction. Virtual reality "is the technology used to provide a more intimate 'interface' between humans and computer imagery. It is about simulating the full ensemble of sense data that make up 'real' experience" (p. 5).

Virtual reality made its grand entrance at a panel session called "Virtual Environments and Interactivity: Windows to the Future" during the 1989 SIGGRAPH Conference on computer graphics. Audience members (myself included) listened to Jaron Lanier (1989), a pioneering developer of virtual reality, explain the concept:

> It's a simulation of a reality that can surround a person that's created with computerized clothing. It's rather like the physical world in that it's an externally perceived reality that you perceive through your sense organs and the physical world. You perceive sensation on the outside of your eyes and your ears and your skin, and what you do in a virtual world is you put on clothing that generates stimulation right on top of those sense organs. (p. 7)

VR research attempts to create technologies that engage all of the senses in the process of interacting with computers. For example, VR interfaces enable people to explore virtual worlds and hold objects. Taking hold of a virtual object simulates the feeling of pressure. Or in Mead's vocabulary, holding the virtual object stimulates oneself to exert an inner mental effort—pressure. In these systems, the "virtual object" feels like the "real object." The system simulates the feeling of holding a real object through the use of tactile feedback controllers. But this is an example of only one type of VR interface now under development. Current VR research

> can be split into four broad categories: desktop systems (navigating through 3-D on a monitor), partial immersion (navigating through 3-D on a monitor with enhancements such as gloves and 3-D goggles), full-immersion systems (head gear, gloves, and bodysuits), and environmental systems (externally generated 3-D, but with little or no body paraphernalia). (Reveaux, 1993, p. 34)

Examples of these four categories include, respectively, the following: 3-D computer games including Microsoft's Flight Simulator, interacting with a computer monitor wearing 3-D glasses, VR arcade games in which players wear a head-mounted display helmet and data gloves, and projecting three-dimensional computer-generated images on walls of physical space. In addition to these four general categories, innovative developers are also adding puppetry and a-life to virtual environments.

"Over the past few years, several real-time animated digital puppets have been created for entertainment and promotional purposes" (Graves, 1993, p. 38). A well-known project is a system developed for Nintendo. It is a 3-D head of Mario, of the *Super Mario Brothers* computer game. "The Mario puppet is controlled by an actor who wears a face armature that has sensors to track the actor's head, face, and lip movements" (p. 38). The actor's movements control the computer-animated head of Mario. Another example of a digital puppet is "Neuro-Baby," a project under development at the Fujitsu laboratories in Japan. Neuro-Baby is a digital puppet that "seems to have a mind of its own, learning from its interactions with human beings through the use of *neural-network* software" (Reveaux, 1993, p. 38). A neural network is "a form of computation inspired by the structure and function of the brain" (Illingworth, 1990, p. 303). Neural network research involves researchers from a variety of disciplines:

> The work has attracted scientists from a number of disciplines: neuroscientists who are interested in making models of the neural circuitry found in specific areas of the brains of various animals; physicists who see analogies between the dynamical behavior of brain-like systems and the kind of nonlinear dynamical systems familiar in physics; computer engineers who are interested in fabricating brain-like computers; workers in artificial intelligence (AI) who are interested in building machines with the intelligence of biological organisms; engineers interested in solving practical problems; psychologists who are interested in the mathematics of such neural network systems; philosophers who are interested in how such systems change our view of the nature of mind and its relationship to brain; and many others [including entertainment and game companies]. (Rumelhart, Widrow, & Lehr, 1994, p. 87)

VR developers claim that applying neural network and a-life research to virtual reality "provides the interest, action, and real-time changes in behavior that occur in a living world. A-life makes the virtual world as intriguing as the real world" (Kelly, 1994, p. 21). In an entertainment context, "a-life lets the inhabitants of a world adapt to their environment, learn, and evolve in response to new players and new circumstances" (p. 21). In addition to entertainment, developers of these environments are working on a-life applications for business to predict financial trends and in education to "construct virtual worlds that explain themselves as they evolve" (p. 21). Rucker (1992) states: "Present day applications of Alife [sic] programs include computer graphics that draw themselves, methods of finding solutions to intractably difficult problems, and, of course, robotics. In the future we can expect to see large numbers of Alife [sic] organisms wandering around in cyberspace—this will keep virtual reality from being sterile and boring" (p. 32).

THE "ARTIFICIAL VERSUS REAL BEHAVIOR" PARADOX

Although VR developers and cyberpunk enthusiasts welcome the idea of immersing ourselves in cyberspace, there are warnings about possible consequences. L. Casey Larijani (1994) states that there is "concern about the exaggerated susceptibility and vulnerability exhibited by subjects within immersive environments" (p. 8). When the medium disappears in virtual reality, events we perceive in virtual situations "become incorporated into our own, ever-evolving 'realities'" (p. 8). According to Larijani, some researchers fear that virtual reality will open doors to excessive and abusive behavior in virtual environments. Exaggerated behavior will then become integrated with normal behavior in the real world. This idea represents a potential cyberspace paradox in progress. Simultaneously, while researchers are building virtual worlds to better understand scientific and medical knowledge, the individuals who immerse themselves in virtual environments may be altering their individual knowledge of real-world experience.

Today, examples of behavior alteration in the real world based on cyberspace relationships are beginning to be discussed. For example, the introductory issue of *Wired* magazine ran an article about a woman whose real life changed as a result of her "online" or digital persona. In real life the woman was described as "a rather mousy person—the shy type who favored gray clothing of a conservative cut—and was the paragon of shy and retiring womanhood" (Van Der Leun, 1993, p. 74). In contrast, her digital persona was called "The Naked Lady," in which she was a sexy, lewd, bawdy, man-eating female. As months of cyberspace interactions with men progressed, a transformation occurred in the woman's real life. "She got a trendy haircut. Her clothing tastes went from Peck and Peck to tight skirts slit up the thigh. . . . Her speech became bawdier, her jokes naughtier" (p. 74). In short, she became her digital persona.

Reports of real-world behavioral changes as the result of VR and cyberspace interactions raise new concerns about the possible affects of digital technologies on human behavior. These concerns "include the ethical or political issues of specific VR technologies, consideration of VR as related to the arts, theories of scientific management systems and questions of cognitive learning and behavior" (Larijani, 1994, p. 10). What will happen when the "generalized others" we relate to are VR simulations, digital personas, and artificial life forms? Will a baseball game played in cyberspace invoke the same responses as a game played on a baseball field? As VR technology improves these are topics that will require serious discussion.

THE PHYSICAL BODY IN MEDIATED SPACE

In contrast to the VR interface approach that integrates the body into cyberspace, ubiquitous computing wants to turn physical space into a computer interface. This goal of ubiquitous computing is at odds with virtual reality. Where VR wants to fool the user into leaving the everyday physical world behind, ubiquitous computing wants to integrate computers into physical space. Because human activity occurs in the real world, ubiquitous computing makes computers disappear into the background of physical environments. For example, computerized objects such as wall-sized interactive screens and clip-board-sized computer terminals will be placed in physical spaces.

Ubiquitous computing is based on earlier research on media spaces. Media spaces are "computer-controllable networks of audio and video equipment used to support synchronous collaboration" (Gaver, 1992, p. 17). Media spaces create the appearance of a physical visual environment with the use of computers, projection screens, and video cameras: "The concept of media spaces is not new, Captain Kirk of the television program Star Trek communicated with other captains of other space ships via a huge projection screen. Captain Kirk could see and hear the person and the person's surroundings, and the other person with whom he was communicating could see and hear him as well" (Barnes & Greller, 1994, p. 10). Presently, media spaces enable the two-way transmission of auditory and visual information across geographic space.

Although media spaces span geographic space, they attempt to send and receive the visual and auditory messages people would experience in face-to-face communication. By setting up large screens with video cameras in physical spaces such as meeting rooms, hallways, and recreational areas, media spaces attempt to provide interpersonal interaction that is close to face-to-face encounters. People interact with each other in the following ways: through chance encounters in hallways and recreational areas, video phone conversations, group discussion, formal presentations, and social activities. Of all the cyberspace technologies, media spaces are the closest to actual reality because they create synchronous or real-time acoustic and visual environments that are based on physical environments. Moreover, they are based on normal human behavior patterns in real-world activities. But instead of being face to face in the same room, people's "telepresence" is transmitted through video, audio, computer, and telephone technologies: "*Telepresence is defined as the experience of presence in an environment by means of a communication medium.* In other words, presence refers to the natural perception of an environment, and *telepresence* refers to the *mediated* perception of an environment" (Steuer, 1992, p. 76; emphasis in original).

The concept of telepresence developed in teleconferencing and telerobotics applications. *Teleconferencing* is setting up a meeting in a special location that can transmit the images and sounds from other locations. For example, a conference room is set up where people sit on one side of a table and look at a group of people sitting on the other side. In reality, the table is next to a projection screen. The first group is in one location and the second group geographically somewhere else. The screen helps to simulate the illusion that both groups are meeting in a single space. Information such as gestures, facial expression, eye movement, and other nonverbal signals that are lost in standard telephone conversations are transmitted through telepresence. Thus, teleconferencing solves the problem of trying to be in two places at the same time. Additionally, the concept of telepresence can be applied to the telephone: "For example, while you're talking on the telephone to someone, it is as though your ears were in some remote place. You can hear what's going on miles away and then create sound (through the telephone) without actually being there" (Aukstakalnis & Blatner, 1992, p. 247). The difference between the telephone and teleconferencing is the addition of visual information to verbal electronic exchanges. However, adding the visual information to these exchanges is altering the meaning of face-to-face communications. With teleconferencing systems, face-to-face communication is no longer two people in the same room. The meaning is expanded to include the ability to see a person's face in a media space.

Telepresence research originally began at NASA as a way of controlling robots: "Since it is better to send machines than humans into hazardous environments like space, the NASA research team aimed to provide a wrap-around technology that would give the machine operator the feeling of 'being' in the place of the machine being operated" (Woolley, 1992, p. 126). For example, robots would be sent outside to repair space ships, while the human operator remained safely inside the space craft. Scott Fisher (1989), a NASA researcher working on telepresence, describes his project:

> What our particular lab, NASA Ames in California, is trying to do is . . . to make you really have the sense of being present in that remote environment and be able to interact with it as much as possible. Really the bottom line here is to go

> from personal computer to personal simulator in a sense. To be able to simulate whatever it is you'd like to move around inside of. (p. 14)

To simulate the illusion of actually being in another location, the NASA researchers placed cameras in a robot that were "connected to a head-mounted display so that the wearer could see what he or she would see if actually there. Similarly, a glove or exoskeleton (that is, a series of hinges and struts clamped to the body, like an articulated splint) could be used to reproduce the wearer's movements in the robot's arm and hand or to provide tactile feedback" (Woolley, 1992, p. 126). Communication between the robot and operator has a complete range of sensory feedback and response. The operator is now telepresent through robot information links.

THE ORWELLIAN PARADOX

Telepresence through ubiquitous computing, media spaces, and teleconferencing has Orwellian implications. Although people are mentally and physically immersed in cyberspace, their actions and locations can be monitored and digitally recorded because these technologies require the user to be physically interacting with computer systems. For example, in ubiquitous computing environments individuals wear an "active badge": "With an active badge system, every computer you sit down at is your computer, with your custom interface and access to your files, because your active badge sends it information via infrared signals" (Rheingold, 1994, p. 94). The paradox of this system are the Orwellian possibilities. Individuals can freely connect to cyberspace through any computer system, but, at the same time, the locations of researchers wearing the active badges can be monitored at all times by a central system. Individual freedom of motion is counteracted by the surveillance of physical location. Similarly, media spaces and teleconferencing activities can be recorded digitally or on videotape while individuals are communicating in these environments.

THE SELF IN CONTEMPORARY CYBERSPACE

Today, the popular computer-based communication environment is networking. Computer networks are growing at a rapid pace. For example, the "mother of all networks" is called the *Internet*. In online computer vernacular, it is referred to as *cyberspace*. This contemporary cyberspace enables people to travel across time and space without a physical body. But in contrast to ubiquitous, media, and teleconferencing spaces, computer networking systems do not include personal visual information. Heim (1993), in *The Metaphysics of Virtual Reality,* states that "being a *body* constitutes the principle behind our separateness from one another and behind our personal presence" (p. 100; emphasis in original). Eliminating visual information about the physical body in cyberspace communication has positive and negative implications. On the one hand, eliminating the body makes us more equal because we no longer have access to the visual information of sex, age, or race. But on the other hand, the quality of human relationships narrows, because unlike face-to-face communication, we do not have a full range of visual and verbal sensory information: "No other form of social relating can reproduce the plentitude of symptoms of subjectivity present in the face-to-face situation" (Berger & Luckmann, 1966, p. 29).

As a result of cyberspace communication, "the boundaries between the subject, if not the body, and the 'rest of the world' are undergoing a radical refiguration, brought about in part through the mediation of technology" (Stone, 1991, p. 101). The current use of computer networks significantly alters our relationship to physical bodies in the communication process. People can now communicate and develop relationships without ever meeting each other in a face-to-face situation (Rheingold, 1993). These technologies enable people to communicate with each other in electronic space instead of real space. People exchanging messages in electronic space are creating new "symbolic" (Gergen, 1991) or "virtual" communities (Rheingold, 1993): "Symbolic communities are linked primarily by the capacity of their members for symbolic exchange—of words, images, information—mostly through electronic means" (Gergen, 1991, p. 214). The formation of symbolic or virtual communities raises the issue of how people will develop a self-identity when they communicate through electronic media instead of face-to-face interaction. In Mead's terms, what happens when the generalized other becomes the "electronic other?"

The relationship between media and developing a sense of self is the topic of a number of books (Gergen, 1991; Meyrowitz, 1985; Poster, 1990). These authors argue that "electronic media have changed the significance of space, time and the physical barriers as communication variables" (Meyrowitz, 1985, p. 13). We can now speak to someone in New York while sunning in California: "The technological achievements of the past century have produced a radical shift in our exposure to each other" (Gergen, 1991, p. xi). Advances in radio, telephone, transportation, television transmission, computers, and cyberspace are exposing us "to an enormous barrage of social stimulation. Small and enduring communities, with a limited cast of significant others, are being replaced by a vast and ever-expanding array of relationships" (p. xi). As a result of these technologies, our amount of social participation is expanding.

We are now exposed to views, values, and visions that we would not normally come in contact with through face-to-face encounters. Electronic media "have rearranged many social forums so that most people now find themselves in contact with others in new ways. And unlike merged situations in face-to-face interaction, the combined situations of electronic media are relatively lasting and inescapable, they therefore have a much greater effect on social behavior" (Meyrowitz, 1985, p. 5). Because the formation of self depends on social behavior, media effects on social behavior will consequently affect the development of self. For example, Gergen (1991) and Poster (1990) argue that electronic media is fragmenting self-conceptions. In electronic media "the self is decentered, dispersed, and multiplied in continuous instability" (Poster, 1990, p. 6). Gergen (1991) describes this condition as the "saturated self": "The evening at home, once quiet, relaxed, and settling, is now—by dint of telephone, automobile, television, and the like—a parade of faces, information, and intrusion. One can scarcely settle into a calming rut, because who one is and the cast of 'significant others' are in continuous motion" (p. 67). Moreover, Gergen argues, "the fragmentation of self-conceptions corresponds to a multiplicity of incoherent and disconnected relationships" (p. 7). Relationships that form in cyberspace fall under this description. Computer network users interact with each other through disconnected and many times incoherent e-mail messages. Additionally, a myriad of electronic relationships can invite "us to play such a variety of roles that the very concept of an 'authentic self' with knowable characteristics recedes from view" (p. 7). Through electronic discourse, people can experiment and play with digital personas, such as The Naked Lady.

The lack of personal visual information in network exchanges allows people to test new personalities and even create totally fictitious ones. For example, in "The Strange Case of the Electronic Lover," Lindsy Van Gelder (1991) describes how a prominent male New York psychiatrist was "engaged in a bizarre, all-consuming experiment to see what it felt like to be female, and to experience the intimacy of female friendship" (p. 365). As a result of his experiment, many of the women he developed electronic relationships with felt that they had been "mind raped" by the fraud. In cyberspace the unity of personality associated with physical presences dissolves because individuals create digital characters of self that engage in correspondence with other digital personas. Thus, the ecology of self once grounded in physical reality becomes separated and distributed in a network of digital relationships. According the Gergen (1991), "the fully saturated [or digital] self becomes no self at all" (p. 7).

To summarize, Poster (1990) states when computer communication replaces face-to-face communication the subject is affected in the following ways: (a) new possibilities for playing with identities is possible, (b) gender cues are removed, (c) existing hierarchies in relationships are destablized, and (d) the subject is dispersed and dislocated in space and time. He further states: "The subject is changed in computer communications, dispersed in a postmodern semantic field of time-space, inner/outer, mid/matter" (p. 115). The subject is no longer represented as a physical human being. In cyberspace the physical self is represented by bits and bytes of information that disperses through the electronic nervous system of the network. Although, the physical body disappears in contemporary cyberspace interaction, the body can be used as a metaphor to understand a communication paradox in progress.

THE COMMUNICATION PARADOX

Cyberspace can be directly related to McLuhan's (1964) use of the body as a metaphor to describe communication systems:

> Today, after more than a century of electric technology, we have extended our central nervous systems itself in a global embrace, abolishing both space and time as far as our planet is concerned. Rapidly, we approach the final phase of the extension of man—technological simulation of consciousness, when the creative process of knowing will be collectively and corporately extended to the whole of human society, much as we have already extended our senses and our nerves by the various media. (p. 19)

McLuhan's vision of extending our physical bodies through electric media has been realized in cyberspace. It extends our senses and annihilates physical space as it enables us to encounter the collective views of human society. We can now create, duplicate, and distribute a digital persona throughout the World-Wide Web of computer systems. However, although we are bridging the barriers of time and space through global communications media, we are simultaneously destroying the unity of self. As our communications technologies extend our senses into a united global embrace, the ecology of self dissolves. This is the final paradox of cyberspace.

REFERENCES

Aukstakalnis, S., & Blatner, D. (1992). *Silicon mirage: The art and science of virtual reality.* Berkeley: Peachpit Press.
Baird, W. (1993). *Crashcourse.* New York: Ace Books.
Barnes, S., & Greller, L. (1994). Computer-mediated communication in the organization. *Communication Education, 43*, 1-10.
Baudrillard, J. (1983). *Simulations.* New York: Seiotext (e).
Benedikt, M. (1991). *Cyberspace: First steps.* Cambridge, MA: MIT Press.
Berger, P. L., & Luckmann, T. (1966). *The social construction of reality.* New York: Anchor Books.
Bova, B. (1989). *Cyberbooks.* London: Mandarin Paperback.
Bukatman, S. (1993). *Terminal identity.* Durham, NC: Duke University Press.
Dreyfus, H.L. (1979). *What computers can't do.* New York: Harper & Row.
Fisher, S. (1989, December). Virtual environments and interactivity: Windows to the future. *Computer Graphics: SIGGRAPH '89 Panel Proceedings, July 31-August 4, Boston, Massachusetts, 23*(5), 7-18.
Foster, A.D. (1990). *Cyber way.* New York: Ace Books.
Gardner, H. (1985). *The mind's new science.* New York: Basic Books.
Gaver, W.W. (1992). The affordance of media spaces for collaboration. In *ACM*

1992 Conference on Computer-Supported Cooperative Work, Sharing Perspectives, October 31 to November 4, 1992, Toronto, Canada (pp. 17-24). New York: Association for Computing Machinery.

Gergen, K.J. (1991). *The saturated self: Dilemmas of identity in contemporary life.* New York: Basic Books.

Gibson, W. (1984). *Neuromancer.* New York: Ace Books.

Gibson, W. (1986). *Count Zero.* New York: Ace Books.

Gibson, W. (1988). *Mona Lisa Overdrive.* New York: Bantam Books.

Gibson, W. (1991). Academy leader. In M. Benedikt (Ed.), *Cyberspace: First steps* (pp. 27-29). Cambridge, MA: MIT Press.

Graves, G.L. (1993, January). Invasion of the digital puppets. *New Media*, pp. 38-39.

Hafner, K., & Markoff, J. (1991). *Cyberpunk: Outlaws and hackers on the computer frontier.* New York: Simon & Schuster.

Haraway, D.J. (1991). *Simians, cyborgs, and women: The reinvention of nature.* New York: Routledge, Chapman & Hall.

Heim, M. (1991). The erotic ontology of cyberspace. In M. Benedikt (Ed.), *Cyberspace: First steps* (pp. 59-80). Cambridge: MIT Press.

Heim, M. (1993). *The metaphysics of virtual reality.* New York: Oxford University Press.

Hintz, H.W. (1960). Whitehead's concept of organism and the mind-body problem. In S. Hook (Ed.), *Dimensions of Mind* (pp. 100-109). New York: New York University Press.

Hollinger, V. (1992). Cybernetic deconstructions: Cyberpunk and postmodernism. In L. McCaffery (Ed.), *Storming the reality studio: A casebook of cyberpunk and postmodern fiction* (pp. 203-218). Durham, NC: Duke University Press.

Illingworth, V. (1990). *Dictionary of computing* (3rd ed.). Oxford: Oxford University Press.

Jamison, P.K. (1994, February 28). Contradictory spaces: Pleasure and the seduction of the cyborg discourse. *The Archnet Electronic Journal on Virtual Culture* [On-line serial]. Available: LISTSERV@KENTVM.KENT.EDU Archived as JAMISON V2N1.

Kelly, R.V., Jr. (1994). Move over, Dr. Frankenstein. *Virtual Reality Special Report, Premiere Issue*, pp. 19-25.

Kroker, A. (1993). *Spasm: Virtual reality, android music and electric flesh.* New York: St. Martin's Press.

Lanier, J. (1989, December). Virtual environments and interactivity: Windows to the future. *Computer Graphics: SIGGRAPH '89 Panel Proceedings, July 31-August 4, Boston, Massachusetts, 23*(5), 7-18.

Larijani, L.C. (1994). Homo Faber or Homo Sapiens? *Virtual Reality Special Report, Premier Issue*, pp. 7-10.

Levy, S. (1991, November). Cyberspaced. *MacWorld*, pp. 61-66.

Levy, S. (1992). *Artificial Life: A report from the frontier where computers meet biology.* New York: Random House.

Lyotard, J. (1991). *The inhuman.* Stanford: Stanford University Press.
McCaffery, L. (1992). *Storming the reality studio: A casebook of cyberpunk and postmodern fiction.* Durham, NC: Duke University Press.
McLuhan, M. (1964). *Understanding media: The extensions of man.* New York: Signet Books.
Mead, G. H. (1959). *The Philosophy of the present.* LaSalle, IL: Open Court.
Mead, G. H. (1962). *Mind, self, & society.* Chicago, University of Chicago Press.
Meyrowitz, J. (1985). *No sense of place.* New York: Oxford University Press.
Minsky, M. (1986). *The society of mind.* New York: Simon & Schuster.
Novak, M. (1991). Liquid architectures in cyberspace. In M. Benedikt (Ed.), *Cyberspace: First steps* (pp. 225-254). Cambridge, MA: MIT Press.
Piercy, M. (1991). *He, she and it.* New York: Knopf.
Porter, S. (1992, March). Virtual reality. *Computer Graphics World*, pp. 42-43.
Poster. M. (1990). *The mode of information.* Chicago: University of Chicago Press.
Reveaux, T. (1993, January). Virtual reality gets real. *New Media*, pp. 32-41.
Rheingold, H. (1993). *The virtual community: Homesteading on the electronic frontier.* Reading, MA: Addison-Wesley.
Rheingold, H. (1994, February). PARC is back! *Wired*, pp. 91-95.
Rose, F. (1984). *Into the heart of the mind: An American quest for artificial intelligence*: New York: Harper & Row.
Rushkoff, D. (1994). *Cyberia: Life in the trenches of hyperspace.* San Francisco: HarperCollins.
Rucker, R. (1982). *Infinity and the mind.* New York: Bantam Books.
Rucker, R. (1992). Artificial life. In R. Rucker, R.U. Sirius, & Mu, Q. (Eds.), *Mondo: 2000 A user's guide to the new edge* (pp. 64-67). New York: HarperCollins Publishers.
Rumelhart, D.E., Widrow, B., & Lehr, M.A. (1994, March). The basic ideas in neural networks. *Communications of the ACM*, pp. 87-92.
Shelley, M. (1963). *Frankenstein.* New York: Signet Classic.
Sirus, R.U. (1992). Cyberpunk. In R. Rucker, Sirius, R.U., & Mu, Q. (Eds.). *Mondo: 2000 A user's guide to the new edge* (pp. 64-67). New York: HarperCollins.
Sobchack, V. (1993). New age mutant ninja hackers: Reading Mondo 2000. *The South Atlantic Quarterly Review, 92*(4), 569-584.
Springer, C. (1993). Sex, memories, and angry women. *The South Atlantic Quarterly Review, 92*(4), 713-733.
Stephenson, N. (1992). *Snow crash.* New York: Bantam Books.
Sterling, B. (1988). *Islands in the net.* New York: Ace Books.
Sterling, B. (1992). Preface from Mirrorshades. In L. McCaffery (Ed.), *Storming the reality studio: A casebook of cyberpunk and postmodern fiction* (pp. 343-348). Durham, NC: Duke University Press.
Steuer, J. (1992). Defining virtual reality: Dimensions determining telepresence. *Journal of Communication, 42*(4), 73-93.

Stone, A.R. (1991). Will the real body please stand up?: Boundary stories about virtual cultures. In M. Benedikt (Ed.), *Cyberspace: First steps* (pp. 81-118). Cambridge, MA: MIT Press.

Thomson, A. (1993). *Virtual girl.* New York: Ace Books.

Tomas, D. (1991). Old rituals for new space: Rites de passage and William Gibson's cultural model of cyberspace. In M. Benedikt (Ed.), *Cyberspace: First steps* (pp. 31-47). Cambridge, MA: MIT Press.

Turin, D. (1993). Welcome to the machine: Clever Hans and his expert systems future. *Mondo 2000, 11*, 47-51.

Van Der Leun, G. (1993). This is a naked lady. *Wired, Premier Issue*, pp. 74,109.

Van Gelder, L. (1991). The strange case of the electronic lover. In C. Dunlop & R. Kling (Eds.), *Computerization and controversy* (pp. 354-375). Boston: Academic Press.

Weiner, N. (1954). *The human use of human beings: Cybernetics and society.* Garden City, NY: Doubleday Books.

Weiser, M. (1991, September). The computer for the 21st century. *Scientific American*, pp. 95-104.

Weiser, M. (1993, July). Some computer science issues in ubiquitous computing. *Communications of the ACM*, pp. 75-84.

Wiener, L.R. (1993). *Digital woes: Why we should not depend on software.* Reading, MA: Addison-Wesley.

Woolley, B. (1992). *Virtual worlds.* Oxford: Blackwell.

Zachmann, W.F. (1992, March 31). Simulation: The ultimate virtual reality. *PC Magazine*, p. 107.

✧✧✧✧ 14

The Cybergym: Virtual Reality in the Health Club

Elizabeth Weiss

At first glance, the cerebral activity of computing and the nonphysical world of cyberspace seem quite distant from bodybuilding, exercise, and the health club. But the two are already in the process of converging, as Elizabeth Weiss demonstrates in this analysis of an often unacknowledged site of contemporary virtual reality. She examines the consequences of joining cyberculture with our often narcissistic compulsion for physical fitness and discusses how this new urban space alters the manner in which we interact with our own bodies.

In other sections of this book, further consideration of the body in cyberspace can be found in Jay David Bolter's comments on virtual reality and the mind-body split in Chapter 7, Michael P. Beaubien's study of cyberspace gaming in Chapter 12, Richard Cutler's research on relationships in Chapter 21, and Mark Lipton's essay on cybersex in Chapter 22.

In *Variations on a Theme Park* (1992), author Michael Sorkin chronicles the end of public space and cities as we once knew them and describes the creation of a drastically new kind of urban space: "Recent years have seen the emergence of a new kind of city, a city without a place attached to it. . . . The city described is no longer merely physical . . . this new city occupies a vast, unseen, conceptual space" (pp. xi-xii). We could use these same words to characterize electronic space: a floating, invisible structure in which people interact without face-to-face connections and without associations with a tangible or specific territory.

Sorkin (1992) outlines three characteristics of the new "conceptual city": an obsession with security and surveillance, an emphasis on simulations and faux familiarity—or "the city as theme park" (p. xiv)—and the dissolution of anything distinctive or intrinsic about a specific space. The shopping mall and amusement park are two conspicuous models of this new cyberlike urbanism, or "Cyburbia" (p. xv). But there is another site that combines the qualities of both electronic and urban space in a uniquely frightening way: the ubiquitous health club.

World Gym is a spacious, upscale gym in New York's Lower East Side. The equipment is bright orange and cold steel; the brand is "Cybex." The verisimilitude in name may be coincidental, but one is reminded of cyberspace here by more than just the similarity in sound. Observe the following:

- A woman tells her friends in step class that she will not be at the gym this weekend because she is going to the Caribbean with her sister: "But I'll still get some exercise. We're going to rent bikes," she pauses, as she feels she needs to explain: "I mean, *real ones*."
- A recent Infomercial for a personal, portable "stepper" advertises its product this way: "Tired of going to the gym? Now you can have the convenience of working out in your own home, without the hassle of going out!" The stepper is a simulation of a simulation (the electronic stairclimber) of real stairs. Likewise, the living room becomes a simulation of a simulation (the health club) of the outdoors. Without any trace of irony, the announcer warns us, "Beware of imitation steppers!" ("There's only *one* stepper for you . . . ")

Visually, it is striking how much the grid-like patterns, complicated apparatuses, and sprawling equipment in a gym resemble wire circuitry inside an electronic machine. The "machine aesthetics" of the health club cause many first-time health club users to feel alienated and overwhelmed—a disorientation very similar to what one feels when experiencing virtual reality for the first time. The first difference between these two worlds is the following: although cyberspace provides only an *emotional* high with its illusion of ultimate mental freedom, the gym's disembodying experience is both an emotional and *physiological* one.

The cyberspace navigator enters electronic space solely for the mental journey, but the health club user comes with an agenda of attaining *tangible* results. In time, however, the gym user will find that jacking into an exercise machine is as habit forming as plugging into the matrix can be. And soon the exerciser will return again and again, like the cyberspace addict, just for the ride.

SURVEILLANCE

Upon entering the gym, members must stop at the front desk to input their membership number into the central computer. On the screen appears their photograph, the last time they worked out, and the cumulative number of visits to the gym. The surveillance has begun.

Next are the mirrors: floor to ceiling and wall to wall. The health club user is watched constantly in the mirror, by him- or herself and by others, competitively comparing stamina and bodies. The mirrors make the gym as voyeuristic as the cinema, the circus, or a beauty pageant; it is simultaneously a place of spectacle and a place of spying. Novelist Don DeLillo discusses the current omnipresence of the camera this way: "The twentieth century is . . . the filmed century. . . . The whole world is on film, all the time. Spy satellites, microscopic scanners, pictures of the uterus, embryos, sex, war, assassinations, everything" (quoted in Dery, 1992, p. 46). The gym's obsession with watching and being watched makes the health club a quintessentially postmodern urban space.

The exercise machines complete the panoptic gaze of the health club. The computerized equipment tracks the user's effort: "You must keep up with the machine," it dictates, measuring his or her progress. "You have burned 210 calories," it reports, and then stores the results in the computer memory. The machines stare at the user with more force than any of the other gazes. And unlike the human eye, machines never blink.

The one space of relief from the ubiquitous mirror is the darkened wall that fronts on the street. This is a one-way mirror in which only those outside the gym can look in, amplifying the spectacle phenomenon even further. Many bypassers do stop to peer inside, ogling the indoor exercisers as they electronically reshape their flesh. The gym users become metal balls inside a pinball machine, bouncing around inside a space dominated by electrical circuitry as onlookers watch them through transparent glass.

The one-way communication of the electronics is offset by the only real space of democracy in the gym: the locker room. Downstairs, in another level entirely from the electronic world above, members strip themselves of workout clothes and mindset. Here they talk to each other without the white noise of machines and mirrors. The one small mirror over the sink is used as a bulletin board to exchange information, serving as a form of "unmediated communication," a term used by Baudrillard (1981, p. 183) to describe the power of graffiti.

REMOTE CONTROL URBANITES AND TREADMILL TRAVELERS

Upon beginning his workout, the gym member must choose a machine: lifecycle, rower, or treadmill. The machine charts the activity of the user, displaying how many flights of stairs the stepper has (imitated) climbed, how many miles the user (would have) covered, or how steep the (imaginary) hill is. In *Society of the Spectacle* (1983), Guy Debord defined *the spectacle* as "a social relation among people, mediated by images" (para. 4). William Gibson (1984) echoed this sentiment with his definition of *cyberspace* as a "consensual hallucination" (p. 51). The gym is a space of consensual spectacle, in which its members pretend to be truly engaging in the activity they electronically mimic.

With its choose-your-own-adventure quality, the health club fulfills the second requirement of the new urban, cyberlike spaces; in the gym, every activity is an amusement ride, an appealing and regulated version of reality. One can cross-country ski across a mountain, row across a lake, or even bike across America. But gone are any unpleasant snow moguls, the irregular currents of a lake, or those unpredictable hills in nature. In the gym, one can experience every rugged and risky activity in the world—without the risk or ruggedness. Like Disneyland, the health club offers participants every city in the world, all within safe, clean, concrete boundaries.

The variety of simulated activities offered in the gym is a reflection of the "remote control" quality of modern urbanites. Club exercisers can change their exercise as quickly as they can change channels. Thus the television has its metaphorical place in the postmodern gym (and its physical place too; televisions are available to watch while virtually skiing across that steep mountain).

In that all gyms provide a pleasant sameness for its users, the health club lives up to the last criteria for urban cyberspace locations. No matter how foreign the locale outside the gym walls, inside the users are provided with a generic and interchangeable vision of universality. A tourist who runs outside in every new city he or she visits sees life at street level, taking in the native culture and people face to face during the run. On the other hand, a treadmill user pounds away on the same black rubber over and over in every country; he or she goes nowhere and sees nothing. The "treadmill traveler" is like the protagonist in Anne Tyler's *The Accidental Tourist*, a man who writes books for reluctant travelers who want to cross the globe with as little reminder as possible that they have left home.

VIRTUAL EXERCISE: THE MIND AND THE BODY

Alhough the body is the main event, the gym is also *dis*embodying in that the exerciser appropriates the maternal role, giving birth to a new self in a new body, rejecting the one given by the true mother. In the fitness movement, individuals use technology to replace the woman's life-giving status. Like the Nazi soldiers described by Klaus Theweleit in *Male Fantasies* (1987), gym members train themselves to live like machines, making them "true child[ren] of the machine, created without the help of woman" (p. 160).

This quest to recreate the body through the machine is primarily a result of the commodification of culture. The gym's very purpose is to create marketable bodies that are later bartered in exchange for a promotion, prestige, or sex. The gym member is encouraged to make the machine into "the mother" by delivering a new body from the womb of the machine.

Indeed, one of the most popular classes offered at World Gym is "Body Sculpting." In this class, members sculpt their own bodies just like an artist sculpts an imitation of a body, with clay or marble. The image of a sculptor surveying his or her work is very applicable to the health gym member, in that both survey their work of art (the body) from a distance. The body becomes an entity separate from the inner self, something that must be constantly judged and then altered. By obsessively reforming their bodies, members end up *disembodying* themselves, much like a virtual reality (VR) participant. The bodies become something that can be watched (by themselves or by others), tracked over time, and, most importantly, changed at will—just like in the matrix.

Even in fashion, the gym user resembles one who is jacked into a VR space. Wearing full latex bodysuits, weightlifting gloves, leather belts around the waist, and walkmans that block out all external sound, the gym user could easily be mistaken for a suited up VR traveler. If they took off their goggles and helmet, TRON protagonists would feel right at home in a health club.

PUBLIC SPACE

Like cyberspace, the gym blurs boundaries between any remembrance of the old private and public space separations. The rules and norms of the outside world do not apply within health club walls; there is no other public space in which you can find adults groaning, grunting, and shamelessly moaning: "Feels so good!" And there is no other (public) place in which strangers casually walk around in skin-tight clothing and help position each other in compromising positions.

Artificial Reality pioneer Myron Krueger creates simulations that free adults from the normally confining restrictions placed on them in real life (Morgan, 1992). "Adults in our society allow themselves an incredibly restricted repertoire of physical behaviors. My interactions are operated by the body so people will forget what they are doing with their bodies as they try to achieve an effect on the screen. They find themselves in postures they have not been in since they were children" (p. 97). The same is easily said of any aerobics class.

In that both women and men walk around the gym sweating profusely in astonishingly revealing clothing, the health club is unquestionably a highly eroticized zone. In this building dedicated to the aesthetics of the body, sexuality is more than just a subtext. Gyms are to the singles scene today what bars, dance clubs, and the shopping mall were to the past—and what cyberspace and electronic bulletin boards may be to the future.

GENDER IN THE GYM

The gym truly is home for those users who spend more time in the gym matrix than anywhere else. Lenda Murray is one such example. As part of her training that led to her being crowned Ms. Olympia 1990, 1991, and 1992, she spent 8 hours a day in the gym (where she squatted 425 pounds regularly). Along with her looks and her superhuman ability, her stringent diet (five rations of skinless turkey breast or fish a day, nothing else) makes her sound more android than mortal. Knowing that Ms. Murray pumps her body down to 7% body fat, it is no wonder that wherever she goes, people stare (Ravo, 1992).

With such draconian diet restrictions and work-out regimen, one is again reminded of Theweleit's (1987) description of fascist, "stereometric" soldiers (p. 153) who exercise to the point at which pain means pleasure: "The mechanized body as conservative utopia derives . . . from men's compulsion to subjugate and repulse what is specifically human about them" (p. 162). Theweleit's analysis applies to the cyborg body of Ms. Olympia, illustrating that the drive to repress human qualities in place of technological ones is no longer limited to just men.

But unlike the surprisingly conventional gender dynamics posited by most cyberpunk authors, science-fiction filmmakers, and cyberspace theorists, the gym matrix is gendered in much more egalitarian fashion than the outside world. Men comprise the majority of step classes at World Gym, a matriarchal class run by a small, hoarse-voiced woman yelling moves at her disciples. Treadmills and stepmasters are manipulated as skillfully and as often by both sexes. Even the weightlifting equipment is shared without reluctance or without any of the power dynamics that exist outside the mirrored walls. Despite the artificiality of its visual, utopian pretense, the gym offers surprisingly radical, utopian-like gender dynamics.

THE GYM OF THE FUTURE

In the near future, virtual reality may overlap with the gym in more than just metaphor. Today's cross-country ski machines, body slide machines (imitating ice skating), and other mimetic variations of reality could be combined with the more complicated and sensory-oriented advantages of cyberspace. Each workout would be a new adventure, even more fun than the amusement-park-like opportunities in today's gyms. Gym users would be able to jack into the environment they choose in cyberspace while they simultaneously workout their real bodies. If this gym of the future—"the CyberGym"—becomes a reality, a totally new theory for embodiment and body-mind interaction will be required.

As it is theorized today, the body of the cyberspace traveler is left behind, inactive and motionless, while the subject's mind is freed and deliriously omnipotent. Cyberspace theorist Claudia Springer (1992) writes, "Computers offer a radically new relationship, one that no longer fortifies physical prowess but, instead, passifies the body while engaging the mind" (p. 12). Some fear this separation between mind and body, predicting that, in Gibson's words, the body will become "meat." In this scenario, according to Brenda Laurel (1991), "the mind accelerates into the net, clothed in pixelated radiance, leaving the body forgotten, slumped over a keyboard in some shabby basement room" (p. 14).

Others praise the bodiless nature of cyberspace, celebrating the ability to leave the troublesome, diseased body behind. This desire to abandon the body is a result of the slew of modern fears centered around the body (AIDS, abortion, surrogate motherhood, etc.). But this era characterized by panic over the vulnerability of the body cannot last forever. As soon as the hysteria concerning the fragile body subsides, a new type of cyberspace that actively includes the body may be preferred. Unlike the mind-body split that occurs in Gibsonian cyberspace, the CyberGym would unite both mind and body, liberating them equally, although in radically different ways. The CyberGym would incorporate the emancipation of the mind in the matrix, while simultaneously allowing the body to come along for the ride.

Another cyberwriter has her finger on the inevitable pairing of the mind and the body: "No matter how virtual the subject may become, there is always a body attached. It may be off somewhere else—and that 'somewhere else' may be a privileged point of view—but consciousness remains firmly rooted in the physical. Historically, body, technology, and community constitute each other" (Stone, 1991, p. 109). Unlike the present version of virtual reality, the CyberGym would acknowledge this fact, and work with it.

As we posit the existence of a CyberGym, one valid fear is the possibility that exercisers will come to prefer the simulation to the real. Why ski a real mountain when you can enjoy the view and get the same physical movements without the icy wind? But one advantage of the CyberGym is that it would offer a more social experience for present-day health club members who currently interact only with machines.

Friends and family would be able to keep in closer contact by combining their exercise time with correspondence. Former college roommates living in separate East Coast cities could meet each week for a game of volleyball on a (virtual) Malibu beach. A CyberGym family could play a game of cybertennis together: the father in one city at his screen, the daughter off at college across the country at another screen—each sweating at his or her own station. They would get the same workout unhampered by long distance or a glaring sun. The CyberGym will be good for family values.

According to Donna Haraway (1991), the history of our culture is the history of a "technoculture," in which humans and machines are already intertwined in innumerable ways. Cyborgs already abound in our culture, in the form of Ms. Olympia and Arnold Schwarznegger. But these cyborgs, as well as the more literal machine-human combinations that have emerged from science, incorporate the fusion of a *human mind* with a *mechanical body* (mechanical body part or machine-like body).

But the cyborg of the CyberGym would mean the opposite: a *mechanical mind* (the mind fusing with the machine) combined with a *human body.* Members of the CyberGym would participate in the matrix like TRON explorers, but when they jacked out, they would be more than just mentally exhausted after an aerobic hour of circuit hurdling, grid skipping, and cursor dodging.

Knowing that the modern obsession with health, fitness, and toned bodies is more than a passing trend, the cyberspace-health club unification may be inevitable. After its initial hype, a bodiless cyberspace would ultimately fail as a lucrative pastime. Upwardly mobile middle Americans have the purchasing power to make or break expensive technological products, and the future will soon find double-income couples with children who have less and less time to jack into cyberspace just for fun. But if virtual reality were packaged as a way to experience any environment imaginable, all while simultaneously sweating off pounds on the body that awaits your return—now *that* would sell.

REFERENCES

Baudrillard, J (1981). *For a critique of the political economy of the sign* (C. Levin, Trans.). St. Louis: Telos Press.

Debord, G. (1983). *Society of the spectacle.* Detroit: Black & Red.

Dery, M. (1992). Terrorvision: Panopticism in the age of totally hidden video. *Mondo 2000, 7,* 44-46.

Gibson, W. (1984). *Neuromancer.* New York: Ace Books.

Haraway, D. (1991). *Simians, cyborgs, and women: The reinvention of nature.* New York: Routledge.

Laurel, B. (1991). Art and activism in VR. *Verbum, 52,* 14, 8-25.

Morgan, J. (1992). Real artifice: Myron Krueger's beautiful interface. *Mondo 2000, 7,* 96-97.

Ravo, N. (1992, December 2). Wonder Woman, In the Flesh. *New York Times,* p.B1.

Sorkin, M. (1992). *Variations on a theme park: The new American city and the end of public space.* New York: Noonday Press.

Springer, C. (1992, June). *Muscular Circuitry: The invincible armored cyborg in cinema.* Paper presented at Rhode Island College.

Stone, A.R. (1991) Will the real body please stand up? Boundary stories about virtual cultures. In M. Benedikt (Ed.), *Cyberspace: First steps* (pp. 81-118). Cambridge, MA: MIT Press.

Theweleit, K. (1987). *Male fantasies, Vol. II. Male bodies, psychoanalyzing the white terror* (E. Carter & C. Turner, Trans.). Minneapolis: University of Vermont Press.

◇◇◇◇ 15

Experience in the Age of Digital Reproduction

Margaret Cassidy

Contrary to what many may believe, virtual reality, digital environments, and excursions into cyberspace have already become an integral part of people's lives. The future is already here, as Cassidy points out in this examination of digital experience, simulation, and cybertravel. Drawing on Walter Benjamin's ideas about mechanical reproduction, Daniel Boorstin's concept of the pseudo-event, and the postmodernist notion of hyperreality, she discusses the impact of digital reproduction, alteration, and simulation on our experience of the world. Apart from Section 3, other approaches to digital experience can be found in Herbert Zettl's aesthetic study of virtual reality in Chapter 5, Charles U. Larson's dramatistic analysis of virtual reality in Chapter 6, Terri Toles Patkin's human factors research in Chapter 11, and Mark Lipton's exploration of the experience of cybersex in Chapter 22.

> Recently, a young San Francisco couple exchanged wedding vows using virtual reality. . . . As family and friends watched through virtual-environment monitors, the bride and groom donned special headgear that transported them into the mythical city of Atlantis, where they exchanged their vows. . . . Developers of the wedding software hope that this will lead to a whole new market for virtual-reality centers, which have, until now, been used primarily for pure amusement. (Bruckert, 1994, p. 48)

This blurb came from the November 1994 issue of *Ladies' Home Journal*. Thus, it appears that virtual reality (VR) has become a regular consideration of mainstream America. Technologies that were until recently the stuff of science-fiction novels are now common knowledge and frequently referred to in regular conversation. American children are growing up with the stuff; a recent episode of *The Simpsons* had Lisa Simpson fantasizing about having VR gear in her school. And although the popular program *Mighty Morphin Power Rangers* has been receiving its share of attention for a whole variety of reasons, what is perhaps most interesting about the show is the fact that the term *morph* is now a regular part of the vocabulary of the average American youth. And so, even though the elaborate cyberspace fantasies like those of William Gibson are still more the stuff of science fiction than of actual possibility, we are becoming a society that is more accustomed to the idea of using these new technologies, a society that looks forward to having them.

In such a society, it seems essential to take these changes seriously and to think about their consequences. Many people are still reluctant to be part of any discussion about something like virtual reality. These are the people who will argue that a virtual Atlantis wedding is the choice of one bizarre couple, not a sign of cultural transformation, and, in fairness, they are probably right about that. It is stories like this virtual wedding that lead many communication scholars to believe that discussions of new technologies sound a little too much like sci-fi fantasy, and so they have little interest in taking part in them. But in writing off what is going on, scholars lose out on an opportunity to watch a significant change in a culture's media environment as it happens. Presumably, those who have some awareness of what is happening are in a better position to take part in shaping these events, and so the changes taking place deserve serious attention.

It is probably fair for skeptics to say that we do not presently have anything close to the totally immersive virtual experiences so often described by the visionaries and the pioneers. But there *are* already many new technologies in some homes, schools, places of business, and even, apparently, places of worship that seem to be changing these places in subtle and not-so-subtle ways. Teleconferencing, the Internet, digital image, sound and video editing software, electronic books, and CD-ROMs—all of these are new ways of encoding, representing, and sharing experiences made possible by the computer. What kind of world will it be as more and more of our experiences take place through these new media? Even if fully immersive virtual reality is far off, or never to be, the changes already happening deserve to be studied. And there is plenty of communication scholarship, some of it even written well before the days of virtual reality, that is quite relevant to what is going on today. Looking at this work is a good place to begin thinking about the changes and challenges that we face.

REPRODUCED EXPERIENCE

A good example of a question that is a part of today's discussions, but which has been addressed before, is this: What happens when we are able to mass reproduce an experience, such as we are doing today through computer simulation? Walter Benjamin (1968) might never have imagined some of the developments in reproduction that have taken place in recent years, but his work certainly sheds some light on those developments. In his well-known essay, "The Work of Art in the Age of Mechanical Reproduction," Benjamin explored some of the implications of mass reproduction. His concern was that people's perceptions of original works would be compromised in various ways. Reproductions would decontextualize the original, putting its copies "into situations which would be out of reach for the original itself" (p. 220). Even though it would be the reproduction, not the original, finding its way into a variety of new contexts, Benjamin feared that the authenticity or "aura" of the original would be destroyed.

Furthermore, should good quality reproductions be easily accessible people might start to believe that there is no important difference between the original and the reproduction. John Berger (1977) also expressed this concern in *Ways of Seeing*, arguing that "the uniqueness of the original now lies in it being *the original of a reproduction*" (p. 21; emphasis in original), that an original is nothing much worth seeking out for its own merits, but is rather a template from which to make the really important creation—the reproduced image.

However, neither Benjamin nor Berger was oblivious to some of the possible benefits of such new technologies of reproduction. It is possible to use reproduction to democratize knowledge, to make it available to many more people than was previously possible. People might take an interest in a work of art, a natural wonder, or an historical event as a result of learning about it through some form of reproduction. For example, although a recording of a Beethoven symphony can never capture all of the experience of hearing a live performance, it can reproduce the music well enough for listeners to appreciate it, and perhaps to try to learn more about it—maybe even to go to a live concert. An historic landmark is only significant to those who know the story behind the place; such knowledge might come from a book or magazine, or some other mass-produced source. So although some of the unique authority of a place or a creation might be lost in mass reproduction, such reproduction could also grant more authority and respect to the original by making it known to more people.

Clearly, these ideas are relevant to the technological changes we are witnessing today. At the present time, we have even more sophisticated methods of reproducing "original" experiences and making them available to a large audience. For example, photographers are becoming aware that the CD-ROM is an ideal vehicle for photographic images, which might otherwise be seen only in galleries. Three-dimensional modeling enables us to "walk around" historic landmarks on our computer screens, bringing us to places we might not otherwise get to. Digital audio technology allows us to explore works of music in new ways. One can argue that these new forms of reproduction will take something away from the original works, making them merely models to be converted into the digital information from which they can be reproduced. Under the circumstances, it might never occur to people that there is any good reason to go to a museum or a gallery to see the original image from which their CD-ROMs were made, especially because the computerized version can be experienced without leaving the comfort and safety of home.

On the other hand, it may be that the authenticity of original works can be enhanced by new technology. As with older methods of reproduction, perhaps people will learn about art, history, or music through an interactive media experience, thus enabling them to appreciate the original that they otherwise might not have known about at all. A computer simulation will not be the same as physically being there, but it would be better than nothing.

So it would seem that there is something to be gained, as well as something to be lost, as a result of the mass reproduction of unique experiences. To make things more complicated, today's technologies allow us not only to come closer to the goal of making reproductions that are barely distinguishable from the original, but to alter the original in a variety of ways. What are the implications of using technology to "improve on" an experience?

PSEUDO-EXPERIENCE

Our use of new technologies has contributed to our being a society whose experiences are often technologically altered in imperceptible ways. Daniel Boorstin (1962) is one scholar who thought deeply about what happens when a society's experience of reality is changed by technology. Boorstin's concern was with what he would call the pseudo-event and what impact pseudo-events are having on American culture. By a *pseudo-event*, Boorstin meant an experience that seems completely "real," but is fabricated in some fashion, often without our knowing that some aspects of it are manufactured. As technological advance enabled us to make more and more realistic images, it became possible to substitute these images for the unaltered original experience. It is a desirable thing to do because we can manufacture images of an experience that are more satisfying than the experience itself would be. For example, theme parks that create miniature, "realistic" versions of foreign countries give many visitors the sense that they are actually better off than those who bother to travel to the country itself; after all, the park is closer, cheaper, and does not require you to learn a foreign language. Then there is the advertisement that recently ran for "The Ultimate Gift Idea—Fighter Pilot for a Day" ("Air combat USA," p. 51, 1994). The ad goes on to describe how for $695, one may don flight suit, helmet, and parachute, take off in a fighter plane with an instructor, and engage in a mock air attack. This is a large part of what Boorstin meant by a pseudo-event: an experience that retains many realistic elements, but that "fixes up" the original event by removing the uncomfortable, the distasteful, the difficult, and the demanding from the experience.

Boorstin (1962) was concerned that America had become a nation predisposed to having a dangerously large appetite for pseudo-events, that "we have been notorious as a country where the impossible was thought only slightly less attainable than the difficult. The unprecedented American opportunities have always tempted us to confuse the visionary with the real" (p. 240). Boorstin wrote, "We have become so accustomed to our illusions that we mistake them for reality. We demand them. And we demand that there be always more of them, bigger and better and more vivid. They are the world of our making: the world of the image" (pp. 6-7). The more our image-making technologies develop, the more we demand and the more ways we seek to live in worlds of our own making. The problem with this attitude, according to Boorstin, is that we have come to expect things from reality that reality simply cannot provide, and so we are forever disappointed by it. Consequently, we choose to live more and more in our manufactured illusions, which are more interesting, less painful, and more pleasant than reality.

This might seem to be a perfectly fine situation; if reality is not nice and we can make images that are, then what is the matter? What is the matter, to Boorstin (1962), is what he calls the mirror effect. One important path to wisdom is to be confronted by realities that do not match our expectations. When we face such conflicts, we are challenged to modify our understanding. If, however, we can mold our world to fit the images we have in our heads, we effectively avoid challenges to our incomplete understanding of the world. Boorstin was concerned that we would become more and more limited in our experience by opting for the comfort of the image over the challenges of reality. He worried that we would cease "to give visas to strange and alien and outside notions" (p. 260), and thus exclude from our lives "the very world which would jar our experience, and which we most need to make us more largely human" (p. 256).

Clearly, we are confronted today by more technological change of the sort that inspired Boorstin's work back in 1962. In the past few years, the term *hyperreality* has found its way into the vocabularies of people thinking about the implications of new technology. For those who find such terms to be more confusing than enlightening, this term can be thought of, to a large extent, simply as a new way of describing the pseudo-event. Scholars such as Jean Baudrillard (1983) and Umberto Eco (1986) describe the hyperreal as a combination of reality and image, reality "fixed up" so that it is not quite real—it is better than real. An example Eco gives is a replica of the bill of sale of Manhattan Island written in English, for an American audience, instead of the original Dutch—which he calls a "fac-different" instead of a facsimile (Eco, 1983, p. 11).

Perhaps the best way to demonstrate how Boorstin's work relates to the more recent work of people like Baudrillard and Eco is through the example of travel. There is plenty of talk about how technologies like virtual reality might be used as a substitute for physical travel. On the one hand, virtual vacations could solve some problems of travel. For example, travel has traditionally been restricted to those with the time and resources to make the trip. But it is conceivable that many people who cannot travel extensively could gain access to a virtual travel experience. Certain kinds of expeditions require travelers to be in excellent physical condition, thus excluding many people from experiencing them. But a virtual version would not discriminate on the basis of physical ability. One could also argue that simulation allows us to create whole new worlds to which we may travel; although a simulation might be based on some real location, there is no particular reason why it needs to resemble any place that actually exists. In theory, a person could dream up his or her idealized vacation, then have a simulation made to order. Anyone who is skeptical that this will be possible anytime soon should refer back to the wedding in Atlantis. It is already here.

Now along with the benefits of virtual travel come some potential shortcomings. The kind of travel virtual reality will permit may support Boorstin's (1962) criticism that we have become what he calls "tourists" rather than travelers. In the past, Boorstin argues, travel meant uncertainty, danger, and discomfort. You took your chances and sometimes were deeply rewarded with a profound experience. Simulated travel is travel with no sense at all of crossing any physical distance, with no discomfort whatsoever. And what one encounters there is entirely predetermined by the designers. Even if they allow for a degree of random luck, it too must be preordained in order to exist. Simulated travel is travel without uncertainty; whereas travelers on an African safari know that they may or may not actually see what they set out to see, purchasers of a virtual safari would probably be quite angered if such serendipity were built into the experience. Surely the weather was perfect in virtual Atlantis, and that the couple would have been quite annoyed had they not gotten the weather they paid for. Some would argue, then, that the virtual trip is the better one because you are sure you will get what you are after. Eco (1986) describes this point particularly well in his *Travels in Hyperreality:*

> When, in the space of twenty-four hours, you go (as I did deliberately) from the fake New Orleans of Disneyland to the real one, and from the wild river of Adventureland to a trip on the Mississippi, where the captain of the paddle-wheel steamer says it is possible to see alligators on the banks of the river, and then you don't see any, you risk feeling homesick for Disneyland, where the wild animals don't have to be coaxed. Disneyland tells us that technology can give us more reality than nature can. (p. 44)

What is going on today raises some important questions that we need to think about. Although it is exciting to talk about "unprecedented" changes and to speculate about the wonders that they will bring, such an attitude also suggests that no one has ever taken on any of these issues before, which leaves many people at a loss to make sense of things. In truth, these issues have been debated for a long time. Once we realize that there is something familiar about today's changes, we are in a better position to say something about them. We might not all agree, but at least we can all be part of the conversation.

REFERENCES

Air combat USA. (1994, August 24-30). The ultimate gift idea—Fighter pilot for a day [advertisement]. *Resident,* p. 51.

Baudrillard, J. (1983). *Simulations* (P. Foss, P. Patton, & P. Beitchman, Trans.). New York: Semiotext(e).

Benjamin, W. (1968). *Illuminations* (H. Zohn, Trans.). New York: Harcourt, Brace & World.

Berger, J. (1977). *Ways of seeing.* New York: Penguin Books.

Boorstin, D. (1962). *The image: Or what happened to the American dream.* New York: Athencum.

Bruckert, S. (1994, November). Something old, something really new. . . . *Ladies' Home Journal,* p. 48.

Eco, U. (1986). *Travels in hyperreality* (W. Weaver, Trans.). San Diego: Harcourt Brace Jovanovich.

◇◇◇◇ 16

Getting Over the Edge

Stuart Moulthrop

For some time now, scholars and critics have tried to answer questions such as "Is print dead?" or "Is the book dead?" Computer technologies are the latest in a long line of electronic and/or audiovisual media that have threatened to render typographic form obsolete. The introduction of electronic writing further complicates these questions, as it both extends and undermines print media. Stuart Moulthrop clarifies the issues involved in current discussions and debates over the "new edge" technologies and worldviews, as well as exposing some of the inherent contradictions in print-based discourse in an electronic environment. He also examines the progression that led to the development of hypertext and considers the staying power of traditional print. In Sections I, II, and IV, other views of electronic textuality can be found in Neil Kleinman's historical study of intellectual property in Chapter 4 and Jay David Bolter's arguments concerning print-based discourse and virtual reality in Chapter 7; also relevant to the future of the book are Terri Toles Patkin's discussion of virtual education in Chapter 11, Judith Yaross Lee's survey of text-based computer-mediated communication in Chapter 19, and Lance Strate's exploration of cybertime in Chapter 23.

The only responsible intellectual is one who is wired.
—Taylor & Saarinen (1993, p. 13)

Millennium season has arrived. Every month now the rhetoric of technology salesmen, never much known for subtlety, resets the record for hyperbole. The airwaves are filled with trailers for the future. AT&T promises surfside faxes, power breakfasts in your skivvies, your medical history on a credit card. Maybe you do not desire this stuff just yet, but don't worry . . . *you will.* Meanwhile, on MCI's side of the highway, Anna Pacquin lisps that *everything is information*—digitized, lightspeed quick, annihilating distinctions of time and space. In the new regime *there will be no more "there!"* Or, as we might cynically observe, *there goes the neighborhood.* So begins "our violent descent into the electronic cage of virtual reality," says Arthur Kroker (1994), with trademark hysteria; down we go into the "floating world of liquid media where the body is daily downloaded into the floating world of the net, where data is the real, and where high technology can fulfill its destiny of an out-of-body experience" (p. 36). There goes the body, too, drowned in recombinant buzz. Shuffled off into "bodiless exultation" (Gibson, 1984), we hang out in cyberspace awaiting further prophecies. *Where do you want to go today?* asks Microsoft, but it is less a question of going than of knowing—knowing where we are. We have come to that liminal zone called "The New Edge" (Rucker, Sirius, & Mu, 1992). The gulf between the now and the new yawns impatiently.

This is an ambiguous, ambivalent state. Our millennium calls for heavy irony. Vivian Sobchack (1992), commenting on the cyberhip magazine *Mondo 2000*, says "In my sober and responsible moments I bemoan our culture's loss of gravity and fear the very real social dangers of disembodied ditziness, but holding this Christmas present to myself, all I want is a head shot" (p. 583). It is particularly easy to feel this way if one is of a certain age. Cyberculture may be the last holiday orgy of the yuppies, replete with silicon sugar plums for all. There is something seductively regressive about the New Edge, with its smart drugs, mind machines, data networks, body-piercing narcissism, and dreams of virtual sex without secretions. Personal computing these days seems little more than an exclusive toy shop, especially considering the present craze for CD-ROM and "multimedia." More often than not this buzzword refers to prerecorded sequences of sound and video, a *techne* that seems distinctly familiar. As Greg Ulmer (1990) says, "Everything now, in its own way, wants to be television" (p. 11). Except for television, of course, which wants to be something new, improved, and "interactive," but whose vision of the future turns out to be Oliver Stone's *Wild Palms*, or Beavis and Butthead in cyberspace.

In large part the New Edge may be just another *trompe l'oeil* shadow; although it may not be entirely without significance, even so. In the era of simulation, as Baudrillard (1983) pointed out, the production of illusions becomes a crucial enterprise. Consider the thesis of "digital convergence," the last "vision rollout" put on by John Sculley before he left Apple Computer for wilder company. Taken at its glossiest, this concept means the wholesale integration of personal data services; much the same thing that is intoned over that stolen Peter Gabriel riff in all those AT&T spots. If the industrialists get their way, then nearly all our information will be mediated by a very small number of boxes and perhaps a single skein of cable.

Consequences of this change could be great. No more personal computers, no more television sets, no more fax machines, just a single appliance strung into "the dataline," as Pat Cadigan (1990) calls it. Nor would consumer electronics be the sole area of impact. Imagine a world without bookstores, in which one has only to connect to a publisher's electronic catalog to download, in whole or part, anything that one can plausibly afford. The implications for retailing are astonishing, as Barry Diller and others in the media marketing business have recognized (Carlin, 1993). Sculley's convergence seems likely to be realized any day now; it has considerable momentum both economically and politically. His vision maps closely onto Vice President Gore's National Information Infrastructure (NII) initiative, in which a "partnership" of communications companies, information providers, computer makers, and government will build the fabled digital superhighway. Because this strategy seems equally acceptable to the resurgent right (or at least the Speaker of the House), it seems sure to go forward.

Discussion of the NII usually centers on its implications for business. Under "time-based competition," in which product development cycles can be measured in weeks, some method of fast, copious, and efficient data exchange becomes essential (Peters, 1992; Zuboff, 1988). Complex, densely interrelated tasks must be adequately documented and represented for managers. Large engineering enterprises like the aerospace industry require flexible software tools for complex and dynamically changing work groups (Malcolm, Poltrock, & Schuler, 1991). But the implications of this development go well beyond industrial competition. Autobahns and interstate highways support commerce (and military mobilization), but they also change profoundly the way we organize ourselves as a culture. Just ask anyone who grew up in the suburbs and later returned to the urban core. As Fred Pfeil (1990) points out, the coming of the concrete highways contributed crucially to the atomized, post-Oedipal condition of the "PMC," Pfeil's shorthand for both Professional-Managerial Class and Postmodern Culture. The new fiber-optic data routes might bring similarly sweeping changes to cultural life. But what will these effects be? Can they be understood in terms not saturated by science fiction visions or pitchman hyperbole?

When Arthur Kroker (1994) writes about bodies "downloaded into the floating world of the net" (p. 7), he is of course fantasizing. Whether the "destiny" of "high technology" lies in "an out-of-body experience," even our highest technologies of the moment come nowhere close to that objective. The body, like the material world in general, turns out to be more complex and sophisticated the more closely we examine it. Digital convergence is one thing; digital conversion quite another. Uploading or downloading people into information networks is the stuff of Star Trek's 24th century (i.e., of television), not of the present era. What we transfer into the network, now or in the foreseeable future, is not our literal mind or body but some representation: some text. As Donna Haraway (1991) says: "Writing is pre-eminently the technology of cyborgs, etched surfaces of the late twentieth century" (p. 176). Questions about cyberculture thus lead away from "edges" (new or otherwise) and back toward surfaces—or to scenes of writing.

At the moment our cyborg texts remain heavily invested in preelectronic technologies. We are living in what Jay David Bolter (1991) calls "the late age of print" (p. 2), a moment in history when the old, industrial paradigm of alphabetic literacy collides with the younger agenda of electronic communication. Outlines of a new order have begun to emerge, yet the old regime remains stubbornly present. Alhough promoters of multimedia may try to turn everything into television, for a while the main front of development in electronic media remains verbal and textual; there is good reason to think that the word will not wither away anytime soon (Moulthrop, 1993). *Cyberspace* as we know it in the 1990s is largely a system of texts and intertexts. Consider the current most popular lane on the information highway, the distributed writing system called the World-Wide Web. This vast congeries of information is really nothing like an electronic book or even a virtual library. The flow of information on the Web is much more dynamic and much less invested in stable objects than such metaphors suggest. Yet its component elements are still referred to (and to some extent designed) as "pages." Authors representing themselves on the Web organize their work around the comforting notion of a "home page" (December & Randall, 1994).

If we recognize today's electronic environments as what Bolter (1991) calls "writing spaces" (pp. 10-12) then we may begin to understand the emerging cultural front of cyberspace. Is the library the home we never left? Or is it the object of our frustrated returning, the home to which we cannot come again? The cyberpunks and New Edgers dream about cyberspace in the comfort of predigital media. They operate in the book and magazine markets, old foundations of the print age. They are often, strange as it may seem, staunch defenders of high literacy and even the canon (e.g., Stephenson, 1993). Too often their projections assume that crucial aspects of print culture—analysis, reductive formalism, Aristotelian *agon*, and discrete authorship—will be carried wholesale across the new frontier.

They are probably dead wrong about this. In the environment of electronic communications, write the "media philsophers" Mark Taylor and Esa Saarinen (1993), "all philosophy must be interactive. Monologue becomes dialogue or, more precisely, polylogue" ("Ending the Academy," p. 1). Cyberspace may be a textual domain, but it is not the Gutenberg Galaxy, same as it ever was. Textuality in the new writing space is not constrained by the rigid ordering principles native to preelectronic media. This means that we must fundamentally rethink our position as subjects of electronic textuality. We must come to grips with yet a third kind of "convergence," a phenomenon George Landow (1992) calls "the convergence of contemporary critical theory and technology" (p. 4). This intersection may have more significance, in the short run at least, than either the vision of integrated data services or the dream of human-machine fusion.

The subject of Landow's interest, like that of Bolter, is a relatively modest item on the high-technology agenda, a form of electronic writing called *hypertext*. (For background on this concept, see Bolter, 1991; Halasz, 1987; Landow, 1992; Nelson, 1990; Slatin, 1990.) The term was coined in the mid-1960s by the computing visionary Theodor Nelson (1990) to describe "non-sequential writing"

(p. 3/19), a scheme for using interactive computing systems to deliver documents in variable form, as opposed to the strict sequence imposed by book binding. Hypertexts cannot be translated into print. They retain a dynamic or "interactive" component that no nonelectronic reduction can adequately represent. In hypertext, a body of writing is formally divided into arbitrary units or *lexias* as Landow calls them, borrowing from Roland Barthes. The reader's path from one lexia to another is determined partly by active engagement: The reader selects a word in the present lexia, chooses an option from a menu, issues a command, or otherwise indicates some wish for further development. The program responds with another piece of writing that may or may not match the reader's desires, but that articulates in some way to the previous passage. In the most ambitious, "constructive" versions of this writing system (Joyce, 1994), the reader may not only follow predefined pathways, but may alter the connections and add new lexias to the system, creating complex textual hybrids.

Hypertext is a characteristic product of the late age of print, which is to say, it is deeply ambiguous. Although still dependent on alphabetic literacy, algorithmic programming, linearity, hierarchy, and other trappings of Gutenberg culture, hypertext implicitly challenges the episteme from which it sprang. Although any hypertextual document remains a limited and definable object, this object is much more like Roland Barthes's notion of "text"—a dynamic network of ideas, indefinite in its boundaries and mutable over time—than like a teleologically closed literary "work" (Landow, 1992, p. 23). The precise nature and boundaries of a hypertext are hard to define. The experience of reading for any two people who traverse its verbal space may be radically different: "polylogue," not monologue. When multiple writers are involved, authorial voice and intention come in for serious questioning. In the World-Wide Web, for instance, a single document may contain scores of references to other texts stored at various far-flung points around the Internet. A single reading may involve writings (and writers) from Baltimore to Bombay; and because many documents on the Web are regularly revised and updated, both the authorial corps and the textual corpus are subject to change.

These aspects of hypertextual writing lead Landow to his particular vision of "convergence." As he sees it, the current interest in hypertext represents the happy union of two cultural forces that have worked for 20 years in adjacent ivory towers. On one side of this new synthesis are information scientists, men like Douglas Engelbart and Andries Van Dam, who created the first practical hypertext systems. On the other flank stand poststructuralist theorists like Barthes, Michel Foucault, Jacques Derrida, and Julia Kristeva, whose critiques of print culture, or logocentrism, appear to parallel the hypertextual enterprise. As Landow (1992) sees it, the technology of the printed book:

> engenders certain notions of authorial property, authorial uniqueness, and a physically isolated text that hypertext makes untenable. The evidence of hypertext, in other words, historicizes many of our most commonplace

> assumptions, thereby forcing them to descend from the ethereality of abstraction and appear as corollaries to a particular technology rooted in specific times and places. (p. 33)

Landow does not claim that hypertext represents an "applied grammatology," to borrow Ulmer's phrase, only that there is a compelling and useful analogy between poststructuralist theories of the text and the development of electronic writing. "What is perhaps most interesting about hypertext," Landow (1992) explains, "is not that it may fulfill certain claims of structuralist and poststructuralist criticism but that it provides a rich means of testing them" (p. 11). What Landow means by "testing" here, or what anyone else might mean by it, remains very much at issue. Hypertext enables its users to invent new forms for arranging and passing on information. These forms do not map onto the claims of poststructuralist critics in any simple, literal way. But if Landow is right, hypertext should allow us to *articulate* poststructuralist concepts within the emergent practices of digital culture. *Articulation* here might mean a process of connection in which one creates contingent unities among moving differences (for the roots of this concept, see Grossberg, 1992). This enterprise seems entirely in line with Haraway's cyborg politics. If such a process is possible, then hypertext might lend some substance to all that loose talk about digital highways, electronic frontiers, and a "floating world of liquid media." But this remains to be seen.

At the moment we face a more primary and practical cultural problem: the disturbing presence of the past. Contrary to the testimony of the 1960s, print is not dead, nor is it merely sleeping. The cultural complex of print (a metonymy taking in publishing houses, academic institutions, reviewers, advertisers, and, these days, multimedia conglomerates) is actually *undead*, which is to say that it lingers on, monstrously transformed, haunting us in the dead of night. According to Taylor and Saarinen, who have laid the strongest claim yet to Marshall McLuhan's mad media prophecies, technologies such as hypertext portend a cultural paradigm shift. This would be a change from monologue to polylogue, from edifice to improvization, from *Bildung to bricolage.* "Expert language," they say, "is a prison for knowledge and understanding. A prison for intellectually significant relationships. It is time to move beyond the institutional practices of triviledge, toward networks and surfaces, toward the play of superficiality, toward interstanding" (Taylor & Saarinen, 1993, "Communicative Practices," p. 8). Neologism is an essential part of the game here. *Triviledge* indicates the privilege of institutional learning, or the trivilality of knowledge; *interstanding* names the way of knowing appropriate to hypertext, the exploration of what Joyce calls "interstices" and "contours," or what Gilles Deleuze and Félix Guattari (1987) call "lines of flight" (p. 3). "When depth gives way to surface," Taylor and Saarinen write, "under-standing becomes inter-standing. To comprehend is no longer to grasp what lies *beneath* but to glimpse what lies *between*" (Taylor & Saarinen, 1993, "Interstanding," p. 1). In moving from the page to the interstice, from understanding to interstanding, we ostensibly reverse figure and ground, transforming the condition of textuality.

But how much is genuinely new here? As Pete Townshend might have said: *Meet the new Logos; same as the old Logos.* The problem is that scholars, critics, developers, and designers cling desperately to the same old ways of doing what we do. "Triviledge" represents our ultimate home on the page. Those optical networks and etched surfaces that might redeem us seem strangely hard to engage. Take Taylor and Saarinen's book as a depressingly perfect case in point. Like McLuhan and Fiore's *The Medium is the Massage* (1967), whose design it emulates, *Imagologies* puts up a deeply irreverent front. "The triviledge that legitimizes the academic critic renders him impotent," Taylor and Saarinen proclaim. "Merely a Peeping Tom who gazes from afar but refuses to enter the fray, he becomes nothing more than a limp dick" (Taylor & Saarinen, 1993, "Ending the Academy," p. 7). But how much difference can these words make, even when they are made-up or bawdy words? How much difference can a book make—for even though it is as irreverent and iconoclastic in design as it is in content, *Imagologies* is still very much a book. Taylor and Saarinen (1993) do consider this objection, but their answer fails to satisfy:

> If an electronic text can be published in printed form, is it really electronic? The alternative would be to give up print and publish an electronic text. But the technology necessary for accessing electronic texts is still rather limited. Furthermore, most of the people we want to reach remain committed to print. There is no sense preaching to the converted. Our dilemma is that we are living at the moment of transition from print to electronic culture. It is too late for printed books and too early for electronic texts. Along this boundary we must write our work. ("Telewriting," p. 5)

Much of this argument makes sense—although the sense that it makes deeply undermines the primary claim. There is indeed no point in "preaching to the converted." If we understand hypertext we know that there is no point in preaching at all, just as there is no sense in worrying about the limpness of the next man's transcendental signifier, or your own. If technologies like hypertext really do open possibilities for cultural renewal, then, as Taylor and Saarinen (1993) say, they ought to help us climb out of the muck of triviledge and simple-minded agonistics. This might mean that we can indeed give up print and do something other than write books—that it is not too soon for electronic texts. The new networks ought to provide Landow's testing ground for poststructuralist critique, a space in which we can experiment with alternatives to the Logos as we know it. Have you ever reconceived yourself entirely outside the grounds of Western metaphysics? *You will. . .*

Or maybe you won't. As any scientist knows, most experiments fail. Even after we have given up on print, the majority of "really electronic" text will be hopelessly contaminated with the old ways of knowing. What we must carry forward is a strong sense of foundational irony. The past is always present; we are Gutenberg creatures no matter how hard we play at revolution—there is no such thing as "nonsequential writing." We make our way by recursion, by folding a new order back on and into its predecessor. The relations among media, as McLuhan discovered and as Neil Postman (1992) has clarified, belong to a complex, mutually modifying ecology. Drastic, monumental changes are rare in most ecologies—and disastrous when they do occur. In the place of such upheavals, in our day-to-day survival, we find articulations, contingent complications of the old order that may, in their nontotalizing, fractal context, create some space for "interstanding." Or so we may hope.

So is there really a new world coming? If books are still being written about cyberspace (including this book), then it must be too soon to tell. There is only one thing about which we can be reasonably sure: We must stop writing our work along the boundaries. We must step off the edge and onto the shifting surfaces. This writing is finished, or unfinished. Its electronic address is: *http://raven.ubalt.edu/Moulthrop/essays/edge.html*

REFERENCES

Baudrillard, J. (1983). *Simulations* (P. Foss, P. Patton, & P. Beitchmann, Trans.). New York: Semiotext(e).

Bolter, J. (1991). *Writing space: The computer, hypertext, and the history of writing*. Hillsdale NJ: Erlbaum.

Cadigan, P. (1990). *Synners*. New York: Bantam.

Carlin, P. (1993, February 28). The jackpot in television's future. *New York Times Magazine*, pp. 36-41.

December, J., & Randall, N. (1994). *The World Wide Web unleashed*. New York: SAMS.

Deleuze, G., & Guattari, F. (1987). *A thousand plateaus: Capitalism and schizophrenia* (B. Massumi, Trans.). Minneapolis: University of Minnesota Press.

Gibson, W. (1984). *Neuromancer*. New York: Ace Books.

Grossberg, L. (1992). *We gotta get out of this place: Popular conservatism and postmodern culture*. New York: Routledge.

Halasz, F. (1987). Reflections on NoteCards: Seven issues for the next generation of hypermedia systems. *Communications of the ACM, 31*(7), 836-852.

Haraway, D. (1991). *Simians, cyborgs, and women: The reinvention of nature*. New York: Routledge.

Joyce, M. (1994). *Of two minds: Hypertext pedagogy and poetics*. Ann Arbor: University of Michigan Press.

Kroker, A. (1994). *Spasm: Virtual reality, android music, electric flesh*. New York: St. Martin's Press.

Landow, G. (1992). *Hypertext: the convergence of contemporary literary theory and technology*. Baltimore: Johns Hopkins University Press.

Malcolm, K., Poltrock, S., & Schuler, D. (1991). Industrial strength hypermedia: Requirements for a large engineering enterprise. In P.D. Stotts & R.K. Furuta (Ed.), *Hypertext '91 Proceedings* (pp. 13-24). San Antonio: Association for Computing Machinery.

McLuhan, H.M., & Fiore, Q. (1967). *The medium is the massage.* New York: McGraw-Hill.

Moulthrop, S. (1993). You say you want a revolution? Hypertext and the laws of media. In E. Amiran & J. Unsworth (Eds.), *Essays in postmodern culture* (pp. 69-97). New York: Oxford University Press.

Nelson, T. (1990). *Literary machines.* Sausalito, CA: Mindful Press.

Peters, T. (1992). *Liberation management: Necessary disorganization for the nanosecond nineties.* New York: Knopf.

Pfeil, F. (1990). *Another tale to tell: Politics and narrative in postmodern culture.* New York: Verso.

Postman, N. (1992). *Technopoly.* New York: Vintage.

Rucker, R., Sirius, R.U., & Mu, Q. (1992). *Mondo 2000: A user's guide to the new edge.* New York: St. Martin's Press.

Sobchack, V. (1992). Reading Mondo 2000. *South Atlantic Quarterly, 92*(4), 581-597.

Slatin, J. (1990). Hypertext: Order and coherence in a new medium. *College English, 52,* 870-883.

Stephenson, N. (1993, September 13). Smiley's people. *New Republic,* p. 52.

Taylor, M., & Saarinen, E. (1993). *Imagologies: Media philosophy.* New York: Routledge. [This book is paginated in individual sections. Citations are given by section name and page number.]

Ulmer, G. (1990). *Teletheory: Grammatology in the age of video.* New York: Routledge.

Zuboff, S. (1988). *In the age of the smart machine: The future of work and power.* New York: Basic Books.

◇◇◇◇ 17

Pedagogy and Hypertext

Stephanie B. Gibson

From text to classroom to curriculum and canon, the fluid and disembodied character of cyberspace dissolves forms and disrupts established procedures and relationships. In this chapter, Stephanie B. Gibson examines some of the pedagogical possibilities that may be called forth by a shift from the use of traditional printed text to that of hypertext. Providing an overview of hypertext and hypermedia forms, and an exploration of typography's relationship to education, she casts hypertext characteristics in contrast to the paradigmatic structures summoned by traditional printed text and offers some thoughts on the presence of educational hypertext in the academy. Aside from Section III, other discussions of textuality can be found in Neil Kleinman's study of intellectual property and electronic publishing in Chapter 4, Jay David Bolter's comparison of text and virtual reality in Chapter 7, and Judith Yaross Lee's research on text-based, computer-mediated communication in Chapter 19; a related examination of cyberspace education appears in Terri Toles Patkin's profile of the virtual organization in Chapter 11.

The University of Maryland, Baltimore County (UMBC) was built in 1967 without a computer science building because it was thought that that obscure discipline would not attract students. Now, in 1995, from grade school to graduate school, students are using hypertext as an adjunct to their studies. Those people who were attracted to the study of computers (contrary to the thinking of many more schools than just UMBC) went on to design computer programs that now invisibly pervade our everyday lives. ATMs, Game Boys, and laptops, to name just a few manifestations, are integral parts of American life. A great shift has taken place from traditional, printed text to cyberspatial, electronic text. The movement has been from the tangible and physical to the ephemeral and digital, from text as object to text as environment. It seems only fitting that one of the areas most greatly affected by these developments has been education.

Almost all our contemporary ideas about pedagogy have been anchored firmly in a paradigm informed by the printed word. These assumptions about the world have driven interactions in the classroom to such an extent that the room physically resembles print: We see rows and columns, we hear silence, and up above the cursive alphabet—although most of us have long ago abandoned handwriting for anything other than the most personal of writing—lingers in our memories. Until this moment there has been little challenge to that way of understanding theories about learning and teaching. We now find ourselves at a crack in the window that allows us to examine the present in the blazing light of what is (perhaps, always perhaps) to come.

The impact of this new cyberspatial manner of apprehending text can be seen in a number of different domains. This chapter addresses how ideas about pedagogy have been, and may be, reconfigured by the introduction of hypertext into the educational system at all levels—from kindergarten through postdoctoral work.

WHAT IS IT?

Any program that allows readers to navigate nonlinearly through a body of text, sometimes a single text, but frequently a database of related materials with hundreds of nodes of text linked together forming a network of relevant material, may be considered a *hypertext*. Hypertext is text that exists only in cyberspace. It is impossible to put hypertext into traditional page-bound print; doing so would so radically alter its nature that it would simply no longer be hypertext.

Hypertext is called by many names, the most common being *hypertext, multimedia,* and *hypermedia.* It may also be considered to be many different things: a stand-alone text version on disk or CD-ROM that a student may read on his or her personal computer, or text (or even a database) accessed online through any one of a number of available library or network systems, or a program used in the classroom to create a text—in other words, the possibilities are quite broad. Designers of hypertext and hypermedia packages are concerned with the differences between their products and traditional texts assigned for classroom use (Crane, 1990; Crane & Mylonas, 1988; Newman, 1991). A number of scholars have addressed the question of how hypertext and hypermedia differ from traditional printed text in their epistemological, ideological, political, and cultural biases (Bolter, 1991; Delaney & Landow, 1991; Kaplan, 1991; Landow,

1992; McDaid, 1991; Moulthrop, 1991b; Slatin, 1991). Some investigate how the hypertext environment differs from that of the traditional computer environment (Herrstrom & Massey, 1989; Rubens, 1989; Smith, 1991). Hypertext is not simply more text, or text arranged differently. It is qualitatively different from traditional text and engages us in qualitatively different activities. A horseless carriage is not simply a vehicle that moves without benefit of animal power, it alters our position in the universe. Hypertext, too, calls into being a completely new set of attitudes about who we are and our relationship to our written world, as pointed out by Jay David Bolter and Sue Barnes, among others, in Chapters 6 and 14, respectively, of this volume. Hypertext is not simply a larger book. A few of the physical differences may be illuminating: It contains more, covering the ground that could be covered by hundreds of books in a single hypermedia package. Readers do not have to get up and go to another book; when another text is needed a single keystroke summons it to the screen. It may contain different modalities: printed text, photos, animation, video, diagrams, or sound. It can keep track of the path you have followed through the text. Perhaps, most significantly, it can make connections between a piece of text and more than one other piece of text in a nonlinear fashion that is impossible in traditional print. Sometimes the medium is "write-to" as well as read, meaning any reader can add commentary and links, which then become part of the text.

Because it is so different from traditional printed text, hypertext's appearance in the classroom calls into question many accepted ideas about how text is used. Much like traditional printed text, a significant characteristic in hypertext is control of the text; but the locus of control in hypertext can be very different from that of traditional print. Some important questions grow out of the different nature of this new text. What does hypertext allow readers and writers to do that traditional text does not? What does hypertext allow teachers and students to do that traditional text does not? And what assumptions about the classroom (and curriculum and canon) are called into question as a result of these different interactions?

Several scholars have discussed the movement from traditional print to hypertext as an inevitable shift. O.B. Hardison (1989) maintains that hypertext is part of what he sees as a natural progression—literary, social, and technological—wherein American culture is slowly disconnecting from its history and floating into what he calls paradigmatic isolation—the cutting off of culture from any heretofore familiar paradigms of interaction. George Landow (1992), on the other hand, sees the "convergence of contemporary critical theory and technology"—the coming together of postmodern critique and hypertextual practice—subtitling his book thusly. McDaid (1991) maintains that nothing less than the transformation of consciousness is at stake in a relationship with hypertext. Jay Bolter (1991) says that hypertext will alter the manner in which realities are constructed. And Richard Lanham (1993) insists that the new electronic writing of hypertext will bring us full circle to classical rhetorical forms. Whatever their specific conclusions, these scholars and critics all indicate that hypertext radically alters traditional hierarchical structures both within writing systems and between author and reader. It is in this alteration in the relationship between author and reader that the fundamental differences between traditional print and hypertext lie, and these differences seem likely to cause a shift in pedagogy.

TRADITIONAL TEXTBOOKS IN THE CLASSROOM

The relationship of textbooks to their respective disciplines has been the object of examination for some time. In 1979, Frances FitzGerald showed a relationship between textbooks and contemporary social values. Earlier, Paolo Friere (1970) made a powerful argument that classroom agendas are integrally tied to political agendas. In the years since these and other works, this issue has been addressed by scholars in many disciplines (e.g., English, 1986; Gagnon, 1987; Kaplan, 1991; Knoblauch & Brannon, 1984). A recent study found that although communications textbooks mention issues addressed in professional communications scholarship, the translation process they undergo renders them in an entirely different light (Gibson, 1991). Textbooks are seen, at their most powerful, as a driving force behind curriculum decisions and, at their least powerful, as simple auxiliary tools to classroom interaction. The various truths probably lie somewhere between those two possibilities.

The thought in which scholars engage, in many ways, constitutes a field. Textbooks traditionally represent this thought in a much different format than that of its original presentation. Obviously, the two bodies of text—professional scholarship and textbooks—are asking their audiences to engage in two different activities. Scholars, presumably well versed in the theory and methods of the field, read journals to engage in debate about the current direction of the discipline. Conversely, students read textbooks to gain entry (which may be interpreted in several ways) to the discipline. Briefly, some characteristics that set traditional classroom textbooks apart from other types of text can be seen in the following.

Journals and academic language notwithstanding, textbooks are not inviting reading. They present their text in a manner peculiar to textbooks. Physically they resemble no other type of written text. They are often printed on heavy paper to withstand excessive handling, wide margins are provided for comments by readers, questions are frequently posed at the close of a chapter to test the reader's comprehension of what he or she has read, side bars attempt to illustrate particularly difficult material. These characteristics send readers the message that the text arrives at the interaction with the student with an attitude of authority (Gibson, 1991; Moran, 1971).

Traditional classrooms are a reflection of this noninteractive environment. The design and layout of this classroom is static, like print on a page. No matter how a reader moves, or moves through the pages of a book, the print remains anchored firmly to its place on the page. In a mirror relationship chairs often remain attached to desks (do those things have a name?). Sometimes both are bolted solidly to the floor. Much traditional classroom activity also reflects the unidirectionality of traditional print. The lecture, the blackboard, the overhead projector—these are the staples of a print-driven classroom, all of them traditionally controlled by the teacher. The printed textbook carries with it these same assumptions about the relationship between teachers and students—that one is in charge, the other a mere vessel.

How teachers use textbooks in the classroom is not at issue here; clearly, there are many ways to contextualize textbooks in the classroom. What is fascinating is that the majority of texts in print say that they encourage one thing—critical thinking—while presenting their content in a manner that attempts to both block and trivialize that activity by being markedly uncritical of their own assumptions. When methods other than that which informs the book are acknowledged, it is only in passing, and the prevailing attitude is to explain that such other methods exist, but to dismiss both the concepts and other methodology as neither valid nor valuable. This sort of internal disqualification is accomplished in several ways. First, and most significant, the method and paradigm that drive the book itself are rarely acknowledged. Texts often see relationships in the world they describe as unidirectional, which is the same attitude they take in relating to their audience. Textbooks rarely engage in self-reflection, in which they explain that paradigmatic strictures involve basic assumptions about what is important and that this drives decisions about what appears in the text and how. Even when textbooks discuss the notion that assumptions about reality may be embedded in theory and method, they rarely indicate any recognition of the assumptions embedded in the theory that guides the composition of their own text. The unspoken assumptions of a discipline, as Kuhn (1970) pointed out, are difficult enough to see, let alone question. When underlying assumptions are articulated and examined by the author, it then becomes easier to show how agendas exist in other theoretical methods. When books not only do not do this, but present material as unquestionable truth, contradictory messages are being given. The text wants its readers to become better critical thinkers, but it removes one of the most important tools they can be given for doing this. It does not allow them to examine the text. In examining two message levels of the text—content and pedagogic—clear problems exist. To the uninitiated novice, much of what is contained in traditional textbooks appears to be knowledge carved in stone.

Textbooks are, as Olson (1988) states, "compilations of the given" (p. 30). Presentation of scholarly discourse in journals is different because the very nature of the journal is that it is in flux. The appearance of responses to articles and responses to those responses indicates the existence of an ongoing dialogue—quite different from what happens in textbooks. The literature of scholarship begs a different engagement from its audience. It assumes readers have an extensive background in the field, that they are mature enough thinkers to follow a sometimes complex line of reasoning, and—most important—it asks that readers engage in debate about the thinking and the direction of the discipline. It is clear from the authority with which textbooks approach their audience that they do not wish to be questioned about their methodology. I do not intend to address here the question of whether it is possible, or even desirable, to close the gap between professional scholarship and what students read. It is significant that a major difference exists between the texts of scholars and the activities requested by those texts, and the texts used in the classroom by students and the activities requested by those text. The relationships of the texts to their audiences are different; the overt and covert, content and pedagogical messages are different. And as a result, related educational arrangements are affected.

HYPERTEXT IN THE CLASSROOM

The hypertext form is utilized in quite a wide variety of ways. For instance, *afternoon* by Michael Joyce (1987), *Victory Garden* by Stuart Moulthrop (1992), and *Uncle Buddy's Phantom Funhouse* by John McDaid (1992), are three examples of hypertext fiction. The first two are solely text based: The reader reads a node of text and, depending on his or her selection of navigation methods, moves to any one of several possible text blocks to continue reading. The third example incorporates a multimedia experience that takes advantage of object-oriented programming in presenting the reader with "objects," graphics, sound, and some movement. The reader moves through this text in the same way as he or she navigates through the first two—either by using an arrow set up by the writer or by selecting a bit of text he or she wishes to pursue and clicking on it. Many other educational hypertext packages are available; most incorporate multimedia such as written text, sound, graphics (including illustration and photographs), and frequently video. Many of these packages are extremely large databases of material, compared to what we are accustomed to having access to in one spot, and they allow many different pathways of navigation. For instance, one of the first constructed was the *Perseus Project*. This hypertext package strives to make available (to its credit—it is still, several years into the project, being worked on) much of ancient Greece. There are archeological photographs and diagrams, photos of period artwork, plays in the original Greek with translations, contemporary commentary, maps, and several glossaries, all linked together to allow myriad approaches to the material. All this is available at a single keystroke. *Ulysses* is another example of a hypertext project, described in some detail by Jay Bolter in Chapter 6, which combines video of actors reading Tennyson's *Ulysses*, scholars discussing the piece, the poem itself, and other material. Readers can select portions of the database they wish to study. Yet another type of hypertext is that frequently used in writing classrooms. A writing program, like Storyspace, is used by composition teachers to give students open access to each other's work. In Storyspace, writers may compose nodes of text, link them to any number of other text nodes, and leave the project open for others to add their text nodes and links. Unlike some hypertext fictions and composition programs, these classroom multimedia packages do allow users to also become authors and linkers. All these programs, although fundamentally different in tremendously significant ways, are considered hypertext.

All the qualities of hypertext encourage vastly different habits of thought than does traditional print. Hypertext has been called a democratizing medium because it allows everyone access to both production and decoding. This may be said of it both internally and within its larger environment. Internally, for example, hypertext is able to show clearly interconnectedness between ideas by linking them together. Although this is not completely impossible in print, it is structurally difficult to include massive amounts of material in a single text. It also goes against all accepted authoring practice; the idea behind composing text is, for the most part, to exclude anything that might be only tangentially related and to include only that which is directly pertinent. In particularly large traditional textbooks, it is difficult to show connections among all the disparate material compiled within. In authoring a hypertext it is possible to allow the text to branch in several directions at once, representing many relevant paths of thought. As a result, ideas can be contextualized historically as well as theoretically in ways impossible in traditional print. For example, The *Perseus Project* contains what would amount to several printed books, audio, and even video, all linked together through many different pathways allowing readers to traverse the material searching for many different types of relationships. To do this with traditional printed text would require several trips to the library, several armfuls of books, and an ability to imagine connections and translations that might seem overwhelming to beginning students. What is more, readers are viewing primary material, commentary, and criticism—not solely material that has been digested and represented in a simplified fashion for their ease. Although primary material is not always easy for readers to wrestle with, it can give a picture of the discipline that commentary two or three times removed cannot.

The epistemological and pedagogical ramifications of these qualitative differences between the two types of text are many. Because no margins literally exist, there is neither actual nor figurative marginalization. No text node has any more or less significance than any other node of text because they all appear in the same manner on the screen. Of course, both positive and negative points can be made about this. Some say that not all pieces of information are equal in value or importance. When whatever is summoned to the screen becomes primary, this equalizes Aristotle and the college freshman. Some applaud this new equality; others decry the elimination of gatekeepers saying hypertexts without them lack legitimacy. (It must be noted that not all hypertexts allow readers to also function as writers and link makers; in fact, most hypertexts do not.)

In many hypertexts there is no hierarchy of ideas as is evidenced in a table of contents or outline. Instead of the linear sequencing of items characteristic of most printed texts, nonlinear, web-like organization drives hypertext. After the opening screen announcement of what the package is, there is no one direction one must take through the text; many equally interesting paths are available. In other words, no particular node must be read before moving on to any other node. This, of course, challenges the notions that one concept is more important than another or that certain knowledge must precede other knowledge. This sort of organizing principle spreads ideas or pieces of text out in a manner that shows their relationships not in order of importance, calling into question not only hierarchies of ideas, but the notion of prerequisites.

The dynamic nature of hypertext is another significant difference. Books are static; their layout remains the same no matter how the reader chooses to experience the text. But hypertext moves about on the screen, always presenting the reader with a different primary node. And although CD-ROMs are completed pieces, other hypertext structures, those on the Internet in particular, are dynamic in an even larger sense. Books embody, as Ong (1982) and Bolter (1991) both state, a sense of closure, the idea that what the reader holds in his or her hands is the completed subject, an area that has been both literally and figuratively covered. The kinetic environment of hypertext always allows new material to be added, new relationships to be delineated.

A host of differences are evidenced between traditional print and hypertext in the writing classroom. Scholarship in the field of composition theory has directed attention to how write-to hypertext alters the nature of the interactions among all classroom participants—students, teachers, and all combinations thereof. Space prohibits a thorough consideration about the nature of the composition classroom with hypertext, but a brief glance reveals that composition researchers are also examining radical changes not only in the nature of the interactions and the quality of the work produced, but in the nature of the work produced. Collaborative work produced using write-to hypertext programs such as Storyspace uses entirely different writing and thinking skills than do traditional composition techniques. These techniques approximate dynamic learning structures, such as those described by Knoblauch and Brannon (1984), Treisman (1985), and Douglas (1994a, 1994b), much more closely than does the isolated writing used in most composition classrooms.

SOME IMPLICATIONS FOR CLASSROOM, CURRICULUM, AND CANON

General classroom policy and activities have the possibility of being heavily impacted by these differences in the move from traditional text to hypertext. First, control is shifted away from the teacher to the user of the text. The pedagogical implications in the classroom are that the teacher must relinquish some measure of control, and, as a result of this, the relationship between student and teacher is altered. When using a hypertext package as an adjunct to a course, the student will have access to material not traditionally available in both volume and structure. Although it is certainly possible for students to skip ahead in textbooks, they do not do so often, usually because they have no way of knowing what in the subsequent text is linked conceptually to what they are presently reading. Traditional printed text signals to students: This is what will be covered in class, and usually in this very same order. Not so with hypertext. In using a hypertext, the reader has access to a significantly larger database of material than when using a traditional printed text. Not only is more material available, but this is frequently material used in preparation of the course, in other words, primary text material and scholarly critique. This is material that is almost never made available to students as a matter of course. But in a hypertext database it is highly accessible to them.

Traditional classroom relationships are altered because the teacher no longer has control over who will read what texts, when, or in how much depth. This is not to say that these primary texts have heretofore been unavailable to students if they search for them. But that is the key phrase—searching, on a somewhat grand scale, was necessary. Not many typical students exhibit this type of interest in their course material. When a body of literature is right at their fingertips, however, the question of exploration is different. When students have access to primary material and connecting ideas are made easier to follow, they can often see conceptual maps that teachers frequently keep private. Some of the information they may be reading may even be contrary to the conceptual agenda of the course. Students may now pursue, on their own, links among ideas that may or may not be planned as a part of the course material. If they are part of the course, students may be ahead of the class progression and ask questions that anticipate these links. If they are not planned as part of the class material, students may force the issue, making the instructors examine ideas they had originally planned not to cover. Unless teachers are prepared to dictate each time they are confronted with an unexpected question, student access to hypertext material will force teachers to deal with material they may not have planned for, in a time not their own.

This altered relationship mirrors the internally democratizing elements of hypertext. There is no marginalization within the text of ideas or in the classroom of readers who wish to pursue different paths. When students have control of what they can read, they also have control of what connections they will make. This is not without even considering the enormous database available to them online on the Internet.

These are some of the ideas about teaching that are embedded in the technology of hypertext. This is how relationships in the classroom may be altered, as may be the structure of how people interact with each other and their material, what the teacher can and cannot do, what he or she may expect of the students, and what they may expect of the teacher.

Some have even suggested that hypertext will bring with it a paradigm shift as radical as that ascribed to the shift from manuscript to print (Bolter, 1991; Kaplan, 1991; Landow, 1992; McDaid, 1991). Charles Ess (1991) indicates that students gain a better idea of connectedness and the ability to grasp highly complex material when working with hypertext as opposed to traditional printed textbooks. Both Landow (1992) and Moulthrop (1991a) address the notion that a new rhetoric must necessarily grow out of our use of hypertext both as a composition tool and as a reading instrument. Landow discusses the rhetoric of arrivals and departures because this is what readers do as they read hypertext—leave one screen and arrive at another. This traveling among texts, this linking of ideas together in space, leaves readers with a more developed idea about how a particular piece of text is related to another piece of text. When writing in hypertext, Ess's students came away with clearer notions of how ideas were related to one another.

Hypertext's ability to democratize the classroom by showing interconnectedness, not marginalizing less popularly held points of view, and having no embedded hierarchy, all argue for a more open classroom in which students feel free to ask, and also answer, questions. The kinetic characteristics of hypertext seem to lend themselves to showing students that the world is constantly evolving and that knowledge is not carved in the proverbial stone. Hypertext lends itself to collaborative learning: techniques in which the students are engaged on a fundamental level with the text, with each other, and with the teacher. In learning in which students are allowed to discover connections and realities for themselves we have seen a more complete grasp of material and a greater interest in continuing to learn. Moreover, the dynamic attributes of hypertext provide the possibility of allowing all users to do what only scholars have traditionally done—engage in debate.

Implications for curriculum and canon can be seen in this examination of the microcosm of the classroom. Issues of control are central. If classroom control must shift, the administrative grip on curriculum will also be challenged. In the alteration of access, the politics of choice will be dramatically shifted to the forefront. When access is expanded, as it is when hypertext is used, choice lies much more dramatically with the reader. Control of the canon may be dispersed when access is available to everyone connected with the academy.

A principal change may occur in the material being used to teach courses. Many courses use textbooks instead of primary material. Even in literature courses a leaning exists toward using anthologies frequently containing only parts of works. I have argued elsewhere (Gibson, 1993) that what we offer students in (particularly introductory) textbooks actually constitutes the canon. What makes it through the obstacle course of academic gatekeepers and into the classroom texts constitutes the discipline. All else is scholarly debate. As observed earlier, academic journals request different activities of their readers than do textbooks, among those activities are the milling over of what may be permitted to enter the canon. The body of material that is the core of what we talk about when we refer to a discipline; the core of what we want novices to know about a discipline; material that has passed the test of relevance, understandability, and importance; and finally material that is believed to be true is what is found in textbooks. This is canon. Hypertext, with included supporting material, links to lesser known texts, commentary, and criticism, even other disciplines, reconfigures what is available to students and reconfigures the canon. In addition to reconfiguring the canon in any single discipline, hypertext allows for the mating of several areas of study. In fact, the medium of hypertext has a Postmanesque (1992) way of insisting that more than a single discipline be included in the database.

THE SHIFT

It seems inevitable that classrooms will shift from using traditional print textbooks to hypertext, perhaps not to meet all of their needs, but certainly for many purposes. At a workshop I attended in Summer 1994, at which the *Ulysses* package was discussed, teachers were immediately drawn to it. At that seminar several high school and college English teachers asked excitedly where they could procure the package for their institutions. An oft-heard comment during that summer workshop, and since, is that hypertext is a way to hold student interest. It is dynamic, contains several approaches to the material, and appears to give readers/users a choice about how the material will be experienced and studied. (It also contains minimal printed stimulus, most of that particular package using video as its primary platform.) Will this change initiate a paradigmatic shift? A brief examination of some of the epistemological biases of print and electronic text will provide a clearer answer here.

Just as textbooks construct their own authority and in so doing obscure the foundations of the belief systems that inform them, hypertext can easily do the same. Although many possibilities of openness exist with hypertext, as cited earlier, the fact remains that many hypertexts lead and limit the reader in much the same way as does traditional print. Although with print it is obvious that the artifact is saying "examine me in this particular order, and when you come to the end—stop," with hypertext such a relationship can be constructed without the reader knowing he or she is being so directed. A book has a beginning, middle, and end, and the physical nature of the object informs the user of the appropriate method of engagement. Hypertext is artifactless, except on the metalevel, and so it exists without self-apparent user directions. Directions are embedded at a much deeper level.

As a result of these possibilities, not all hypertext is as free as has been described. It is certainly possible to construct a hypertext so that it leads the reader in as structured a way as does traditional print. They can be more structured, in fact, because in traditional print the reader is free to skip from any one page to any other page. In a computer environment, it is possible to program the user's every move. This goes against the principal of what most hypertext authors maintain as the medium's intention, many of them stating that the nature of the medium is to fight against this type of constraint. Nevertheless, it is possible to lead a reader in hypertext in a manner inconceivable in print, and I have seen several hypertexts that do just this. In hypertext the reader has no concept of what he or she is not seeing because the artifact shows neither size nor content. When the reader does not know the possibilities of the text, it is possible to program gates within the text that do not allow progress through the program until certain other nodes have been read and/or questions (some have quizzes programmed into them) have been answered. This type of hypertext is every bit as directed (and deadly boring) as the traditional printed text with questions at the end of each chapter quizzing a somnambulistic reader on the contents therein. Neither does every hypertext exist in a write-to mode; in fact, few hypertexts allow the reader to contribute. In spite of all that is written about the marvels of allowing readers to add text, create new links, and alter existing paths, few hypertexts allow the reader to do any of this. Even in composition programs, in which these types of contributions are invaluable, not all programs in use allow them. When the text leads the reader on a predetermined path and does not allow contributions, alterations, or wanderings, there is certainly a sense of hierarchy—the text is in charge, and the text will tell the reader what is important. In some highly structured hypertext environments, readers may still have the illusion of constructing the text, but when a choice is path A or path B and the end of the path is always the same stroll through the text, this choice is a deception, making this type of hypertext suspect. Is it worse to have no choice or to have the illusion of choice?

Without the mutability characteristic of the hypertext most people discuss, there is certainly an epistemological attitude of a body of knowledge being "covered" completely—no questions need be asked nor are they, quite literally, permitted.

When hypertext is constructed in this way, the responsibility shift spoken of here does not occur. The teacher need relinquish no control, he or she has just as much as always. The teacher controls the text, how much students may read, and where they may wander. He or she controls what contributions they may make to class and what questions they may ask.

Clearly the possibilities for conundrums peculiar to hypertext are myriad. The same qualities that open possibilities for hypertext also provide the opportunity for problems. In a database so enormous that it includes several thousand nodes of primary and secondary text, where does authority lie? And what of the concept of authorship—will it be entirely done away with? Will, as my students maintain, we become a nation of expert linkers able to draw connections, but without original thought. And what of the concept of closure that Bolter (1991) and Ong (1982) say traditional print affords us? The closure of traditional print leaves readers with the impression of a certain amount of expertise and authority. Both write-to and closed but enormous databases may relieve individual authors (and linkers) of the responsibilities of expertise. Many scholars see the gatekeeping function of print and its politics as an important method of safeguarding the academy. Hypertext presents the possibility of genuine revolution—epistemologically and pedagogically with all the attendant implications for classroom, curriculum, canon, and cultural paradigm.

It seems unlikely, however, that such a revolution will occur. Most scholars today do not view open hypertexts as authoritative acceptable sources. There is great disagreement as to the acceptability as research material of unmoderated lists and World-Wide Web sites. The need, created by books, for a sense of authority, authorship, and authenticity will not fade softly away. Electronic texts will be required to have closure, control of their subject matter, and responsible expert editorial boards in order for them to be acceptable classroom adjuncts. With all this it seems unlikely that there will be any significant challenge to the practice of presenting text as if it had no agenda. Hypertexts must still make assumptions about what is worthy of inclusion, and it remains to be seen if the possibilities of size will allow the inclusion of possibly competing worldviews.

Based on what we know about the functioning of textbooks in the classroom, it seems obvious that it is not the desire of the current educational system that our initiates engage in the same activities as do seasoned scholars. It is not in the interests, politically, socially, or intellectually of any established discipline for newcomers to the field to engage directly in debate. Aside from the oft-cited practical reasons for the necessity of coming into possession of the canon prior to admission into the dialogue, the notion of legitimate challenge has historically been ill received (Fleck, 1939/1979; Kuhn, 1970). Based on the traditional relationships among texts, disciplines, scholars, and novices, relationships driven not simply by a quest for knowledge but by a host of intrigues, it seems probable that future analysis of hypertext in the classroom will continue to indicate the same sort of self-reflective myopia present in traditional printed textbooks.

CONCLUSIONS ARE NOT YET POSSIBLE

At this point most open and write-to hypertexts are being used and positively discussed only in writing classrooms (Douglas, 1994a, 1994b; Forman, 1991; Joyce, 1988). Given the current state of the educational system in this country it seems unlikely that hypertexts with truly "democratizing" qualities will be accepted into mainstream use outside of composition workshops. There may be *some* hope. Seymour Papert (1980) traveled to France in the late 1970s to introduce his computer program Logo into grade-school classrooms. Although a tremendously significant purpose of elementary education—teaching youngsters appropriate social behavior—was omitted from his resultingly optimistic discussion of that experiment, the experiment still yielded primarily positive results.

In spite of the possible "mis"uses of hypertext cited previously, the technology does encode a new worldview, different from that of traditional print. I have discussed the primary differences between the two. Pedagogically, hypertext both allows and encourages more genuine participation by students. It also seems to open up the classroom in ways that would encourage collaborative learning. Whether teachers will be willing to give up some control of their classrooms is a question similar to that brought about by the introduction of the printing press. The academy hated seeing authority shifted, but it was as inevitable as sunrise. Not knowing what may happen in a particular class is uncomfortable and requires a flexibility and a range of material many instructors may be unwilling to embrace. As hypertext breaks down the barriers between disciplines by contextualizing bodies of knowledge historically and conceptually, it will demand a more well-rounded classroom that admits not only opposing points of view, but points of view from seemingly disparate fields. Faculty will be forced to adapt; we are already seeing the results of this in newly formed interdisciplinary departments and schools all around the country.

Hypertext will also have an impact on an epistemological scale larger than classroom pedagogy. It calls into question several different relationships of academic authority. Not only will instructors in individual classrooms have their authority challenged, but the larger ideas of curriculum and canon will be forced to account for themselves in ways heretofore unimagined. As attitudes that inform the construction of hypertext make their way into curriculum planning, and beyond, traditional elements such as prerequisites, required reading, and single-discipline classrooms may find themselves in jeopardy. The wider contextualization allowed by hypertext will most certainly force changes in the manner in which disciplines are conceived and expertise is attributed. When the text is mutable, all notions about authority and authorship are called into question.

The habits of thought encouraged by the dynamic and visual environment of hypertext and other cyberspace applications are already apparent in our culture in the guise of, for example, MTV and computer games. Rhetorical traditions in all venues will be severely challenged by this. It has become convention now, for example, that what is possible visually, whether or not it is logical, is expected. Whether these visuals make traditional and logical sense in the world of the real no longer demands the imperative consideration it used to.

We are already seeing the impact of hypertext both in the classroom and in the culture. Many children and students are more computer literate than we are; and certainly they are less intimidated by the possibilities of computers than we were at their age. This chapter has not even begun to consider the possibilities of Internet capabilities such as the World-Wide Web, a living, growing hypertext. So will this be a democratizing medium as so many think, or will it simply produce a nation of people with short attention spans and good eye-hand coordination, as others contend? I am in favor of anything that asks us to examine our traditional agenda. Particularly when that agenda has been, for the most part, a hidden one. Whether the emergence of hypertext will result in a pedagogical shift remains to be seen, perhaps not by us. But I suspect we will all be examining these questions for some time to come.

REFERENCES

Bolter, J.D. (1991). *Writing space.* Hillsdale, NJ: Erlbaum.

Crane, G. (1990) Challenging the individual: The tradition of hypermedia databases. *Academic Computing, 1,* 22-38.

Crane, G., & Mylonas, E. (1988, November). The Perseus Project: An interactive curriculum on classical Greek civilization. *Educational Technology,* pp. 25-32.

Delaney, P., & Landow, G.P. (1991). Hypertext, hypermedia and literary studies: The state of the art. In P. Delaney & G.P. Landow (Eds.), *Hypermedia and literary studies* (pp. 3-50). Cambridge, MA: MIT Press.

Douglas, J.Y. (1994a). Making the audience real: Using hypertext in the writing classroom. *Educators' Tech Exchange, 1*(3), 17-23.

Douglas, J.Y. (1994b). Technology, pedagogy, or context: A tale of two classrooms. *Computers & Composition, 11,* 275-282.

English, R. (1986). Can social studies textbooks have scholarly integrity? *Social Education, 50,* 46-48.

Ess, C. (1991). The pedagogy of computing: Hypermedia in the classroom. In P.D. Stotts & R.K. Furata (Eds.), *Hypertext '91 Proceedings* (pp. 277-289). New York: Association for Computing Machinery.

FitzGerald, F. (1979). *America revised.* Boston: Little, Brown.

Fleck, L. (1979). *Genesis and development of a scientific fact* (F. Bradley & T.J. Trenn, Trans.). Chicago: University of Chicago Press. (Original work published 1935)

Forman, J. (1991). Computing and collaborative writing. In G.E. Hawisher & C.L. Selfe (Eds.), *Evolving perspectives on computers and composition studies* (pp. 65-83). Urbana, IL: National Council of Teachers of English.

Friere, P. (1970). *Pedagogy of the oppressed* (M.B. Ramos, Trans.). New York: Continuum.

Gagnon, P. (1987, Summer). Democracy's untold story. *American Educator,* pp. 19-25, 46.

Gibson, S.B. (1991). Professional scholarship and introductory communications textbooks (Doctoral dissertation, New York University, 1991). *Dissertation Abstracts International, 52,* 1931A-1932A.

Gibson, S.B. (1993, November). *Textbooks as canon.* Paper presented at the Speech Communications Association Convention, Miami, FL.

Hardison, O.B. (1989). *Disappearing through the skylight.* New York: Penguin.

Herrstrom, D.S., & Massey, D.G. (1989). Hypertext in context. In E. Barrett (Ed.), *The society of text* (pp. 45-58). Cambridge, MA: MIT Press.

Joyce, M. (1987). *afternoon, a story* [Computer software]. Watertown, MA: Eastgate Systems.

Joyce, M. (1988). Siren shapes: Exploratory and constructive hypertexts. *Academic Computing. 4*, 11-14, 37-42.

Kaplan, N. (1991). Ideology, technology, and the future of writing instruction. In G.E. Hawisher & C.L. Selfe (Eds.), *Evolving perspectives on computers and composition studies* (pp. 11-42). Urbana, IL: National Council of Teachers of English.

Knoblauch, C.H., & Brannon, L. (1984). *Rhetorical traditions and the teaching of writing.* Upper Montclair, NJ: Boynton/Cook.

Kuhn, T.S. (1970). *The structure of scientific revolutions* (2nd ed.). Chicago: University of Chicago Press.

Landow, G.P. (1992). *Hypertext: The convergence of contemporary critical theory and technology.* Baltimore: John Hopkins University Press.

Lanham, R.A. (1993). *The electronic word: Democracy, technology and the arts.* Chicago: University of Chicago Press.

McDaid, J. (1991). Breaking frames: Hyper-mass media. In E. Berk & J. Devlin (Eds.), *The hypertext/hypermedia handbook* (pp. 445-458). New York: McGraw-Hill.

McDaid, J. (1992). *Uncle buddy's phantom funhouse* [Computer software]. Watertown, MA: Eastgate Systems.

Moran, T.P. (1971). Education and persuasion: A propaganda analysis of English language textbooks used in New York City academic high schools (Doctoral dissertation, New York University, 1971). *Dissertations Abstracts International,* 32/10-A, 5747.

Moulthrop, S. (1991a). Beyond the electronic book: A critique of hypertext rhetoric. In P.D. Stotts & R.K. Furata (Eds.), *Hypertext '91 Proceedings* (pp. 277-289). New York: Association for Computing Machinery.

Moulthrop, S. (1991b). The politics of hypertext. In G.E. Hawisher & C.L. Selfe (Eds.), *Evolving perspectives on computer and composition studies* (pp. 253-274). Urbana, IL: National Council of Teachers of English.

Moulthrop, S. (1992). *Victory garden* [Computer software]. Watertown, MA: Eastgate Systems.

Neuman, D. (1991). Evaluating evolution: Naturalisitc inquiry and the Perseus Project. *Computers and the Humanities, 25*, 239-246.

Olson, D.R. (1988). Mind and media: The epistemic functions of literacy. *Journal of Communication, 38*(3), 27-36.

Ong, W.J. (1982). *Orality and literacy: The technologizing of the word.* New York: Methuen.

Papert, S. (1980). *Mindstorms.* New York: Basic Books.

Postman, N. (1992). *Technopoly: The surrender of culture to technology.* New York: Knopf.

Rubens, P. (1989). Online information, hypermedia, and the idea of literacy. In E. Barrett (Ed.), *The society of text* (pp. 3-21). Cambridge, MA: MIT Press.

Slatin, J. (1991). Reading hypertext: Order and coherence in a new medium. In P. Delaney & G.P. Landow (Eds.), *Hypermedia and literary studies* (pp. 153-170). Cambridge, MA: MIT Press.

Smith, C.G. (1991). Reconceiving hypertext. In G.E. Hawisher & C.L. Selfe (Eds.), *Evolving perspectives on computer and composition studies* (pp. 224-252). Urbana, IL: National Council of Teachers of English.

Treisman, P.M. (1985). A study of the mathematics performance of black students at the University of California, Berkeley (Cooperative learning, remedial, honors programs, affirmative action) (Doctoral dissertation, University of California, Berkeley, 1985). *Dissertation Abstracts International, 47,* 1641A.

◇◇◇◇ 18

Cinematic Representations of Cyberspace

Paul Lippert

Cyberspace, although computer-generated, has seen many representations in cinema, itself a media space. Paul Lippert uses films such as TRON as a jumping-off point to discuss the signficance of computer media's peculiar mix of the analogic and the digital. Noting how the concrete and the abstract have historically functioned as metaphors for each other, he connects symbolic form with social class, the elite leaning toward literacy and the masses toward speech and imagery. Ultimately, he is critical of postmodernists who celebrate cyberspace as a metaphor for computing and cyberpunk as a lifestyle. In the other sections of this book, alternate critical discussion of virtual space can be found in Herbert Zettl's analysis of the metaphysics of virtual reality in Chapter 5 and Jay David Bolter's comparison of virtual reality and text in Chapter 7; other related critiques of a more general nature include John M. Phelan's essay in Chapter 2, and Ronald Jacobson's discussion of policy in Chapter 9; see also Lance Strate's arguments concerning cyberspace versus cybertime in Chapter 23 as a variation on Lippert's distinction between concrete and abstract forms.

Two neon-lit figures with dim yet unmistakably human faces engage in a life-and-death Frisbee match, supported by a gridwork of similar neon lines that hang in a black void. Cartoon-like, yet strangely iridescent motorcycles race on an illuminated plane, leaving linear barriers of light behind them. With these images, Walt Disney Productions introduced the general public in 1982 to what is now known as cyberspace. The film they appear in, TRON, has since become a major case study for postmodernists interested in the cultural impact of computer technology. Basically a children's film, with good-guys-beat-bad-guys plot and seemingly prepubescent characters, it is considered to be a cultural landmark for its depiction of such "space."

Yet in considering these brightly colored and excitingly kinetic images, it is possible to be distracted from the fact that what is being depicted (i.e., the computer's functions) is in actuality not a space at all but, in practical terms, its opposite. In a certain sense, one can even say that space was the *problem* that the computer was invented to *solve*. Bureaucracies, needing to process ever-increasing amounts of information, were faced with a growing impediment of space; the space of ever-lengthening forms and documents, ever-widening file folders, ever-multiplying file cabinets, ever-more crowded offices, ever-growing distances between offices, people, and sources of information. The computer helped to remove this impediment by storing and processing information in what is to a great extent a nonspatial medium. When we use the term *cyberspace*, we are using the concept of space as a metaphor for something that in some ways can be made to function like a concrete space, but that is actually much more abstract. Such cinematic representations of the computer's functions as can be found in *TRON*, or any one of a number of other recent science fiction movies, utilize the actual space of the screen for such metaphoric purposes. In this case, it is not the linguistic *concept* of space alone, but the *directly visible* spaces on the screen's surface that are used as metaphors for abstractions about the computer.

But how can such graphic spatial metaphors be used to capture the complex, invisible nature of the computer's influence on our lives? Why would they be chosen over more literal, language-based methods of explanation? Most important, what are the social implications of this choice? This chapter contextualizes these questions through an examination of the media environment in which they arise in order to suggest possible answers to them.

The use of spatial metaphors for abstractions is nothing new. As Walter Ong (1967) has pointed out, the cultural transition from orality to literacy is marked by a shift from a temporal to a spatial phenomenology of the word. In the early days of print culture, knowledge began to be cast into object-like form and subjected to a logic of spatial arrangement on the depthless, denatured surface of the printed page. When applied to physical entities, like planets, whose characteristics are manifest by means of their positions in actual space, like orbits, this logic led to productive developments in the natural sciences. When applied to more abstract entities, it tended to reify them, to conceptualize them as if they actually had the characteristics of objects situated in space. A prime example of this is the very notion of *system*. Originally this term was applied specifically to the schematic representation of planets in their orbits. So influential was the concept, as advanced in such works as Copernicus's *De Revolutionibus* in 1543, that suddenly all sorts of phenomena began to be represented in such diagrams as systems. Even human psychology took on a geometric form (Ong, 1951).

It is a paradoxical feature of writing, and especially of print, that they facilitate the contemplation of the abstract by rendering it in the concrete form of object-like, visible words situated on the space of the page (Havelock, 1963, 1976). Because both language and the alphabet are digital symbol systems, the form of the signifier is purely arbitrary and conventional. At least ideally, it is nothing more than a technical convenience; it need not affect the semantic status of the signified. In fact, it functions best when its physical form is transparent (Havelock, 1976). Inevitably, an analogic habit of mind tends to come into play, especially when new questions are being addressed. As the increasingly abstract nature of new knowledge makes it ever more difficult to grasp, not only the signifiers but the signified concepts themselves are concretized (reified), translated, consciously or not, into spatial form. Poststructuralist writing well exemplifies this habit, from the work of Michel Foucault, in which all sorts of phenomena are reduced to "things" in "places," to a recent author (Bukatman, 1993), who asserts about his book on cyberspace: "*Terminal Identity* constructs a trajectory that propels the subject into the machine" (p.17). Not only is the cultural impact of computer use here depicted through the image of a human subject actually inhabiting a machine (as in the science fiction movies), the very text that describes this state of affairs itself figures as a sort of mechanical device that somehow puts it there.

As the print environment is gradually supplanted by electronic technologies, it is ironic not only that these spatial metaphors continue to proliferate, but they are even being applied to a technology that in large part was developed specifically for its nonspatial character. And yet, cyberspace is not usually described in terms of the dull, lifeless space of the printed page. Instead, it is a colorful, exciting, dynamic, even dramatic space that is depicted in most writing on the subject as well as in the movies. The cybernetic Frisbee players of *TRON* have their equivalents in serious writing on the subject that describes human subjects leaving their "obsolete" bodies to enter the "dramatic arena" of cyberspace (Bukatman, 1993, p. 201). How can we account for this?

Two important features of this writing are related to the fact that its subject is a technology. First, the metaphor, to a large degree, precedes the phenomenon. Unlike natural phenomena, technologies are conceived before they actually exist. Second, the phenomenon can be altered so as to correspond to the metaphor, as well as vice versa. Technology can be adapted to popular tastes. Therefore, writers are addressing themselves to something that is not only in the process of becoming, but whose path of development is subject to alteration. It is even possible that self-fulfilling prophesies are being made. But if they are not based on the experience of a completed, existent phenomenon itself, where do these prophesies come from?

Part of the answer, I believe, can be found by placing the computer in the context of the history of the development of communication media. From the very beginnings of human communication to the advent of the print era (one might even say, to the development of the telegraph), media have rather consistently evolved in the direction of increasing digitalization of form. After this point, as the age of electronic media began, this process seemed to reverse direction, as media became increasingly analogic and began to evolve toward the representation of direct experience (Levinson, 1979). The computer, obviously, represents a branch from this line of evolution that reverses the direction of change yet again toward digitalization. So we now can see two fairly distinct lines of media evolution heading in opposite symbolic directions. If the digital abstractions of print tended to give way to analogic spatial metaphorizing, just what might be expected from the even more digital computer? Although it had no intrinsic equivalent to the space of the printed page, it soon adopted the video monitor from its analogic cousin—the television—whose content traditionally and even still today derives largely from film.

Considered apart from its analogic content, television actually has an affinity with the computer. In their near-instantaneous operation, in their rendering space in effect irrelevant, in their connecting of displaced, decontextualized information, both represent a break from the linear continuity and spatial context of the printed page. And with the addition of the video monitor to the computer's standard apparatus, both are capable of the same kind of visual display of content. Both are capable, that is, of a visual display suitable to the symbolic content of film.

Although basically an analogic medium, film has a spatial bias similar to that of print. Signifiers are given visual form and are subjected to a logic of spatial arrangement. And yet, its analogic form causes its space to generate meaning differently. For unlike the physical form of digital symbols, that of analogic symbols is not merely a technical convenience. It is directly expressive of meaning. Unlike the use of spatial metaphors in the print environment, which tends to concretize what is abstract, their use in that of film tends to make abstract what is concrete. If a character, for example, is standing in the foreground of a shot, and thus takes up a greater amount of screen space than others within the same frame, although a mere concrete spatial arrangement is denoted, at the same time a more abstract connotation is being expressed about that character's relation to the others. Popular film's essential mode of operation, then, is to represent a concrete narrative through images whose spatial characteristics serve as metaphors for the story's abstract connotations.

This process of using imagery for abstraction did not begin with film. In oral cultures, whose languages are relatively devoid of abstract terms, the dominant form that knowledge takes is concrete, image-evoking narrative. Although abstract meanings are implicit in the storyline, they are not directly expressed in words. Instead, they are symbolized by images called to mind by verbal description. For this reason, Eric Havelock (1963) calls preliterate Greek culture one of "image thinkers." The image, though, as in radio drama, has to be constructed in the mind mainly on the basis of these verbal descriptions. Film is different in that it articulates the image in explicit form on the space of the screen. The mind, in a sense, has its visualizing done for it. But once the mind has possession of the image, the act of using it to represent the abstract is the same with both speech and film media.

These two types of spatial metaphorizing—one, characteristic of print, which concretizes the abstract; the other, characteristic of film and oral narrative, which abstracts the concrete—arise in response to opposite epistemic problems. The former reacts to an overload of abstraction, characteristic of literacy. The latter reacts to a lack of it, characteristic of orality. The computer, interestingly, can be associated with both, although in very different applications. In its mathematical and scientific uses, as when abstract equations are given graphic form, it is functioning like print. In its more recent entertainment uses, as when images of fictional characters and their narrative actions are spatially manipulated to express the more abstract interactions of games, it is functioning like film.

Historically, these two types of spatial metaphors and their related epistemic problems have been associated not just with different media, but with different social classes. Since the invention of writing, orality and literacy (that is, oral and literate modes of thought, embodied for the most part in oral and literate people) have coexisted in what Ong (1967) calls media interface culture. Rhetoric is an art developed by literate elites in order to persuade mostly oral audiences. In many respects, it represents an interaction between the two sensibilities. Such interaction is an important characteristic of the Age of Rhetoric, which came to an end with the advent of typographic culture.

In many respects, the cultural transition from print to electronic media seems to be bringing with it a return to this rhetorical orientation in society (Lanham, 1993). Our present culture, in spite of whatever print era ambitions of universal literacy and cultural equality that may linger, can be understood in terms of media interface. As print and literacy, generally, increasingly become the dominant media of only the elite, and while the masses turn to the speech and imagery of the electronic media's "secondary orality," society is divided epistemically. This societal split corresponds to the split in the path of media evolution described earlier: The elite embrace ever more digital forms, whereas the masses go analogic. In terms of content, as the elite explore ever higher levels of abstraction, popular culture revels in the graphic and the concrete.

Equipped with the video monitor, the computer has been adapted for mass marketing by means of software that creates an analogic user interface. As with traditional rhetoric, literate resources are being used to appeal to an essentially oral sensibility. Giving this highly digital medium an analogic persona facilitates its representation in the mythology of popular film as well. This "selling" of the computer, both as consumer product and as cultural icon, represents an interface not only between the two branches of media evolution, but between two social classes. Whereas one class concretizes the abstract, translating the computer's meaning into the imagistic terms of cinematic space, the other class abstracts the concrete, trying to understand the computer in these terms. Both processes, I believe, are evident in cinematic representations of cyberspace; yet each operates through distinctly different cinematic elements.

The mass audience's tendency to abstract from concrete images has its surest foothold in the narratives of these films. The narrative of *TRON*, for example, exhibits features that are the same as those of the mythologies of oral cultures (Ong, 1982). It centers around the actions of a hero or protagonist with whom the audience establishes a mimetic identification. The plot is agonistically toned, consisting of the struggles between clearly defined forces of good and evil. The new and unknown is presented in the form of magic or even religion, as a machine mysteriously transforms live human beings into digitized data and a "Master Control Program" approaches the status of a deity. Its extremely flat characters seem to have no interiors; for the most part, their presence is expressed kinetically. Technology is represented animistically, with computer programs taking on human form. All these characteristics serve to concretize the narrative, rendering it in a form in which its spatial representations can be used metaphorically to express the abstract.

The tendency of the elite, corporate and intellectual, to concretize the abstract finds its expression in these films' mise-en-scene (the visual elements placed within the frame at any particular time during the course of the narrative). Here we find spatial metaphors not only for concepts about the computer, but for theories of postmodern culture in general. *TRON*'s depiction of absolute Cartesian space divided by abstract linear coordinates, of irradiated light neither reflected nor blocked by anything solid, of decentered presences and actions, of depthless yet semantically inflated surfaces in its mise-en-scene has been interpreted in much postmodernist writing as representing ideas that address both of these highly abstract topics (Bukatman, 1993; Sobchack, 1988). As found in this and several other recent science fiction films, these spatial elements have risen to the status of authoritative pronouncements not just on the supposed wonders of the computer, but on nothing less than the "cultural logic of late capitalism." It is remarkable about these cinematic representations and their critical interpretations that they exhibit such a close similarity between the social viewpoints of the creators of popular cultural commodities and "Marxist" literary critics. That mass culture merchants and supposed counterculturists would engage in such mutual flattery and collaboration is deeply disturbing to this writer. It is a broad phenomenon in our culture today, best epitomized by the recent "hip" commercial William Burroughs did for Nike and discussed in detail elsewhere (Hayward, 1993; Roszak, 1994; Savan, 1994). More significant here is the question of how this common elite viewpoint is received by the mass audience.

Kinetically led into this space through the concrete narrative, the audience is subjected to a visual environment that is rather drastically at odds with common-sense notions of what is natural, or even real. In those films, like *TRON*, whose narratives employ a reassuringly conventional action-adventure plot structure—in which we know in advance that the good guys will beat the bad guys and all problems will be solved by the end of the story—it seems that the mise-en-scene would make little more impression than that of an extended chase scene through an amusement park. In more recent cyberspace-related films, such as *The Fortress, Future Shock, Ghost in the Machine, Homewrecker, Mind Warp*, and *Lawnmower Man*, the "trip" into this new realm tends toward the generic conventions of the horror film: not an encouraging sign. For whatever our "liberated" postmodernists may say about horror visually articulating "anxieties about the body" (Whose body? Whose anxieties?), the nonmonstrous characters in these films seem to want to keep their bodies in one solid piece, untechnologically modified and alive (in the traditional sense of the term). I assume that the audience goes along in reacting negatively to the mise-en-scene.

Yet most revealing of the postmodernist/audience media interface as expressed through the interaction of narrative and mise-en-scene are those works that tend toward the conventions of the detective novel and the film noir. The novel *Neuromancer* (Gibson, 1984), although not a film, plays a prominent role in discussions about representations of cyberspace. What is remarkable about this book's reception is the tendency of the technophilic not even to notice its unremitting pessimism, to, in the author's words, "read me and just take bits, all the cute technology, and miss about fifteen levels of irony" (cited in McClellan, 1989, p. 70). Utopian prophesying tends to be based on descriptions of the story's setting (the print equivalent of mise-en-scene) without taking much account of what effects that setting is having on the characters, their actions, or the plot generally. For those who have an interest in the characters and what happens to them, the conventions of the narrative set up a number of expectations that, depressingly, are never fulfilled: expectations of desire, love, coherence, and purpose. Trapped within a mad technological environment, the characters' human impulses wither.

A similar yet not quite so hopeless example is the film *Blade Runner*, which, although not explicitly centered around conceptions of cyberspace, is considered by many to be a prime example of the expression of the postmodern (and cyberpunk) through its mise-en-scene. What is especially ironic about this film is that the director, who is known primarily for his talents in scene design, was forced by the producers to strengthen the narrative elements of the film before they would release it. This primarily involved the addition of a voice-over narration that stressed the protagonist's struggle to find coherence in his bizarre surroundings as well as to answer questions about his own humanity. A small cult has formed around the later-released "director's cut" of the film, as postmodernists pick over the symbolism of scenic details. Yet it seems to me that the producers knew the mass audience's reaction to this environment and insisted that it be incorporated into the narrative.[1]

[1]For more about reactions to postmodern elements of recent science fiction films, especially the reemergence of film noir elements as signs of opposition, see Lippert (1993).

What this all amounts to, I think, is a situation in which postmodernists and typical audience members see very different things in these films. Although the former embrace concretely glowing schematizations as symbols of conceptually glaring cultural prognostications, the latter struggle to maintain an existential footing on the narrative path. Dazzling one another in their kaleidoscopic dance of antifoundationalist imagery, the postmodernists fail to see the significance, indeed, even proclaim the "obsolescence," of narrative as it is known to the average person. But for the audience, it is the narrative that grounds the experience of images in the human lifeworld, which is where this experience ultimately originates. It is in this lifeworld that humanity has found what Susanne Langer (1939) calls "charged" symbols of life orientation since time immemorial. But as science and technology increasingly have distanced us semantically and experientially from this lifeworld, our ideas and their images have become similarly remote.

As ever-more brave new abstractions materialize on the cinema screen, the audience encounters them on their narrative journey. The narrative paths chosen so far seem to approach these "spaces" and "things" from such a perspective that they seem artificial and unreal to most people. Perhaps it is that they do not understand, that in their concrete modes of thought they cling to nostalgic notions of what is natural. But perhaps it is that they understand only too well, that in such spaces they recognize the alienated existences that they have already begun to live in the "space" of their daily lives.

REFERENCES

Bukatman, S. (1993). *Terminal identity: The virtual subject in postmodern science fiction.* Durham, NC: Duke University Press.

Gibson, W. (1984). *Neuromancer.* New York: Ace Books.

Havelock, E.A. (1963). *Preface to Plato.* Cambridge, MA: Harvard University Press.

Havelock, E.A. (1976). *Origins of western literacy.* Toronto: Ontario Institute for Studies in Education.

Hayward, P. (1993). Situating cyberspace: The popularisation of virtual reality. In P. Hayward & T. Wollen (Eds.), *Future visions: New technologies of the screen* (pp. 180-204). London: British Film Institute.

Langer, S.K. (1939). *Philosophy in a new key.* Cambridge, MA: Harvard University Press.

Lanham, R.A. (1993). *The electronic word: Democracy, technology, and the arts.* Chicago: University of Chicago Press.

Levinson, P. (1979). *Human replay: A theory of the evolution of media.* Unpublished doctoral dissertation, New York University, New York City.

Lippert, P.J. (1993). Beyond postmodernism in science fiction film. In M.T. Newman (Ed.), A *rhetorical analysis of popular American film* (pp. 117-134). Dubuque, IA: Kendall/Hunt.

McClellan, J. (1989, December). From here to reality. *The Face,* p. 70.

Ong, W.J. (1951). Psyche and the geometers: Aspects of associationist critical theory. *Modern Philology, 49,* 16-27.

Ong, W.J. (1967). *The presence of the word.* New Haven, CT: Yale University Press.

Ong, W.J. (1982). *Orality and literacy: The technologizing of the word.* New York: Methuen.

Roszak, T. (1994). *The cult of information* (2nd ed.). Berkeley: University of California Press.

Savan, L. (1994, September 6). Over-the-counter-culture: Corporations harvest hip. *Village Voice,* pp. 50-53.

Sobchack, V. (1988). *Screening space: The American science fiction film.* New York: Unger.

SECTION 4

MEANING: CYBERCOMMUNICATION AND CYBERCULTURE

Communication abhors a vacuum. Electronic communication calls into being electronic space. Computer-mediated communication (CMC) calls into being computer-mediated space. That these new spaces are much more than alternatives to physical space is a point that is central to this volume. As products of communication, they constitute new forms of social space; this is the case for all forms of electronic communication, but doubly so for interactive media such as the telephone and the computer. Although in some ways cyberspace mimics and substitutes for actual locations and forms of transportation, performing social functions and imitating the form of physical reality, in other ways we are introduced to an entirely new set of phenomena. And as part of the process of adapting to such new and different environmental factors, we change the ways in which we communicate, both in format and in content. Communication adjusted to meet the demands and biases of cyberspace is cybercommunication, and as communication and culture are intimately linked (to some they are consubstantial), culture itself is also altered. Thus, the focus of this section is on the ways in which cyberspace is influencing both communication and culture.

Human communication is characterized by the use of symbol systems; we compose our messages by drawing on established codes. This is the subject of the first chapter in this section, Judith Yaross Lee's study of the codes of electronic mail. Surveying the various forms of text-based, computer-mediated interpersonal communication, Lee argues that the symbol systems of cyberspace combine literate, oral, and iconic modes, juxtaposing novel symbols and familiar forms in new and unprecedented ways. Thus, Lee believes that it is through the combinations in particular that a unique and distinctive form of rhetoric has emerged in cyberspace. One of the most discussed phenomena associated with this form of cybercommunication is flaming; it is also one of the most misunderstood, as Philip Thompsen demonstrates in this section's second chapter. His analysis provides extended theoretical discussion of online hostility, offering a model that frames flaming as both a message encoded by a source and a meaning decoded by a receiver and therefore influenced by a variety of factors on both sides of the transaction.

As a site of new forms of communication, cyberspace gives rise to new cultural formations and entirely new forms of culture. CMC is commonly used as an abbreviation for computer-mediated communication, but could just as well stand for computer-mediated culture, also known as cyberculture. Thus, whereas Lee and Thompsen emphasize the codes and modes of cyberspace, Richard Cutler, in the third chapter in this section, focuses on the social implications of computer-mediated communication. His chapter is concerned with the new types of relationships that we enter into in cyberspace and with their impact on self-concept. Drawing on the symbolic interactionist perspective, Cutler argues that such virtual relationships are legitimate, able to satisfy real needs, and ultimately healthy. The following chapter, by Mark Lipton, is also concerned with the impact of computer media on the self, especially the basis of human identity in the body. His exploration of cybersex ranges from sexually oriented chat, cyberpornography, and teledildonics to the more general relationships between cyberculture and gender, sexuality, and self-image. Noting that the human body provides a key anchor for cultural meaning making, Lipton warns of the destabilizing effects of the cyborg lifestyle. In the final chapter, Lance Strate explores the neglected topic of cybertime both as supplement and alternative to the notion of cyberspace. As much a part of any communication context as the sense of place, time according to Strate is central to the formation of culture, community, identity, and, ultimately, meaning. Strate explores the characteristics of cybertime resulting from computer technology's time-keeping functions, from computer media's ability to present symbolically a sense of "virtual time" and from the individual's experience of time when interacting with and through computers.

Throughout this section, the core issue is the problem of generating meaning in a electronic environment. As new codes and new forms of signification are developed against the ground of the cyberscape, new meanings and new ways to make meaning are born. Moreover, meaning cannot be confined to cyberspace itself. Cyberculture has its origins in the "new culture" of computer professionals and hobbyists, which itself is changing as more and more members of the general public find themselves going online. At the same time, the impact of cyberspace and cybercommunication extend beyond the electronic domain. American culture and Western culture in general are influenced by and converging with cyberculture, itself becoming increasingly synonymous with global culture.

◊◊◊◊ 19

Charting the Codes of Cyberspace: A Rhetoric of Electronic Mail*

Judith Yaross Lee

At present, communication in cyberspace generally takes place by entering data through an alphanumeric keyboard. As such, cybercommunication by electronic mail, conferencing, discussion group, or live "chat" is an extension of such older forms as writing, printing, and typing. Thus, the media code of electronic mail and related genres borrows heavily from the conventions of typography and letter and memo writing, as Lee makes clear in this chapter. She argues, however, that e-mail diverges significantly from preelectronic writing and printing, and even from such channels as the electronic book and hypertext, by retrieving elements of oral media such as telephone conversations, oral performance, and face-to-face communication; e-mail produces a sense of immediacy and informality missing in more traditional relationships between writer and reader. Lee therefore argues that

*My thanks to the many people who have generously helped me research and compose this chapter: Rita Rahoi of the School of Interpersonal Communication at Ohio University, for her skillful assistance in the library and her patient downloading of some 500 e-messages; Joe Amato of the Humanities Department at Illinois Institute of Technology, for his gracious sponsorship of this project to the members of the *Technoculture* list; Sue DeWine, Director of the School of Interpersonal Communication at Ohio University, for sharing her e-mail correspondence; and Lance Strate, of the Communications Department at Fordham University, for his sensitive commentary on an earlier draft of this essay.

e-mail is a hybrid medium, "a junction where orality and literacy, in their extreme or purest forms, meet." Moreover, e-mail also brings into play nonverbal iconic elements such as the emoticon or smiley face :-) as well as other innovations in the use of typographic characters for visual and affective communication. Thus, Lee demonstrates that communication through this new cyberspatial code constitutes a new and highly significant form of rhetoric. Outside of Section IV, a different type of rhetorical analysis can be found in Charles U. Larson's Burkean exploration of virtual reality in Chapter 6, whereas other examinations of textuality include Neil Kleinman's historical study of intellectual property in Chapter 4, Jay David Bolter's comparison of text and virtual reality in Chapter 7, Stuart Moulthrop's discussions of the future of the book in Chapter 16, and Stephanie Gibson's overview of hypertext and education in Chapter 17.

Communicating in any medium calls for choosing from the sign systems we call codes, which constitute form and content, matter, and manner. Some codes are imposed by the medium, some sanctioned by social authorities, others entirely novel, still others adapted from ancillary purposes. Not every choice succeeds, but even failure invokes social and textual meanings, and the result is always rhetoric. Any new medium can illustrate how rhetors adapt existing codes to new situations, but electronic mail (e-mail) offers a unique look into the emerging codes of cyberspace. Often referred to as *computer-mediated communication* (CMC) because it involves the online composition and retrieval of electronically transmitted text, e-mail actually embraces several distinct genres: personal correspondence (dyadic communication), public announcements (varying from small group notices to mass messages, akin to flyers and junk mail), discussion lists (sometimes called *bulletin boards*, or simply *lists*, which involve messages between dyads and among small groups of members), and e-conferences (which attempt to replicate small or large group discussion). Through its particular union of the textual and the oral, e-mail constitutes cyberspace: it is a social site where messages—rather than people, meet. This chapter presents a rhetoric of electronic mail[1]—describing, classifying, and explicating the codes used in e-mail messages—in order to map the new territory we call cyberspace.

In the 30 years since Marshall McLuhan (1964) claimed in *Understanding Media* that "the medium is the message,"[2] examinations of orality and literacy have confirmed that language changes when communication media shift. Such examinations have, however, focused more on characterizing the effects of print than on interpreting the impact of electronic interaction. The

[1]I am following the examples of Kenneth Burke in *A Rhetoric of Motives* (1950) and Wayne Booth in *The Rhetoric of Fiction* (1961) and *A Rhetoric of Irony* (1974) in using rhetoric to denote a communication phenomenon, the analysis of that phenomenon, and the text presenting the analysis.

[2]The phrase serves as the title of the first chapter of *Understanding Media*.

classic history of economics and politics in the Renaissance and Reformation by Elizabeth Eisenstein (1979), *The Printing Press as an Agent of Change*, probably the most authoritative account of how media affect culture, antedates the computer revolution. The provocative discussions of rhetoric and secondary orality in Walter Ong's *Orality and Literacy* (1982) and Eric Havelock's *The Muse Learns to Write* (1986), among other scholarship from the early 1980s (Pattison, 1982; Tannen, 1982; Scribner & Cole, 1981), likewise appeared before the personal computer left its mark on the writing of individuals. The theorists who have undertaken to explain the impact of the computer on written language, on the other hand, largely ignore electronic mail and, perhaps because of our culture's bias toward print, emphasize instead the product-oriented aspects of electronic communication. Michael Heim (1987), for example, looks at word processing in *Electric Language;* Jay David Bolter's *Writing Space* (1991) and George P. Landow's *Hypertext* (1992) look at hypertext narratives. Richard A. Lanham (1993) does consider the rhetorical dimension of many varieties of *The Electronic Word,* as he calls it in a text tantalizingly issued in both conventional codex and Macintosh diskette, yet his cultural argument remains high above the daily reality of e-mail—as does Mark Poster's analysis in *The Mode of Information* (1990), although his chapter "Derrida and Electronic Writing" describes some e-mail phenomena. Discussions explicitly about e-mail, by contrast, for the most part ignore philosophical, cultural, and rhetorical implications (an exception is Thompsen & Ahn, 1992, whose title makes the point: "To Be or Not to Be: An Exploration of E-Prime Copula Deletion and Flaming in Electronic Mail"). Instead, discussions of e-mail tend to focus rather narrowly on how organizations can set up and manage effective networks (see, e.g., Caswell, 1988; Radicati, 1992; Vallee, 1984).

The hybrid nature of e-mail has important consequences for the form and content of its messages, whose textual conventions are evolving and stabilizing with use. With its immediate electronic transmission of typographic text, e-mail stands midway between the telephone call and the letter. As the materiality and formality of the typed letter yield to the immediacy and intimacy of the telephone call, e-mail messages not only contain less contextualizing or background information than the business letter, but also flaunt informal vocabulary, phonetic spellings, and colloquial sentence structures. Appropriately enough, considering that cyberspace is quite literally neither here nor there, correspondents in this virtual community use codes reflecting both orality and literacy. In addition to its own insiders' jargon, e-mail has given rise to new paralinguistic signs (including nonverbal symbols such as the happy face and typographical glyphs such as the column of greater than signs [>] used to indicate words downloaded or quoted from a previous message) that exploit the technology of the computer keyboard and screen. This chapter examines writers' rhetorical choices in two dominant genres of e-mail messages: individual correspondence and the Internet bulletin board (or *list*), in which people metaphorically post messages for anyone interested to see. Discussion in the *Technoculture* and *Voices* lists featured here ranges from the personal to the professional—academic considerations of technology and culture in the former, a women's hypertext collective in the latter. The e-textual counterparts of naturally occurring talk exemplify e-mail in its social contexts, whereas the list members' sophistication as writers and e-mail users gives them particular insight into e-mail phenomena. Contrasting messages from both e-mail genres with their conventional textual and oral counterparts shows how cyberspace is changing the written word.

Social psychologists have observed that the absence of "a distinctive etiquette" forces users of new communication technologies to learn new ways of behaving toward information and each other (Kiesler, Siegel, & McGuire, 1984). E-mail conventions, as constructed democratically online, constitute just such an etiquette, in both the descriptive sense of "common practice" and the prescriptive sense of "appropriate practice." Prescriptive rhetoric has tended to dominate discussion, however, largely because Anglo-American writing has institutionalized the elitist concept of "reputable custom." As the Scottish theorist George Campbell (1776/1963) defined it in his influential *Philosophy of Rhetoric*, "reputable custom" arises from the premise that "the generality of people speak and write very badly" (p. 141). Campbell's work incorporated some of the 18th-century's most advanced ideas about psychology and philosophy, but his notion of reputable use reflects the social politics of the late Middle Ages, when the medieval *ars dictaminis* (art of letter writing) offered instruction in the rhetorical practices of the elite.[3] From a political standpoint, the *ars dictaminis*, like Campbell's notion of reputable use, extended the elite class's power of credible written communication down to the lower classes.

E-mail rhetoric, on the other hand, reflects the democratizing power of computers. Despite the universal recognition of e-mail's ability to flatten hierarchies, many people fail to see how that same power elevates common use over reputable use. In the 10 years since Peggy Porter (1984) asked plaintively, "Where is the Emily Post or Miss Manners to help us enter this alien culture which we have newly encountered?" discussions of e-mail etiquette have tried to comply by offering lists of do's and don'ts.[4] Their efforts are as futile as those of

---

[3]Until fairly recently, etiquette books explicitly aimed to teach members of lower classes the behavioral rules of the aristocracy. In that sense, they also followed the pattern of the *ars dictaminis*. Such instruction presumes, of course, that people outside those elite groups need skills to function within them. Even today, candidates for upper management seek guidance in acquiring suitable manners, and parents chide their children for behavior that seems "vulgar"—common. More obviously, contemporary models for correct business letters, wedding invitations, and the like abound.

[4]More recently, Philip Elmer-Dewitt (1994) of *Time* asked, "If e-mail represents the renaissance of prose, why is so much of it so awful?" (p. 66). See also Goode and Johnson (1991), who recommend that users proofread messages for spelling errors before pressing the send button, and tailor content and tone to the culture of the intended audience, among a dozen other "guidelines . . . in the spirit of encouraging electronic mail and networking" (p. 64). More experienced users seem to recognize the futility of such recommendations. Dern (1994), for example, includes a section on "Netiquette" in his chapter on Internet citizenship, but he focuses on social rather than linguistic rules.

English teachers who insist that *everyone* needs a singular pronoun, not *their*. The top-down rhetorical practices of literate culture do not apply to oral culture, in which everyone does *their* own thing.

E-mail's immediacy and democratic power have their nearest parallels in oral communication, but e-mail is not an oral medium; rather, e-mail converts correspondence into a virtual conversation. In this new genre of mock-oral prose, much as in such older examples as Mark Twain's *Adventures of Huckleberry Finn* (1884/1985), literate and oral codes mingle and swap juices.[5]

RHETORICAL IMPLICATIONS OF E-MAIL FORM

Even familiar functions take new forms as codes adapt to cyberspace. E-mail messages, for example, alter the basic format of the typewritten memorandum, which standardizes correspondence with its rigid to-from-date-subject template. As McLuhan (1964) has argued, such standardization is one of the hallmarks of alphabetic literacy, and it has carried over into e-mail, which transmits typographical messages electronically. Most e-mail systems require a sender to fill in a memo template with its prescribed "To," "From," and "Subject" lines. Because it reveals both sender and receiver at the very beginning, e-mail has no need for the conventional "Dear John" or "Sincerely, Sue" of paper correspondence. The absence of a salutation and closing alters the familiar dynamic of correspondence, revealing in the process important differences between electronic and paper language.

From the reader's standpoint, the receipt tracing (e.g., "Received 25-Jan-1994 02:24pm") at the bottom of the screen or printout signals the end of the message. As the last element in the message, the tracing confirms the end of communication in much the same way as the blank space at the end of a letter or memo. Formalist theory suggests that the blank space at the bottom of a page confirms (with the redundancy typical of complete communication) elements in the text, such as the closing phrase and the writer's name, that declare the message complete. That is, as the textual equivalent of the phone call's "thanks for calling" or "good talking with you," the closing phrase provides a transition between the body of the message and the final textual element, the signature or

---

[5]I am indebted to Shelly Fisher Fishkin (1993) for the connection between *Huckleberry Finn's* mixed codes (African-American and Euro-American, in her case) and Huck's preference for a "barrel of odds and ends . . . [where] things get mixed up, and the juice kind of swaps around, and the things go better" (p. 2). Although mock-oral prose is most familiar in Mark Twain's writing, it was already a familiar technique to Americans by the 1830s in the Down East writings of Seba Smith's Jack Downing (see, e.g., Blair & Hill, 1978).

name indicating that the correspondent is, quite literally, signing off. The power of writing to reorder time and space asserts itself in the convention by which writers reveal themselves by name only at the end.[6] Thus the blank space that follows the text reassures the reader that the writer has said goodbye (unless there is a P.S., or postscript, which by definition means "after the writing"). These conventions need to be invented for the computer writing space. Because a blank screen would bring anxiety, not reassurance, basic e-mail systems signal "end of text" with additional text, the receipt tracing. The Prodigy system, which markets e-mail services to a wide consumer market, deflects anxiety with graphics rather than text; its e-mail software creates a metaphorical paper letter on the screen, framing the message, including any blank space not filled by text, with a graphic border around the edge of the screen to simulate a piece of paper.

In contrast to the Prodigy solution, the typical e-mail writing space invites correspondents to revise how they signal the end of their messages. Although some writers import the conventional "Sincerely yours, Joe," from paper mail, the usage has not caught on. In fact, John Seabrook (1994), writing in the *New Yorker* of his early e-mail exchanges with Bill Gates of Microsoft, reports that he began to view his own use of "Dear Bill" and "Yours, John" as an "etiquette breach" (p. 48) after observing how Gates began and ended his messages abruptly, without either salutation or closing phrase. Reliance on the familiar boundary markers of the paper letter underlines not only our tendency to understand new technologies in terms of older ones—as early rhetorics imposed the values of oral performance on writing—but also our insecurity with the lesser redundancy of electronic communication, compared with print. Electric language is, as Mark Poster (1990) has observed, immaterial.[7] Conventions based on material media like ink and paper do not quite fit.

The immateriality of the written trace contrasts sharply with the multiplication of copies of stored versions—whether in backup disks or tapes or in printouts—as anyone in a so-called paperless office can attest. Richard Lanham (1993) has recognized the basic paradox involved: "The electronic word embodies a denial of nature" (p. 18) so that we now can have our cake, eat it, *and* give it away to someone else! Despite e-mail's similarity to talk, which remains the most ephemeral communication medium in general use, at least one e-mailer suspects that "the memory for digital signs will be _longer_ [sic] than that of written signs. Perhaps even as long as the life of signs on clay tablets!" He has reason to think so: A total stranger once presented him with a printout "nicely

[6]The convention also suggests that personalized stationery represents an effort to assert the political over the technical.

[7]The term *electric language* is from Michael Heim (1987). On the power of the computer to "dematerialize the written trace," see Poster (1990, p. 111). The immateriality of all language is, of course, an ongoing topic among contemporary theorists—especially followers of Derrida—who begin by exploding the structuralist union of sign and signified as a metaphorical convenience and extend the argument to include all attempts to inscribe thought.

preserved under a plastic cover" of a posting he had made some three years earlier (*TNC*, 1993, March 29, 2:29 p.m.). Nonetheless, some danger exists of what one scholar called "fetishizing . . . the digital sign," which in its immateriality grants digital language particular powers or limitations of signification, a viewpoint that ignores "the failure of the sign (any sign) to capture the saturation of meaning or narrative/descriptive closure it appears to promise" (*TNC*, 1993, April 3, 9:14 a.m.). At the very least, the paradox that makes e-mail texts at once both durable and fragile comes across in the greater redundancy of some components than others.

The reliance on print-based boundary conventions may be more common among novice users and writers who export regular computer text via e-mail than among correspondents composing online. But frequent e-mailers adopt one of three distinct conventions. Many sign off with only a word or phrase: "Thanks!" is common; Gates ended one letter "Enough for now" (Seabrook, 1994, p. 54). Others use informal renderings of their names. Prevailing usage favors first name only or initials (sometimes in lower case and usually without periods or spaces between the letters), but communication between strangers sometimes leads to use of first and surnames (almost never including middle names or initials). Familiarity is the general rule. Among friends, that can lead to intimate in-talk, as when an American professor on leave in Israel signed himself "Dovidl," the diminutive of his Yiddish—not Hebrew—name, which would be used mainly by family members. Given the redundancy of any of these solutions to the problem of closure, however, many writers opt for a third practice: They simply stop writing. Adopting this approach requires strong faith in e-mail technology and the durability of the electronic word.

Requiring the user to fill in the e-mail template before beginning a message means that every e-mail message designates an addressee from the very start. E-mail thus confirms Mikhail Bakhtin's claim that every utterance "is oriented toward an addressee" (Voloshinov, 1973, p. 85). It also identifies the sender. Most e-mail software automatically generates a "from" line revealing at the very least the sender's user Id, if not the complete electronic address (e.g., "PP609" or "LEEJ"). The address communicates other information as well. Internet messages reveal through their address syntax the name of the sender's computing unit, the institution or organization, occasionally the brand of computer system (*vax*, for instance, referring to the DEC mainframe), and the network domain (e.g., *bitnet, edu, gov, uk, com*).

Every element of the address thus has the potential (not always exploited) to carry social meaning as well as technical information. Although user Ids may simply contain someone's name or assigned code, they may also express personal interests or politics (e.g., "feminist"). Subdomains sometimes contain puns or acronyms, as when Ohio University changed its code from *UCLS* (University Computing and Learning Services) to *CATS* (Computer and Technology Services). Of greater social interest, however, is the network or top-level domain, which identifies networks as American or international, and indicates which of the former belong to educational, government, or commercial systems. The Internet grew out of links among research and governmental computing systems, so addresses on these networks have higher status than those of such Johnny-come-latelies as America Online (whose domain is *aol*). Another indicator of status is one's proximity to the "Net"—that is, the number of subdomains in one's address. The shorter one's address, the higher one's status (Lohr, 1994), perhaps because a longer address provides more information about a sender, thereby defining the person more by function and membership than by personal traits. Viewed through a metaphorical mailbox or list of new messages received, these addresses function much like envelopes, allowing the receiver to attach priorities to messages even before reading them. The template thus links e-mail to its literate origins in the memorandum.

As a negative consequence of the template's information, e-mail has acquired what Andrea Ovans (1992) has called "the pitfalls of the memo culture" (p. 128), whereby people pretend not to have received a message, answer only those messages that suit them, or toss into the wastebasket (if only metaphorically) messages they dislike. But other consequences of the template are more positive. Having the sender's name at the beginning of a message, and sometimes at the end as well, gives e-mail a more casual, personal character than a printed letter. Although the ease of e-mail fosters the distribution of junk messages and unnecessary "I agree" replies, it can also discourage formal, institutional pronouncements. Sending an anonymous or institutional message may require a user to exert special effort, such as logging on under a new account or shifting to another predefined memo layout. From a visual standpoint, shifting layouts seems the electronic equivalent of changing from one kind of stationery to another, but from a rhetorical perspective it represents exchanging one's individual persona for institutional facelessness. In fact, a recent case study suggests that such official messages tend to appear on paper rather than e-mail (Deatsch, 1994). The less formal purpose of e-mail thus combines with its personal face to compress the distance between writer and reader. In that sense, by discouraging anonymity, e-mail captures for writing some of the personal presence of face-to-face communication.

The Textual Self

Not that anonymous messages or false representations are impossible. People are always free, in whatever medium they use, to adopt a new persona for a new interaction. I remember as a teenager playing a game in which my friends and I gave false names and telephone numbers to boys we met at the beach, and college students routinely come home for winter vacation with new nicknames or modes of interaction. Internet folklore recounts many examples of falsified genders, ages, and other personal factors. A recurring theme focuses on the opportunity to hide behind one's e-mail text—for good or ill.

Charting the Codes of Cyberspace

The ill effects of the invisible persona have received the mos[illegible] Deborah Tannen (1994), editorializing in a sidebar to a *Newsweek* featu[illegible] mail, specifically blames "the anonymity of networks" for emboldening som[illegible] to "deluge women with questions about their appearance and invitations to s[illegible] (p. 53)—to harass them in ways that society no longer permits. Although sexual harassment merits serious concern in any context, Tannen's explanation amounts to blaming the messenger for bad news. Because list users commonly enforce social conformity by the practice of *flaming*, overwhelming a violator's mailbox with angry replies sent via the e-mail answer function (a practice that would be impossible if e-mail were truly anonymous), anonymity and network morality are more likely contributing factors than first cause.

That honor probably goes to gender imbalance. A recent study by Eric Jorgensen (n.d.) of MIT estimates that Internet discussion lists are about 87% male.[8] Why would the male-dominated groups of cyberspace be more willing than the male-dominated clubs and workplaces of a few years ago to make women welcome? Or to discourage their members from making sexually provocative comments to women? Jorgensen's decision to censor his own message in anticipation of being flamed illustrates how flaming promotes social conformity, but because complaints constituted only 0.00657, rather than the 0.50 he expected, it is unclear whether the strategy was successful or unnecessary.[9] Women have already begun insisting that online intimidation stop (Price, 1993), and experience suggests that network users' tolerance for online harassment will diminish as the political power that women have achieved in other arenas extends to cyberspace. After all, only recently have sexual jokes come to constitute harassment, as opposed to camaraderie, and many Americans today—25 years after the feminist movement was launched—resist even that change.

In contrast to the antisocial few, many other men and women find opportunities for play in the chance to fabricate a textual self. A cartoon in the *New Yorker* a few years ago showed two canine computer buffs gloating that "on the Internet no one knows you're a dog." Similarly, a group of women reportedly collaborated on a series of love letters, a deception they saw as "Cyrano on the internet [sic], with the innocent male cast as Roxanne" (*TNC*, 1993, March 29, 2:29 p.m.). The mere conception of such a ruse indicates that paper texts have no patent on insincerity or fiction. And what's in a name, anyway? Everyone on the *Technoculture* list knows that "Tomato" is Joe Amato, so the pseudonym is no disguise. But it does differentiate this persona from those developed in his other writing and in his personal relationships.

---

[8]Jorgensen's survey of Internet USENET demographics resulted in a sample of 4,566: 86.5% men (*N* = 3,948) and 13.5% women (*N* = 615).

[9]Network administrators also have a vested interest in avoiding inflamatory messages because the resultant flames can cause the computer system to crash. The manager of the system that forwarded two lawyers' advertisement to the Internet was pretty irate himself. "They crashed our computer about 15 times . . . because of the volume of incoming complaints," he fumed. "I lost an entire week dealing with [it]" (Lewis, 1994, p. C1).

Women's anger at online harassment reflects e-mail's simulation of social presence. Virtual presence is, of course, what gives cyberspace its sense of place, but it also explains some of the more unusual phenomena of computer communication, including flaming. Conventional correspondence does not lend itself particularly well to heated discussion because of the extended time lag between turns. The whole affair tends to fizzle out after a few angry exchanges have been composed, committed to paper, and sent off—partly because moods and objects of attention shift over time, partly because the effort needed to maintain the fight becomes disproportionate to benefits received from doing so. Telephones offer combatants much more gratification by allowing voice-to-voice confrontation, but one party can gain the upper hand by hanging up. If, as this comparison suggests, verbal fights are a phenomenon enhanced by physical presence, then their appearance on e-mail confirms that cyberspace functions as a physical location where people behave as they do in conventional spaces.

Such an interpretation explains why, as one *Technoculture* member put it, "people feel obligated to 'leave' the list (whether in a tizzy or a huff or just a sad, sad shufflin' away) instead of bringing up another topic to see what happens" (*TNC*, 1993, March 12, 12:19 p.m.). It also explains the case of a woman "who was forced off a list by physical threats from one of the other subscribers" (C. Guyer, personal communication, December 9, 1993) because the threat of violence shows how e-mail communication collapses the distinction between virtual and real communities. The very terms *lurking* and *lurker* for a nonparticipating observer of bulletin board discussions suggest the in-group's hostility to nonparticipants—characterized by Internet slang as voyeurs peeking in from the outside—and the idea that lists are clubs for "members only" intensifies the sense of space defined by the participants. One must either participate or leave; lurkers are trespassers. In such a community, in which the metaphorical has become functional, the gendered communication patterns familiar to real-space groups continue to operate. A member of a women's hypertext collective contrasted "the kind of offense/defense maneuvering and displays which happen on other lists like TNC" with the "exceedingly polite" communication of the women's group running the *Voices* list (C. Guyer, personal communication, December 9, 1993). In contrast to the multiple flames within six months of *Technoculture* postings, *Voices* had none. Other women's lists appear equally tranquil (Kantrowitz, 1994).

The memo template's subject line points to a second manifestation of e-mail's lesser redundancy: Writers do not need a full sentence to contextualize their remarks ("I am writing in regard to your letter of November 4, 1993") and may sometimes avoid any reference to their motives for writing. Seabrook (1994) described the subject line as "a little like . . . a publicity release for what you have to say" (p. 52), but the announced subject may in fact have nothing to do with the message. Rather than look up or retype a cumbersome Internet address, senders may choose to reactivate it by invoking the reply mode to an old message. (I have carried on six months of conversation with one friend on varied subjects under the subject line "Re: Testing," which was my answer to her original message to verify my address.) Typically, however, the subject line provides most of the context the writer deems necessary. It may even be the whole message. A writer who titled a message "Lunch Monday noon at Uptown Chinese?" would have little, if anything, to add in the body of the message, whereas a writer who entered "Lunch" in the subject space of the template might need a message as long as "Are you free for lunch on Monday? How about noon at Uptown Chinese?" By contrast with e-mail's opportunities for brevity, telephone calls (as Harvey Sacks, 1992, points out) commonly contain a reason for the call early in the message.

E-mail replies also tend to lack contextual information. Indeed, a reply may consist of only a single word, such as "Thanks!" or "Great!" or a phrase, such as "oh, john. really!" (*TNC*, 1993, March 25, 2:47 p.m.). E-messages may lack substance in ways that paper texts cannot partly because the subject line makes additional explanation redundant, but largely because the reply function compresses actual time between conversational turns. Virtually speaking, no time has elapsed between utterance and reply if I answer a message as soon as I read it. So it makes perfect sense for someone to respond to a message titled "Idea" by writing "Good input! I'm still thinking...." (Sue DeWine, personal communication, May 11, 1994, original ellipses). An e-mail message requires less contextualizing content than a letter or paper memo because the context is already present, as in oral conversation. The same does not apply, however, to the response that reaches *its* destination divorced in time and space from the stimulus message. Only the subject line ("Re: Idea") links a reply to the prior message, requiring the reader to complete the context through memory. The reply itself, of course, becomes an immediate context for the next response, in true dialogic fashion.

Two alternatives have emerged for handling messages when elapsed time disrupts the reading-reply cycle. One is a new convention circulating among members of bulletin boards. A list member who wants to reply to a topic no longer current, a specific message, or a specific comment in a longer message may quote relevant portions of the stimulus message. Instead of using quotation marks, the familiar literate symbol, to frame or enclose retyped text, e-mail writers typically *import* the text from the previous message into the reply, signaling the importation with a row of mathematical greater-than signs (>) running down the left margin. This convention brings the past into the present, creating the illusion of zero-elapsed time in replying to it. As the reliance on typographical symbols suggests, this convention adapts the customs of letter writing ("In regard to your letter of May 3, when you requested . . . ") and thereby reflects e-mail's debt to the codes of literacy. The second alternative applies to private e-mail and discussion lists as well as to oral conversation in groups. So much time may have passed between the original message and the opportunity to reply that a context for reply is lost. The result is silence. This circumstance, familiar to students whose teachers finally call on them long after their response had any relevance, represents another similarity between e-mail and oral conversation: Context is created *between* turns rather than by turns. In "snail mail," by contrast, the expected time lag between turns diminishes the irrelevance of a delayed answer, even as it increases the need to contextualize that answer.

The virtual conversation created by such turn-taking leads to another affinity between e-mail and oral communication: Breaking off is hard to do. Although an e-mail sequence may end after the requested information has been provided, commonly a few superfluous turns follow the completion of business: "Glad I could help" might be followed by "Thanks again," which itself might lead to "Looking forward to seeing you at the meeting in October," and (in an extreme case) a final "I'll be there!" Such chatter serves no function related to content; rather, each message confirms receipt of the previous nicety. This phenomenon, however, can exist only when it costs little in time and effort. Interminable goodbyes belong to the jokelore about discussions with friends and neighbors on the front steps (Garrison Keillor once illustrated the problem in song) because the phenomenon belongs to the world of oral, social conversations. The effort and money required for a business letter—or, in some cases, a long distance telephone call—mean that few verbal responses will be generated solely to confirm the receipt of prior messages.

The memo form affects the language of e-mail messages as well as their structure. Perhaps because the memo form has a conventional association with informal, internal communication—between people who already know each other or who share institutional links—the vocabulary and grammar of e-mail lack the formality of many other genres of professional communication. Joshua Meyrowitz (1985) claims that "the more slowly messages are encoded, sent, and received, the more formal their typical content" (p. 110), but a case study of one manager's written communication indicates that encoding and transmission time may themselves be functions of social purpose (Deatsch, 1994). The messages in that study revealed a distinct pattern between medium and purpose: letterhead for official personnel matters, memo format for formal requests and announcements (thereby creating a paper trail for future reference), e-mail for informal requests, announcements, and individual persuasion.

Institutional factors enhance e-mail's informality by establishing a sense of direct communication between equals. High-ranking executives such as Bill Gates of Microsoft answer their own e-mail, whereas secretaries act as gatekeepers over their telephone calls and paper mail. In the process, e-mail exerts democratizing pressure as it bypasses the hierarchies of power and status that telephones preserve. The template itself, with its institutional blandness, eliminates other hierarchical power issues, especially those associated with elegant or prestigious stationery, providing a greater sense than paper allows of communication between equals. Additional factors may also help flatten hierarchies, but the linguistic evidence is clear: The aristocratic formality of writing is diminished—some would say eliminated—in e-mail. In its place, *vox populi, vox Dei.*

E-MAIL TEXT AS VISUAL TALK

Slanguage and Mock-Oral Writing

The insiders' jargon that creeps into e-mail content helps drive the informality while also benefiting from it. E-mail's origin as a hackers' medium has a role in the phenomenon, but now even people who cannot tell a spool drive from a punch card speak knowingly about "lurkers on the Net" (people who read but do not contribute to discussion lists) and "snail mail" (regular postal service). Some terms use initials as acronyms or shorthand: btw (by the way), MUD (Multi-User Dungeon), MOO (multi-User, Object-Oriented), MUSE (Multi-User Simulation Environment), GOK (God only knows), OIC (Oh, I see!). Like other forms of specialized language, jargon helps create and define e-mail communities, and new members embrace the lingo as signs of belonging. (Prodigy provides a glossary for new users.) E-mail replaces the redundancy of formal communication (for instance, a name repeated on the letterhead, in the signature, and typed below) with informal brevity.

Colloquial vocabulary and syntax thereby rule the day. Sentences need not be either complete or grammatical. "Trying to get ahold of you, but the addresses aint working" is a typical example (*TNC*, 1993, March 11, 10:04 a.m.). Punctuation tends to be haphazard ("lets find the common ground by which we may construct bridges between mechanical, electronic and social engineering. My my. I"m [sic] all for that" (*TNC*, 1993, March 12, 8:07 a.m.). Abbreviations abound: One writer curses, apparently in mock anger, "yer a great b-word," whereas another describes a friend as "enthusiastic about the conf at MIT" (*TNC*, 1993, March 11, 6:17 p.m.; S. J. Weininger, personal communication, October 17, 1992). As these examples suggest, deviations from formal grammar usually signify efforts to visualize talk. It would make no *phonetic* difference, for example, if Joe Amato's request to me (personal communication, February 3, 1993)—"I wonder if you could do me a favor (more work, she sez)"—had the correct spelling *says*, but the friendly, casual quality of the text would be lost. The ongoing discussion on computer-mediated conferences and electronic bulletin boards, in particular, fosters such mock-oral writing, which has a long tradition in American popular culture as the textual representation of the colloquial speaker. A skilled writer can imply vocal modulation with considerable precision. One contributor to the *Technoculture* list represented four changes of pitch and tone—musing, aspirated, dropped, raised—in as many sentences: "Lemme see, here. Hoo-kay. (I know I'm gonna regret this, but....) Anyways" (*TNC*, 1993, March 12, 12:19 p.m.; original ellipses). E-mail merges the literate emphasis on sight with the breezy informality of talk, with its many variations of sound.

Emoticons

More important than e-mail's linguistic variations, however, are the visual symbols called *emoticons*. Illustrations constituted by punctuation marks and other symbols (primarily nonalphanumeric) from the keyboard, emoticons adapt both oral and literate codes. In some ways, emoticons are miniature, screen-based versions of the banners and graphic printouts (e.g., Bugs Bunny composed of *X*'s and *O*'s) that hackers developed more than 20 years ago. Their reliance on characters from the computer keyboard reflects their literate origins. On the other hand, emoticons have more in common with hieroglyphics than with the alphabetic, phonetic writing on which Western literacy is based, and emoticons' visual representation of the speaker or listener's frame of mind brings nonverbal aspects of oral communication to written text. As a hybrid code, the emoticon is a perfect fit for a hybrid medium.

Emoticons have acquired various textual and social uses. Because they are read sideways, an element of play enters the text even before the reader decodes the symbols. Some emoticons exist mainly as jokes, passed along from one person to the next as examples of wit. This category tends toward elegant or complex examples, such as those featured by Tom McNichol (1994) in his introduction to the Internet for readers of *USA Weekend*, a national newspaper supplement:

Charlie Chaplin C):-(EQ)
Ronald Reagan 7:-)

As these examples illustrate, joking emoticons have very little use in constructing messages. They offer denotation nearly devoid of connotation.

When emoticons do contribute to the meaning of a message, however, they intensify the verbal text rather than substitute for words or phrases. In her study of switching between oral and written language, Denise Murray (1988) saw emoticons (she called them "icons") as transitional signs and predicted that their use would decline as other conventions developed—particularly asterisks (to indicate verbal stress), multiple vowels (for changes in intonation), and multiple question marks and exclamation points (for emphasis). But she mistakenly grouped orthographic conventions for visualizing sound with signifiers of attitude. E-mail writers use pairs of asterisks to indicate that the bracketed word, usually an adjective or adverb but occasionally a verb form, should receive verbal stress. Similarly, multiple question marks or exclamation points signal the reader to intensify the degree of rising intonation in a question or the loudness of an assertion. Both features appear quite clearly in this insistent statement, "Of course none of you are *obliged* to get involved with this!!" (*Voices*, 1994, February 12, 3:49 p.m.), and they indicate that the convention amounts to little more than an adaptation of conventional punctuation to the computer keyboard. Similarly, the list member who wrote "Like I said a looooooong time ago, I like to tell stories" (*TNC*, 1993, March 14, 1:10 p.m.) relied on conventional rules of English phonics, not specialized codes of cyberspace.

Using emoticons, on the other hand, does require understanding a specialized code. Who among the uninitiated would recognize 8-0 as a sign of astonishment, or know when to use (8-o for "Oh, no! It's Mr. Bill!"? These examples, although extreme, nonetheless illustrate that emoticons are inherently different from alphabetic signs—a difference that explains, in part, why we view them from a different angle. Rather than represent sounds, they represent attitudes. That is, emoticons are literate symbols with no grounding in oral language.

The Body in the Text

Ranging from the simple sideways smiley face :-) to elaborate caricatures of public figures, the connotative emoticon serves a simple function: to express an attitude toward the statement that precedes it. The reader must determine from the context, however, whether the emoticon signifies the writer's own attitude or a representation of the attitude that he or she wishes to invoke in the reader. When telecommunications expert Tom Reid (local communication, February 16, 1994, 6:19 p.m.) concluded a systemwide announcement about the establishment of new modem lines and protocols with the statement "You don't have to know what all this jargon means! ;)" the winking face represented his own face, offering good will to the bewildered and confiding technical knowledge to the hackers. In a somewhat different use of a smiley—"If you wish to change something already there you can ask the author of the note to do it! Or argue about it ! :-)" (*Voices*, 1994, February 8, 5:52 p.m.)—a member of a writing collaborative indicated that controversy and conflict were normal, even enjoyable, aspects of the group process. The smiley face can also, however, attempt to suggest or impose an attitude on the reader. The list member who wrote "George, what do you say? I admit I haven't finished your book :-)" (*TNC*, 1993, March 12, 10:04 a.m.) clearly intended the smiley to represent the desired approval from George, urging him to abandon any irritation he might feel about the preceding discussion. As these uses suggest, the emoticon contributes to written communication a sign system usually limited to oral communication: facial expression.

E-Mail as Performance Space

This inscription of the body into the text, particularly when combined with text as visual speech, explains the tendency of discussion list participants toward the dramatic and oratorical. Alluding to the dialogue conventions of popular dramas enhances the mock-oral dimension of the electronic text. One aggrieved list member portrayed himself as a character in a western, using phonetic spellings to represent the stereotypical cowboy's accent. "Wahl, I kin see we don't want no FED'RAL AGENTS on this list," he charged in the body of his message (*TNC*, 1993, March 12, 2:34 p.m.), and its explicit orality and western inspiration encompass the title as well. The subject line, "WANTED (not)," invokes the posters of criminals in the sheriff's office as it begs the reader to imagine a spoken voice chanting "not!" in the manner of current slang. The dramatic impulse extends from cultural icons to more elaborate metaphors, such as the one constructed by this writer *cum* prospector or tour guide, who represents his writing space as a site with three dimensions:

> Hi...uh, wait just a sec, there's some snow drifted across my information superhighway <<STAMP!>> <<STAMP!>> there, got it off my boots, don't want to track it into your nice dry Macintoshes.
>
> Where was I? Right—I want to suggest that . . . (*TNC*, 1993, March 14, 11:24 a.m.)

The playful qualities of these messages remind us, as Meyrowitz (1985) has taught, that electronic media blur work and play, humor and seriousness, along with generational, social, and physical boundaries. In addition, these examples reveal that e-mail—with its blurring of present and past, here and there—inspires writers to try controlling the sound and duration of their messages, just as they would if they were physically present.

Readers join writers in seeing the discussion list as drama. (Readers become writers, of course, when contributing to the discussion.) From their vantage point as spectators, however, dramatic performance concerns not sound and time, but space. Kali Tal, for instance, envisions the list as a dance floor. Defending another list member's post, she argued that discussions need not be orderly and coordinated, but ought to allow each member to choose a suitable mode for participation:

> And it aint that I think the dood is always right . . . or even always on the right track. It's a style thing, a voice thing, a rhythm thing. He doan wanna arm wrestle. He wants to *dance*. Me too. It's a big floor. There's room for us all. (TNC, 1993, March 14, 11:12 p.m.)

Istvan Cizerny-Ronay makes a similar, if less metaphorical, observation. In comparing screen with stage, he recognizes that beyond the oratorical element lies a physical component that he identifies as "presence," using quotation marks to distinguish physical from virtual presence.

> The screen is like a stage. . . . the one thing that holds me fascinated is the performance. . . . the ease of exchange makes opinions and even hard information pre-texts for imaginative "presence." . . . I don't separate the "issues" from the voices. I guess I take the ideas more seriously, the more involved I get with the voice. Not every voice will do. (*TNC*, 1993, March 13, 5:49 p.m.)

Although Cizerny-Ronay *compares* screen with stage, he *identifies* discussion with performance, text with voice, voice with body. He and Tal envision virtual dramas in which they take part, dramas several steps closer to "reality" than the theoretical, metaphorical dramas envisioned by Erving Goffman (1959). In the process, Cizerny-Ronay illustrates the power of the e-mail text to embody the writer while also creating a site for the writer's performance. E-mail thus demonstrates in practice Bakhtin's claim in Part III of *Marxism and the Philosophy of Language* that "a word is a territory shared by both addresser and addressee" (Voloshinov, 1973, p. 86).

AT THE JUNCTION OF ORALITY AND LITERACY

More important for the purposes of this chapter, the embodiment of the writer in the text clarifies the nature of e-mail's hybridness. Rather than represent a middle ground moderating the characteristics of oral and written language, e-mail constitutes a junction in which orality and literacy, in their extreme or purest forms, meet. One reason is obvious: e-mail adapts the technology of the keyboard, a by-product of print, to the requirements of talk. For instance, the convention of upper and lower case letters, a visual and spatial distinction devised for print, becomes a means for indicating loudness. Similarly, the emoticon converts the finite alphanumeric keyboard into a source of nearly infinite signs. Unlike manuscript characters (which can be varied infinitely) or moveable types (which can be turned sideways or upside down), the standard keyboard restricts the placement of its 107 characters[10] to specific horizontal and vertical positions. Creative combinations of characters in the emoticon's sideways axis allow writers to transcend the keyboard's limitations, controlling and varying the glyphs through which they express meaning as speakers have always controlled and varied their sounds. Reading e-mail is thus akin to reading a musical score: To the initiated, both sound and emotion reside in the text.[11] An experienced e-mail reader can hear the unhappiness in the following report from a member of the *Technoculture* list (*TNC*, 1993, April 9, 9:39 a.m.):

> my first VW [virtual world] experience a few years ago . . . was a virtual kitchen containing virtual appliances. The very first thing that I did was to go over to the stove and put my disembodied hand on one of the burners—I wanted to hear it sizzle. A MAJOR disappointment :- (

Like virtual reality simulators, e-mail seeks to unify textual and physical experience. By requiring us to bend at the neck and look sideways at the message, emoticons transform reading from a mental to a physical process. Both readers' and writers' bodies can be inscribed in the e-mail text.

---

[10]Ten numeric characters and their shift-key alternates, 26 alphabetic characters in upper and lower case, 11 punctuation and mathematical marks with shift-key alternates, and an additional 10 keys, slash, asterisk, and period on the number pad.

[11]For a fascinating discussion of the historical process wherein musical texts became "the music," see Dehnert (1990).

The virtual physicality of reader, writer, and message—despite all our sensory evidence to the contrary—explains some of the difficulties of fitting e-mail into existing rhetorical, social, and legal structures. One writer saw the rhetorical problem in terms that illustrate as well as describe it:

> the notions of textuality I am trying to enact, to emplot myself within, won't fit the technology: this is a space, someone might say, for a ludic post-modernism, the freeplay of digitized signifiers, one in which my insistence on a deliberated, hold-things-together impulses and rhetoric (or poetics, for that matter) is an anachronism that could, should I persist, cost me my sanity. (Or somebody might also say, "Lighten up, jerk!"). (*TNC*, 1993, March 15, 7:14 a.m.)

The conflict expressed here points to parallels between the introduction of e-mail and the introduction of print. According to the classic interpretation by Elizabeth Eisenstein (1979), print decentralized control of information and thus paved the way for Protestant and secular disruptions of political control by the scribal information culture of the Roman Catholic Church. E-mail, similarly, presses against the boundaries of grammar and rhetoric defined by print culture. Moreover, it presses against the boundaries of work and play. In a culture that has seen the work week increase and leisure decline, this paradox of electronic communication points to one of contemporary life's great ironies: Labor-saving devices make more work.

A second paradox centers on e-mail's underlying metaphor, by which we toss messages into a "wastebasket," "open" our "mail," and receive notices of undeliverable messages from a "postmaster." Of course, we really identify bits of magnetic tape for erasure, convert stored signals to glyphs on our screen, and receive error messages from computers that cannot find a match between the addressee's user Id and the one on the message. The metaphorical process, however, elides the distinction between immaterial and material. Speech and the electronic trace on the screen become indistinguishable from writing on paper or magnetic tape. Therefore is e-mail public like speech or television? Or is it private like manuscript writing?[12]

This distinction goes beyond questions of rhetoric or technology to matters of law. When an alumnus of the University of Michigan sought access to senior administrators' e-mail under the state's freedom-of-information law, on the premise that e-mail is analogous to written documents, the university declined on two grounds: first, that e-mail is more akin to telephone calls, which

[12]An interesting problem arose in the process of my writing this chapter because some members of *Technoculture* considered their postings private correspondence covered by copyright (which gives control of a letter to the writer, according to the most recent legislation), whereas others saw their work as public presentations. Because all the postings are archived and thus available, like any published text, to whoever chooses to look them up, I saw them as subject to the fair use provisions of publications. Although I have cited by name only those contributors who gave me permission to do so, I have cited by date and title other postings whose writers did not specifically grant permission.

go unrecorded and therefore fall outside the boundaries of the law; second, that the federal Electronic Communications Privacy Act shields the university from screening e-mail to determine whether it concerns public business covered by the state law (DeLoughry, 1994).

As the courts struggle to define how such print-based legal concepts as tampering with the mail and intellectual property apply to electronic communication, the more nebulous questions of social use remain equally challenging for the lay public. May one send a message of condolence by e-mail? A wedding invitation? Must one reply immediately to an e-mail message? The absence of a response within a few days may offend the writer, who may feel like a visitor stranded on the front doorstep knowing that the person inside is ignoring the bell. In that sense, although e-mail systems offer some of the advantages of writing over speech—the chance to deliver an entire thought without interruption, the chance to plan out one's remarks for maximum effect—the receiver holds all the cards in an e-mail conversation, as in other modes of communication. A reader can refuse to open a letter, avoid replying, let the phone ring without answering (or hang it up afterwards), and so on, thereby reminding us that in cyberspace, as in other media, a message is a gambit, an invitation that one may accept or decline. E-mail receivers have further control over the physical form of the message, which they can print on whatever paper and in whatever fonts they choose. In this case, as in others, e-mail intensifies the essential characteristics of both writing and speech.

Although e-mail's rhetorical features express distinctions from conventional writing, telephony, and speech, the conventions of e-mail are as dematerialized and fluid as cyberspace itself, for this hybrid is almost certainly transitional. When interactive digital video merges with e-mail, as computer researchers now predict (Markoff, 1994), the resultant video mail will displace literate textual codes with nonverbal ones. Although this new communication medium will almost certainly rely on familiar facial and body "language," users will find themselves in unfamiliar waters as they attempt, anew, to chart its codes. Nonetheless, the example of e-mail makes clear that communication itself creates cyberspace. Perhaps more important, e-mail demonstrates that natural languages are flexible enough and users creative enough to adapt to new media. As writing and print stabilized and diffused aristocratic dialects and usage, so e-mail is generating new vocabularies and modeling a new rhetoric.

In this sense, e-mail fulfills the goal of alphabetic literacy. As the alphabet renders sound in visual space, so e-mail converts writing to speech. By allowing readers and writers to meet in cyberspace, e-mail repairs the disjunction between authors and their discourse that philosophers from Plato to Derrida have found problematic. Plato's lament in the *Phaedrus* that writing renders a speaker silent becomes Derrida's (1967/1976) complaint in *Of Grammatology:* Writers must die for writing to speak. Although he agrees with Derrida on almost nothing else, Walter Ong (1982) noted, similarly, in *Orality and Literacy,* that writing by definition is "discourse [that] has been detached from its author" (p. 78). Not so for the e-mail writer. The electronic text embodies the author—the virtual speaker who meets the reader, who becomes embodied by a similar process in response. Thus, although e-mail derives from both writing and speech, it does not homogenize traits from each into a synthetic mixture or blend. Rather, like a child, it has some traits from one parent and some from the other, and the combination has a life of its own.

REFERENCES

Blair, W., & Hill, H. (1978). *America's humor: From Poor Richard to Doonesbury.* New York: Oxford University Press.

Bolter, J.D. (1991). *Writing space: The computer, hypertext, and the history of writing.* Hillsdale, NJ: Erlbaum.

Booth, W.C. (1961). *The rhetoric of fiction.* Chicago: University of Chicago Press.

Booth, W.C. (1974). *A rhetoric of irony.* Chicago: University of Chicago Press.

Burke, K. (1950). A *rhetoric of motives.* New York: Prentice-Hall.

Campbell, G. (1963). *Philosophy of rhetoric* (L.F. Bitzer, Ed.). Carbondale, IL: Southern Illinois University Press. (Original work published 1776)

Caswell, S.A. (1988). *E-mail* (Converging Technology Series). Boston: Artech House.

Deatsch, J.A. (1994). *Investigating the stereotypes: One woman manager's written language.* Unpublished manuscript.

Dehnert, E. (1990). The consciousness of music wrought by musical notation. In J.W. Slade & J.Y. Lee (Eds.), *Beyond the two cultures: Essays on science, technology, and literature* (pp. 99-116). Ames: Iowa State University Press.

DeLoughry, T.J. (1994, January 26). U. of Mich. refuses to release e-mail of administrators. *Chronicle of Higher Education*, p. A28.

Dern, D.P. (1994). *The Internet guide for new users.* New York: McGraw-Hill.

Derrida, J. (1976). *Of grammatology* (G.C. Spivak, Trans.). Baltimore: Johns Hopkins University Press. (Original work published 1967)

Eisenstein, E.R. (1979). *The printing press as an agent of change: Communication and cultural transformation in early-modern Europe.* New York: Cambridge University Press.

Elmer-Dewitt, P. (1994, July 4). Bards of the Internet. *Time, 144*(1), 66-67.

Fishkin, S.F. (1993). *Was Huck black? Mark Twain and African-American voices.* New York: Oxford University Press.

Goffman, E. (1959). *The presentation of self in everyday life.* New York: Anchor.

Goode, J., & Johnson, M. (1991, November). Putting out the flames: The etiquette and law of e-mail. *Online, 15*(6), 61-65.

Havelock, E.A. (1986). *The muse learns to write: Reflections on orality and literacy from antiquity to the present.* New Haven, CT: Yale University Press.

Heim, M. (1987). *Electric language: A philosophical study of word processing.* New Haven, CT: Yale University Press.

Jorgensen, E. (n.d.). *Background: The survey and why I did it.* Unpublished manuscript.

Kantrowitz, B. (1994, May 16). Men, women & computers. *Newsweek*, p. 55.

Kiesler, S., Siegel, J., & McGuire, T.W. (1984, October). Social psychological aspects of computer-mediated communication. *American Psychologist, 39*(10), 1123-1134.

Landow, G.P. (1992). *Hypertext: The convergence of contemporary critical theory and technology.* Baltimore: Johns Hopkins University Press.

Lanham, R.A. (1993). *The electronic word: Democracy, technology, and the arts.* Chicago: University of Chicago Press.

Lewis, P.H. (1994, April 19). An ad (gasp!) in cyberspace. *The New York Times*, pp. C1-C2.

Lohr, S. (1994, June 6). Can e-mail cachet = jpmorgan@park.ave? *The New York Times*, pp. A1, C4.

Markoff, J. (1994, March 13). The rise and swift fall of cyber literacy. *The New York Times*, pp. 1, 5.

McLuhan, M. (1964). *Understanding media: The extensions of man.* New York: McGraw-Hill.

McNichol, T. (1994, January 21-23). Fellow travelers on the info highway. *USA Weekend*, pp.4, 6.

Meyrowitz, J. (1985). *No sense of place: The impact of electronic media on social behavior.* New York: Oxford University Press.

Murray, D.E. (1988). The context of oral and written language: A framework for mode and medium switching. *Language in Society, 17*, 351-373.

Ong, W.J. (1982). *Orality and literacy: The technologizing of the word.* London: Methuen.

Ovans, A. (1992). Can e-mail deliver the message? *Datamation, 38*(11), 128.

Pattison, R.P. (1982). *On literacy: The politics of the word from Homer to the age of rock.* New York: Oxford University Press.

Porter, P. (1984). 'Dear PP05': Interpersonal communication and the computer: Entering a brave new world. *Library Hi Tech, 2*(1), 22-27.

Poster, M. (1990). *The mode of information: Poststructuralism and social context.* Chicago: University of Chicago Press.

Price, W.T. (1993, August 6). Harassment goes on-line. *USA Today*, pp. 1B-2B.

Radicati, S. (1992). *Electronic mail: An introduction to the X.400 message handling standards.* New York: McGraw-Hill.

Reid, T. (1994, February 16, 6:19 p.m.). *Higher speed modem pool for off-campus use.* Ohio University All-in-1.

Sacks, H. (1992). May 8: Reason for a call: Tellability. In G. Jefferson (Ed.), *Lectures on conversation* (pp. 773-783). Oxford: Blackwell.

Scribner, S., & Cole, M. (1981). *The psychology of literacy.* Cambridge, MA: Harvard University Press.

Seabrook, J. (1994). E-mail from Bill. *New Yorker, 69*(45), 48-61.
Tannen, D. (1994, May 16). Gender gap in cyberspace. *Newsweek*, pp. 52-53.
Tannen, D. (Ed.). (1982). *Spoken and written language: Exploring orality and literacy*. Norwood, NJ: Ablex.
Thompsen, P.A., & Ahn, D.K. (1992). To be or not to be: An exploration of e-prime, copula deletion and flaming in electronic mail. *Etc., 49*, 146-164.
TNC. [*Technoculture* Internet discussion list]. LISTSERV@GITVM1.GATECH.EDU. (INDEX TNC).
TNC. (1993, March 11, 10:04 a.m.). Re: Calling David Sewell.
TNC. (1993, March 11, 6:17 p.m.). Re: More advice (was: re: voice and authority).
TNC. (1993, March 12, 8:07 a.m.). Re: Unwanted?
TNC. (1993, March 12, 10:04 a.m.). Re: Bob Black's rant.
TNC. (1993, March 12, 12:19 p.m.). Re: Bob Black's rant.
TNC. (1993, March 12, 2:34 p.m.). WANTED (not).
TNC. (1993, March 13, 5:49 p.m.). Re: Authority.
TNC. (1993, March 14, 11:12 p.m.). Amato's staying power.
TNC. (1993, March 14, 11:24 a.m.). Authority & community.
TNC. (1993, March 14, 1:10 p.m.). Re: Back again, hopping mad.
TNC. (1993, March 14, 11:12 p.m.). Amato's staying power.
TNC. (1993, March 15, 7:14 a.m.). Re: Amato's staying power.
TNC. (1993, March 25, 2:47 p.m.). Re: Brief tangent/fractal expansion.
TNC. (1993, March 29, 2:29 p.m.). Re: The evanescence of public e-text.
TNC. (1993, April 3, 9:14 a.m.). Re: Texte a texte a fetishism.
TNC. (1993, April 9, 9:39 a.m.). Re: Helmets and tears.
Twain, M. (1985). Adventures of Huckleberry Finn. In W. Blair & V. Fischer (Eds.), *The Mark Twain library*. Berkeley: University of California Press. (Original work published 1884)
Vallee, J. (1984). *Computer message systems*. New York: Data Communications.
Voloshinov, V.N. [Bakhtin, M.]. (1973). Verbal interaction (L. Mattejka & I.R. Titunik, Trans.). In *Marxism and the philosophy of language* (pp. 83-98). New York: Seminar Press.
Voices. [Internet discussion list]. VOICES-L@ECL.WUSTL.EDU.
Voices. (1994, February 8, 5:52 p.m.). Extra links.
Voices. (1994, February 12. 3:49 p.m.). Project and paper for C&W conference.

◊◊◊◊ 20

What's Fueling the Flames in Cyberspace? A Social Influence Model

Philip A. Thompsen

As in any other communication environment, social interaction in cyberspace also includes behavior that may be judged antisocial, such as the widely discussed phenomenon of flaming in computer-mediated communication and cyberculture. Although flaming, as an expression of hostility through the codes of cyberspace, may seem to be a simple and straightforward form of communication, in this chapter Thompsen demonstrates that there is considerable disagreement as to the definition and nature of this phenomenon. Rather than viewing flaming simply as a certain type of message or behavior, Thompsen suggests that flaming involves a relationship established through computer media, and therefore that the interpretation of another's message or behavior as flaming is equally a part of the concept of flaming; in other words, flaming can be understood as an act of decoding as much as an act of encoding. He argues that a broader approach that takes into account the negotiation of meaning, as it is influenced by a variety of factors, offers a better understanding of this phenomenon than explanations that focus on the limited communication modes available through e-mail. Apart from this section of the book, other perspectives on the social character of cyberspatial communication include Gary Gumpert and Susan J. Drucker's essay on social space in Chapter 1, John M. Phelan's critique of cyberculture in Chapter 2, Terri Toles Patkin's profile of the virtual organization in Chapter 11, Michael P. Beaubien's discussion of hostile language use and power in MUDs in Chapter 12, and Sue Barnes's ecological approach to cyberspace in Chapter 13.

Consider the following scenario: You have recently subscribed to what you thought was a rather serious e-mail discussion list for scholars in your field. You are reading the messages, trying to follow the discussion, looking for ideas. Seemingly out of the blue, two of the participants get angry, call each other names, use profanity, and hurl out ad-hominem arguments. Then things turn really nasty. You check the return addresses on these messages and discover, much to your surprise, these are not sophomoric punks who have little respect for civility. These are people you know, respect, even admire. What is going on here? Why are otherwise decent folks beating each other up with digital bits of vivid vitriol?

Welcome to the flame wars. If you are wondering what is behind these spontaneous combustions in cyberspace, you are not alone. The phenomenon of flaming has caught the attention of many who engage in computer-mediated communication (CMC), from casual "net-surfers" to serious scholars. The literature on flaming ranges from exaggerated tales of terror to carefully controlled experimental investigations. Yet despite a decade of speculation on the causes and consequences of flaming, there is still little agreement on what is fueling the flames in cyberspace. Many believe the technological constraints of computer media encourage people to lose themselves and let their emotions fly. Others think the population of cybernauts simply has an unusually high concentration of hotheads. And still others feel flaming is merely a reflection of human nature, not much different from other forms of conflict.

Who is right? Perhaps they all are, for what causes flaming depends on how flaming is defined and how narrow the causal boundaries are drawn. The diversity of explanations for flaming reflects more than a rigorous debate over the effects of CMC—it reveals a theoretical fuzziness that hinders the advancement of substantive knowledge claims. To bring flaming into sharper focus, this chapter draws on the "social influence model of technology use" (Fulk, Schmitz, & Steinfield, 1990, p. 121) to provide a structure for the integration of research findings. Although previous studies are cited in support of the model's propositions, the model as a whole remains untested. It is offered, therefore, not as an authoritative representation of the "way things are," but rather as a source for developing testable questions about flaming from within a comprehensive theoretical framework.

Before the model is presented, the chapter first looks at how flaming has been defined, both as an abstract theoretical construct and as a measurable research operationalization. Next is a critique of the major theoretical perspectives guiding inquiry into flaming. In response to this critique, a social influence model of flaming is advanced. The model's propositions are formally stated, and each of the factors identified in the model are described. The chapter concludes by considering the implications and limitations of this model.

DEFINING FLAMING

The term *flaming* apparently evolved from the "hacker" computer subculture. One of the earliest definitions found in the literature is offered in *The Hacker's Dictionary* (Steele et al., 1983): "to speak rabidly or incessantly on an uninteresting topic or with a patently ridiculous attitude" (p. 158). Although this definition suggests flaming is merely an annoying peculiarity that should not be taken seriously, the term appears to have been broadened over time to include a variety of generally negative antisocial behaviors, including the expression of hostility, the use of profanity, and the venting of strong emotions.

Here is a sampling of some of the definitions of flaming found in the popular and scholarly press:

- speaking incessantly, hurling insults, [and] using profanity (Baron, 1984)
- the practice of expressing oneself more strongly on the computer than one would in other communication settings (Kiesler, Siegel, & McGuire, 1984)
- rudeness, profanity, exultation, and other emotional outbursts by people when they carry on discussions via computer (Eckholm, 1984)
- emotional outbursts of rudeness, profanity, or even exultation among users of computer conferencing systems (Spitzer, 1986)
- heated, emotional, sometimes anonymous, venting by a participant (Selfe & Meyer, 1991)
- rabid, abusive, or otherwise overexuberant outbursts sent via computer (Stewart, 1991)
- impoliteness, swearing, charged outbursts, and often a high use of superlatives (Hawisher, 1992)
- the hostile expression of strong emotions and feelings (Lea, O'Shea, Fung, & Spears, 1992)
- the heated exchange of messages expressing hostility or defensiveness toward others on a computer network (Thompsen & Ahn, 1992)
- insults, swearing, and hostile, intense language (Walther, 1992)
- the spontaneous creation of homophobic, racist, and misogynist language during electronic communication (Dorwick, 1993)
- vitriolic online exchanges (Dery, 1993)
- the tendency to react more critically or with greater hostility over this medium, leading to an escalation of conflict (Rice & Steinfield, 1994).

These definitions for flaming may not at first seem incongruent. But a closer examination reveals some subtle differences. Some emphasize the emotional quality of a message, whereas others focus on the expression of hostility. Some place the locus of flaming in the sending of a message, some in the reception of a message, and some in the exchange of messages. This diversity of definitions begs a number of questions. Is flaming a behavior, a message characteristic, a subjective reaction, or a linguistic genre? Does flaming arise from a relaxing of inhibitions or an intensifying of interpersonal friction? Is flaming reflective of strong tempers, incessant banality, or immature histrionics?

To be fair, theoretical constructs are inherently abstract (Judd, Smith, & Kidder, 1991), and perhaps this diversity of conceptual definitions should be of less concern than the extent to which researchers agree on operational definitions of flaming. In other words, what do researchers measure when they claim to measure flaming? Here the situation is clearly problematic. In their reviews of past research, both Anderson and Walther (1992) and Lea et al. (1992) have noted that flaming has not been consistently operationalized in past research. Widely divergent operational definitions have been employed by researchers in the effort to measure flaming.

For example, many studies have defined flaming in terms of uninhibited behavior, but have operationalized "uninhibited" in very different ways. Some studies counted insults and name calling (Siegel, Dubrovsky, Kiesler, & McGuire, 1986; Weisband, 1992), whereas others measured flirting and the expression of personal feelings toward others (Kiesler, Zubrow, Moses, & Geller, 1985). Sproull and Kiesler (1986) used self-report measures of "increased willingness to communicate bad news or negative information" and the "flouting of social conventions" (p. 1508). Lea and Spears (1991) counted uses of paralanguage and swearing. Still others have employed the categories of Interaction Process Analysis (Bales, 1950) to assess negative socioemotional content (Hiltz, Johnson, & Turoff, 1986; Rice & Love, 1987; Thompsen & Foulger, 1993).

Certainly multiple operationalizations of a construct can be useful in establishing convergent and discriminant validity (Campbell & Fiske, 1959). The diversity of operational definitions may reflect a healthy debate in the research community over the essence of flaming. Yet the work to date has provided little evidence for establishing the conceptual validity of flaming as a research variable. It may not be overstating the case that flaming has been appropriated in some studies as a provocative term to use in the service of advancing various perspectives on media effects. Flaming has been a "hot" topic for CMC research, but as the following critique suggests, we may have been burned in the rush to contain the blaze.

A CRITIQUE OF PREVIOUS EXPLANATIONS OF FLAMING

A number of nomological nets have been cast to catch the elusive essence of flaming. Deindividuation theory (Festinger, Pepitone, & Newcomb, 1952; Zimbardo, 1969), which suggests that anonymity and reduced self-awareness leads to uninhibited behavior, is one of the most frequently cited explanations for flaming (Kiesler et al., 1984; Lea & Spears, 1991; Spears, Lea, & Lee, 1990;

Sproull & Kiesler, 1991). From this perspective, computer users experience an erosion of self-control by being submerged in a massive matrix of anonymous voices. Citizens of cyberspace develop a kind of mob mentality, in which social norms and constraints are presumably less influential than in "normal" settings. People lose their sense of social identity—they become "deindividualized"—exposing a dry hotbed of uncivilized humanity in which flames are easily ignited.

Social presence theory (Short, Williams, & Christie, 1976) is another popular explanation for flaming. This perspective holds that the inability of CMC systems to transmit much of the social information present in face-to-face interaction leads to more impersonal communication (Hiltz et al., 1986; Rice, 1984; Steinfield, 1986). When people talk face to face, they have a keen sense of the "social presence" of each other; eye contact, facial expression, tone of voice, and other cues contribute much to the quality of the interaction. When people talk online, however, this sense of social presence is greatly reduced by the limitations of the computer as a communication medium. As a result, computer conversations are more impersonal, more blunt, and more likely to produce the kind of friction that leads to flaming.

A third explanation for flaming is offered by the information richness theory (Daft & Lengel, 1986). This perspective holds that CMC systems are relatively inferior for communicating "rich," multifaceted information. Ranking communication media according to their ability to transmit information richness places face-to-face meetings and telephone calls toward the top of the list and e-mail and computer conferencing toward the bottom. Information-rich media foster the reinforcement of a message through extraverbal channels, so less effort is needed to communicate clearly. But information-poor media constrain messages to a limited range of expression—such as the ASCII character set used in many CMC systems—and consequently more information is needed to compensate for this narrow "bandwidth." Because electronic mail messages are typically short and contributions to a computer conference rarely exceed a few lines, ambiguity abounds, intentions are easily misinterpreted—and the slightest spark can touch off a flame war.

Although some empirical evidence has been offered in support of these theories, research findings a ; largely inconsistent. (For a review of the extant research on flaming, see Lea et al., 1992.) As one critique put it, "in the rush to describe and catalogue effects, theories may have developed and become reified prematurely" (Walther & Burgoon, 1992, p. 52). As a whole, this body of theoretical work has been widely criticized (Baldwin & Holmes, 1992; Culnan & Markus, 1987; Fulk et al., 1990; Walther, 1992; Williams, Rice, & Rogers, 1988). The critique offered here focuses on four points of concern.

First, the influence of time is typically ignored. Most explanations of flaming have adopted some variant of what Culnan and Markus (1987) called the "cues filtered out" perspective. Flaming is said to arise because some of the social and communicative cues used to regulate interaction and inhibit hostile behavior in face-to-face communication—such as indicators of status, facial expression, and tone of voice—are "filtered out" by the computer medium. But there is evidence that, given the time often denied them in experimental comparisons, CMC users develop strategies to overcome the lack of communicative cues (Blackman & Clevenger, 1990; Holmes & Berquist, 1990; Walther & Burgoon, 1992). The influence of time may be crucial in understanding flaming in electronic mail discussion lists and other forms of asynchronous CMC, in which interactions take place over relatively long periods of time. Similarly, the immediacy of response in synchronous forms of CMC, such as the real-time computer conferencing popularized in the "chat rooms" of commercial online services, suggests that the influence of time may be an overlooked factor in understanding how the lack of communicative cues contributes to flaming.

Second, explanations of flaming have typically displayed a bias toward face-to-face communication. As Culnan and Markus (1987) point out, the "cues filtered out" perspective assumes that face-to-face communication is the standard by which CMC should be compared, and "ignores the possibility . . . that the electronic media have capabilities not found in face-to-face communication" (p. 431). In his study of computer conferencing at IBM, Foulger (1990) found evidence that computer media "allow people to communicate in new ways, and perhaps more effectively than has been possible in the past" (p. 89). A perspective that begins with the assumption that face to face offers "the most" and CMC can only provide something "less" may miss valuable insights.

Third, previous explanations of flaming suffer from what Roth (1987) has dubbed "meaning realism." Flaming is said to be found in the objective attributes of a message. From these perspectives, a flame is a flame is a flame; all reasonable observers will be able to tell a flame apart from a message that is not a flame (a flicker perhaps). Few of the extant explanations for flaming consider the interpretation of a communication interaction, yet it may be more theoretically satisfying to acknowledge that flaming emerges when a reader attributes this quality to messages. Flaming does not exist in a vacuum; it requires the "fuel" of interpersonal interaction and the interpretation of that interaction by social actors. From this perspective, flaming is an emerging quality attributed to a sequence of messages by human actors involved in an interpretive process of meaning creation (Anderson & Meyer, 1988; Leeds-Hurwitz, 1992). Put simply, a flame is not a flame until someone calls it a flame.

Finally, explanations of flaming have typically looked for causes in the distinctive characteristics of technology, rather than in the social settings in which technology is used (Baldwin & Holmes, 1992; Fulk et al., 1990). Computer communication media are seen as having relatively fixed, invariant attributes that influence all users in similar ways. Flaming is assumed to be an effect of technology, whereas possible social influences are minimized or ignored. But examination of social influences can be most illuminating (Compton, White, & DeWine, 1991). Lea and Spears (1991) argue that "earlier research underestimated the role of social contextual factors and normative processes in CMC," and that "compared with face-to-face interaction, the social and normative context may be of even greater importance in computer-mediated communication" (p. 299). It is conceivable that flaming may be related less to supposed constraints of technology than to social norms that value uninhibited behaviors (Lea et al., 1992).

In sum, previous explanations of flaming have largely failed to incorporate the element of time, exhibited a myopic bias toward face-to-face interaction, suffered from meaning realism, and typically ignored the role of social influence. Although flaming has been researched from a variety of perspectives, the claims that have been made about flaming arguably rest on shaky foundations. What CMC research needs, to use the words of Steinfield and Fulk (1990), is a stronger "theoretical infrastructure—a tree to which individual findings can be grafted to generate the synthesis and integration needed to support knowledge claims" (p. 13). The following model is an attempt to move toward that goal.

A SOCIAL INFLUENCE MODEL OF FLAMING

A theoretical perspective on technology that offers promise for providing a more solid foundation for grounding claims about flaming is Fulk et al.'s (1990) "social influence model on technology use." This model evolved from an earlier version, a "social information processing model" (Fulk, Steinfield, Schmitz, & Power, 1987), which in turn drew on the work of Salancik and Pfeffer (1978). Although none of these works originally addressed flaming, they provide a basis for developing a model of flaming that can address many of the weaknesses of previous explanations while yielding new and potentially useful insights.

The social influence perspective holds that the choices people make regarding technology use are neither entirely rational nor entirely subjective, but rather are "subjectively rational." Explanations of media use need to move beyond rational models based on the supposedly invariant influence of technological constraints on behavior and consider the widely variable influence of social environments on the subjective interpretation of behavior. Fulk et al. (1990) argue that:

> The limitation of traditional media use theories is their over-reliance on rational processes to explain the entire range of media-choice situations. A realistic understanding of behavior requires knowledge not simply of objective features of the environment, but also the social milieu that alters and adjusts perceptions of that environment. (p. 127)

A social influence perspective on flaming thus considers both the behavior of flaming and the social negotiation of what that behavior means. To use the terms of Fulk et al. (1990), flaming is both a media use and a media evaluation—a CMC behavior and an interpretation of that behavior. Technological characteristics of the computer medium—such as the lack of nonverbal cues—may indeed contribute to the behavior of flaming, but from the social influence perspective, this is only a partial explanation. A more complete explanation of flaming would account for the sense-making norms that influence people to interpret some CMC behavior as flames. The social influence perspective focuses the effort to explain flaming on articulating the factors that contribute to these two sides of flaming—the behavior of flaming and the interpretation of those behaviors as flaming.

So what are these factors? Fulk et al. (1990) identify a number of factors in their model which, when extended to flaming, provide a framework for integrating previous research. This framework is built on two propositions:

Proposition 1: The behavior of flaming is a function of (a) social influence, (b) media experience and skills, (c) media evaluations, (d) task evaluations, and (e) situational factors.

Proposition 2: The interpretation of flaming is a function of (a) social influence, (b) media experience and skills, (c) media features, and (d) prior use of other media.

These propositions are presented schematically in Figure 20.1. Note that two factors influence both the behavior and the interpretation of flaming: (a) social influence and (b) media experience and skills. These two major influences on flaming are considered next, followed by a discussion of those remaining factors that the model associates with either the behavior or interpretation of flaming.

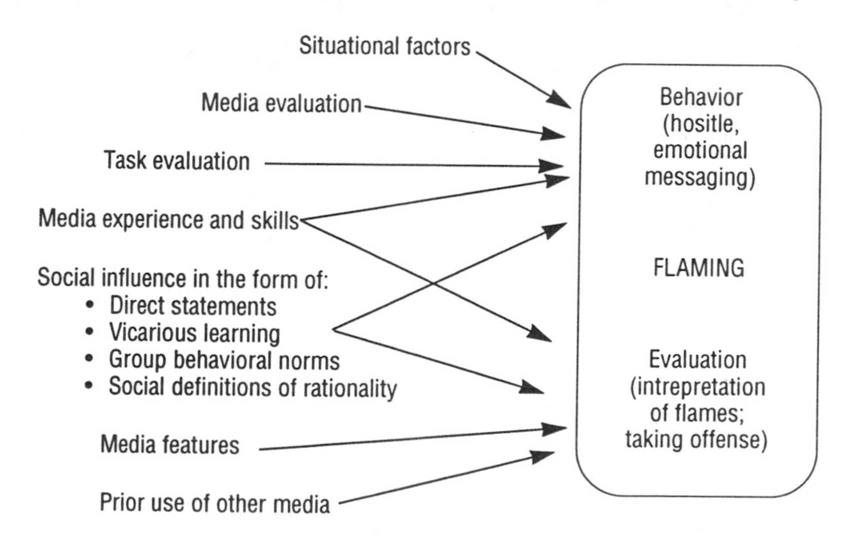

Figure 20.1. A social influence model of flaming

SOCIAL INFLUENCE

Unlike those explanations for flaming that have focused on technological limitations, social influence occupies a central role in this model, affecting both the behavior and the interpretation of flaming. According to Fulk et al. (1990), social influence may be exerted in at least four ways: (a) direct statements by others, (b) vicarious learning from others, (c) group norms, and (d) social definitions of rationality. Although social influence is not necessarily limited to these four manifestations, these categories provide a useful framework for understanding the impact of social influence on flaming.

Direct Statements

There is some evidence that flaming may be moderated (or intensified) by direct statements by others outside of the CMC context (Thompsen, 1994). In settings in which CMC is supplemented by face-to-face communication, direct statements relating to an incident of flaming can help douse the fire or fan the blaze. Furthermore, direct statements may contribute to the interpretation of flaming behavior. A hostile e-mail message from someone who is perceived by his or her peers as antagonistic outside of the CMC context is likely to be interpreted (and crafted) differently than a flame from a "cyberspace cowboy"—someone who may be mild-mannered in person, but dons a flamboyant CMC persona when online (perhaps as compensation for failures in interpersonal relationships; see Turkle, 1984).

Vicarious Learning

People undoubtedly learn much about flaming by watching others flame. When users witness a "flame war," they vicariously learn the techniques and consequences of flaming specific to that incident. One need not participate in a flame to learn about flaming; indeed, many people stay on the sidelines in CMC discussions, preferring to remain quiet spectators, known as *lurkers* in network jargon (Brown, 1984; Romiszowski & deHaas, 1989). Although this area of social influence has yet to be fully explored with respect to flaming, the model suggests a reasonable hypothesis that vicarious learning has a significant influence on both the behavior and the interpretation of flaming.

Group Behavioral Norms

Although some proponents of deindividuation theory hold that computer media reduces the influence of group behavioral norms, there is some evidence that the opposite is true. Lea and Spears (1991) found group norms to be a significant predictor of flaming, particularly those norms related to the appropriateness of uninhibited behavior. Groups in which uninhibited, aggressive argumentation is the norm are likely to experience quite different flaming behaviors than groups in which the norm is passive acceptance of leadership. In some groups, flaming may be a reflection of shared group norms rather than a violation of common rules of civil discourse.

Social Definitions of Rationality

What is perceived as rational behavior in one CMC forum (e.g., the USENET newsgroup alt.flaming) could be perceived as quite irrational in another (e.g., the newsgroup misc.kids). Lea et al. (1992) suggest that flaming may be reflective of a "computer hacker subculture" that embraces social definitions of rationality that "run counter to the expectations and standards of industrial or educational organizations from which perspective they might be considered deviant or uninhibited" (p. 23). The definitions of rationality at work in a social environment may be the key difference between those groups that condemn flaming as blatantly vicious hostility and groups that celebrate flaming as an artistic expression of cyberspace machismo.

To review, the model asserts that social influence is one of the major factors contributing to flaming, whether flaming is viewed as an objective behavior or as a subjective interpretation. Social influence, as revealed through direct statements, vicarious learning, group behavioral norms, and social definitions of rationality, represents a potentially significant influence on flaming, one that has yet to receive much attention from the research community. The incorporation of social influence into a comprehensive model of flaming may help illuminate this research opportunity by offering a more culturally sensitive and less technologically dependent explanation.

MEDIA EXPERIENCE AND SKILLS

Although social influence plays a significant role in this model, flaming is also held to be a function of the experience and skills of those who use computer media. Fulk et al. (1990, p. 125) argue that social information is "more influential for individuals who have less experience and knowledge" of a particular communication technology. In general, those with greater experience and skill in using CMC systems are more likely to be influenced by other factors (such as media features) that reduce the overall significance of social influence in predicting media behavior. Media experience is thus seen as modifying the impact of social influence processes in both the production of flaming behaviors and the interpretation of those behaviors as flaming.

This proposition seems warranted given the literature on flaming. Those with extensive experience in using CMC systems are likely to be more aware of proper "e-mail etiquette" (Goode & Johnson, 1991) than novice users and thus less likely to start a "flame war" inadvertently. Experienced users are also likely to have encountered a range of flaming behaviors, from a "mild scorch" to a "roaring blaze." This experience may temper their tolerance levels for hostile messages, influencing the interpretation of what constitutes a salient incident of flaming. Experienced users develop skills in "flame management," such as clearly delineating flaming content with the phrases FLAME ON and FLAME OFF (Sproull & Kiesler, 1991), or using pictographs or emoticons (symbolic icons made with punctuation marks) to indicate a facetious tone (Blackman & Clevenger, 1990; Miller, 1992).

Novice users may start flames by simply revealing their ignorance of CMC norms, such as typing in ALL CAPS (the electronic equivalent of shouting), failing to use descriptive message headers, posting personal messages to public forums, or sending "listserver" commands (such as "signoff," a command intended to be interpreted by a computer program) to a widely distributed electronic mail discussion list. Novice users may also fail to recognize attempts by experienced users to modify aggressive arguments (such as using IMHO before a comment, which is a common abbreviation for "in my humble opinion"), possibly contributing to an evaluation of messages as flames that were intended by the sender to be only mildly assertive.

The proposition that media experience influences the behavior and interpretation of flaming demands further research. As with social influence, the degree of experience one has with CMC systems is a potentially significant predictor of flaming and how flaming messages are interpreted. The social influence model also suggests additional factors that contribute to flaming. Those factors influencing the behavior of flaming are considered next, followed by those that influence the interpretation of flaming.

OTHER FACTORS INFLUENCING THE BEHAVIOR OF FLAMING

In addition to social influence and media experience, the model suggests three additional factors that influence the behavior of flaming. These factors are media evaluations, task evaluations, and situational factors.

Media Evaluations

How people evaluate the computer as a communication medium is likely to influence the behavior of flaming. Research has shown there are differences in the way people evaluate CMC's appropriateness for socioemotional communication (Rice & Love, 1987). Those who feel the medium is inadequate or inappropriate for the expression of emotions would seem to be less likely to craft flaming messages than those who may be more comfortable in expressing emotions in this manner. Flaming may also be related to anxiety or feelings of frustration in learning to use CMC systems (Siegel et al., 1986). Someone who evaluates a CMC system as difficult to use may take out her or his frustrations in belligerent messages to anonymous others on a computer network. Flaming may arise from conflicting evaluations of the CMC system being used and the most appropriate ways to use it.

Task Evaluation

In some organizations, CMC systems are regarded as important channels for serious work: E-mail may be replacing the memo as the preferred method of internal communication. Flaming is officially discouraged in some organizations as an inappropriate waste of resources (see Foulger, 1990, for a description of the antiflaming policies at IBM). Other organizations may have a much "looser" attitude toward nontask use of CMC, even encouraging socioemotional communication in the desire to increase organizational camaraderie (Sproull & Kiesler, 1991). Flaming behavior may vary in both quantity and quality in these two task evaluation contexts. An explanation of flaming should thus account for how users view the purpose of a particular CMC medium or transaction.

Situational Factors

As mentioned earlier, time may be a significant situational factor in flaming, especially in asynchronous CMC. Flaming may be influenced by the length of discussions, which may occur over days or weeks. The number of messages received in a given unit of time, the time between messages, and the time of day a message is read may be situational factors related to flaming. Location of CMC use may be another significant situational factor. CMC users may access communication networks in a variety of places: at the office, at home, on the road. Flaming behavior may be less common in messages originating in "serious" locations, such as an office, than in more casual settings. Situations also vary in the degree of privacy offered; flaming as behavior may be influenced by the presence of other people during a CMC interaction. There is some evidence that the mere presence of others influences CMC behavior (Robinson-Stavely & Cooper, 1990). Flaming within a geographically separate group may be of a different caliber and hold different consequences than flaming within a co-present group communicating with the aid of group decision-making software.

To summarize, the social influence model suggests that the behavior of flaming is a function of the two central factors of social influence and media experience. In addition, media evaluations, task evaluations, and situational factors contribute to the behavior of flaming. Although some evidence from previous research has been cited in support of these propositions, there exists a need for further research to explore how these factors work together. Such an effort could help bridge together some of the seemingly contradictory strands of previous research, which has primarily focused on the behavioral dimension of flaming. Perhaps an even more important research opportunity is an investigation into the factors that contribute to the interpretation of flaming, an area that has largely been ignored by previous research.

OTHER FACTORS INFLUENCING THE INTERPRETATION OF FLAMING

The social influence model holds that flaming is more than just behavior; it also incorporates the interpretation of behavior. Why do some people consider a message to be a roaring flame, whereas others consider the same message to be a harmless chide? The model suggests that, as with the behavior of flaming, social influence and media experience are important factors. The model goes on to identify two additional factors influencing the interpretation of flaming: media features and the prior use of other media.

Media Features

The characteristics of CMC systems may influence how individuals interpret messages received through such systems. Users read messages on a variety of hardware and software configurations, from large mainframe systems to portable personal digital assistants. The interpretation of flaming may differ between those who have a user-friendly electronic mail program with a graphical interface and those who read messages on systems that have painfully slow display rates or that lack message filtering capabilities. Some systems even have sophisticated "kill" commands to screen out messages from specific individuals or messages with objectionable words. Flaming may be influenced by the degree to which users are aware of (and make use of) these and other media features that enable "flame management" strategies.

Prior Use of Other Media

Just as previous experience with flaming can influence how one interprets flaming, how people react to and make use of other media can influence evaluations of behavior in CMC contexts. The interpretation of flaming may be influenced by previous experiences with flaming-like behavior in other media, such as complaint letters, prank phone calls, and televised debates. How one interprets these similar behaviors in other media is likely to influence how one interprets flaming as it is encountered in computer media. People also bring to a flaming situation different expectations of the advantages and disadvantages of media use, based largely on previous experience. There is evidence that preusage expectations of media use influence media evaluations (Rice, Grant, Schmitz, &

Torobin, 1990). Thus, behavior patterns based on prior use of other media may contribute to a set of interpretive rules that aid in the sense making of flaming behaviors. Because individuals vary in the media experiences they bring to the CMC context, taking account of these diverse experiences can contribute to a more complete explanation of how people interpret flaming.

In summary, the social influence model holds that the interpretation of flaming is a function of social influence, media experience, media features, and prior use of other media. It should be stressed that this proposition, as with the rest of the model, is offered more for its heuristic value than its predictive value. The model is suggested as a framework for integrating previous research and for developing research questions to guide future research. Some of those questions, as well as some of the limitations of this model, are considered in the conclusion to this chapter.

CONCLUSION

The social influence model of flaming developed here seeks to provide a more complete understanding of flaming than previous efforts. Rather than limit the explanation of flaming to the influence of technological constraints on those who use technology, this model acknowledges the influence of humans on human behavior and in the negotiation of what that behavior means. The model allows the integration of many of the characteristics of flaming previously identified by research as well as suggesting some intriguing questions for future investigation.

For example, why is flaming more common in some CMC settings than others? To what extend do users frequently exposed to flaming develop a tolerance for it? What fire-fighting strategies do users develop for putting out flames? Are group norms really less influential in CMC, or can group norms be more influential? Rather than promote a lack of social context, could CMC systems in some settings actually increase awareness of the social context? Is flaming the result of a lack of "information richness," or the result of too much of a different kind of richness, an emotional intensity that cannot be attributed to the technology alone, but to the social environment in which the technology is used?

Indeed, could it be that, as Goodwin (1994) suggested, "flames are the friction born of minds rubbing too closely together?" (p. 69). As Goodwin put it: "The problem of flaming is not that we don't understand each other. It's that we understand each other all too well. We're mainlining each other's thoughts" (p. 69). As provocative as this idea may seem, it nevertheless strikes a resonant chord with many who have experienced flaming directly. For those who have been burned in a flame war, flaming is more than a technologically caused psychological neurosis—it is also clearly a social phenomenon, reflecting rational purpose, human conflict, and subjective interpretation. The model developed in this chapter acknowledges this social dimension of flaming in a way previous theories have not, and, by so doing, arguably provides a more complete perspective for understanding flaming.

Of course, the model of flaming outlined here is not without its weaknesses. The Fulk et al. (1990) model focused more on media choice than on media behaviors once that choice was made; the evidence remains limited for concluding that the extension of the model in the directions suggested here are warranted. Although the social influence model can account for many diverse strands in previous research, the model essentially remains untested. Furthermore, this model is less parsimonious than other theories that have been employed to account for flaming. The more comprehensive explanation for flaming offered by this model may necessitate complicated and perhaps impractical research designs in order to test its propositions fully.

Is it worth the effort? Is flaming a phenomenon that warrants the serious attention of scholars of communication? Or is flaming simply part of a passing phase in the development of computer-mediated communication? The jury is still out. Some believe flaming is an antisocial effect of CMC and thus provides an intriguing dependent variable for assessing the negative impact of computer technology on human communication. For others, flaming offers a unique opportunity to advance our understanding of conflict and interpretive sense making from within an environment that allows relatively unobtrusive observation (Rice et al., 1990). But for many flaming is simply not a big deal. Flaming happens. It is part of life on the electronic frontier.

As with previous frontiers, law-abiding citizens will eventually displace the outlaws. What has been learned about flaming in the past decade of research could thus be of little consequence in the future, as cyberspace becomes a more civilized place. This is particularly likely if claims about flaming continue to be based on the shifting sands of technological characteristics, claims that could easily wash away as the technology changes and as the application of that technology becomes more sophisticated. If scholarship on flaming is to have lasting value, researchers should move toward examining flaming not simply as an effect of communication technology, but as a reflection of the social negotiation of meaning through communication media.

REFERENCES

Anderson, J.A., & Meyer, T.P. (1988). *Mediated communication: A social action perspective.* Newbury Park, CA: Sage.

Anderson, J.F., & Walther, J.B. (1992, May). *Relational tone in computer-mediated communication: A meta-analysis of past research.* Paper presented to the International Communication Association, Miami, FL.

Baldwin, C., & Holmes, M.E. (1992, May). *Social presence and verbal immediacy: A linguistic critique of media determinism.* Paper presented to the International Communication Association, Miami, FL.

Balcs, R.F. (1950). A set of categories for the analysis of small group interaction. *American Sociology Review, 15*, 257-263.

Baron, N.S. (1984). Computer mediated communication as a force in language change. *Visible Language, 18*, 118-141.

Blackman, B.I., & Clevenger, T., Jr. (1990, November). *The promises, possibilities and pragmatics of using pictograph surrogates in on-line messaging: Implications for managing the adoption of computer-mediated communication technology.* Paper presented to the Speech Communication Association, Chicago, IL.

Brown, E. (1984, January). Fear and lurking on CB simulator. *PC World*, pp. 182-191.

Campbell, D.T., & Fiske, D.W. (1959). Convergent and discriminant validation by the multitrait-multimethod matrix. *Psychological Bulletin, 56*, 81-105.

Compton, D.C., White, K., & DeWine, S. (1991). Techno-sense: Making sense of computer-mediated communication systems. *Journal of Business Communication, 28*, 23-43.

Culnan, M.J., & Markus, M.L. (1987). Information technologies. In F. M. Jablin, L. L. Putnam, K.J. Roberts, & L.W. Porter (Eds.), *Handbook of organizational communication: An interdisciplinary perspective* (pp. 420-443). Newbury Park, CA: Sage.

Daft, R.L., & Lengel, R.H. (1986). Organizational information requirements, media richness, and structural design. *Management Science, 32*, 554-571.

Dery, M. (1993). Flame wars. *South Atlantic Quarterly, 92*, 559-568.

Dorwick, K. (1993, April). *Beyond politeness: Flaming and the realm of the violent.* Paper presented to the Conference on College Composition and Communication, San Diego, CA.

Eckholm, E. (1984, October 2). Emotional outbursts punctuate conversations by computer. *New York Times*, pp. C1, C5.

Festinger, L., Pepitone, A., & Newcomb, T. (1952). Some consequences of deindividuation in a group. *Journal of Abnormal and Social Psychology, 47*, 382-389.

Foulger, D.A. (1990). *Medium as process: The structure, use, and practice of computer conferencing on IBM's IBM PC computer conferencing facility.* Unpublished doctoral dissertation, Temple University, Philadelphia.

Fulk, J., Schmitz, J., & Steinfield, C.W. (1990). A social influence model of technology use. In J. Fulk & C. Steinfield (Eds.), *Organizations and communication technology* (pp. 117-140). Newbury Park, CA: Sage.

Fulk, J., Steinfield, C.W., Schmitz, J., & Power, J.G. (1987). A social information processing model of media use in organizations. *Communication Research, 14*, 529-552.

Goode, J., & Johnson, M. (1991, November). Putting out the flames: The etiquette and law of e-mail. *Online*, pp. 61-65.

Goodwin, M. (1994, April). ASCII is too intimate. *Wired*, pp. 69-70.

Hawisher, G.E. (1992). Electronic meetings of the mind: Research, electronic conferences, and composition studies. In G. E. Hawisher & P. LeBlanc (Eds.), *Re-imagining computers and composition: Teaching and research in the virtual age* (pp. 81-101). Portsmouth, NH: Boynton/Cook.

Hiltz, S.R., Johnson, K., & Turoff, M. (1986). Experiments in group decision making: Communication process and outcome in face-to-face versus computerized conferences. *Human Communication Research, 13*, 225-252.

Holmes, M.E., & Berquist, C. (1990, November). *Gender display in synchronous computer-mediated discourse: A case of channel constraints and opportunities.* Paper presented to the Speech Communication Association, Chicago, IL.

Judd, C.M., Smith, E.R., & Kidder, L.H. (1991). *Research methods in social relations.* Fort Worth, TX: Holt Rinehart and Winston.

Kiesler, S., Siegel, J., & McGuire, T.W. (1984). Social psychological aspects of computer-mediated communication. *American Psychologist, 39*, 1123-1134.

Kiesler, S., Zubrow, D., Moses, A.M., & Geller, V. (1985). Affect in computer-mediated communication: An experiment in synchronous terminal-to-terminal discussion. *Human Computer Interaction, 1*, 77-104.

Lea, M., O'Shea, T., Fung, P., & Spears, R. (1992). "Flaming" in computer-mediated communication: Observations, explanations, implications. In M. Lea (Ed.), *Contexts of computer-mediated communication* (pp. 89-112). London: Harvester-Wheatsheaf.

Lea, M., & Spears, R. (1991). Computer-mediated communication, de-individuation and group decision-making. *International Journal of Man-Machine Studies, 34*, 283-301.

Leeds-Hurwitz, W. (1992). Social approaches to interpersonal communication. *Communication Theory, 2*, 131-139.

Miller, M.W. (1992, September 15). A story of the type that turns heads in computer circles: Digital smiley faces are used in e-mail conversations by the lateral-minded. *Wall Street Journal*, pp. A1, A11.

Rice, R.E. (1984). Mediated group communication. In R.E. Rice & Associates (Eds.), *The new media: Communication, research and technology* (pp. 129-154). Beverly Hills, CA: Sage.

Rice, R.E., Grant, A.E., Schmitz, J., & Torobin, J. (1990). Individual and network influences on the adoption and perceived outcomes of electronic messaging. *Social Networks, 12*, 27-55.

Rice, R.E., & Love, G. (1987). Electronic emotion: Socioemotional content in a computer-mediated communication network. *Communication Research, 14*, 85-108.

Rice, R.E., & Steinfield, C. (1994). New forms of organizational communication via electronic mail and voice messaging. In J.H. Andriessen & R. Roe (Eds.), *Telematics and work* (pp. 109-137). Hillsdale, NJ: Erlbaum.

Robinson-Stavely, K., & Cooper, J. (1990). Mere presence, gender, and reactions to computers: Studying human-computer interaction in the social context. *Journal of Experimental Social Psychology, 26*, 168-183.

Romiszowski, A.J., & deHaas, J.A. (1989). Computer mediated communication for instruction: Using e-mail as a seminar. *Educational Technology, 29*(10), 7-14.

Roth, P.A. (1987). *Meaning and method in the social sciences: A case for methodological pluralism.* Ithaca, NY: Cornell University Press.

Salancik, G.R., & Pfeffer, J. (1978). A social information processing approach to job attitudes and task design. *Administrative Science Quarterly, 23,* 224-253.

Selfe, C.L., & Meyer, P.R. (1991). Testing claims for on-line conferences. *Written Communication, 8,* 162-192.

Short, J., Williams, E., & Christie, B. (1976). *The social psychology of telecommunications.* New York: Wiley.

Siegel, J., Dubrovsky, V., Kiesler, S., & McGuire, T.W. (1986). Group processes in computer-mediated communication. *Organizational Behavior and Human Decision Processes, 37,* 157-187.

Spears, R., Lea, M., & Lee, S. (1990). De-individuation and group polarization in computer-mediated communication. *British Journal of Social Psychology, 29,* 121-134.

Spitzer, M. (1986). Writing style in computer conferences. *IEEE Transactions on Professional Communications, PC 29*(1), 19-22.

Sproull, L., & Kiesler, S. (1986). Reducing social context cues: Electronic mail in organizational communication. *Management Science, 32,* 1492-1512.

Sproull, L., & Kiesler, S. (1991). *Connections: New ways of working in the networked organization.* Cambridge, MA: MIT Press.

Steele, G., Woods, D., Finkel, R., Crispin, M., Stallman, R., & Goodfellow, G. (1983). *The hackers dictionary.* New York: Harper & Row.

Steinfield, C.W. (1986). Computer-mediated communication in an organizational setting: Explaining task-related and socioemotional uses. In M. L. McLaughlin (Ed.), *Communication Yearbook* (Vol. 9, pp. 777-804). Newbury Park, CA: Sage.

Steinfield, C.W., & Fulk, J. (1990). The theory imperative. In J. Fulk & C. W. Steinfield (Eds.), *Organizations and communication technology* (pp. 13-25). Newbury Park, CA: Sage.

Stewart, D. (1991, September). Flame throwers: Why the heated bursts on your computer network? *Omni,* p. 26.

Thompsen, P.A. (1994). An episode of flaming: A creative narrative. *ETC: A Review of General Semantics, 51,* 51-72.

Thompsen, P.A., & Ahn, D.-K. (1992). To be or not to be: An exploration of E-Prime, copula deletion and flaming in electronic mail. *ETC: A Review of General Semantics, 49,* 146-164.

Thompsen, P.A., & Foulger, D.A. (1993, May). *Effects of pictographs and quoting on flaming in computer media.* Paper presented to the International Communication Association, Washington, DC.

Turkle, S. (1984). *The second self: Computers and the human spirit.* New York: Simon and Schuster.

Walther, J.B. (1992). Interpersonal effects in computer-mediated interaction. *Communication Research, 19,* 52-90.

Walther, J.B., & Burgoon, J.K. (1992). Relational communication in computer-mediated interaction. *Human Communication Research, 19,* 50-88.

Weisband, S.P. (1992). Group discussion and first advocacy effects in computer-mediated and face-to-face decision making groups. *Organizational Behavior and Human Decision Processes, 53,* 352-380.

Williams, F., Rice, R.E., & Rogers, E.M. (1988). *Research methods and the new media.* New York: Free Press.

Zimbardo, P.G. (1969). The human choice: Individuation, reason, and order versus deindividuation, impulse, and chaos. In W.J. Arnold & D. Levine (Eds.), *Nebraska symposium on motivation: 1969* (pp. 237-307). Lincoln: University of Nebraska.

◇◇◇◇ 21

Technologies, Relations, and Selves

Richard H. Cutler

In changing the way in which we communicate, new media provide us with the opportunity to enter into new and different kinds of relations with others. Thus, computer media and cyberspace technologies allow us to form virtual relationships, join virtual groups and organizations, and build virtual communities. This in turn alters the roles that we play and our very sense of identity. Cutler examines the new social situations characteristic of cyberspace, drawing on Joshua Meyrowitz's analysis of television in No Sense of Place *(1985). Noting that computer-mediated communication is distinguished by its high level of interactivity and active participation, Cutler considers the processes of group formation, socialization, and the creation of power structures in cyberspace. Positively evaluating computing's impact on the sense of self, he concludes that communication in cyberspace is not especially isolating, fragmenting, or addictive. In Sections I, II, and III, alternate perspectives that take a more critical view of cyberspatial relationships can be found in Gary Gumpert and Susan J. Drucker's survey in Chapter 1 and John M. Phelan's essay in Chapter 2; other discussions of online communities and relationships appear in Terri Toles Patkin's study of the virtual organization in Chapter 11 and Michael P. Beaubien's discussion of MUDs in Chapter 12; for further examination of the concept of the self in cyberspace, see Jay David Bolter's comparison of text and virtual reality in Chapter 7 and Sue Barnes's environmental analysis in Chapter 13.*

This chapter advances a perspective for understanding the social consequences of applying cyberspace technology to communication. Established at the outset is the premise that as people adopt new technologies for information exchange the social context[1] in which they live and work is altered by the technology. To understand what changes, if any, will be created for social relations and society as the cyberspace phenomenon grows, I suggest that we begin with three basic understandings. First, adopting the new communication technologies results in changed social situations. Second, with the changed social context comes a widening range of possible relationships. Third, changed relationships result in new social roles. New links among society's members are unconstrained by the usual boundaries of space, place, or even time. For instance, individuals may send or read e-mail or messages on electronic bulletin boards at any time; they may have real-time, interactive conversations with one or more participants regardless of real-world location; and they can contribute to the creation of imaginary places that others interact with from anywhere. Driving the three changes is the interaction afforded by the technology of cyberspace. In the body of this chapter interaction is applied to the function of changed role play in the formation of groups, socialization, and power structure. Like Meyrowitz (1985), I take a "situational approach,"[2] but my focus is on the interactive quality of communication contents and processes found in cyberspace. Interaction is the characteristic of cyberspace technology that differentiates it from other public electronic media such as television. I argue that interaction as a feature of new social situations is the key to the creation both of changed self-concepts and new group identities. Meyrowitz's situational approach is appropriate because the role changes described in this chapter occur in a larger context of new communities composed of participants who may belong to many other communities and who continually move in their online communications among groups. Finally, I discuss the importance of the new interactions in cyberspace for the quality of life of individuals in the information society. Whether we can accurately predict the social impact of cyberspace, the goal of this chapter is to establish the perspective that the proliferation of cyberspace technologies changes who we think we are and how we relate to others.

---

[1]Meyrowitz (1985) recognizes that social context has been "underdefined." I applaud his efforts at definition and find that my idea of social context includes his notion of "social situation" with its implicit ties to the defining nature of media. He states, "I argue that electronic media create new types of social situations that transcend physically defined social settings and have their own rules and role expectations" (p. 333).

[2]In his preface to *No Sense of Place*, Meyrowitz (1985) describes the situational approach. He says, "Sociologists have long noted that people behave differently in different social 'situations,' depending on where one is and who one is with. . . . The theory developed here extends the study of static situations to the study of changing situations, and extends the analysis of physically defined settings to the analysis of the social environments created by media of communication" (pp. viii-ix)

CYBERSPACE TECHNOLOGY AND SOCIAL CONTEXT

Communication technologies change the sense of time and space within which a society conducts its affairs. Consider, for example, how the telegraph made possible the wire news services, coordinated train travel, and the stock market ticker tape. Each of these technologies has varied senses of time and space. For example, a continent traversed by wire news seems closer at hand than the one seen as it moves across a passing train window. The speed of news from distant places, the setting of time zones, and the ability to participate in commodity markets from afar were instrumental in creating a sense of an American nation (Carey, 1989). Alteration of the sense of time and place across an entire society is an effect frequently overlooked as new products such as personal computers are marketed for their personal entertainment or efficient productivity value. But, as scholars from McLuhan (1964) to Marvin (1988) have pointed out, the time- and space-changing characteristics of a new communication technology furnish the possibilities for new social situations, initially by and for the most powerful, controlling elements of society. For example, an electronic mail system may be installed to speed message traffic up and down an organizational hierarchy. That system also allows me to contact other employees easily. Suppose that I can more readily solve a problem if I can get the advice of a colleague in another part of the organization, perhaps in another city. Using this new e-mail technology, I set up a direct and immediate communication link without obtaining the permission of my boss or her supervisor and without going through any receptionists. The change in social context afforded by the technology fosters changes in relationships. Furthermore, not only have I formed a collaboration on topics of mutual interest, but I have engendered a relationship that redefines our social roles as colleagues. The opportunities for new roles and communication have literally been created by the individual addressing capability of the technology, and my changed behavior has been enabled by the switched connections of our computers that leap over the physical space that separates us and that bypass the social power hierarchies. As a result of the new relationship, I conceive of myself in a changed role as a colleague and collaborator with a shared allegiance based on mutual skills and professional interests rather than departmental identity. With new relationships and altered roles come changed communication behaviors by members of the society. As I explain, here, new communication behaviors result in new senses of self and group identity.

USES AND EFFECTS OF CYBERSPACE TECHNOLOGY

The dynamic process of changed technology, relations, and selves with respect to television was well argued by Meyrowitz (1985) a decade ago. Since then, the application throughout the information society of networked, interactive computer-based communication technologies (read: cyberspace) has occasioned a reexamination of the social and psychological effects of electronic media on people's lives. The technology of cyberspace is comprised basically of computers, modems, and software protocols linked by international telecommunications networks to provide an infrastructure called *computer-mediated communications* (CMC). This infrastructure enables individuals to converse in cyberspace. Among the many definitions of *cyberspace* (see Benedikt, 1991), one of the most workable is Howard Rheingold's (1993): "the conceptual space where words, human relationships, data, wealth, and power are manifested by people using CMC technology" (p. 5). What Rheingold, long-time denizen of The Well—an electronic forum known for its diverse if not eccentric participants—suggests in his definition is that, first of all, CMC is a medium created out of converged technologies in which words and relationships share some sort of "space"—with not only data, but with manifestations of wealth and power. So, CMC is more than data and connection systems; it is a social situation as well. Pretty intense scene, huh? Well, he could simply be describing nothing more impressive than your bank's lobby. But, wait, there is more. Rheingold (1993) adds, "Virtual communities are social aggregations that emerge from the Net when enough people carry on those public discussions long enough, with sufficient human feeling, to form webs of personal relations in cyberspace" (p. 5). Sounds kinda hip and "new age-y," doesn't it? Your attention arrested, and having just learned that new communication technologies alter social situations, you might ask, "Well then, what do we already know about the uses and social consequences of cyberspace? And what's this about virtual communities as 'social aggregations'? Are they like virtual reality with a bunch of people?"

For the past two decades, cyberspace technologies have been mostly applied to work environments. The infrastructure, hardware, and software are expensive when you start from scratch. The current literature surrounding CMC is almost entirely task-based and focused on cost, efficiency, and productivity with little attention given either to the changes effected on the people or to the social relations created from using the communications technologies. All is not lost, however. Some communication researchers (Hiltz & Turoff, 1978; Kiesler, Siegel, & McGuire, 1984; Steinfield, 1986) have noted that increased efficiency also broadens the number of possible communication interactions and leads to other forms of human contact (Rice, 1980; Rice & Love, 1987). In other words, communication researchers have discovered what I discussed earlier about the general effect on social situations when a new communication technology is adopted. That is, people form social relationships besides the agreements and procedures that are necessary to implement any new technology. The additions to productivity from adopting CMC technologies are "first-level effects," but the unanticipated changes to the social and psychological components of organization that result are "second-level" effects, equal in importance to those of the first level (Sproull & Kiesler, 1991).

Now, communication scholars are often accused of making discoveries that "burst through open doors." So, I would not want to impress on you that the use of communication technologies for social communication is anything new. Be that as it may, extending the range and control of human communications has accompanied the invention of the printing press, the routes of mail service, the networks of telegraph and telephone wires, and, most recently, electronic messaging over networked telecommunications systems. By making the messages increasingly mobile, people can communicate with each other at increasingly distant places with less and less need for personal physical movement.

CYBERSPACE TECHNOLOGY AND ROLE CHANGES

We do know from CMC studies and the work of scholars such as Meyrowitz (1985) that new communication technologies change society by affording new communication links among its members, and that those new relationships are accompanied by the adoption of new roles.[3] That individuals cannot communicate without some sort of role to prescribe appropriate language and status should be an obvious corollary. Meyrowitz uses the wonderful example of a young person relating the activities of a holiday abroad and the different social roles assumed in the telling, depending on the social situation: with parents, close friends, or neighbors. Accordingly, Meyrowitz demonstrates that new communication technologies change society in three areas of role play—group identity, socialization, and power hierarchy. This general perspective can serve to describe the changes to be noted and anticipated in cyberspace. The discussion that follows examines changes in the three areas of role play.

First, changes in group identity can be seen in the many voluntary associations that have appeared as everyday millions of people interact electronically. From 1988 to 1992, the number of networked personal computers (PCs) quadrupled from 6.8 million to 31 million,[4] thus increasing geometrically an individual's opportunities for new affiliations. Large, commercial bulletin board systems (BBSs), such as America Online, CompuServe, MCI Mail, and Prodigy are offering discussion groups along with marketing information and consumer products. Noncommercial BBSs have been established at an astonishing rate in the major population centers of the United States, rising from 40,000 in 1992 (Steinert-Threlkeld, 1993) to 60,000 nationwide by 1993 (Rheingold, 1993). The vast majority of electronic bulletin board systems are locally run by volunteer

[3]The term role comes from George Herbert Mead (1934), who defined it as "a socially prescribed way of behaving in particular situations for any person occupying a given cultural or social organizational position" (p. 36).

[4]According to estimates by the Market Intelligence Research Corporation (Steinert-Threlkeld, 1993).

sysops (system operators), who usually own the PC and supervise the "board" with a cross between benevolence and voyeurism, serving anywhere from a handful to hundreds of participants (Allen, 1988). Most of these bulletin boards are frequented by local users for games and entertainment, sharing public domain software, and posting general information and discussion. In addition, the newsgroups and mailing lists accessible through the Internet serve an additional 5 to 10 million people internationally. Some BBSs offer a special interest and draw long distance participants. The appearance of extensive online environments dedicated to conversation and sharing ideas and information, such as The Well in San Francisco, Echo in New York, Habitat in Japan, the international IRC (Internet Relay Chat), and LambdaMOO at Xerox's PARC, suggests that people with access to computers hooked up to telephones are readily expanding their social contacts beyond organizational affiliations and local bulletin boards. Among the most advanced interactive multiuser groups, found mostly on academic computers connected to the Internet, are MUDs, MOOs, MUSHes, MUCKs, and TinyMUDs. Multi-User Dungeons (MUDs) are board games of sorcery and combat skill that are written into the text-based world of Internet. The Tiny MUDs, MUSHes, and MOOs, their more social cousins, are unique in their combination of role play and interactive communication in a textually described social context made possible by object-oriented software. Like BBSs, but highly interactive, these volunteer associations are generally formed around mutual interests, word play, and the exchange of information. MUD software provides an interface for participation of each member of the group in the process of reading and commentary on the text at a speed approaching face-to-face conversation.

Speaking of group affiliations, what about those "social aggregations" that Rheingold (1993) calls "virtual communities?" Ever since Robert Boyle settled a scientific argument with philosopher Thomas Hobbes in 1669 by getting the support of peers who had all read Boyle's paper, virtual communities of readers have formed around the same document (Stone, 1991). But in cyberspace, groups are not simply organized around a medium or a text. The interaction of individuals with mutual interests leads to the sharing of accumulated knowledge and the creation of specialized language and other cultural products. Groups take on the character of communities in their diversity of individuals who create cultural products: the textual histories of jokes, word play, threads of conversation, negotiation of the meaning of events in the physical world, and, in the case of MUDs and MOOs, the programming of objects that can be discovered, explored, and manipulated like objects in the real world. In addition to the focus on topics of mutual interest, each group offers social interaction as well as interesting collections of textual archives, running jokes, personal stories, and histories. In sum, the opportunities for individual affiliation with new, electronically configured groups are enormous.

Interaction in cyberspace groups also creates changes in socialization roles. Newcomers ask questions and are schooled in the opinions of those more knowledgeable. The process frequently goes something like this: A common communication is the question "Does anyone know . . . ?" Solicitations for advice or comments serve as pretexts for requesting acceptance into the group. In addition to receiving answers to their questions, "newbies" (newcomers) receive models for the proper social protocols for conducting discourse: for example, when to use uppercase to "SHOUT", asterisks around a word for *emphasis*, and emoticons (smiley ;-) faces) for mood. Through shared stories and news about "real life" (RL), the attentive newcomer soon learns who are considered outsiders and what are the tenets of belief of the group. Besides serving to consolidate group identity, stories and commentary foster the value system to which continued membership implies tacit agreement.

Meaning is negotiated through discourse. Group members feel free to add supporting or contradicting information, opinions to comments, or to take the thread of conversation off into a related issue that draws further remarks, jokes, innuendoes, insults, and rebukes. A consensus is struck as many members seem to support a particularly articulate point of view. Dissenters fade and, if the difference of opinion is serious enough, may not be heard from again. Within the group, personal e-mail communication continues privately between participants who find they have more to share than they want to make public. Friendships and romances often develop. Thus, the language of the group as well as its ideology—in short, its culture—is arrived at through a dynamic process of socialization to what is meaningful. Inappropriate behavior is rewarded with "flames"[5] and even ostracism (Reid, 1992).

Besides learning the culture of the group and changing from the newcomer role in the socialization process, the initiate learns who to respect, who to challenge, and who can be counted on to defend or attack one's views. In time one's roles change in the power hierarchy based on a balance between competence in the subject matter of the group, the ability to articulate personal views, and the time one wants to invest in the group's threads of conversation and flame wars. Given the rapid growth of virtual communities or lifestyle enclaves, the power structure of groups is usually fluid with longer term members holding their positions by dint of being carriers of more accumulated cultural history and the foci of relationship networks. In all, cyberspace affiliations are remarkably egalitarian. The exceptions are the MUDs and similarly combat-oriented enclaves, in which the object of play is to differentiate positions in the hierarchy; but even there, power is accessible through programming and playing prowess. Above the more or less shallow hierarchy of newcomers and initiates, the usually silent administrator or group moderator has the power to censor "postings" (messages), censure acts, and even remove participants when they threaten the cohesion of the group. After all, the administrator is usually a volunteer and has a personal interest in the focus

---

[5]Rather than being simply disruptive behavior, the practice of flaming—irate, hostile messages—may be seen as an example of using an emotional tone because other media channels do not exist (Thompsen, 1993).

of the group. Without group cohesion, dialogue about the topic would disappear. And above the group's administrator, the staff and directors of the online service, the computer center, or the owner of the machine providing the Internet access holds power over the group's virtual meeting space and, hence, its continued existence. Real-world power structures still can determine the existence of virtual communities and have a nasty way of intruding. Recently a group devoted to discussing "fringe" sexual behavior and performing virtual sex acts was found operating from a government computer by an employee serving as the group's administrator. The group's virtual activities were suspended, and the employee had to face the discomfort of an FBI investigation. Needless to say, once the privacy of the group was breached, members were concerned for their own real-world job security as well as continued lifestyle.

In summarizing the changes to social roles in the three broad categories of role play, note that interaction is a key ingredient to facilitating change. In the next section I distinguish between the role changes facilitated by television, as observed by Meyrowitz (1985), and the role changes that cyberspace technology enables.

INTERACTION

In his discussion of roles, Meyrowitz (1985) builds on the work of Erving Goffman (1959), who uses analogies between roles played on the dramatic stage and those played in social life. Goffman proffers the idea of stages to distinguish between role behaviors in public (front stage) and private (backstage). Meyrowitz applies Goffman's analogy to mediated behavior and makes the point that television publicly portrays for all ages and sectors of society behavior that was once private, thus blurring the distinction between the two stages and the roles played there.

One way to understand how television and cyberspace technology differ in their effect on role changes is to strip away the prominent characteristics and functions that they both share until one function best characterizes each. Television blurred the boundaries between social roles by showing what was previously privy only to certain social groups, socialization processes, and hierarchies. What television shows is not restricted to viewers possessing special knowledge as was, for example, the secrets shared only among male initiates in traditional societies. Little interaction occurs between the medium and the users. Cyberspace, by contrast, has interaction as its distinctive media characteristic. That is, in order to use the technology of cyberspace one must be active, whether manipulating the technology or navigating through it to communicate with others. Interaction begins with the technology, and many newcomers struggle with the welter of technical jargon and procedures needed to negotiate cyberspace. The need to consult others for help in mastering the technology drives many novice cybernauts[6] to user groups to enhance their communication skills. Spurred by

[6]Just as the phenomenon of virtual reality was making its public debut, Howard Rheingold

successes of communication proficiency attained and the willingness of others to share information, many participants begin to converse about personal interests. Going online simply to converse becomes an objective and source of satisfaction. One variant of interaction with others for its own sake—multiplayer gaming—has become so popular that national services now link players to interactive databases (Michalski, 1993). For others who may have entered cyberspace when it was used primarily for data transfers and storage, interaction is limited to retrieving information as from a huge data bank.

The important point to be made here is that the technology of cyberspace affords a level of conversational interaction through text heretofore unavailable by any other medium, even the fastest mail or fax service. It is this characteristic of interactivity that distinguishes cyberspace from other role-changing technologies such as television. As Howard Rheingold (1993) noted, "Virtual communities are social aggregations that emerge from the Net when enough people carry on those public discussions long enough, with sufficient feeling, to form webs of personal relationships in cyberspace" (p. 5). People simply do not bump into each other as much in other communication technologies. Although ham radio, CB radio, and the telephone are interactive technologies, they lack the ease of group interaction that is afforded by discourse over what Rheingold calls the Net. Furthermore, the permanence of electronic addresses and the accretion of moderated, conversational threads that may be reviewed and responded to at any time provide a sense of place and stability that are unlike the conversations that occur and then are gone. Compared to face-to-face and point-to-point modes of communicating, interaction via cyberspace technologies can be called "many to many."

Interaction includes asking, telling, commenting, discussing, joking, correcting, arguing, and agreeing. With many participants in the forum, interaction becomes the means by which users establish their social identity as being aloof, persuasive, critical, a mediator, inciting, decisive, collaborative, or a conciliator to make peace to preserve membership in the group or to keep the group from disintegrating. Interaction describes the active profusion of textual discourse that pursues, yet may not achieve, consensus as to what are the group's prevailing views. And hierarchical positioning is based partly on the skillful use of language facilitated by the interactivity of the technology. Furthermore, the ability to hold a hierarchical position within the group appears to be a function more of the sharing of information and its persuasive articulation—both interactive tasks—rather than by "restriction of information and on limiting subordinates' access to all but a few onstage situations" as Meyrowitz (1985)

(1991) published *Virtual Reality*, in which he compared those who are changing the way we will live in the future with the infonauts of a decade ago, that "fanatic subset of computer enthusiasts . . . who" developed the personal computer that has "helped change the way we live today." About cybernauts, Rheingold said, "an even smaller and at least equally fanatic subset of that subculture began to think not only about what lay beyond the horizon but what might be found beyond that" (p. 135).

avers are the usual means to maintaining power (p. 65). This finding is a major departure from long-standing observations about the nature of power distribution among individuals in a group. The deciding factor to be recognized, though, is that the social situation created by a text-based, interactive technology is one in which an individual must disclose information in order to have a presence. Without the narrow communication channel of text, a person does not exist. The degree to which an individual has an identity online is a function of the individual's participation, and participation is based on control of disclosure. As I show in the next section, individuals adopt many different disclosure strategies in an attempt to create a personal identity.

INTERACTION, SELF-CONCEPT, AND CONTROL OF DISCLOSURE

Cyberspace technology facilitates interaction. Individuals use the technology to establish and change their roles in the group and at the same time evolve who they think they are, that is, their self-concept vis-à-vis others. Self-concept has many definitions, but they all center around the idea of one's vision of self. Why would an individual change behavior and self-concept merely to please others? The process of interaction to achieve socialization and self-concept was described by a colleague of Mead, Charles Horton Cooley (1964), in his notion of the "looking glass self." Cooley stated the power of the personal imagination is to see oneself as others do and to act accordingly. He said, "Our personality grows and takes form by divining the appearance of our present self to other minds" (p. 207). The effect of others on role definition differs by social situation. In the social situation in work environments, roles are largely defined by tasks and the power structure—that is, by others. On the other hand, role definition in voluntary environments is one of building individual self-concept.

Meyrowitz (1985) describes the differences in communication behavior in changed social situations in terms of new roles. But in the electronic world of cyberspace, as in the face-to-face world, the objective for many behaviors is to form relationships: "In interpersonal communication one presents one's vision of self to those intimate others from whom one seeks and needs support in order to sustain one's view of self" (Cushman & Cahn, 1985, p. 28). Humans need support from "intimate others." They want more than simply behavior that is consistent between the self and roles played. They want to trust others with intimate expressions. Thus, the process of role definition in a voluntary environment is a function of building self-concept through the control of disclosure of personal information. The more one discloses personal information, the more others will reciprocate, and the more individuals know about each other, the more likely they are to establish trust, seek support, and thus find satisfaction. Without disclosure and interaction nothing happens. In a condition of encounters with strangers, prudence and caution dictate control of disclosure. Control of disclosure creates a kind of currency that is spent to keep interaction moving. For illustration, here are some of the disclosure strategies actually observed in a virtual community. Note that not all strategies disclose equally, but that all are functions of control:

- Admit or feign ignorance; ask for help, ideas—act like a novice seeking initiation.
- Declare personal information, display vulnerability thereby challenging others to do the same.
- Avoid revealing personal information but participate at a distance through ironic commentary, refinement of points, word play, and critical analysis about the nature of the communications among participants.
- Establish authority based on respect for experience by sharing personal history.
- Establish trust by sharing intentions, motivations, or goals.
- Share only with those who disclose personal information.
- Establish a presence through disputation, flaming, correcting, and chiding.[7]

Each of the disclosure strategies presents a behavior role applicable to group interaction (see Bales, 1950). As personal information and attitudes are disclosed, trust develops. Participants do not necessarily agree on points of view, but learn to tolerate each other. As trust develops, so does a sense of intimacy, caring for the other, and attachment of special value to the history of the relationships, that is, maintenance of the community. A group identity builds, and many participants make plans to dispose of the media barrier and meet face to face.

INTERACTION AND IMPLICATIONS OF BUILDING SELF-CONCEPT

People meet online, and then relive, expand, and reflect on the experience. Interaction produces changes in two directions: toward self-concept building as described earlier, and group identity building. So, by acting out roles or taking on expanded or new identities, participants become changed selves. They use the interactive, face-to-face nature of the technology that created the opportunity to

---

[7]For five months in 1994, the author observed the interactions of a group of communicators on a group list, a moderated forum, somewhat like a BBS, but more focused on their area of mutual interest. Because the sexual lifestyle of members of the list might be characterized as "fringe" when compared to the values of what they call "Ozzie and Harriet America," they had great stake in cleaving together for mutual support and open discussion of their issues.

further personal transformation and formation of groups. What are we to make of these changes? Are they good, bad? It is hard not to observe cybernauts without being empathetic to their all-too-human searches for understanding themselves and others. I continue to be struck by the free-wheeling speech, the frank advice, censure, and voices of sympathy, balance, and reason. I take the conversations as expressions of identity-seeking confirmation and/or companionship.

Are the changes isolating? Fragmenting? Addictive? Vis-à-vis the traditional view of face-to-face relations as the most desirable mode of interaction; yes to all three. The conversational nature of interactive media in cyberspace is more to be compared to the immediacy of face-to-face interaction. However, in times of change, leaving old roles, seeking change, and forming new relationships, time spent with media—whether shared experiences or not—must be at the cost of face-to-face interactions; in other words, mediated communication is by its nature isolating. Our lives are full of mediated experiences at the cost of face-to-face relations: reading print publications is a personal, isolating act; listening to the radio forecloses talking and listening to others; watching television is absorbing even in the presence of others; advertisements constantly use "attention-getting" devices. Mediated communication, regardless of richness, cannot approach the inherent interactivity of face-to-face communication. Clearly, not all communication is best done face to face. The many channels of expression that accompany face-to-face communication—dress, appearance, symbols of status, and body language —can also be used as social barriers to participation and interaction. Visual appearance can send symbolic signals that speak of authority or unresponsiveness. Immediate audio feedback may interrupt the formation and expression of complicated ideas. When conversation is reduced to text, many people feel more confident about expressing their opinions. Thus, it is important to differentiate between the possibilities for interactive communication made available by the technology—or lack of it—and the social situation in which the communication occurs. For instance, the technology may supply only text, or it may provide full-motion video with synchronized audio. However, barriers to communication are equally likely to be socioeconomic as they are to be inherent in the medium. Access to a medium such as printing or computing may require a form of literacy, but it will also be most available to those of the socioeconomic class that can afford it. In short, the argument that mediated communication will always be inadequate compared to face-to-face interaction because it is inherently isolating simply does not hold up in light of the diversity and functionality of a variety of media. Let's examine the more specific concerns of isolation then.

Many people in densely urban areas and remote rural towns experience profound feelings of loneliness spawned from isolation and lack of trust. For those unhappy souls with limited opportunities for satisfying face-to-face relationships, the many online groups found in cyberspace offer not just information, but conversation—like AA—anytime day or night, when they need companionship; and, if personal information is disclosed, advice, comfort, or a reality-adjusting rebuke is easily received without physical risk.

Even those persons closer to the business and organizational uses of new communication technologies are likely to share in the benefits of new experiences such as communicating in cyberspace. And there are advantages. With mediated interaction, barriers are few. Telephone conversations are as intimate as whispers in the ear. Voice mail offers one-to-one or one-to-many broadcasting of personal messages without the intervening protocols of salutations, face-saving style (Hiemstra,1982), answering, and rescheduling of missed calls. Electronic correspondence allows for direct communication without the compromises of immediate feedback; likewise, textual communication—whether paper or electronic—allows for consideration of meaning and crafted clarity. CMC researchers (Hiltz & Turoff, 1978; Kiesler et al., 1984) have long known that online communication in cyberspace tends to involve a lone participant faced only by a computer screen. The resulting feeling of anonymity is paralleled by a feeling of autonomy. Participants are more likely to send messages without considering consequences, or to overreact by flaming. Conflict resolution, which requires a negotiated meaning and thus is highly interactive, only works in a mediated environment in which the interaction is high or the channels for different levels of communication are rich. In both cases time is of the essence. When time is not a critical factor, deliberation and specificity of meaning can be enhanced through mediated, particularly textual, communication. Today's teleconferences, chat lines on Internet Relay Chat (IRC), and in object-oriented electronic spaces such as MOOs, provide rapid feedback and interaction that approaches the speed and rich overlays of meaning found in face-to-face conversations. Like mediated communication, in general, then, the isolating aspect of textual communication in cyberspace has advantages as well.

Fragmenting? Among the analysts of contemporary life, Kenneth Gergen (1991), a psychologist and postmodernist, sees the participation of individual selves in the larger mediated culture as one in which the sense of self is both overwhelmed by increased contacts and diffused into a multitude of relationships:

> Through the technologies of the century, the number and variety of relationships in which we are engaged, potential frequency of contact, expressed intensity of relationship, and endurance through time all are steadily increasing. As this increase becomes extreme we reach a state of social saturation. (p. 61)

The technologically created social context is one of saturation and results not in fragmentation—as one might suppose—but in building different kinds of community:

> In this context, it may be said that the technologies of social saturation actually contribute to the kind of social interdependence we call community. They enable new communities to form wherever communication links can be made—among truckers on CB radios, businessmen on electronic mail, hackers with home modems, and so on. New potentials for interdependence are a significant by-

> product of the socially saturated world. At the same time, however, with each new potential for symbolic connection, the traditional face-to-face community loses its coherence and its significance in the life of its participants. For the participants are no longer possessions of the local community only, or even primarily, rooted in the local soil. (p. 215)

If Gergen (1991) is right, we could be creating an information society in which interaction takes place increasingly by media punctuated by face-to-face meetings such as conventions. What are perceived to be fragmenting social practices may in fact be results of the shifting of social relationships engendered by the highly mobile, mediated environment in which our lives and work are increasingly built. Even if we work at home, our work is liable to be somewhere else via communication technologies. Thus, we find individuals who have been mobile, rootless, and without a sense of what Meyrowitz (1985) would call "place," attaching themselves to the interactive media of cyberspace for the sense of belonging to the society that they find being constructed there.

Addiction to media can mean different things. *Addiction* may be the easy term that explains the experience to those not having it. Eschewing face-to-face or other mediated interaction in favor of interaction in cyberspace is the basic behavior. Some addiction may be attributed to the tendencies of some personalities to escape emotional issues associated with real-world demands. One plausible reason for the reported adoption of a (usually) new medium to the exclusion of other forms of social intercourse is the easy access to new relationships that were once unavailable. As Sherry Turkle (1984) has so ably pointed out in her classic study, *The Second Self*, individuals may see in an object a reflection of themselves, by working to master the object they work on transforming their own personality. The functioning of Turkle's concept is not unlike Cooley's (1964) "Looking Glass Self" alluded to earlier. If we want to change, we commit ourselves to forming an identity online by adjusting to what garners positive feedback from others. A second plausibility for fixing attention on a new group of people with whom one can identify is that the interactions can be very supportive and gratifying, especially if one feels like the proverbial "ugly duckling." Many communities that proliferate in cyberspace provide support that individuals would not find in the limited acquaintances of their own family, work group, or home community. For those having a satisfying experience online, accepting the term *addiction* may be easier than explaining to close family members that they are the source of the dissatisfaction. In addition, as sociologists Bellah, Madsen, Sullivan, Swidler, and Tipton (1985) have explained, most educated individuals have moved up and out of their home community, away from all the sources of support—and restraint—that had provided them with a sense of belonging to a community. Third, America has a long history of investing dreams for a new beginning, for utopia, in new communication technologies, especially since the telegraph (Carey, 1989; Czitrom, 1982; Marx, 1964; McLuhan, 1964). For those faced by barriers of language, accent, skin color, communication and mobility handicaps, appearance, or a lack of social graces—usually the provenance of the middle and upper classes—interactive media are a haven promising a new chance to partake of the American dream.

Then too, just as we call a new technology and the uses to which it is put by names based on previous experience—"horseless carriages" is my favorite—so we find terms such as *addiction* reflective of our past and current concerns and an easy descriptor for what we do not understand except by its grasp on the attention of others. When the term *addiction* is applied to a series of new technologies—as has been done to telephones, television, video games, and computers—to describe something that is clearly not physiological yet difficult to withdraw from, perhaps we ought to suspect that the term masks something else. We need to look more deeply for the roots of the habits. Addiction comes from great need. In physical addiction to pharmaceuticals, the drug is the means to a feeling of well-being, and withdrawal is painful because of a chemical relationship with the drug. In online *addiction*, the feelings of well-being come from interacting with other humans. Habituation is to playful interaction and self-concept building in an atmosphere of acceptance. Slipping away to cyberspace is easy; it is always there. Personal risk comes only from the emotional investment—sometimes mistakenly called *addiction*—that is not easily given up. Withdrawal from online relationships is like leaving friends and lovers. The relationships are real. Leaving a relationship in cyberspace can be as devastating as in real life due to the emotional engagement.

Relationships formed online do not always remain in cyberspace. As intimacy and trust develop out of mutual disclosure of motivations and needs, the desire to love and care for newfound friends and lovers increases the need to meet face to face. Some portion of all online socializing involves plans for meeting privately and in groups. To call the relationships made online "Do-it-yourself dating" would be to overlook the importance of learning how people describe themselves in word play, what people like and dislike, and what they have done before meeting them; quite the reverse of singles bars and video dating services. Avodah Offit, a New York psychiatrist and sex therapist, bought her first personal computer in the late 1970s and was introduced to e-mail in 1987. Her novel, *Virtual Love*, is written as e-mail correspondence between two psychiatrists and details the immediacy and power that e-mail brings to written communication and intimate relationships (Lohr, 1994). We should all be so addicted!

Speaking of other media, compared to the shared meanings of mass media such as television, radio, films, books, newspapers, and magazines, virtual communities are characterized by participants who both create the topics and form the audience. As such they are less subject to manipulation by professional program producers and schedulers. Although discussion is public on line, reading is private. Although information is shared it can be public or private; the individual is in control of disclosure, thus protecting privacy. Unlike parasocial relationships formed between audiences and performer personalities, cyberfolk really converse with and get to know each other. In that respect, cyberspace communication is more like letter writing and phone calls: intimate, subject to personal reflection and editing, and controlled disclosure and identity building by the roles taken on. Unlike the mass media in which the audience has little role discretion as viewers, online interactors can adopt a variety of roles as they sort themselves out along lines that emerge as important vis-à-vis others in the task of constructing communities and society. I cannot help but find the use of interaction for the creation of self-concept and group identity in the face of technological transformation as anything other than healthy.

REFERENCES

Allen, T.B. (1988, September). Bulletin boards of the 21st century are coming of age. *Smithsonian*, pp. 83-93.

Bales, R.F. (1950). A set of categories for the analysis of small group interaction. *American Sociological Review, 15*, 257-263.

Bellah, R.N., Madsen, R., Sullivan, W.M., Swidler, A., & Tipton, S.M. (1985). *Habits of the heart: Individualism and commitment in American life*. New York: Harper & Row.

Benedikt, M. (1991). Cyberspace: Some proposals. In M. Benedikt (Ed.), *Cyberspace: First steps* (pp. 119-224). Cambridge, MA: MIT Press.

Carey, J. (1989). *Communication as culture: Essays on media and society*. Boston: Unwin Hyman.

Cooley, C.H. (1964). *Human nature and the social order*. New York: Schocken.

Cushman, D.P., & Cahn, D. (1985). *Communication in interpersonal relationships*. Albany: State University of New York Press.

Czitrom, D.J. (1982). *Media and the American mind*. Chapel Hill: University of North Carolina Press.

Gergen, K.J. (1991). *The saturated self: Dilemmas of identity in contemporary life*. New York: Basic Books.

Goffman, E. (1959). *The presentation of self in everyday reality*. Garden City, NY: Doubleday Anchor Books.

Hiemstra, G. (1982). Teleconferencing, concern for face, and organizational culture. In M. Burgoon (Ed.), *Communication yearbook* (Vol. 6, pp. 874-904). Beverly Hills, CA: Sage.

Hiltz, S.R., & Turoff, M.(1978). *The network nation: Human communication via computer*. Reading, MA: Addison-Wesley.

Kiesler, S., Siegel, J., & McGuire, T.W. (1984, October). Social psychological aspects of computer-mediated communication. *American Psychologist, 39*(10), 1123-1134.

Lohr, S. (1994, August 28). Therapy on a virtual couch. *The New York Times*, p. F7.

Marvin, C. (1988). *When old technologies were new: Thinking about electric communication in the late nineteenth century*. New York: Oxford University Press.

Marx, L. (1964). *The machine in the garden.* New York: Oxford University Press.
McLuhan, M. (1964). *Understanding media: The extensions of man.* New York: New American Library.
Mead, G.H. (1934). *Mind, self, and society.* Chicago: University of Chicago Press.
Meyrowitz, J. (1985). N*o sense of place: The impact of electronic media on social behavior.* New York: Oxford University Press.
Michalski, J. (1993, June 21). Community, part I. *Release 1.0,* pp. 6, 15-16.
Reid, E.M. (1992,). Electropolis: Communication and community on internet relay chat. *Intertek, 3.3,* 7-13.
Rheingold, H. (1991). *Virtual reality.* New York: Summit Books.
Rheingold, H. (1993). *The virtual community: Homesteading on the electronic frontier.* Reading, MA: Addison-Wesley.
Rice, R.E. (1980). Impacts of organizational and interpersonal computer-mediated communication. *Annual Review of Information Science and Technology, 15,* 221-249.
Rice, R.E., & Love, G. (1987). Electronic emotion: Socioemotional content in a computer-mediated communication network. *Communication Research, 14*(1), 85-108
Sproull, L., & Kiesler, S. (1991). *Connections: New ways of working in the networked organization.* Cambridge, MA: MIT Press.
Steinert-Threlkeld, T. (1993, January 23). *Dallas Morning News.* p. F1.
Steinfield, C. (1986). Computer-mediated communication in an organizational setting: Explaining task-related and socioemotional uses. In M.L. McLaughlin (Ed.), *Communication yearbook* (Vol. 9, pp. 777-804). Beverly Hills, CA: Sage.
Stone, A.R.(1991). Will the real body please stand up? Boundary stories about virtual cultures. In M. Benedikt (Ed.), *Cyberspace: First steps* (pp. 81-118). Cambridge, MA: The MIT Press.
Thompsen, P.A. (1993, February). *A social-influence model of flaming in computer-mediated communication.* Paper presented to the Western States Communication Association, Albuquerque, NM.
Turkle, S. (1984). *The second self: Computers and the human spirit.* New York: Simon & Schuster.

◇◇◇◇ 22

Forgetting the Body: Cybersex and Identity

Mark Lipton

However cerebral and Platonic our conceptions of cyberspace may be, it is a locus of human activity and is therefore influenced by the fact that we are biological and sexual beings. It is inevitable that social interaction in cyberspace includes the romantic and the libidinous. One of the earliest commercial uses of computer technology was for dating services and matchmaking, and computer-mediated communication simply eliminates the middleman; electronic versions of personal ads are also available to interested individuals. Online live chats include "sex talk" or "hot chats," extensions of telephone sex and party lines, whereas new forms of digitized and computer-programmed pornography are available though a variety of sources. Along with sex, the legal and moral issues surrounding sexuality, including sexual harassment and molestation, are imported into cyberspace. At the same time, others point to a cybersexual future based on virtual reality and "teledildonics." In this chapter, Lipton surveys the various forms of sexually oriented content associated with cyberspace, warning that we may be creating a hedonistic "global bath-house"; he also points to a possible epistemological shift that favors tactility and the notion that "feeling is believing." The significance of these profane aspects of computing transcends content, Lipton goes on to argue, potentially altering the social construction of gender, sexuality, and identity. Cybersex changes our cultural conceptions of the body, undermining our assumptions about its naturalness and stability in favor of a technological construct that he refers to as the "community body." Noting that our systems of communication and signification depend on biologically based bodies, he also warns that cybersex may be entropic, that it may result in a breakdown of meaning and cultural coherence. Other than in this section of the book, discussions of sex and the body can also be found in Michael P. Beaubien's analysis of cyber-rape in Chapter 12, Sue Barnes's study of self and ecology in cyberspace in Chapter 13, and Elizabeth Weiss's arguments concerning the virtual health club in Chapter 14; see also Gary Gumpert and Susan J. Drucker's work on cyberspace as a social environment in Chapter 1, and Herbert Zettl's analysis of the aesthetics of virtual reality in Chapter 5.

> We have modified our environments so radically that we must now modify ourselves in order to exist in this new environment. We can no longer live in the old one. Progress imposes not only new possibilities for the future but new restrictions.
>
> —Norbert Wiener, *The Human Use of Human Beings* (1954)

> "So long as you can forget your body you are happy," said Lady Bennerley. "And the moment you begin to be aware of your body, you are wretched. So, if civilization is any good, it has to help us to forget our bodies, and then time passes happily without our knowing it."
>
> —D.H. Lawrence, *Lady Chatterley's Lover* (1928)

> Nature kicks back.
>
> —Felix Guattari, "The Three Ecologies" (1989)

Cyberspace, simply put, is a virtual "space" where humans engage each other via electronic technology—that is, when they are not fully co-present with each other in a shared spatial context. The creation of a virtual "space" is one example of progress imposing modifications on our environment. And typically, excitement flourishes as cyberspace is regarded as the newest human frontier. After all, cyberspace is continually expanding as rapidly developing computer technology creates dozens of increasingly strange "spaces," where humans, or their abstracted representations, encounter one another and nonpresent "objects" in ways that would have been unimaginable even 20 years ago. In many respects, electronically generated cyberspace amplifies entropy—the natural tendency of all orderly systems to move toward a state of disorder. It does so because cyberspace challenges, undermines, and ultimately throws into disorder all the "rules" that govern human interaction in the "real" spaces that we have shared for some 20 million years. And nowhere does cyberspace generate more entropy, more chaos, than in that most fundamental arena where humans have until now engaged each other "in the flesh"—the realm of sexual relations. My objective in this chapter is to address the ways in which cyberspace generates disorder in the realm of what may broadly be called "sex."

By *sex* I mean to include all things people understand as sexual. Freud (1920/1966) uses the word in a similar manner, including in its meanings "something which combines a reference to the contrast between the sexes, to the search for pleasure, to the reproductive function and to the characteristic of something that is improper and must be kept a secret" (p. 376). I also include in the broad meaning of sex its reference to such things as differences in gender identity, the social and behavioral roles ascribed to biological males and females, and the varieties of sexual behaviors and preferences in humans—including those Freud called "perverse people" (p. 377).

Cyberspace is not, of course, the first technological development to affect sexual conceptions, values, and behavior. Many earlier technologies have altered the social and psychological meanings of sex simply by making it more visible. In 1877, for example, Eadweard Muybridge's photographic representations shifted from moving horses to naked male and female bodies, and, as Williams (1989) writes, "If Muybridge's first audiences came simply to learn the new truths of bodily motion, they stayed to see more because this new knowledge was also infused with an unsuspected visual pleasure" (p. 39). Just how powerful that "visual pleasure" is may be seen in the unflagging demand for more, and more varied, visual representations of human sexuality and sexual behavior. In 1992 alone, sales and rentals of "adult" videos generated some 1.6 billion dollars, and Madonna's *Sex* sold out its half-million-copy print run in a matter of days (Desmarais, 1993).

The connection between sex and profit is, of course, an ancient one, and the realization that sex sells accounts for much of the sexually oriented content of television, film, and magazines. As Ross (1989) observes in his analysis of the relationship between such media and sex, sexually explicit content "aim[s] at the market-targeted body (usually male) in ways which are likely to excite that body, and the popularity of this or that film or magazine is evidence of its success" (pp. 195-196). Given the selling power of sex, it comes as no surprise that sexually oriented material should also come to occupy a significant portion of the interactive "spaces" created by our newer, computer-mediated technologies: Connecting cyberspace with sex is a sure way to populate the circuits.

I use the term *cybersex* in its narrow sense, in the first part of this chapter, to refer to the various ways in which users of computer-mediated interactive technologies employ sexually oriented content to excite the eye and the ear and, through them, the sexual pleasure centers of the body. But there is more to sex than meets the eye—or the ear, the hand, and the rest of the sensory apparatus that gives us sexual pleasure. In the second part of this chapter, therefore, I use *cybersex* in its broader meaning to refer to the implications of cyberspace technologies for the ways in which we define and identify ourselves and others, and relate to one another, through our bodies.

CYBERSEX AS CONTENT: SEXTALK, CYBERPORN, AND TELEDILDONICS

One of the distinguishing features of human beings—some would say *the* distinguishing feature—is our ability to store our experiences and evoke them again inside ourselves through the agency of words. Because words and grammatical rules allow us, moreover, to take experience apart and recombine it in novel ways, language also gives us the capacity to evoke in ourselves experiences we have not had but can in this way imagine. Through our capacity to imagine, we can excite in ourselves strong sensory feelings—those associated with awe, dread, and terror, but also those associated with calm, joy, and intense pleasure. It is not surprising to find in a creature with such capacities, therefore, that language should play a significant role in evoking and mediating sensual and sexual feeling.

The use of words—thought, spoken, or written—to excite and modify sexual feeling in oneself and in others long predates the development of computer technology. Erotic (or obscene) letters are earlier examples of "telesex" communications that rely on the word to excite the mind and body sexually, and "sextalk" is the extension of these communications into cyberspace.

Basically, *sextalk* is any kind of electronically mediated conversation that has as its major objective the sexual arousal of one or more of the participants (see, e.g., Gumpert, 1987). Phone sex and what are called "hot chats" online are examples. Just as there are specialized phone-sex 900 numbers that you can call to talk to the person of your fantasy—or rather, to a professional paid to *simulate* the person of your fantasy—there are bulletin board systems that you can call with your modem and computer to chat with other "real" people, that is, people not paid to simulate your fantasy but presumably engaged in pursuing their own sexual ends in the conversation. There are many national and international bulletin boards that vary in the range of services they provide. ECHO (East Coast Hangout) and The Well (Whole Earth 'Lectronic Link) are examples of multiple-use bulletin board systems that offer their subscribers entry into many different kinds of conversations, only some of which are "hot chats." Also called *compusex, hot chats* have been described as "lascivious on-line banter, [which] if done correctly, leads to one-handed typing, resulting in a digitally-induced climax" (Robinson & Tamosaitis, 1993, p. 154). Other bulletin board systems, like Penthouse Online or the Pleasure Dome, are specifically devoted to sex. These bulletin board systems feature hot chats with real people, but also allow the user to download pornography—sexually explicit images or photographs either of other users or of popular models. Features such as downloading pornography, however, move beyond "sextalk." They rely on symbols and technologies that are image-driven rather than word-driven, and their products fall into a second category of cybersex "contents": what is widely called *cyberporn.*

In most versions of cyberporn, the user interacts electronically with a computer program that has constructed a fantasy scenario subject to manipulation by the viewer. For the most part, cyberporn consists of erotic pictures and videos and "dirty" computer games. *Softporn Adventure* (1980), a text-based game in which the object was to "score" three times, and *Leisure Suit Larry in the Land of the Lounge Lizards* (1984), an updated version of the same game with animated graphics, additional script, music, and Larry (the "dork" who tries to get laid), were early examples of soft cyberpornography available on floppy disk. These were followed, in the late 1980s, by *MacPlaymate*, which offered more graphic representations and more sophisticated programming, capable of responding to a larger number of user manipulations. In this game, the user disrobes the on-screen woman, Maxie, and then, by using adult sex toys, the user helps Maxie reach climax, complete with cries of pleasure. The greater technical and sexual sophistication of *MacPlaymate* was followed by the development of new software for use with CD-ROM. CD-ROM can store more information than standard fixed and floppy disks (about 200 pictures versus one or two) and today is a necessary piece of hardware for cyberporn users because adult videos and high-resolution graphics require huge amounts of disk space. *Virtual Valerie*, the first erotic computer "game" widely available on CD-ROM, went a step beyond the virtual Maxie and brought cyberporn software into the open and onto the pages of mainstream computer magazines, spurring demand for additional erotic CD-ROM software.

With its enhanced ability to store and access data, CD-ROM is a key part of the technology needed for the projected future of cybersex, that is, for what some have called *teledildonics*: virtual sexual experience that occurs through and in virtual reality. With respect to technology, teledildonics would require adding electronically produced tactile stimulations (if it activates nerve endings in the body) or mental *simulations* (if it operates directly on pleasure centers in the brain) to the complex of existing technologies that allow us to "virtually" see, hear, and manipulate computer-generated representations of others and objects. The complex technologies and interfaces that would be required have not yet been developed, but they have long been imagined—at first rather crudely, as in such futuristic popular films as *Barbarella* (1968), in which the sexy 41st-century space adventurer overloads an orgasm machine, and Woody Allen's *Sleeper* (1973), with its images of vibrating eggs and an orgasmatron. However, more recent filmic visions of cybersex in virtual reality, notably *Lawnmower Man* (1992) and *Wild Palms* (1993), have narrowed the gap between technologies merely imagined and those now being actively pursued in hardware and software laboratories. It is increasingly difficult to tell how much of teledildonics is still imaginary and how much is approaching reality. In *Virtual Reality* (1991), Rheingold gives us this projection of the next step in cybersex:

> Before you climb into a suitably padded chamber and put on your 3D glasses, you slip into a lightweight . . . bodysuit. . . . Embedded in the inner surface of the suit, using a technology that does not yet exist, is an array of intelligent sensor-

> effectors . . . that can receive and transmit a realistic sense of tactile presence (p. 346)

Teledildonics, or virtual sex, requires more than the wearing of a technologically advanced bodysuit called smart skin. It also requires virtual reality software that allows the participant to alter the virtual representations of his or her own body. Thus, one might assume the guise of a favorite sex symbol or create for oneself additional or different body parts to experience. As Robinson and Tamosaitis (1993) put it: "The possibilities are limited only by your imagination. The program makes the rules, and you choose the program" (p. 243). Rushkoff (1994) puts it somewhat differently in recounting how teledildonics was described to him:

> It would go like this: you either screw your computer, or screw someone else by modem. If you do your computer, you just call some girl out of its memory. Your cyber suit'll jack you off. If you do it the phone-sex way, the girl—or guy or anything out there, actually—there could be a guy who's [sic] virtual identity is a girl or a spider even. (p. 46)

In a 1990 article published in *Mondo 2000* (a publication that describes itself as the "guide to cyberlife"), Rheingold claimed that "teledildonics is inevitable given the rate of progress in the enabling technologies of shape-memory alloys, fiber-optics, and super-computing" (p. 54). Teledildonics, he predicted later (1991), is not likely to be next year's fad. But it will be, in his judgment, "an early-to-mid-twenty-first-century technology" (p. 347).

FORMING THE COMMUNITY BODY

Taking Rheingold's vision as the ultimate possibility, it becomes appropriate to discuss cybersex in its broader meaning. Cybersex is more than sexually oriented content in that the technology of teledildonics recontextualizes sexually oriented content. With teledildonics, an individual projects a virtual body into a virtual space and has intimate contact with other virtual bodies. What sexual pleasure will become, and how this sexual pleasure will simulate and stimulate the body, will very much depend on cybersex technology. This technology, then, is a radical modification of the *environments* in which humans interact, but as Wiener points out, humans must modify *themselves* if they are to live in such new environments. Thus, the broader implications of "cybersex" include human self-transformation. Modifications must begin when one attempts to define and identify oneself and others and continue as individuals relate to one another through the body. For example, when participants represent their virtual body, the means of defining oneself changes from an unconscious process to a conscious action. The individual can now modify the signs that represent a human body, changing how one identifies oneself and thus how one identifies others. In reality, my body is represented by its physical characteristics, and all people will unconsciously read my body as a human body. But with cybersex, I have the power to change how my body is represented; thus, I have conscious control over how I identify myself not only to others, but to myself.

Such modifications of ourselves are necessary in that developing cyberspace technologies aim to create a fantastic space that McLuhan (1964) called the "global village." Cyberspace is fostering a democratization of information systems, granting accessibility to all people and thus equality for all peoples (assuming, of course, one can afford the technology). Given the speed at which this technology is being developed, it is not too difficult to imagine a world in which we all really are connected on a regular basis. Phone companies, for example, are continually reminding us how close we are (or should be) to each other. And if cybersex technologies are more advanced then the telephone, then we are indeed moving closer to a global village. There is no question about the appropriateness of the word *global* because cyberspace aims at a global public. Problems arise, however, when the word *village* is used to describe the kinds of human interaction involved in the social atmosphere of cybersex. Rather, a more fitting metaphor for cybersex would be that of a *global bathhouse*, in which interaction is driven primarily by the need for pleasure. And, more importantly, although cybersex technology certainly brings us closer together, in many ways it also drives us further away from those symbolic constructions by which we define ourselves. In the real world, there are codes on which I rely in constructing my identity. My surname is an example of one such code. Where I come from, what I do, and where I live are other examples that inform my sense of self. In other words, identity used to be defined on the basis of community, with respect to family, occupation, religion, or even neighborhood. But cybersex technology removes us from our local community, pushing us into a single orgiastic "community body."

The "community body" may be a more revealing metaphor than the global village in that it takes into account two significant issues. One issue is that chaotic identities are promoted when neither bodies nor communities are situated in time and space. When there are no separate communities to shape our identities, the result is a diffused ideology so shared that individuals become indistinguishable members of a "mass society." When each body is represented as anatomically unique, I am unable to identify with other participants based on my preconceptions of their bodies or their communities, and, in turn, no one is able to identify with me. Too much individuality, minus any anchoring affiliations, and there is no meaningful identity, only white noise. A second significant issue is that the community body acknowledges the close relationship between the technology and the body. Signification or meaning can only be made when the body is coded, transmitted, and received by technology. Cybersex technology, then, will control bodies and how they signify meaning. As a result, the collection of signifieds that we unconsciously read as the body in the real world will inevitably be meaningless within cyberspace. In other words, everything from your hair color to your ethnic heritage can be erased from your virtual identity unless it is coded specifically for cybersex technology. And although simpler bodily codes such as hair color may be represented in cybersex, more complicated codes of community such as ethnic specificity will be more difficult to retain and more easily omitted. Although you may have the option to code your skin tone black, this signifier cannot be related to any community when others have purple skin or paisley skin. Symbolic constructions of identity cannot be based on community in cyberspace if, for example, I present a hairy spider as my virtual body. Thus all participants must rely on cybersex technology, rather than community, to determine what the virtual body signifies.

The technology of cybersex, then, defines the community body, and as the technology further develops, our processes of signification will develop in tandem. If my virtual body is represented as a spider, how will others be able to interpret my virtual representation as something meaningful when who I am is erased in the process of signification? The community body decenters the subject, forcing a reexamination of those aspects of identity at greatest risk of becoming more entropic in cyberspace: the self, the body, and conceptions of gender and identity with respect to oneself and others.

CYBERSEX, THE SELF, AND THE OTHER

Cyberspace causes people's positions to shift both physically and metaphysically. As Poster (1990) explains: "We are being changed from 'arborial' beings, rooted in time and space, to 'rhizomic' nomads who daily wander at will . . . across the globe, and even beyond it through communications satellites, without necessarily moving our bodies at all" (p. 15). And Wiener (1954) suggests that "to see and to give commands to the whole world is almost the same as being everywhere" (p. 97). Both these views posit a shift from the diachronic to the synchronic: with cyberspace, our sense of time and space shifts from the Western, linear historical framework to an instantaneous, multifaceted simultaneity of experience focusing on the present moment, what Wiener means by "being everywhere." And when, as an individual, I have the capacity to be everywhere simultaneously, where I am and who I am are up for grabs. Therefore, by privileging the "rhizomic" or synchronic, that is, allowing us to be everywhere at the same point in time, cyberspace actually forces the markings of an individual's personal history to be mapped differently.

This semiotic shift has awesome implications as an individual develops a concept of self. Mead (1962) views the self as "something which has a development; it is not initially there, at birth, but arises in the process of social experience and activity, that is, develops in the given individual as a result of his relation to that process as a whole and to other individuals within that process" (p. 135). Thus, according to Mead, the self is, in effect, the individual's ability to take the attitude of an other and to act toward him- or herself as does that other (p. 171). One might say that identity is additive and growth continuous: The person I am today may or may not be the person I will be in five years. In part, the person I become, the identity I select, will be based on those other people in my life with whom I surround myself. Additive identity and continuous growth are two related ideas, which offline are limited by community and viewed diachronically. For example, I developed an initial sense of self and identity by responding to my mother. By internalizing her responses, I was able to identify myself as her son and respond accordingly.

When the construction of the self happens online in cyberspace, as is occurring at an increasingly rapid rate, taking the attitude of the other becomes awfully complex. It is not just me and my mom anymore. But it is also not just me and my family, or me and my community. Without fixed and distinct communities, the range of potential interactions becomes infinite. There are, after all, so many "others," so many unique identities to choose from. And, of equal importance, in a synchronic, ahistorical framework, each person one meets must be viewed as foreign, as "other." When the codes that situate where and who one is are no longer based on the Western diachronic perspective, individuals must always present themselves as others because there are no past referents on which to rely in constructing identities. With cybersex, I do not know who my partners really are beyond my fantasy and theirs. For instance, people alter their gender and/or sexuality on the Internet to see how a partner's responses may change their experience. Consequently, there will be no fixed self, but multiple selves, and identity will be further fragmented with each interaction in cyberspace. If I change my gender for cybersex, for example, I have to rely on my partner's responses to know what to say and how to say it. What I say changes each time I interact with someone because there is no single fixed (dominant) response to steer my identity, or my perception of my partner's identity, in any specific direction.

When there are no fixed responses to steer our identities, constructions of the self will change. Online identities in cyberspace offer the individual more possibilities: Identity becomes fragmented as we change who we are in a multiplicity of ways. How we construct and reconstruct the self very much depends on the increasing number of different people we meet and how they respond to us. If one is to be a satisfied participant in the community body, multiple selves are not only possible, but necessary, inevitably dictated by the technology. Multiple selves and fragmented identities are two key patterns in cyberspace, and both patterns rely on the notion of a constructed body.

THE BODY IN CYBERSEX: FREE, FLOATING, DISAPPEARING

In 1928, when D.H. Lawrence described Lady Bennerley's position on a "good civilization," forgetting the body began with an emancipation from the reproductive function, leaving more "room for fun" (p. 77). Lawrence described a character who sees the body not as a tool, but as an obstacle; the desire to transcend the body predates cybersex technology. We should not be surprised, then, that producers of cybersex technology also aim to transcend the body. In *Cyberspace: First Steps*, Stone (1991) suggests that "the discourse of visionary virtual world builders is rife with images of imaginal bodies, freed from the constraints that flesh imposes. Cyberspace developers foresee a time when they will be able to forget about the body" (p. 113). The way to forget about the body in cybersex is to imagine a virtual body.

Teledildonic technology requires the participants to construct an imaginary body in three significant ways. First, all participants must input some virtual representation of their own bodies, reconstructing the body for virtual reality and recoding it for cybersex technology. This technology allows the body to be transformed: We are able to alter physical representations of the human body to appear more (or less) attractive to others. Software programs yet to be developed will allow the body to be represented as nonhuman, that is, as other living and nonliving entities. Because teledildonics software enables such mutations of the body, the way the body is coded becomes characteristically atypical: Every virtual body is different each time. Second, the body that one chooses to present relies on the quality of a partners' hardware. Even if I present my real body without alteration, my body must still be encoded, transmitted, and received before it can be decoded. Thus, how other participants view my body very much depends on the quality of their receivers. The most sophisticated receivers, however, are nevertheless susceptible to noise or interference, and the likelihood that all cybersex technology will be able to encode and decode information in exactly the same way seems remote. And third, virtual bodies destabilize and disorganize the decoding process. When a body continually mutates, it relinquishes control of how it is perceived. When I know nothing about the people with whom I interact, they may decode my body in ways I do not intend. Because perception becomes consciously different and the decoding process confusing, the body becomes increasingly imaginary. As a result of these three elements, in cybersex one never knows what others really look like. In fact, one can safely assume that the bodies people present are *not* their real bodies. Therefore, the virtual, imaginary body offers the possibility of forgetting about the real body.

When the imaginary body contacts other imaginary bodies, the real human body can no longer be a set signifier, a standard point of reference (in that everyone recognizes what constitutes a human body). But when teledildonics allows us to manipulate our virtual bodies, the standard human body becomes just one manifestation in a sea of endless possibilities. Even though the dominant notion of the body may not change, what it signifies probably will. People with disabilities, for example, may be treated with greater equality when physical differences are not regarded as impairments. It is important to recognize, however, that bodies are not just signifiers of meaning, but codes on which we rely in comprehending that which is contained within the body and that which emanates from the body; for instance, learned responses and community. This is, in part, what Butler (1990) means when she describes the body "not as a ready surface awaiting signification, but as a set of boundaries, individual and social, politically signified and maintained" (p. 33). As the set of codes used to recognize and understand another body changes, those elements that function as a result of the body become more complex. As our information machines become capable of coding bodily sensations, for example, pleasure and eroticism will begin to take on very different meanings.

To be a satisfied participant will require a strong sensual relationship between body and technology. When, as Rheingold (1990) suggests "you can run your cheek over (virtual) satin and feel the difference when you encounter (virtual) human flesh" (p. 52), it becomes difficult to tell the difference between the technological and the biological. Haraway (1991) illustrates this idea in "A Cyborg Manifesto":

> Late twentieth-century machines have made thoroughly ambiguous the difference between natural and artificial, mind and body, self-developing and externally designed, and many other distinctions that used to apply to organisms and machines. Our machines are disturbingly lively, and we ourselves frighteningly inert. (p. 152)

As cyborgs, we must expect changes in how the body will function and signify meaning as we adapt to the new environment of cybersex. It will therefore become increasingly important yet increasing difficult to recognize one another. When the body is a collection of floating signifiers, dominant notions of the body such as gender wil. change, remaking meaning.

GENDER AND IDENTITY, IN SELF AND OTHER

Freud (1933/1965) illustrates how sex is one of the first characteristics used to identify individuals. As he put it: "When you meet a human being, the first distinction you make is 'male or female?' and you are accustomed to make the distinction with unhesitating certainty" (p. 141). In other words, gender is the primary code used to identify both the self and the other by recognizing ither similarity or difference. Moreover, gender identity influences almost all dis fundamentally structuring the ways we make meaning. But when the physical body to be identified, or when a virtual body can be manipul transformed at will, the codes that structure the meanings we make of take on new functions. When the body no longer explicitly represents the actual individual, as in cybersex, the arbitrariness of biological differences becomes apparent. Butler (1990) raises such questions when she asks:

> Can we refer to a "given" sex or a "given" gender without first inquiring into how sex and/or gender is given, through what means? And what is "sex" anyway? Is it natural, anatomical, chromosomal, or hormonal, and how is a feminist critic to assess the scientific discourses which purport to establish such "facts" for us? (pp. 6-7)

These are key questions in cyberspace, for the technology being developed for cybersex immediately forces a reformulation of gender: Sex no longer defines the body. Dominant notions, such as the biological codes of sex and gender, will no longer serve to situate the body in developing cyberspace technologies. As a result, it becomes increasingly easier to think of gender, gender roles, and even sex as social constructions.

Meyrowitz (1985), for example, explains the role electronic media play in the merging of masculinity and femininity: "The changes in conceptions of gender roles may have something to do with the merging of male and female information-systems through the widespread use of electronic media" (p. 188). For Meyrowitz, both media and physical places are nothing more than information systems. In his view, as barriers that separate gender roles break down, androgynic possibilities become more apparent. Unfortunately, Meyrowitz's discussion of gender roles does not question the scientific discourse of sex and gender, and, furthermore, he limits his discussion of electronic media to the visual representations of television. Had Meyrowitz foreseen later developments, surely he would have extended his analysis of androgyny beyond gender roles and would have recognized the merging not only of roles, but of actual genders. Cybersex erases gender as the key code used for identifying both the self and the other. Instead, gender becomes one of many malleable codes for constructing personal narratives. What it means to be a man or a woman will no longer be relevant when people accept such inscriptions as mere social constructions, obsolete patterns of identification.

This may be difficult to imagine, but we can look at those forms of cybersex that already exist to see how the codes of sex and gender are being manipulated. According to an article in *Mondo 2000*, the most commonly asked question during online discussions is "MorF?" (Petrek & St. Jude, 1992, p. 114). This question provides a clear illustration of how gender fragments as a key code in identity. Literally, "MorF?" is an abbreviation for the question "male or female?" But figuratively, "MorF?" plays on the pronunciation of this abbreviation: *morph* refers to constructed, imaginary, changeable bodies. It is possible that gender will further fragment, as cybersex technology becomes more advanced. With teledildonics, for example, a gender-related query like "MorF?" seems meaningless. Such a question relies on technologies that emphasize the eye as the primary sensory organ, such as the computer screen. When the focus shifts from the visual perspective to the acute sense of touch, gendered inscriptions will be further fragmented. For example, most people will look away when receiving a medical injection. The visual tends to overshadow the tactile, and by not looking at the needle, the injection seems less painful. When tactile sensitivity begins to rival the visual, looking away is no longer an option: Welcome to a world in which feeling is believing. In such a world, the biological distinctions of sex and gender are obsolete.

CONCLUSION: GLOBAL VILLAGE OR GLOBAL BATH HOUSE?

When sex and gender are not sufficient codes of the body, the body must signify meaning in new ways. The imaginary body is, in part, the solution offered by the producers of cybersex technology. But when the body is reconstructed as imaginary, the identity of the self is granted additional freedom, further removing the codes of the self and the body from a set of signifiers that are globally understood to a set of signifiers that must be globally constructed. In cyberspace, if you cannot decode my body as either male or female, then you must decide which signifier to read first out of the many possibilities. And when the context of the situation, that is, the virtual environment, gives you no hints as to where to begin, your decision will be highly entropic. In more than one sense, you will be fumbling alone in the dark. Like a customer at a bath house, you will have a few brief moments to decide whether to permit some other virtual body to stimulate your body. And when tactile sensitivity is stronger than visual perception, how another "feels" will be much more important than what he or she or it looks like.

How meaning will be reconstructed is still very unclear, especially, it seems to the producers of cyberspace technology. Although they consider "imaginal bodies, freed from the constraints that flesh imposes" (Stone, 1991, p. 113) to be an exciting new direction, they need also to understand that transcending the body and altering the dimensions of community will not occur without effects. Just as Wiener (1954) warns that new possibilities come with new restrictions, restrictions too often overlooked, Guattari (1989) illustrates the seriousness of the potential consequences. He points out that "nature kicks back" (p. 17), referring to the "technico-scientific power of humanity" exemplified in the Chernobyl and AIDS crises. It is possible that natural revolutions against technological developments such as teledildonics will occur, and we should begin to consider how to deal with such occurrences. Guattari (1989) suggests that:

> If we are to orient the sciences and technology toward more human goals, we clearly need collective management and control—not blind reliance on technocrats in the state apparatuses, in the hope that they will control developments and minimize risks in fields largely dominated by the pursuit of profit. (p. 17)

How cybersex and cyberspace ought to be managed and controlled are issues that urgently need to be addressed, and further research would surely help orient our attention to these issues. As we are propelled into the future, we must do our best to ensure that the meanings constructed in our world do not change our global village into a virtual bath house.

REFERENCES

Butler, J. (1990). *Gender trouble: Feminism and the subversion of identity.* New York: Routledge.

Desmarais, N. (1993, October). Neuromimesis, cyberlesque, teledildonics, and cyborgasm. *CD-ROM World*, p. 66.

Freud, S. (1965). Femininity. In J. Strachey (Trans.), *New introductory lectures on psycho-analysis* (pp. 139-167). New York: Norton. (Original work published 1933)

Freud, S. (1966). The sexual life of human beings. In J. Strachey (Trans.), *Introductory lectures on psycho-analysis* (pp. 375-396). New York: Norton. (Original work published 1920)

Guattari, F. (1989). The three ecologies. *New Formations, 8*, 14-30.

Gumpert, G. (1987). Talk*ing tombstones and other tales of the media age.* New York: Oxford University Press.

Haraway, D.J. (1991). *Simians, cyborgs, and women: The reinvention of nature.* New York: Routledge.

Lawrence, D.H. (1928). *Lady Chatterley's lover.* New York: Bantam.

McLuhan, M. (1964). *Understanding media: The extensions of man.* Markham, Ontario: Mentor.

Mead, G.H. (1962). *Mind, self, and society from the standpoint of a social behaviorist.* London: University of Chicago Press.

Meyrowitz, J. (1985). *No sense of place: The impact of electronic media on social behavior.* New York: Oxford University Press.

Petrek, M., & St. Jude. (1992). Putting it on the line. *Mondo 2000*, pp. 112-115.

Poster, M. (1990). *The mode of information: Poststructuralism and social context.* London: University of Chicago Press.

Rheingold, H. (1990, Summer). Teledildonics: Reach out and touch someone. *Mondo 2000*, pp. 52-54.

Rheingold, H. (1991). *Virtual reality.* New York: Simon and Schuster.

Robinson, P., & Tamosaitis, N. (1993). *The joy of cybersex: An underground guide to electronic erotica.* New York: Brady Publishing.

Ross, A. (1989). *No respect: Intellectuals and popular culture.* New York: Routledge.

Rushkoff, D. (1994). *Cyberia: Life in the trenches of hyperspace.* San Francisco: HarperCollins.

Stone, A.R. (1991). Will the real body please stand up? Boundary stories about virtual cultures. In M. Benedikt (Ed.), *Cyberspace: First steps* (pp. 81-118). Cambridge, MA: MIT Press.

Wiener, N. (1954). *The human use of human beings: Cybernetics and society.* New York: Houghton.

Williams, L. (1989). *Hard core: Power, pleasure, and the "frenzy of the visible."* Berkeley: University of California Press.

◇◇◇◇ 23

Cybertime*

Lance Strate

Throughout this volume we have focused on the concept of cyberspace as a site of human interaction, an electronic "place" made possible by computers and computer networks. But the concept of time is just as integral to understanding a given context, situation, scene, or environment as that of space. Moreover, time is a key element in the formation of cultures, communities, identities, and meanings, as Lance Strate notes in this last chapter. Thus, he introduces and examines the idea of cybertime both as an alternative, and as a complement to the concept of cyberspace. Strate argues that the computer functions both as a clock—keeping, measuring, and producing time both for the outside world and its own internal microworld—and as a medium—generating "virtual time" through stories, games, and audiovisual presentation. He also points to the ways in which computing and computer-mediated communication, as activities, involve a variety of temporal experiences. Outside of this section of the book, another view of time can be found in Joseph Barrett's analysis of cybercapitalism in Chapter 10; time is also implicit in the ecological approach employed by Sue Barnes in Chapter 13, and in Herbert Zettl's aesthetics of virtual reality in Chapter 5; also see James R. Beniger's views on cyberspace and control in Chapter 3, and Jay David Bolter's discussion of the self in Chapter 7. An alternative to the opposition between time and space can be found in Paul Lippert's focus on the concrete and the abstract in Chapter 18.

---

*I would like to thank John M. Phelan, Edward Wachtel, Gary Gumpert, Raymond Gozzi, Jr., Ron Jacobson, and Stephanie Gibson, for their input and feedback. My only regret is that I was not able to implement more fully their suggestions.

You no longer have to be an Albert Einstein (1954) to know that space and time are interdependent and inseparable, two aspects of the singular phenomenon of physical reality. Nor do you still have to be a Kenneth Burke (1945), Harold Innis (1951), or Edward T. Hall (1959, 1984) to know that the same is true of social reality. And so, it follows quite clearly that the cyberspace that is associated with computing and computer-mediated communication has a counterpart: *cybertime.* But whereas the concept of cyberspace has proven to be both popular and powerful, the idea of cybertime has been all but ignored. Consequently, we tend to stress the similarities between computer technology and more traditional notions of physical place; we view computer media as a *where*, not a *when*. Along the same lines, there is a tendency to focus on computer technology's convergence with and subsumption by telecommunications and telematics and on cyberspace as the byproduct of the electronic transmission of messages and data over distance rather than over time. This imbalance not only hinders our attempts to assess the impact of computer media, but also influences political and economic decision making, as politicians, government officials, and the communications industry are guided by transportation and spatial metaphors of information superhighways and infrastructures. Moreover, whereas the emphasis on computer-mediated communication points us in the direction of cyberspace, as our focus shifts to computer-mediated *culture*, to the long-term construction of communities, psyches, and shared systems of signification, we need to consider the concept of cybertime.

This is not to say that the concept of time has been entirely ignored in discussions of computer technology, but the discussion has been fragmentary and diffused. My intent, therefore, is to begin the exploration of cybertime in a more systematic manner. There has been a long history of discussion and contention concerning the nature of time in general and our relationship to it (see, e.g., Whitrow, 1980, 1988), and this chapter samples some of the ideas and arguments concerning time that are relevant to the study of computer media.[1] Cybertime itself represents the intersection of several different phenomena. First, there is the computer's time-telling function—how it constructs an internal sense of time and measures the passage of time in the outside world, in order to coordinate actions and events. Second, there is the computer's representational function—how, as a medium, it conveys a sense of dramatic, fictional, or symbolic time, as well as a sense of past, present, and future. Third, there is our own subjective experience of time as we interact with and through computer media—how computing constitutes a human activity and an event that influences our perception of time and our sense of self and community.

---

[1]The literature on time is vast, transcending field, discipline, and specialization, and I make no claims to providing a comprehensive review or survey of this topic, let alone resolving any of the long-standing debates associated with it.

MEASURING TIME: THE COMPUTER AS CLOCK

Typically, the origins of the computer are traced back to devices that aid in numerical calculation such as the abacus or to machines that perform a control function such as Jacquard's automatic loom (Kidwell & Ceruzzi, 1994; Sternberg, 1991); as a revolutionary technological innovation, comparisons have also been made to the steam engine (Toffler, 1981) and to the Gutenberg printing press (Provenzo, 1986). Often overlooked, however, is the computer's close kinship with the mechanical clock developed during the late Middle Ages. J. David Bolter (1984), one of the few to make this connection, argues that the computer is an extension

> of the clock rather than the steam engine. The clock provided information more conveniently and eventually more accurately than the sundial had done before, but it did not intrude physically upon life except by ringing the hour. . . . Like early computers, early clocks were expensive and delicate, and it required a major corporate effort to acquire one. As clocks became common, however, they became not merely useful but unavoidable. Men and women began to work, eat, and sleep by the clock, and as soon as they decided to regulate their actions by this arbitrary measurer of time, the clock was transformed from an expression of civic pride into a necessity of urban life. The computer too has changed from a luxury to a necessity for modern business and government. (p. 38)

Computers and clocks are both devices that manufacture no physical products, but instead produce pure information; the arbitrariness of the uniform hours and minutes produced by the clock means that, like the computer, the clock is a technology of simulation.[2] Moreover, as Lewis Mumford (1963) makes clear, the clock's main function is to coordinate and synchronize activities and events. It is an early technology of control, a forerunner of cybernetics and computing (Beniger, 1986; Weizenbaum, 1976; Wiener, 1967). Clocks are also early forms of automata, self-operating machines, and therefore ancestors of the modern von Neumann computer (Bolter, 1984; Levy, 1992); thus, both the clock and the computer have provided metaphors for the body, the mind, and the universe.

Beyond parallels and pedigree, the electronic computer actually functions as a clock, which is essential to its ability to carry out instructions and manipulate data: "The central processor of the computer contains within it an electronic clock, whose extremely rapid pulses determine when one operation has ended and another is to begin" (Bolter, 1984, p. 38). The clock's frequency (number of cycles per second, measured by the million in megahertz) determines the computer's processing speed, and it is not unusual for computers to incorporate additional clocks to perform other functions (Wyant & Hammerstron,

---

[2]In fact, I would suggest that clock time fits quite nicely into Baudrillard's (1983) concept of hyperreality. This, of course, calls into question the exclusive association of simulation with the postmodern, as opposed to earlier eras.

1994). Like dedicated timepieces, the computer clock can be used to measure duration, determine the present point in time, and even provide alerts along the lines of an alarm clock. The function of the clock is to tell the time of the outside world, but whereas traditional timepieces only measure time's passage and are not seen as creating time out of the whole cloth, the central processor does generate time for the computer's internal world. This electronic heartbeat *is* time insofar as the computer's microworld is concerned. Cybertime therefore corresponds to Sir Isaac Newton's (1934)[3] notion of time: "Absolute, true and mathematical time, of itself, and from its own nature, flows equably without regard to anything external" (p. 6). Although absolute time fits most people's intuitions about the nature of time, it is generally accepted among scientists and philosophers that time does not exist independently of action, motion, and event, but is in fact generated by physical change (hence, time's relativity in relation to speed). Of course, the computer exists in this same physical universe and draws energy from the outside world, but otherwise, the microworld is a closed system, and the computer makes absolute time manifest internally.

Cybertime is absolute time, and it is digital time. By this I refer to something more than digital clocks and watches, although they themselves are not without significance. Introduced at the end of the 1960s, digital timepieces along with electronic calculators signaled the beginning of an ongoing consumer electronics boom; again, computer genealogies typically include the calculator, but slight the digital clock (e.g., Kidwell & Ceruzzi, 1994). And, like calculators, the new timepieces generated a degree of controversy insofar as they short-circuited long-standing methods of "figuring" (in this case due to their mode of representing time). One of the objections to the digital display of time is that the traditional clockface provides a context that includes every possible time of day, out of which we calculate the "correct" time. The digital display, on the other hand, is decontextualized time, presenting only the present moment, which only needs to be read. Thus, the clockface's time provides a sense of past and future, so that we reckon the time as so many minutes before or after the hour; the digital display is entirely present-centered, representing the time as nothing more than a discrete quantity. These differences in display, and the underlying sense of time implied by them, represent significant differences in worldview and ideology, as Jeremy Rifkin, author of *Time Wars* (1987), makes clear:

> A digital timepiece displays numbers in a vacuum—time unbound to either a circadian reference or the past and future. By eliminating the circle, the digital watch helps eliminate the notion that time is cyclical and related to the larger rhythms of the earth and solar system. . . .The digital watch is a fitting metaphor for a society in which the time orientation is becoming increasingly separated from the ecological rhythms of the planet and in which the expediency of the

---

[3]I acknowledge that use of the APA editorial style in this manner generates a temporal anomaly, admit that I take a certain perverse pleasure in it, and apologize for any discomfort it may cause.

> moment takes precedence over a sense of historical reflection and future projection. (p. 121)

However significant, the debate over display only scratches the surface of the computer's digitization of time. For internally, within the microworld of the computer's central processor, its sense of time is digital as well. Human time is generally analogic, that is, we tend to think of time as continuous and, therefore, infinitely divisible. We may watch the clock, counting the seconds and minutes as they tick by, noting the chimes marking the hour, but we generally see this as a byproduct of the clock's mechanics, not time's true nature; we perceive time as flowing seamlessly, rather than hiccuping periodically. Cybertime, in contrast, is based on a series of separate and distinct electronic pulses; just as is the case with the microworld's absolute time, these electronic pulses do not simply mark time—they are what passes for time in cyberspace (Bolter, 1984). Cybertime is therefore based on indivisible units, making manifest the concept of the chronon, the shortest unit of time. The notion that time, like matter, is made up of atoms was popular among intellectuals during the Middle Ages (Whitrow, 1980, 1988), its best known exponent being the 12th-century philosopher Moses Maimonides (1963), who wrote:

> Time is composed of instants. . . . There are many units of time that, because of the shortness of their duration, are not divisible. The division of time ends with the instants that are not divisible. For example, an hour consists of sixty minutes, a minute of sixty seconds, and a second of sixty thirds. And thus this division of time ends up accordingly with parts constituting, for instance, tenths or something even briefer, which cannot in any respect be separated in their turn into parts and are not subject to division. (p. 196)

The concept of temporal atomicity was consistent with the highly religious worldview that prevailed during the medieval period within Jewish, Islamic, and Christian cultures. As G.J. Whitrow (1988) explains, the "atomistic view of time was associated with a drastically contingent and acausal concept of the world, its existence at one instant not implying its existence at any subsequent instant" (p. 79). Rather than assuming an automatic continuity from event to event, this view required the continuous active intervention of God to keep time moving. There is more than a passing similarity here between the God of Abraham and the god of the machine; even with surge protectors, anyone working with computers for any length of time is aware of the uncertain temporal continuity of their microworlds. A momentary discontinuity in the flow of electricity and the computer may freeze—time stops! Thus, the computer's digital time has something in common with theistic time or sacred time.

In the modern era the best-known proponent of temporal atomicity was Descartes, also for theological reasons (Whitrow, 1980). What is of particular significance is that whereas Descartes's deductive approach looked backward to medieval theology for its support, his dream of a reality based entirely on mathematics comes the closest to being realized in the form of the computer's microworld. Apart from the concept of the chronon, the quantification of time that resulted from the clocking of discrete hours, minutes, and seconds led to the commodification of time (Mumford, 1963) and the uniquely Western notion that "time is money" (Lakoff & Johnson, 1980). The division of time into multiple uniform units facilitates the pricing of time and, therefore, the buying and selling of time, a key foundation of the industrial revolution and modern capitalism. It follows that the computer's digital time, and its further easing of temporal commodification, may well form the basis of postmodern or late capitalism (Jameson, 1991).

Digital time is not just a quantitative measurement of time, but rather a quantitative concept of time—time as a sequence of numbers. As Bolter (1984) puts it: "An ordinary clock produces only a series of identical seconds, minutes, and hours: a computer transforms seconds or microseconds or nanoseconds into information" (pp. 102-103). Anything that takes the form of information can be processed by the computer, subjected to statistical and symbolic manipulation. Digital time is entirely arbitrary, completely divorced from natural rhythms and human perceptions, therefore, entirely controllable and malleable.

Cybertime is absolute time, digital time, and it is quicktime. An emphasis on speed is consistent with what Innis (1951) refers to as space-biased societies; societies such as our own in which the emphasis is on communication over distance, territorial expansion, and the extension of centralized control (also see Beniger, 1986). Furthermore, space-biased cultures are present-centered, neglecting tradition and history, unconcerned with maintaining continuity between past and future. Increased speed enhances our ability to transmit messages over space and thereby control territory, while spotlighting the immediate and the ephemeral (Postman, 1985). From a somewhat different perspective, Alvin and Heidi Toffler (1993) state: "'third wave' societies—with economies based on information, communications and technology—run at hyper-speeds" (p. 17). And Paul Virilio (1986, 1991) argues that speed is the fundamental property of postmodern culture; in the age of relativity, the speed of light is the only constant. The electron has set the pace for a century and a half, since the introduction of telegraphy. To the electronic media's instantaneous transmission of information, the computer in turn has contributed to the processing of information at electric speed. And it has given us a way of measuring the instantaneity of electronic technology. As Bolter (1984) puts it, "anyone who works with the computer is introduced to a second temporal world, a world of nanoseconds (billionths of a second)" (p. 100). The nanosecond represents cybertime's chronon, its indivisible temporal atom. The speed of the nanosecond's passage renders it essentially subliminal, as Rifkin (1987) makes clear:

> Though it is possible to conceive theoretically of a nanosecond, and even to manipulate time at that speed of duration, *it is not possible to experience it.* This marks a radical turning point in the way human beings relate to time. Never before

> has time been organized at a speed beyond the realm of consciousness. . . . The new "computime" represents the final abstraction of time and its complete separation from human experience and the rhythms of nature. (pp. 23-24)

Rifkin (1987) sees this "new nanosecond culture" (p. 19) as an outgrowth of our emphasis on efficiency and centralization, our space bias; "bigger is better" leads to "faster is better." We have come to expect the instantaneous, so that it no longer excites us; we see no need to comment on how fast our messages are delivered through electronic mail, but it becomes quite natural to refer to preelectronic mail (the kind that the post office delivers) as *snail mail.* And we no longer find it very evocative to speak of jet speed, but we become quite conversant in jet lag. When sitting at a computer terminal, delays of a few seconds seem interminable and five minutes an eternity. Hyperspeed breeds impatience, haste, and intolerance, both online and in the real world. The instantaneity of electronic speed is commonly said to annihilate distance, leaving us with "no sense of place" as Joshua Meyrowitz (1985) puts it. But it also annihilates duration, leaving us with no sense of time—if cyberspace is a "nonspace" (Gibson, 1984, p. 51), cybertime is a nontime. Time as well as space breaks down as we approach the speed of light, so that the computer's quicktime is often associated with timelessness and hyperspeed with the break down of historicism (see, e.g., Critical Arts Ensemble, 1994; Rifkin, 1987; Rushkoff, 1994).

Internally, the fact that cybertime is absolute, digital, and quick makes possible a high level of synchronization; externally, the computer's hyperspeed makes it a powerful technology of control. The tendency to place computers in command of events, activities, and procedures has been well documented and subject to intense criticism (see Bolter, 1984; Roszak, 1994; Weizenbaum, 1976). The computer further extends the use of clocking, introduced in the 19th century to control labor and production (Beniger, 1986; Lubar, 1993). There is no question that here we find the totalitarian potential of computing, as well as its affinity with capitalism. And yet, at the same time, the computer's ability to control and coordinate in the interests of speed and efficiency have allowed for more flexible notions of time. The computer introduces the idea of *time-sharing,* initially a process by which mainframe computers are able to accommodate multiple users. Moving at hyperspeed, the computer is able to move back and forth among different users and programs, fulfilling a command here, a line of a program there, balancing a variety of tasks so quickly that the user is barely aware of the computer's divided attention. The introduction of time-sharing to mainframe computers made interactive programming via video terminals possible and led to the first electronic mail systems; a variation of time-sharing among different computers linked in networks made more sophisticated forms of computer-mediated communication, such as the Usenet news and discussion groups possible (Rheingold, 1993; see also Gelernter's, 1991, discussion of "tuple space"). Elsewhere, the term *time-sharing* as well as the general principle by which it works has been adopted by the travel industry to create more flexible vacation options. Many businesses have adopted the related idea of *flex time* as an alternative to traditional 9-to-5 job hours (although this tends to be a smokescreen for downgrading jobs from full time to part time), and in financial markets various forms of programmed trading rely on similar principles (Perkinson, in press). Thus, the computer's extreme synchronization results in a more elastic form of time, replacing what Hall (1984) refers to as monochronic time, a linear, one-thing-at-a-time sense of the temporal. Cybertime is therefore polychronic time, which involves many things simultaneously; polychronic time is characteristic of many non-Western cultures and, as Marshall McLuhan (1964) argues, of electronic cultures.

In order to survive, every society requires a degree of synchronization from its members. For most of the history of our species, the rhythms of nature such as the sunrise and sunset, new moon and full moon, equinox and solstice, were sufficient for this purpose. When temporal technologies such as the calendar and the clock were introduced, however, they by and large served to further control and coordinate the actions of human beings (Mumford, 1963). The town clock, with its elevated clock face and its far-reaching chimes, established a local area of synchronized time that served the needs of most Western societies from the 14th through to the 19th century. The invention of the telegraph made it possible to extend this area from the local to the regional in the form of time zones (Beniger, 1986; Carey, 1989). Since that time, the many forms of telecommunications that have been developed, as well as the mass production of increasingly more accurate clocks and watches, have further enhanced coordinated action and procedures.

There is a certain irony, then, to the fact that whereas our technologies are highly synchronized in their use of time, our societies are still largely working with a 19th-century system of time keeping. We all may be wearing extraordinarily accurate watches, but the times that they are set to may differ by as much as 10 or 15 minutes. If past trends are any indication, this lack of synchronization will become intolerable, especially for a nanosecond culture; remedies have already begun to appear in the form of broadcast-controlled timepieces and VCR clocks. We can therefore look forward to the integration of computers and computer networks into one great global clock. The cyberspatial infrastructure would most probably be joined with a superstructure of orbital satellites; contemporary satellites such as the United State's Navstar already broadcast the time to the millionth of a second (Raley, 1994). The centralization of time keeping and its instantaneous dissemination through the global matrix seem to be the next logical developments, especially given the increasing rate of global hyperspeed transactions and the shift to a 24-hour society. I believe that we will eventually find ourselves referring more and more often to Greenwich mean time (or some new international standard) rather than our regional time, and that new timepieces will be marketed that are capable of receiving broadcast time signals (perhaps in conjunction with cellular communications products), thereby maintaining synchronization with the world clock. In a sense, absolute time would be established on a global level, or we might say that a "global microworld" would be established; when the world becomes contained within a cyberspatial network, cybertime will become the world's time. Although this would further separate clock time and natural time, the obsolescence of regional time zones may allow local time to resurface, resulting in the proliferation of heterogeneous time zones on one level, even while time is homogenized on another; of course, the internal time of the individual computer would be the most local time of all.

Thus far, the concept of cybertime has been contrasted with our conceptions regarding real time. Real time is relative and formed by physical change, whereas cybertime is absolute and independent of its microworld. Real time is continuous and infinitely divisible, whereas cybertime is digital and atomistic. Real time is tied to the rhythms of nature and human perception, whereas cybertime is quicktime, based on the hyperspeed of the nanosecond. Also, in modern, literate, Western cultures, real time is monochronic, whereas cybertime is highly polychronic, involving extraordinarily complex forms of synchronization. It would be incorrect, however, to place cybertime in antonymic opposition to real time; insofar as the computer functions as a traditional clock, measuring the time of the outside world, cybertime encompasses real time as one of its temporal modes. In fact, the term *real time* refers both to the time of the physical universe and human perception and also to the *interface* between the computer's present and the present of the physical world. When the two coincide and remain synchronized, the computer is said to be functioning in real time. The concept of real time is therefore connected to the microworld's ability to become attuned to the outside world (an ability that computer technology shares with other media). The interface is not monodirectional, however, so that real time also refers to the ability to synchronize that outside world's activities to cybertime's digital drumbeat.

REPRESENTING TIME: THE COMPUTER AS MEDIUM

In addition to its ability to measure and display time, the computer also functions as a medium, meaning that it can represent time symbolically, communicate a sense of time that is not necessarily *the* time, and thereby produce virtual time. *Virtual time* here refers to a virtual reality's internally generated sense of time and may be used in reference to both computer-generated virtual worlds and the illusion of reality created by all forms of media.[4] Different media may generate

[4]This notion of "virtual time" is distinct from Jean Piaget's, which refers to a conceptual time involving the imagination, and Suzanne Langer's, which refers to symbolic form—both are discussed by Edward Wachtel (1980) in his research on perception. They are not unrelated, however, as virtual reality is a conceptual, symbolic, and imaginary "reality" given perceptual (if not actual) existence.

different types of virtual time, but the computer is a "metamedium" (Pimentel & Teixeira, 1993, p.10), capable of incorporating all existing media. Cybertime is therefore what Hall (1984) refers to as *metatime*: "All those things that philosophers, anthropologists, psychologists, and others have said and written about time: the innumerable theories, discussions, and preoccupations concerning the nature of time" (p. 27). It is a concept of time that includes all other concepts and representations of time, such as the timeline, calendar, and clock face; game time, in which each move in a game represents a unit of time, independent of how long it takes to make the move; narrative time, in which the idea of time is conveyed through verbal description; dramatic time, in which the time represented through performance may move faster or slower than the corresponding clock time; and ritual or sacred time, in which the everyday sense of time is suspended, and the participants are plunged into an eternal present or archetypical moment from the past (Eliade, 1959, 1974; Kirk, 1974).

As audiovisual media, including current and projected forms of virtual reality technology, computers can deal with a wide variety of temporal formats: There is real time that may be transmitted, along the lines of live television, and delayed time that is recorded; a one-to-one time scale may be used so that playback occurs at the same rate as the original event, or the recording may be replayed in fast motion or slow motion, and the rate itself may be varied; motion itself may be frozen, as in photographs or when freeze frame is employed, and motion may be played back in reverse; the recording may be otherwise distorted through editing, cutting, or mixing it with other material to fill out the event (Robinett, 1992; Zettl, 1990). In all these ways, computers can generate a sense of virtual time, the illusion that the sense of time that is presented or represented is truly real time. Additionally, the perception of time may be mediated by the perception of space, specifically the scale of the environment. Hall (1984) discusses the experiments of Alton De Long, in which subjects were supplied with dollhouse-like models and asked to imagine themselves engaged in activities within them. The results indicate that as the scale of the environment decreases, individuals increase the rate at which they interact, process information, and perceive time's passage; thus, in an environment one-twelfth the size of reality, five minutes feels like an hour. These experiments were completed without the benefit of virtual reality (VR) technology, but are clearly relevant to VR and related notions such as telepresence.

Ultimately, what makes cybertime's virtuality distinctive is the great variety of modes by which time can be represented, the unprecedented possibilities for combining the different modes in various ways, the enhanced potential for controlling and manipulating those modes on the part of the user (both as source and receiver), and the enhanced potential for immersion in those modes through VR technology. Cybertime's digitality is the key here, for when time is composed of discrete units of information, it becomes highly malleable, a property that holds true for all digital modes of expression (Lanham, 1993). The combined properties of control and flexibility exhibited here appear contradictory, but are reconciled through computing's ability to achieve complex forms of synchronization. And whereas the computer's virtual time includes natural and traditional temporal modes, it also undermines these older representations by making them part of a large collection of alternatives. Along the same lines, the computer undermines our traditional conceptions of dimensionality.

The idea of dimension is associated with the quantification of attributes, a concept clearly compatible with computing. The attribute of dimension can itself be measured, so that we commonly refer to the three-dimensional space that we live in, to the two-dimensional representations of that space on screen, canvas, or paper, and to the one-dimensional lines we use to form boundaries and maintain order. Dimensionality is a gauge of complexity and a measure of freedom: Movement in three spatial dimensions, for example, is more complex and affords a greater degree of freedom than movement in two. The concept of dimensionality can be applied to any set of attributes. Thus, Herbert Marcuse's (1964) "one-dimensional man" is an individual who is shielded from the complexities of the world and consequently subject to a loss of freedom. We might conclude, then, that our fundamental social and intellectual conflicts are conflicts between one-dimensionality and multidimensionality (see also Atkin, 1981). From McLuhan's (1962, 1964) point of view, the one-dimensional individual, mindset, and society that Marcuse describes is the product of the *linearity* of alphabetic literacy and typography and the resultant mechanical and industrial technologies;[5] in contrast, both oral and electronic cultures are described as multisensory and therefore multidimensional.

The idea of dimensionality also provides a common ground for time and space. By adding time as a fourth coordinate to the spatial dimensions of length, width, and height, we are able to integrate time and space into the unified concept of spacetime. Thus space and time are represented as mathematical coordinates occupying a form of logical space. It is for this reason that time is commonly referred to as the fourth dimension in popular culture. This designation is a misnomer, however, as Rudy Rucker (1984) explains:

> Nobody goes around saying width is *the* second dimension and height is *the* third dimension. Instead we just say that height and width are space dimensions. Rather than saying time is *the* fourth dimension, it is more natural to say that time is just one of the higher dimensions. (p. 139)

In the place of time, we could use some other quality—color, for example—as our fourth dimension. Or we might imagine a fourth spatial dimension, referred to as hyperspace, and including four-dimensional objects such as hypercubes; although impossible to visualize, four-dimensional space can be represented mathematically, especially with the aid of computing.

---

[5]See Jacques Ellul's (1968) study of propaganda for a discussion of the intimate relationship between propaganda and literacy, which in this context serves as the "missing link" between Marcuse and McLuhan.

Alluding to this hyperspace, the terms *hypertext* and *hypermedia* refer to a multidimensional network of verbal and audiovisual items. Thus, hypertext theorists such as Bolter (1991) and George Landow (1992) see in electronic writing the potential to break away from the constraints of one-dimensional linear text and the tyranny of the two-dimensional page. The multidimensionality of hypertext transforms the notion of text from an object held by the reader into an environment through which the reader navigates. Time can be represented in this format just as easily as space, so that the reader may explore a hypertextual network that links representations of different moments or eras. As Bolter (1991) points out, hypertext and hypermedia make available "an electronic space in which the text can comprise a network of diverging, converging, and parallel times" (p. 139). Hypertext has the potential to provide a sense of time that is less fixed and more complex than traditional linear storytelling. Although much of the critical attention has been directed to hypertext, and the ways in which it differs from traditional literature, this same potential is present in a variety of computer software, from word processors and spreadsheets to games and VR simulations (see, e.g., Novak, 1991; Woolley, 1992).

What is significant about these new forms is not that they include the higher dimension of time; after all, time is represented in narrative and dramatic forms such as oral storytelling, novels, and television. Time itself, however, tends to be presented as one-dimensional and generally linear in these older forms, whereas computer software is relatively more open to multidimensional temporal modes. Thus, it becomes feasible to represent and to navigate through parallel timelines (as noted above), or timelines that exist at an angle to each other (MacBeath, 1993), or two separate time dimensions that move in opposite directions from each other (Whitrow, 1980). A computer-mediated narrative can easily present both objective time and the corresponding sense of subjective time held by a human agent, which Zettl (1990) sees as equivalent to the horizontal and vertical dimensions of space. Multiple dimensions of subjective time could be represented if more than one character is involved. Multidimensional time can of course be imagined and discussed without the aid of computing, but this technology makes it possible to simulate it, experiment, and play with it in an unprecedented manner.

Multidimensionality is not the only alternative to one-dimensionality, however. The notion of the fractional dimension, developed through the application of computer power, represents a new way to measure complexity, the complexity of the irregular and the chaotic (Gleick, 1987). The fractal geometry that this idea generated has become a mainstay of motion picture special effects and video games and is essential for the creation of effective VR programming (Hayward & Wollen, 1993). Beyond the visual, fractal mathematics allow computers to model and simulate all manner of systems that otherwise behave unpredictably over time, such as economic trends and meteorological patterns. Thus, they contribute to a more realistic depiction of temporal phenomena as they are better able to capture the randomness and chaos of the real world.

Fractal time itself is a more irregular idea of time, closer to human experience than the uniform rate of clock time. Thus, a computer simulation might vary the tempo of time: "Within a region of cyberspace, time itself may pulse, now passing faster, now slower" (Novak, 1991, p. 240).

Although computers deal with the extreme complexity of higher dimensions and fractals, they do so by reducing phenomena down to a state of extreme simplicity, in the form of binary code. This code represents phenomena through combinations of two possible states, be they zero or one, on or off, or yes or no; like a point in geometry, the mathematical concept of the binary unit or bit has no dimensions (although the space in which a bit of information is stored in memory or on a disk has dimension). The function of a bit of information according to Norbert Wiener (1967), founder of the field of cybernetics, is to reduce uncertainty, possibilities, choice; the ultimate goal is to reduce the degree of freedom to zero. And although there are clear distinctions between human and technological systems, the two interface, overlap, and are influenced by each other, as Wiener makes clear. Here, then, we can see the totalitarian implications of the computer traced to its zero-dimensional code; what Baudrillard (1983) would consider its DNA. There is, of course, a great sense of security associated with the elimination of degrees of freedom, a key point for Marcuse (1964), and individuals who become immersed in computing also derive pleasure from the lack of ambiguity characteristic of the microworlds they create and explore; they may also come to expect the same of the real world (Levy, 1984; Roszak, 1994; Turkle, 1984, 1986). The point, however, is that the zero-dimensional is an alternative to the one-dimensional. Zero-dimensional time would correspond to the frozen time of the photograph or freeze frame and to the experience of timelessness or the "eternal now" associated with sacred time.

Ultimately, whether computing eliminates dimensionality or expands it depends on how the technology is used, the choices that are made. Underlying those choices, however, is a more basic and general effect of computing—its undermining of traditional notions of dimensionality, of the one-dimensional, the three-dimensional, and the four dimensions of spacetime. Whether we are moving into unimaginably high numbers of dimensions, dealing with fractional dimensions, or reducing phenomenon down to zero dimensions, the notion of dimensionality itself has been made multidimensional. In the microworld, it is possible to move easily from one form of dimensionality to another, placing us in the realm of the *metadimensional.* Cybertime is not characterized by any fixed dimensionality, but rather is open to a wide variety of dimensional modes, to metadimensionality; this is consistent with the idea that cybertime is a form of metatime.

Dimensionality, along with digitality, are ways of representing and conceptualizing time through mathematics, and hence tend to be somewhat abstract. Although the metaphor of time as money relies on the quantification of time, currency and commodity make for more concrete comparisons than number alone. Even more concrete is the use of space to make time more accessible and user-friendly. We attempt to grasp the temporal by spatializing it through the linear metaphor of the timeline, the two-dimensional graph metaphor of the calendar page, or the circular metaphor of the traditional clockface. Even the concept of spacetime subordinates time to space by turning time into a fourth *spatial* dimension. The tendency to spatialize time can be seen as another manifestation of Western culture's space bias. And although it is clearly rooted in modern, typographic culture's emphasis on linearity, electronic media such as the computer are associated with nonlinear forms of spatialization. The flowchart, the fundamental diagramming of computer programming, with its nonlinear, tree-like structure (Bolter, 1984), is a highly spatialized representation of events unfolding in time and has become a key image in contemporary culture (e.g., in recent television commercials). This same idea of programming structure, applied to electronic writing, yields the medium of hypertext; thus, there is a tendency to spatialize time in hypermedia. The dimension of time may be represented by travel from node to node, but it may be absent from the individual nodes themselves; each textual item would tend to present time as fixed and frozen. In this respect, the criticism of well-known software designer Brenda Laurel (1993) is noteworthy, as she discusses the quality of reversibility in computing:

> What if I failed to save a copy of my spreadsheet before I monkeyed around with a scenario that turned out to be disastrous? What if that scenario altered a significant amount of my data? The theory of hypertext suggests one solution, where various stages of a "document" . . . can be saved and linked to the current version. This solution is unsatisfactory in that it is likely . . . to create a bewildering proliferation of documents. I don't really want to page back through versions of my work; I want to turn back the clock. The dimension of change is best represented through time, not fixed states. A simple chrono-scrollbar would suffice. Yes, the implementation is hard, but the hardest part is probably visualizing the appropriate representation in the first place. (pp. 114-115)

Here Laurel (1993) is able to overcome the space bias of computer software and contemporary culture, in general, and suggest an alternative interface that better represents the temporal dimension. Her preferred metaphor is that of the theater and the experience of dramatic events and actions unfolding through time, rather than the spatial metaphor of hypertext and hypermedia and the idea of navigation through spaces or worlds. Hypertext theorists do not entirely ignore time; for example, Bolter (1991) points out that "the computer makes possible a kind of historical atlas in which invasions and battles, colonization, and the growth of populations and cities are shown in time as well as space" (p. 81). Still, in hypermedia and in software in general, spatialization is the norm. Although less explicitly time-based, Arthur Kroker (1993) and Steven Jones's (1993) criticisms of virtual reality are related to Laurel's point. Both Kroker and Jones note that discussions of virtual reality tend to focus on the visual aspect and downplay the creation of acoustic virtual reality. Although the visual can register change over time, it also can give us the impression of frozen time, of the timeless. Thus visual VR simulations (at present) often present us with spaces to explore, and although the exploration takes place over time, the environment explored does not change over time—it is a frozen space. The acoustic, on the other hand, can only exist in time: "All sensation takes place in time, but sound has a special relationship to time unlike that of other fields that register in human sensation. Sound only exists when it is going out of existence" (Ong, 1982, pp. 31-32). Sound therefore gives us the impression of temporal continuity and never implies timelessness. Thus, media with a strong aural component (including drama) function as representations of time itself, independent of spatial metaphors.

The spatialization of time in the form of discrete, unconnected, and decontextualized units or moments, as is possible in hypermedia, is also a characteristic of the postmodern condition, as described by Fredric Jameson (1991):

> Different moments in historical or existential time are here simply filed in different places; the attempt to combine them even locally does not slide up and down a temporal scale . . . but jumps back and forth across a game board that we conceptualize in terms of distance.
>
> Thus the movement from one generic classification to another is radically discontinuous, like switching channels on a cable television set; and indeed it seems appropriate to characterize the strings of items and the compartments of genres of their typologization as so many "channels" into which the new reality is organized. (p. 373)

The connection between temporal discontinuity and television's flow is made more explicitly and clearly by Neil Postman (1985), whereas Susan Sontag (1977) traces it further back to the innovation of photography. The key point is that the audiovisual media, while continuing to represent time in a spatial format, have dispensed with print media's emphasis on linearity and continuity; we are therefore left with historical moments lacking a coherent relationship. In this way history, a form of knowledge, is transformed into nostalgia, a set of commodities (such as images and styles removed from a continuous historical context) to be bought and sold. This tendency affects computing and is in turn affected by the computer, in whose memory banks commodified historical information may be deposited or withdrawn. To the extent that cybertime takes the form of nonlinear, spatialized time, computing favors the dissolution of history as a narrative form. At the same time, computer technologies are revolutionizing the way we look at the past by the expansion of our capacity for record keeping; for information storage, processing, and retrieval; and for the preservation of audiovisual material. Alvin Toffler (1981) provides an enthusiastic look at the possibilities:

> Today we are about to jump to a whole new stage of social memory. The radical de-massification of the media, the invention of new media, the mapping of the earth by satellite, the monitoring of hospital patients by electronic sensors, the computerization of corporate files—all mean we are recording the activities of

> the civilization in fine-grain detail. . . . We shall before long have the closest thing to a civilization with total recall. Third Wave civilization will have at its disposal more information, and more finely organized information, about itself than could have been imagined even a quarter-century ago. (pp. 176-177)

There certainly is much to be said for enhancing our social memory, our ability to retain and access historical information. But there is also much that is disturbing about this vision of "total recall," as Theodore Roszak (1994) argues: "Most of what will fill that social memory will be the dross of everyday life: every phone call, every check passed, every credit card purchase, every traffic citation, every airline ticket. Of what use is this to a healthy culture and a vital political life? Obviously none" (p. 211).

As Michael Benedikt (1991) points out (without irony), cyberspace is the realm of the "permanently ephemeral" (p. 11). And as Postman (1985, 1992) argues, decontextualized information is irrelevant, leaving us only with information overload; data do not substitute for history. Like Roszak (1994), Kroker (1993) rejects the idea that more information storage is better, and that "memory" is an appropriate metaphor for that computer function:

> The computer has no memory, if by memory we mean the presence of political judgment and aesthetic reflection. Perfectly recalling everything in the cold language of data, it is incapable of the act of forgetting so necessary for mediating politics and history. In this case, computer memory is always cynical, always about the actual disappearance of embodied memory and the vanishing of aesthetic judgment. (p. 31)

Beyond the problem of information glut, there are very legitimate fears concerning the loss of privacy, fears that our every move leaves behind a trail of electronically recorded transactions. These permanent electronic trails make us vulnerable to anyone with the resources to gather and process the information (Gandy, 1993; Roszak, 1994). Thus, total recall becomes totalitarian recall. We are in the process of becoming a surveillance society, each of us subject to the computer's "panoptic sort" (Gandy, 1993), largely for the benefit of corporations and government. What makes this even more problematic is that these digital cybertime trails are in no way composed of indexical signs; the trail is left in binary code that is arbitrary and therefore easily altered; in the microworld, memory is virtual. And although this may in some instances serve to delegitimize computer memory, more often it seems to breed a sense of fatalistic, bureaucratic indifference. Consider how hard it is to correct a mistake in your credit history, or to convince a company that its computer records are erroneous. Both accidental and purposive manipulations of records and evidence are simple to carry out in a digital medium, and such tampering is undetectable, presenting us with the possibility of Orwellian history—history that is contingent on the needs and whims of those in control of the (operating) system. To the extent that individuals are aware of this, it also serves to remind us that all histories are socially constructed. This form of multidimensional time—a branching, hypertextual past made up of alternate histories and unconnected moments—parallels the postmodern breakdown of objectivism.

Given the hyperspeed of computing technology, surveillance can occur in real time. Total recall becomes total see-all. Thus, David Gelernter (1991) argues that some time in the near future the following scenario will become commonplace:

> You will look into a computer screen and see reality. Some part of your world—the town you live in, the company you work for, your school system, the city hospital—will hang there in a sharp color image, abstract but recognizable, moving subtly in a thousand places. This Mirror World you are looking at is fed by a steady rush of new data pouring in through cables. It is infiltrated by your own software creatures, doing your business. (p. 1)

Like Toffler (1981), Gelernter is enthusiastic about computer power and its potential to revolutionize such activities as news gathering, traffic control, hospital organization, and the political process. It is therefore difficult to decide which is more frightening: the implementation of the system that he describes, or Gelernter's seeming obliviousness to the threat it poses to freedom and privacy. Moreover, he misses the irony of installing *mirror worlds* in a culture characterized by rampant narcissism (Lasch, 1979). Mirror worlds, as symbolic representations or maps of the present (and the past), also represent the computer's potential to both control and contain the outside world through hyperspeed surveillance and information processing and the ability to respond immediately.

Moreover, computer-mediated control is extended into the future. Computer programs are plans for future actions to be taken by the computer, consisting of instructions that are to be carried out at some point in the future. Although flexibility may be included in the program, computers "lock future events into a predetermined course in a way schedules cannot" (Rifkin, 1987, p. 115). (One of the consequences of programming the future was the stock market crash of 1987.) Aside from actually determining the future, computer models are used to forecast the future (Warner & Buzbee, 1994; Rifkin, 1987). The danger here is not just from erroneous models and predictions, but from the possibility of self-fulfilling prophecies (e.g., a computer projection of a stock market crash might easily make investors nervous enough to cause one). In other words, the boundary between forecasting and programming is permeable; both are forms of representation, and prophecy has always been as much if not more about persuasion than prediction. Ultimately, the future becomes a simulation, one that may or may not be modeled on physical reality:

> The age of progress is about to give way to the age of simulation. The new simulated vision of the future incorporates the Promethean appetites of the former age while rejecting the restraints that have shackled it to historical consciousness. . . . The

> future is no longer viewed as something that unfolds in strict linear fashion along a historical plane. Rather, it is something that is continually being reprogrammed to suit the transitory needs of each emergent reality. . . . The new future image conceives of reality as a vast reservoir of information to be fashioned into simulated experiences. (Rifkin, 1987, pp. 171-172)

Virtual time yields virtual futures, hypertextual, multidimensional futures. In some ways, the prospect appears liberating, opening possibilities for change. In other ways, it trivializes the future, making it "permanently ephemeral," replacing notions of fate and progress, evolution and revolution, with game playing. The future as a reality to be prepared for is replaced by the future as a virtual reality, a timeless state that is experienced in the present. Thus, the future is brought under the control of the present. The simulation may be played out from past to present to future, repeatedly, but it exists in the present. Even if multiple futures are simulated, they are futures that are always-already manifest in the programming. Along the same lines, the forecast is an attempt to bring knowledge of the future into the present, thereby process the future as information. Given that knowledge, we can then act to control that future; and with or without the forecast, the program creates a predetermined future: "In the computer age, temporal power will be defined as having access to and control over raw data extracted from past experience, and being able to effectively program future realities" (Rifkin, 1987, p. 197). Total recall becomes total see-all becomes total be-all and end-all.

Gary Gumpert (1987) explains how magnetic tape produces ambiguity in the perception of the present, the now, as it becomes impossible to tell whether a broadcast is live or recorded. The computer's digital recordings, programmed simulations, hyperspeed surveillance, and virtual realities extend this ambiguity to include the future as well. In cybertime, we see the distinction between past, present, and future begin to breakdown as the three tenses become indistinguishable and essentially interchangeable. In some ways, cybertime makes manifest the argument put forth by St. Augustine (1961) in the fifth century:

> It is abundantly clear that neither the future nor the past exist, and therefore it is not strictly correct to say that there are three times, past, present, and future. It might be correct to say that there are three times, a present of past things, a present of present things, and a present of future things. Some such different times do exist in the mind, but nowhere else that I can see. The present of past things is memory; the present of present things is direct perception; and the present of future things is expectation. (p. 269)

St. Augustine (1961) suggests that only the present is objectively real, whereas past and future exist solely in the mind; as the computer is an extension of the mind, it likewise creates "a present of past things and future things." In cybertime, past and future collapse into the present, contributing to the almost mystical sense of timelessness sometimes associated with cyberspace (e.g., Rushkoff, 1994); this is also consistent with the spatialized, decontextualized, and commodified time discussed by postmodernists. Moreover, the computer's treatment of past and future matches the physicist's concept of spacetime, in which time is simply another set of coordinates to be graphed; the spacetime model spatializes time, making it static and fixed. In human terms, what cyberspacetime implies is a technological version of Calvinism, a fatalistic concept of a predetermined future; it is exactly this point of view that Kurt Vonnegut satirizes in *Slaughterhouse Five*, as it suggests that change is impossible and that any efforts to influence the future or avert disaster are futile. This present-centered concept of time is zero-dimensional time, time reduced to absolute certainty. But cyberspacetime also implies the other extreme, that time is infinitely malleable, that we ourselves can anticipate and predetermine the future. The problem then is hubris and isolation from the natural time world. Both extremes undermine traditional notions of the past and the future.

EXPERIENCING TIME: COMPUTING AS ACTIVITY AND EVENT

Human interaction with and through computer media includes our use and experience of time or cyberchronemics. For example, it is commonly noted that electronic mail and computer conferencing are asynchronous forms of interaction: Participants need not transmit and receive at the same point in time. This flexibility combined with the speed of electronic transmission makes e-mail a highly efficient mode of interpersonal communication (Sproull & Kiesler, 1991). Used for networked group communication, the asynchronous character of e-mail eliminates many time-related cues, such as how long a particular task takes to complete, or when it is due. This may result in a deregulation of behavior, a loss of control over the group's output, and even an increase in the time it takes to complete a task, but it also allows for increased creativity, participation, and satisfaction. Although asynchronous communication all but guarantees that the e-mail messages we receive were composed at some point in the past, there is a tendency to experience them as if they were being communicated in the present. This sense of immediacy can also be present when reading other people's electronic discussions in the archives of bulletin boards, listservs, and so on, as Dery (1993) notes:

> on-line conversations exhibit a curious half-life; as the reader scrolls down-screen, scanning the lively back-and-forth of a discussion that may go back weeks, months, or even years, he experiences the puns, philippics, true confessions, rambling dissertations, and Generation X-er one-liners as if they were taking place in real time—which, for the reader watching them flow past on his screen, they are. (p. 561)

As noted earlier, in cybertime distinctions between past, present, and future fade, and our sense of time's passage becomes distorted. Waiting for only a few seconds seems to drag on forever, whereas time truly flies when engaged in computing. Immersed in the microworld, time seems to slow down relative to the outside world; it is almost as if Einstein's theory of relativity and the fact that the faster the speed, the slower the relative rate that time passes, applies to "travelers" along the hyperspeed infobahn. And as Rifkin (1987) relates:

> The really good video game players are able to block out both clock time and their own subjective time and descend completely into the time world of the game. It is a common experience for video game junkies to spend hours on end in front of the console without any sense whatsoever of the passage of clock time. According to Craig Brod, one of the growing number of psychologists specializing in computer-related distress, "those who live with computer workers invariably complain that disputes over time are a major source of friction."
>
> Long-term computer users often suffer from the constant jolt back and forth between two time worlds. As they become more enmeshed in the new time world of the computer, they become less and less able to readjust to the temporal norms and standards of traditional clock culture. They become victims of a new form of temporal schizophrenia, caught between two distinctly different temporal orientations. (p. 25)

These other experiences of time, or experiences of other time, suggest a comparison between cybertime and Mircea Eliade's (1959, 1974) concept of sacred time:

> The computer has an infinity of times in potential, ready to be actualized. Flashy splinters of time, speedy batches of time, dumb loops, programs that open up like fans according to the number of frames you assign them. Michaux speaks of "a time that has a crowd of moments". . . . Paul Virilio of "an intensive time . . . (that) . . . is not complete any more, but indefinitely fractionated in as many instants, instantaneities as the techniques of communication allow it". . . . The computer is also home to "real time," 30 frames per second, a time that fits exactly Eliade's definition of sacred time. "Religious man lives in two kinds of time, of which, the more important, sacred time, appears under the paradoxical aspect of a circular time, reversible and recoverable, a sort of eternal present that is periodically reintegrated by means of rites." "Real time" too is an eternal present of symbols, reversible and recoverable, an ontological time that never gets exhausted and that can be reintegrated at any time. Eliade's sacred time is nonhistorical. It is the time that "floweth not," that does not participate in profane duration. (Stenger, 1991, p. 55)

As metatime, cybertime would include the concept of sacred time. And although entry into cyberspace is not generally viewed as a religious experience, there is a sense in which this electronic environment is a mythical landscape, a magical realm in which incantation has efficacy, in which objects exhibit intelligence, resurrection is a matter of course (e.g., in games), and a sense of total control is possible (Davis, 1993; Hayward & Wollen, 1993; Rheingold, 1993). It is in this sense that Douglas Rushkoff (1994) refers to "man's leap out of history altogether and into the timeless dimension of Cyberia" (p. 4). The term *Cyberia* is a variation of cyberspace, but he uses it to include New Age mysticism, psychedelic drug culture, and raving, as well. The connections are not unreasonable: "Virtual reality is the closest simulation to what a world free of time, location, or even a personal identity might look like. Psychedelics and VR are both ways of creating a new, nonlinear reality where self-expression is a community event" (p. 58). It is no wonder, then, that Timothy Leary is a VR booster. Rushkoff describes virtual environments as a form of sacred space and virtual time as a form of sacred time, a mystical, Zen-like experience. It is interesting to note that this promises both the elimination of time, timelessness (zero-dimensional time), as well as its infinite expansion in nonlinear form. The sense of temporal dislocation in cybertime is a key characteristic of the experience of computing, whether it is compared to religious epiphany, drug-induced hallucination, or the dream state.

Cybertime is in some ways a form of sacred time, a mythic time or dreamtime (Kirk, 1974). And although it has become commonplace to compare the experiencing of audiovisual media to the act of dreaming, no other media provide the same sense of active personal presence as the computer; no other media allow us to construct and encounter other versions of ourselves: dream selves. As a number of scholars have pointed out, computer-mediated communication has led to a great deal of play and experimentation with multiple roles, personalities, and identities (Rheingold, 1993; Sproull, & Kiesler, 1991; Stone, 1991). Cyberspace is implicated in the fragmenting, saturating, or populating of the self (Gergen, 1991) and the decentering of the subject (Poster, 1990). We find ourselves dealing with a multitude of dream selves. Other meanings take hold here as well: Our dream selves are ideal versions of ourselves, fantasy selves; one day, through VR technology, they will also provide us with our ideal body images (Rheingold, 1991). In the psychoanalytic literature, there is a clear connection between the notion of the double, the shadow, the mirror image, and the condition of narcissism (Rank, 1971); thus, virtual doubles feed into our culture of narcissism (Lasch, 1979). Our cyberselves are digital creatures, made not of flesh and blood, but of data and information. They are unaffected by time, suffering neither from age nor injury, essentially immortal (Novak, 1991); the double, in psychoanalysis, may also signify death or its denial (Rank, 1971). Although our physical selves are subject to the ravages of time, our dream-self doubles are the masters of cybertime.

The double is sometimes seen as a threat, a frightening image of ourselves, or a doppelgänger intent on taking our place (Rank, 1971). One such double produced in cyberspace is the shadow left behind electronically and processed through the panoptic sort, through surveillance and the gathering of information about us; it is the double we encounter, for example, in a credit report (Gandy, 1993). This meeting with our data doubles cannot help but be disturbing, as it reflects the effort to reduce us down to a zero-dimensional state, to boil all of our individual qualities and histories down to a yes-or-no answer. In the face of this changeling, we often try to assert the integrity of our individuality, to express our outrage over this violation of our privacy, and, especially if our doppelgänger is a poor reflection of ourselves, to object to its inaccuracy. This generally provides mixed results, and it seems that the only logical course of resistance in a surveillance society is through the time-honored method of aliasing. With privacy eliminated by the panoptic sort, the only place we can hide is behind a multitude of masks; through the generation of doubles we may use the system against itself, creating information glut or *spamming* the data gatherers.

Much of our online doubling is not a matter of choice, however. When viewed spatially, it is reasonable to conclude that the self becomes more divided as more time is spent in communicating with greater numbers of people (Gergen, 1991). As time is subdivided into nanoseconds, and the time it takes to complete tasks such as the sending and receiving of messages decreases, our communication commitments increase, and we are pulled in more and more different directions. Because the past does not fade in cybertime, neither do past relationships, nor past versions of ourselves that remain current in e-mail, listserv, and bulletin board archives. This form of cybernetic cloning seems to promote identity diffusion, multiple personality disorders, and schizophrenic behavior. As we spend more and more of our time in cyberspace, experiencing cybertime, we may simply have to suffer this condition gladly and learn to cope with it somehow, or we may be able to use it to forge a more integrated, metadimensional sense of self. We will certainly have increased opportunities to encounter our own unconscious through our cyberspace doubles. The immediate and improvisational nature of computer-mediated communications allows for more of a direct tap into the unconscious mind than the more careful process of face-to-face public communication and the deliberate composing of written messages. Through flaming, we encounter our id or shadow; through experimentation with online gender reversal, our anima or animus. Doubles and dream selves are deeply connected to the unconscious.

Sherry Turkle (1984, 1986) refers to the computer itself as "the second self" because we tend to use it as a Rorschach test, projecting ourselves onto the technology. As our relationship with the technology has evolved from communicating with computers to communicating within them, the computer becomes the place where our second selves dwell, a dreamscape. Thus, our encounter with cyberspace may, over time, perform a therapeutic function akin to psychoanalysis. Moreover, according to Walter Ong (1982), there is less of a barrier between the conscious and unconscious mind in oral cultures than in literate ones. Writing and print allow us to explore the conscious mind self-consciously, but at the price of repressing the unconscious. The electronic media, and especially computer media, have unstopped the bottle of the unconscious, and what comes out will not be easy to deal with. The immediate effect seems to be a certain fragmenting or fractalizing of the self. Over time, however, a new synthesis between the conscious and the unconscious may well emerge, a more integrated mindset of the sort that Carl Jung (1971) was concerned with. As Ong (1982) puts it, "human consciousness evolves" (p. 178), and a new consciousness may therefore emerge through a synthesis between our physical selves and the dream selves we generate in cybertime.

In addition to consciousness, the computer joins with other media in altering our sense of community. In referring to these new forms of affiliation, Gary Gumpert (1987) speaks of media communities, Kenneth Gergen (1991) discusses symbolic communities, and Howard Rheingold (1993) uses the term virtual communities. Communities, it must be remembered, are something more than just a gathering or a group. Community ties can only emerge over time; they are not so much a matter of spatial proximity as they are a function of patience, growth, and continuity. Traditional communities, villages, and tribes tend to be stable and singular associations. Clearly, this notion of community is being undermined by our new technologies, as individuals and groups are connected into global networks, electronic tribes dispersed through cyberspace. The unique characteristics of cybertime make it possible to maintain multiple associations, to change group membership frequently and without difficulty, and to develop fairly strong ties in short periods of time. This more fluid arrangement yields a kind of liquid tribalism. Tribalism at hyperspeed is amorphous and constantly changing, multiple and overlapping. This is not the homogenous global village, but rather a dense web of interconnected tribal networks, multidimensional and fractalized. The microworld is indeed a *small world,* one in which the real world's *six degrees of separation* (see Milgram, 1974) approaches zero. Of course, we will be increasingly open to the panoptic sort as well. As Kroker and Weinstein (1994) put it: "You will pay for information with information; indeed, you will be information" (p. 11). What they are implying is that we will become our own liquid assets. But our own value will be based on gregariousness; on the number of relationships, associations, and networks we are a part of; on the number of doubles we have in play; on our ability to navigate the networks at hyperspeed, on our nomadic power (Critical Arts Ensemble, 1994). Print-mediated culture may have fostered individualism (McLuhan, 1962, 1964), but computer-mediated culture promotes networking, tribal associations, and various forms of virtual (and possibly global) communities.

The network is usually seen as a spatial concept, but we must remember that time too is a network of relations among different events. Cybertime is networked time and also a network of different concepts of time. As metatime, it has a certain liberating potential. But it also threatens us with overload and a loss of coherence, with the breakdown of the signifying chain, the connection of signifier to signified and of one sign to another needed to generate meaning; this is the schizophrenic breakdown associated with the postmodern condition (Jameson, 1991). Cybertime does not eliminate, but rather subsumes one-dimensional time, clock and calendar time, and the sense of historical time that has taken us so long to develop. We need not lose touch with the one-dimensional, but instead can use it as an anchor to a more stable and coherent sense of time. What is needed is a balance between these tendencies and a balance that also includes the zero-dimensional tendencies of cybertime. Timelessness is a much sought after experience, but it should not come at the expense of history and tradition, and certainly not at the expense of the future. The ways in which we use and experience time are, after all, the key to cultural survival.

REFERENCES

Atkin, R. (1981). *Multidimensional man.* New York: Penguin.

Augustine, St. (1961). *Confessions* (R.S. Pine-Coffin, Trans.). New York: Penguin.

Baudrillard, J. (1983). *Simulations* (P. Foss, P. Patton & P. Beitchman, Trans.). New York: Semiotext(e).

Benedikt, M. (Ed.). (1991). *Cyberspace: First steps.* Cambridge, MA: MIT Press.

Beniger, J.R. (1986). *The control revolution: Technological and economic origins of the information society.* Cambridge, MA: Harvard University Press.

Bolter, J.D. (1984). *Turing's man: Western culture in the computer age.* Chapel Hill: University of North Carolina Press.

Bolter, J.D. (1991). *Writing space: The computer, hypertext, and the history of writing.* Hillsdale, NJ: Erlbaum.

Burke, K. (1945). *A grammar of motives.* Berkeley: University of California Press.

Critical Arts Ensemble. (1994). *The electronic disturbance.* Brooklyn: Autonomedia.

Carey, J.W. (1989). *Communication as culture: Essays on media and society.* Boston: Unwin Hyman.

Davis, E. (1993). Techgnosis: Magic, memory, and the angels of information. *The South Atlantic Quarterly, 92*(4), 585-616.

Dery, M. (Ed.). (1993). Flame wars: The discourse of cyberculture [Special issue]. *The South Atlantic Quarterly, 92*(4).

Einstein, A. (1954). *Relativity, the special and the general theory: A popular exposition* (rev. ed.; R.W. Lawson, Trans.). London: Methuen.

Eliade, M. (1959). *The sacred and the profane* (W. Trask, Trans.). New York: Harvest/HBJ Books.

Eliade, M. (1974). *The myth of the eternal return or, Cosmos and history* (W. Trask, Trans.). Princeton, NJ: Princeton University Press.

Ellul, J. (1968). *Propaganda: The formation of men's attitudes* (K. Kellen & J. Lerner, Trans.). New York: Alfred A. Knopf.

Gandy, O.H., Jr. (1993). *The panoptic sort: A political economy of personal information.* Boulder, CO: Westview.

Gelernter, D. (1991). *Mirror worlds or the day software puts the universe in a shoebox . . . How it will happen and what it will mean.* New York: Oxford University Press.

Gergen, K.J. (1991). *The saturated self: Dilemmas of identity in contemporary life.* New York: Basic Books.
Gibson, W. (1984). *Neuromancer.* New York: Ace Books.
Gleick, J. (1987). *Chaos: Making a new science.* New York: Viking Penguin.
Gumpert, G. (1987). *Talking tombstones and other tales of the media age.* New York: Oxford University Press.
Hall, E.T. (1959). *The silent language.* New York: Doubleday.
Hall, E.T. (1984). *The dance of life: The other dimension of time.* Garden City, NY: Anchor.
Hayward, P., & Wollen, T. (Eds.). (1993). *Future visions: New technologies of the screen.* London: British Film Institute.
Innis, H. A. (1951). *The bias of communication.* Toronto: University of Toronto Press.
Jameson, F. (1991). *Postmodernism, Or, The cultural logic of late capitalism.* Durham, NC: Duke University Press.
Jones, S. (1993). A sense of space: Virtual reality, authenticity, and the oral. *Critical Studies in Mass Communication, 10*(3), 238-252.
Jung, C.G. (1971). *The portable Jung* (R.F.C. Hull, Trans.). New York: Viking.
Kidwell, P.A., & Ceruzzi, P.E. (1994). *Landmarks in digital computing.* Washington, DC: Smithsonian Institution Press.
Kirk, G.S. (1974). *The nature of Greek myths.* New York: Penguin.
Kroker, A. (1993). *Spasm: Virtual reality, android music, and electric flesh.* New York: St. Martin's Press.
Kroker, A., & Weinstein, M.A. (1994). *Data trash: The theory of the virtual class.* New York: St. Martin's Press.
Lakoff, G., & Johnson, M. (1980). *Metaphors we live by.* Chicago: University of Chicago Press.
Landow, G.P. (1992). *Hypertext: The convergence of contemporary critical theory and technology.* Baltimore: John Hopkins University Press.
Lanham, R.A. (1993). *The electronic word: Democracy, technology, and the arts.* Chicago: University of Chicago Press.
Lasch, C. (1979). *The culture of narcissism: American life in an age of diminishing expectations.* New York: Norton.
Laurel, B. (1993). *Computers as theatre.* Reading, MA: Addison Wesley.
Levy, S. (1984). *Hackers: Heroes of the computer revolution.* New York: Dell.
Levy, S. (1992). *Artificial life: A report from the frontier where computers meet biology.* New York: Random House.
Lubar, S. (1993). *Infoculture: The Smithsonian book of information age inventions.* Boston: Houghton Mifflin.
MacBeath, M. (1993). Time's square. In R. Le Poidevin & M. MacBeath (Eds.), *The philosophy of time* (pp. 183-202). New York: Oxford University Press.
Maimonides, M. (1963). *The guide of the perplexed* (Vol. 1; S. Pines, Trans.). Chicago: University of Chicago Press.
Marcuse, H. (1964). *One-dimensional man: Studies in the ideology of advanced industrial society.* Boston: Beacon Press.

McLuhan, M. (1962). *The Gutenberg galaxy.* Toronto: University of Toronto Press.
McLuhan, M. (1964). *Understanding media: The extensions of man.* New York: Mentor Books.
Meyrowitz, J. (1985). *No sense of place.* New York: Oxford University Press.
Milgram, S. (1974). The small-world problem. In J.B. Maas (Ed.), *Readings in psychology today* (3rd ed.; pp. 324-330). Del Mar, CA: CRM Books.
Mumford, L. (1963). *Technics and civilization.* New York: Harcourt Brace Jovanovich.
Newton, I. (1934). *Newton's principia* (A. Motte, Trans., F. Cajori, Ed.). Berkeley: University of California Press.
Novak, M. (1991). Liquid architectures in cyberspace. In M. Benedikt (Ed.), *Cyberspace: First steps* (pp. 225-254). Cambridge, MA: MIT Press.
Ong, W.J. (1982). *Orality and literacy: The technologizing of the word.* New York: Methuen.
Perkinson, H. (in press). *No safety in numbers: How the computer quantified everything and made people risk-aversive.* Cresskill, NJ: Hampton Press.
Pimentel, K., & Teixeira, K. (1993). *Virtual reality: Through the new looking glass.* New York: Intel/Windcrest/McGraw-Hill.
Poster, M. (1990). *The mode of information.* Chicago: University of Chicago Press.
Postman, N. (1985). *Amusing ourselves to death.* New York: Viking.
Postman, N. (1992). *Technopoly: The surrender of culture to technology.* New York: Alfred A. Knopf.
Provenzo, E.F., Jr. (1986). *Beyond the Gutenberg galaxy.* New York: Teachers College Press.
Raley, J. (1994). Global positioning systems. In A. Grant (Ed.), *Communication technology update* (3rd ed.; pp. 302-313). Boston: Butterworth-Heinemann.
Rank, O. (1971). *The double: A psychoanalytic study* (H. Tucker, Jr., Trans.). New York: New American Library.
Rheingold, H. (1991). *Virtual reality.* New York: Touchstone.
Rheingold, H. (1993). *The virtual community: Homesteading on the electronic frontier.* Reading, MA: Addison Wesley.
Rifkin, J. (1987). *Time wars: The primary conflict in human history.* New York: Touchstone.
Robinett, W. (1992). Synthetic experience: A proposed taxonomy. *Presence: Teleoperators and Virtual Environments, 1*(2), 229-247.
Roszak, T. (1994). *The cult of information: A neo-Luddite treatise on high-tech, artificial intelligence, and the true art of thinking* (2nd ed.). Berkeley: The University of California Press.
Rucker, R. (1984). *The fourth dimension: A guided tour of the higher universes.* Boston: Houghton Mifflin.
Rushkoff, D. (1994). *Cyberia: Life in the trenches of hyperspace.* New York: HarperCollins.

Sontag, S. (1977). *On photography.* New York: Farrar, Strauss and Giroux.

Sproull, L., & Kiesler, S. (1991). *Connections: New ways of working in the networked organization.* Cambridge, MA: The MIT Press.

Stenger, N. (1991). Mind is a leaking rainbow. In M. Benedikt (Ed.), *Cyberspace: First steps* (pp. 49-58). Cambridge, MA: MIT Press.

Sternberg, J. (1991). The abacus: The earliest digital computer and its cultural implications. *New Dimensions in Communications: Proceedings of the 48th Annual New York State Speech Communication Association Convention, 4,* 69-71.

Stone, A.R. (1991). Will the real body please stand up? Boundary stories about virtual cultures. In M. Benedikt (Ed.), *Cyberspace: First steps* (pp. 81-118). Cambridge, MA: MIT Press.

Toffler, A. (1981). *The third wave.* New York: Bantam.

Toffler, A., & Toffler, H. (1993, October 31). Societies at hyper-speed. *The New York Times,* Section 4, p. 17.

Turkle, S. (1984). *The second self: Computers and the human spirit.* New York: Simon and Schuster.

Turkle, S. (1986). Computer as Rorschach. In G. Gumpert & R. Cathcart (Eds.), *Inter/media: Interpersonal communication in a media world* (3rd ed.; pp. 439-459). New York: Oxford University Press.

Virilio, P. (1986). *Speed and politics: An essay on dromology* (M. Polizzotti, Trans.). New York: Semiotext(e).

Virilio, P. (1991). *The lost dimension* (D. Moshenberg, Trans.). New York: Semiotext(e).

Wachtel, E. (1980). *Visions of order: The influence of technology on space conception.* Unpublished doctoral dissertation, New York University, New York City.

Warner, T.T., & Buzbee, B. (1994). The future of weather and climate prediction. In C.A. Pickover (Ed.), *Visions of the future: Art, technology and computing in the twenty-first century* (pp. 43-52). New York: St. Martin's Press.

Weizenbaum, J. (1976). *Computer power and human reason.* San Francisco: Freeman.

Whitrow, G.J. (1980). *The natural philosophy of time* (2nd ed.). Oxford: Oxford University Press.

Whitrow, G.J. (1988). *Time in history: Views of time from prehistory to the present day.* Oxford: Oxford University Press.

Wiener, N. (1967). *The human use of human beings: Cybernetics and society.* Boston, MA: Avon.

Woolley, B. (1992). *Virtual worlds: A journey in hype and hyperreality.* Oxford: Blackwell.

Wyant, G., & Hammerstron, T. (1994). *How microprocessors work.* Emeryville, CA: Ziff-Davis Press.

Zettl, H. (1990). *Sight sound motion: Applied media aesthetics* (2nd ed.). Belmont, CA: Wadsworth.

Epilogue: Cyberspace, Shmyberspace

Neil Postman

Throughout this volume we have maintained that cyberspace is a phenomenon that needs to be taken seriously and analyzed critically. Some have written in praise of cyberspace, computers, electronic media, and the information society. Others raise critical questions about their uses, effects, and the policies surrounding them. But for the most part we have taken for granted the presence of electronic technologies and their continued evolution. It is for this reason that we have given the last word to Neil Postman. In the epilogue to this volume, he raises the most basic question of all—Do we actually need cyberspace technologies? Is there a problem that cyberspace is needed to solve? Postman suggests that the difficulties contemporary information technologies were meant to address were, in fact, resolved in the 19th century. Thus, we suffer from too much information and from empty simulations that take the place of genuine experience. Far from a dismissal, Postman reminds us that in fulfilling new functions, older, more important, ones may be ignored; in creating new forms, more traditional and satisfying ones may be forgotten; and that in generating new codes and meanings, we may become lost in a Babel-like state of incoherence. Even if you do not agree with Postman's argument, you might take him up on his challenge to justify cyberspace on the basis of genuine human needs.

> "We feel that even when all possible scientific problems have been answered, the problems of life remain completely untouched."
> —Ludwig Wittgenstein

Here is a problem that people faced in the 19th century. It was only one among many, but it was taken quite seriously: A message could travel only as fast as a human being could travel—about 35 miles per hour (on a train). Nineteenth-century people also worried about another communication problem: Language, either spoken or written, was very nearly the only form messages could take. And they also worried about this one: Most people did not have access to the increasing volume of information that science, commerce, medicine, and other fields of knowledge were generating.

When human beings are presented with problems, they often embark on creative efforts to solve them. This is exactly what happened in the 19th century. The problem, taken as a whole, was this: How can we get more information to more people, fast, and in diverse forms? The good news is that beginning with the invention of telegraphy and photography in the 1840s, and for 100 years afterward, *we solved the problem*. For those who are unfamiliar with the 19th century, here are some of the inventions that contributed to the solution: telegraphy, photography, the rotary press, the transatlantic cable, the electric light, radio, movies, the x-ray, the penny press, the modern magazine, and the advertising agency. Of course, in the first half of the 20th century, we added some important inventions so that once and for all we need not worry about information scarcity or the limitations of space, time, and form.

From millions of sources all over the globe, through every possible channel and medium—lightwaves, airwaves, ticker tapes, computer banks, telephone wires, television cables, satellites, printing presses—information pours in. Behind it, in every imaginable form of storage—on paper, videocassette and audiotape, on disks, film, and silicon chips—is an even greater volume of information waiting to be retrieved. Yes, we solved the problem in spectacular fashion. But in doing so we created a new problem never experienced before: information glut, information incoherence, information meaninglessness. To put it bluntly, information has become a form of garbage, not only incapable of answering the most fundamental human questions, but barely useful in providing direction to the solution of even mundane problems. What has happened is that the tie between information and human purpose has been severed. Information is now a commodity that is bought and sold; it comes indiscriminately, directed at no one in particular, in enormous volume, at high speeds, disconnected from theory, meaning, and purpose.

Several prescient people saw the problem coming and warned us to prepare for it. Among them were Martin Heidegger, Aldous Huxley, Lewis Mumford, Harold Innis, Jacques Ellul, and Marshall McLuhan. But none expressed the dangers more eloquently and precisely than Edna St. Vincent Millay. In her wonderful poem, "Huntsman, What Quarry," she wrote:

> Upon this gifted age, in its dark hour,
> Falls from the sky a meteoric shower
> Of facts . . . they lie unquestioned, uncombined.
> Wisdom enough to leech us of our ill
> Is daily spun; but there exists no loom
> To weave it into fabric . . .

No loom to weave it into fabric. This is the problem we have to confront, and with as much intelligence and energy as we can muster. Why, then, do we tarry so long in addressing it? Well, for one thing, there is the matter of plain denial. I refer to those who are encased in a 19th century mentality and do not, therefore, acknowledge that we have solved the problem of information scarcity. To understand their outlook we may use the example of the automobile. The automobile was the solution to the problem of how to increase speed and mobility, of how to shrink distance, of how to collapse time. This it accomplished quite well, but in so doing created other problems, including poisoning the air, choking our cities, and dispersing families. To those who are burdened by a sense of denial, the answer to these newly created problems is to add cruise control, electric windows, and telephones to our cars. But such innovations are trivial; they do not, in fact, enhance the basic contribution of cars, and they distract us from confronting the most urgent problems created by cars.

This is the sort of outlook we may associate with people who are enthusiastic about virtual reality machines. Finding themselves insufficiently stimulated by real reality, they seek a solution by escaping from it, exciting themselves through a technologically simulated experience. The same may be said for those immersing themselves in e-mail and other forms of computer-mediated communication. Finding themselves short on real friendships, perhaps even afraid to make them, they seek a solution in simulated friendships, pathetically surfing the net to locate a kindred spirit, who like spirits everywhere will have no material existence. And the same may be said for those who spend uncountable hours watching television so that they may escape from the terrifying prospect of formulating an unpackaged original thought. All these souls have this in common: They refuse to acknowledge what their real problem is—respectively, boringness, friendlessness, thoughtlessness.

You will think, at this point, that I do not like such people and have no sympathy for them. But this is not so. Who among us has not been faced with these problems? Who among us has not tried to weave a fabric to our lives by employing some ridiculous simulation, a momentary distraction, a pretense at living? My point is the same one Wittgenstein made about science (in the quote at the beginning of this essay): Technology does not touch life's deepest problems. We may think it will, as so many thought in the 19th century, when the aim of technological development was to reduce ignorance, superstition, and suffering. And to some extent, they were right to hope so. And to some extent, technology did address those problems. But the technology celebrated now is just cruise control and electric windows.

The engineers, computer gurus, and corporate visionaries who claim to speak for the future are, in fact, addressing problems that have already been solved. It is time for us to give up the notion that we may find solutions to our emptiness through technology. We must now turn to our poets, playwrights, composers, theologians, and artists, who, alone, can create or restore the narratives that will give a meaningful pattern to our lives. They are our weavers who can liberate us from cyberspace and put us back in the world.

Author Index

N

O

P

T

U

Subject Index